STRATEGIC LEADERSHIP

Top Executives and Their Effects on Organizations

WWW.GORDON.EDU/CEL

DIG DEEP, REACH OUT, AND START UP!

STRATEGIC LEADERSHIP

Top Executives and Their Effects on Organizations

Amos Tuck School of Business, Dartmouth College

DONALD HAMBRICK

Columbia University Graduate School of Business

WEST PUBLISHING COMPANY

Minneapolis/St. Paul

New York

Los Angeles

San Francisco

Copyeditor: Marilyn Taylor
Text Design: Lois Stanfield, LightSource Images
Artwork: Carlisle Communications
Composition: Carlisle Communications
Indexing: Maggie Jarpey

WEST'S COMMITMENT TO THE ENVIRONMENT

In 1906, West Publishing Company began recycling materials left over from the production of books. This began a tradition of efficient and responsible use of resources. Today, 100% of our legal bound volumes are printed on acid-free, recycled paper consisting of 50% new paper pulp and 50% paper that has undergone a de-inking process. We also use vegetable-based inks to print all of our books. West recycles nearly 22,650,000 pounds of scrap paper annually—the equivalent of 187,500 trees. Since the 1960s, West has devised ways to capture and recycle waste inks, solvents, oils, and vapors created in the printing process. We also recycle plastics of all kinds, wood, glass, corrugated cardboard, and batteries, and have eliminated the use of polystyrene book packaging. We at West are proud of the longevity and the scope of our commitment to the environment.

West pocket parts and advance sheets are printed on recyclable paper and can be collected and recycled with newspapers. Staples do not have to be removed. Bound volumes can be recycled after removing the cover.

Production, Prepress, Printing and Binding by West Publishing Company

 TEXT IS PRINTED ON 10% POST CONSUMER RECYCLED PAPER   Printed with **Printwise** ∞
Environmentally Advanced Water Washable Ink

British Library Cataloguing-in-Publication Data. A catalogue record for this book is available from the British Library.

LIBRARY OF CONGRESS CATALOGING-IN-PUBLICATION DATA

Finkelstein, Sydney.
    Strategic leadership : top executives and their effect on organizations / Sydney Finkelstein, Donald Hambrick.
        p.   cm. -- (West's strategic management series)
    Includes index.
    ISBN 0-314-04605-4 (soft : alk. paper)
    1. Leadership. 2. Executive ability. 3. Strategic planning.
I. Hambrick, Donald C.   II. Title.   III. Series.
HD57.7.F556   1996   95-45380
658.4'092--dc20   CIP

This book is dedicated to our wives and daughters,
Gloria and Erica Finkelstein
and Peg and Claire Hambrick

BRIEF TABLE OF CONTENTS

CONTENTS

INTRODUCTION TO WEST'S STRATEGIC MANAGEMENT SERIES

Co-Editors Michael A. Hitt, R. Duane Ireland and Robert E. Hoskisson

Interest in the strategic management discipline among academics and practicing managers alike continues to grow. Changes in the competitive landscape, based on increased global competition and dynamic technological advances have created new competitive challenges and placed more emphasis on understanding how to strategically manage organizations. Strategic management deals with all types of firms (e.g., large and small; established and entrepreneurial) and types of industries (e.g., emerging, mature). The critical goal is to understand how to compete successfully and "win" in the marketplace. This series of books sheds light on critical strategic management phenomena that help us understand how to gain and sustain competitive advantages in the marketplace (i.e., obtain superior returns for stakeholders).

Each book in the series focuses on a specialized, important topic in strategic management. The topics are examined in terms of cutting-edge research and each book provides an in-depth treatment of the topic. The books are written by prominent scholars with special expertise in the topic area. Each book provides a rigorous, insightful analysis of the topic on which it focuses.

These books may be useful as core texts in specialized courses, supplements to core courses, and particularly as resource guides for strategic management research. While topics represent specialized and important areas of strategic management, each book provides a new piece in the puzzle for understanding how to develop and sustain strategic competitiveness.

The series is a living library. As our knowledge expands, so will the treatments and topics involved in the series. As emerging topics become critical to our understanding of strategic management in the dynamic competitive landscape, books examining those topics will be added. These books will explore the boundaries of the field of strategic management. While they are not intended to establish the limits to the field, they will clearly define the new frontiers of strategic management. We hope that they create a greater understanding of strategic management and stimulate create a greater understanding of strategic management and stimulate expansion of our knowledge in this critical domain.

Introduction to Finkelstein and Hambrick's Strategic Leadership

Sydney Finkelstein and Don Hambrick have developed a thorough, in-depth treatment of strategic leadership. The topic of strategic leadership has become increasingly important in strategic management theory and practice. These two authors have made important contributions to our understanding of strategic leadership through their prior research and writing. This book represents a compilation of their and others' research on the important topic of strategic leadership.

This book should be read by all who study and practice strategic management. Clearly, the chief executive officer and the top management team are critical decision makers for the firm. Finkelstein and Hambrick show that the decisions made by these individuals and/or the team, along with their actions have important effects on firm performance. We congratulate Syd and Don on an outstanding book and are pleased to offer it to you as a part of the West Strategic Management Series.

PREFACE

This book marks an important place in the intellectual journey we started about ten years ago. Trained as strategy researchers and teachers, we become exceedingly uneasy with prevailing strategy frameworks. We were particularly concerned because the major descriptive and prescriptive strategy models then in vogue omitted anything having to do with senior executives. Yet, all around us—in our research, consulting, and everyday observation—we saw ample evidence that organizational outcomes are eminently traceable to the individuals at the top of the firm. We concluded that if we want to understand why organizations do the things they do or why they perform the way they do, we must examine and understand top executives. That is, we extended our interest from strategy to "strategists," or a perspective we now call "strategic leadership."

It turns out we were not alone. Research on top executives has burgeoned in recent years. Academic conferences on strategy and management regularly feature sessions dealing with various issues involving senior executives—succession, cognitions, compensation, top management teams, board-management relations, and so on. Today, it is rare to pick up an issue of a major management or strategy journal without finding articles on some topic of strategic leadership. Researchers from a wide array of disciplines—sociology, social psychology, finance, accounting, and economics—as well as from the subfields of management—strategy, organization theory, and organizational behavior—are energetically engaged in examining strategic leadership.

All this activity has been a mixed blessing. The intellectual ferment and diversity is stimulating, and many important ideas and findings have been established. However, ambiguity and confusion abound. So much work has been done, so quickly, and on so many fronts that extracting the chief thrusts and patterns—even comprehending basic terminology—is exceedingly difficult.

What do we really know about strategic leadership? What are the major research findings? How can we reconcile and integrate the many strands of theory and empirical inquiry regarding top executives? And, especially, where do we, as strategy scholars, go from here? This book contains our answers to these fundamental questions. We focus on both synthesis and knowledge creation, using the vast body of available literature as a springboard to suggest a research agenda for the future.

Many people helped make this project a reality. Mike Hitt, Duane Ireland, and Bob Hoskisson asked us to write a book on strategic leadership for the new West Series on Strategic Management, and they were unfailingly encouraging, constructive, and patient through the entire undertaking.

We are grateful to Deans Ed Fox, Colin Blaydon, and Paul Danos at the Amos Tuck School and Dean Meyer Feldberg at Columbia University for creating the intellectual climate that supported this project, as well as for providing the time and resources needed for its completion. Our colleagues at both schools have been strong supporters of the book and have greatly influenced our thinking. They deserve our thanks: Rich D'Aveni, Bill Joyce, Vijay Govindarajan, Dennis Logue, Scott Neslin, Brian Quinn, Kaye Schoonhoven, and Jim Seward at Tuck; and Eric Abrahamson, Warren Boeker, Joel Brockner, Noel Capon, Ming-Jer Chen, Jerry Davis, Kathy Harrigan, Bob Lear, Bill Newman, Mike Tushman, Ruth Wageman, Kirby Warren, John Whitney, and Bob Yavitz at Columbia.

We were fortunate to have numerous valued colleagues who reviewed chapters or otherwise stimulated or refined our thinking, including Sylvia Black, Brian Boyd, Bert Cannella, Kathy Eisenhardt, Jim Fredrickson, Marta Geletkanycz, John Haleblian, Dawn Harris, George Huber, Yong-Min Kim, Arie Lewin, Ian MacMillan, John Michel, V. K. Narayanan, Nandini Rajagopalan, Rhonda Reger, Larry Stimpert, Anisya Thomas, Jim Walsh, Margarethe Wiersema, and Batia Wiesenfeld. The empirical analysis of research on strategic leadership in Chapter 9 was greatly aided by the assistance of Meredith Ceh and Todd Clark, both former MBA students at the Tuck School, and research assistants Ramesh Narasimhan and Nakul Krishnaswamy. Thanks also go to the many colleagues who responded to our mail survey described in that chapter. Mark Graham was very helpful in smoothing out the edges in some of our writing.

Thanks go to Rick Leyh, our editor at West, both for championing the project and for his professionalism in shepherding the book through the production process. We also owe our assistants, Marcia Diefendorf at Tuck and Barbara Sorich at Columbia, a debt of gratitude for their expertise and patience in typing many drafts and effectively managing the flow of communications between Hanover and New York.

Finally, special thanks and appreciation go to our families for supporting our efforts and putting up with yet another reason to work through the weekend. They make it all worthwhile.

THE STUDY OF TOP EXECUTIVES

*Borden Inc. was once a mighty packaged foods compa-
ny with several well-known brands. It also had a small
but very profitable, hence powerful, chemicals division.
Between the mid-1960s and 1993, Borden was run
by a succession of chief executives whose expertise and
backgrounds were in chemicals, not foods. From their
experience in chemicals, these exeutives knew how to
generate large profits: specialty products and highly targeted applications. This then became their formula in
foods, with over 90 acquisitions of small, mostly regional food companies. In foods, however, there are massive
national economies of scale, particularly in distribution
and advertising. By the early 1990s, Borden had
become an inefficient patchwork of declining brands and
loosely related products, with no profits and a collapsed
stock price. In 1995, Borden was taken over for a price
of about one-third its value just a few years before*
(SCHIFRIN 1994).

The Borden story illustrates two
important points. First, top executives
can have a very significant effect on
their companies. Borden was not trapped in a
declining industry in which all players lost
two-thirds of their market value. Borden's
executives were not impelled to make those
90 acquisitions. They exercised *choice*, and for
whatever reasons, the results were not what
they anticipated. Second, executives are finite

in their repertoires. In the heat of competitive battle—and without our advantage of hindsight—executives cannot detachedly comprehend all facets of their situations, assess all options, and then select one that has a textbook correctness. Instead, executives take mental shortcuts, often gravitating to the familiar, the tried-and-true. Certainly, they are greatly swayed by their experiences.

THE ESSENCE OF STRATEGIC LEADERSHIP

The study of executive leadership from a strategic choice perspective, or more concisely, *strategic leadership*, focuses on the executives who have overall responsibility for an organization—their characteristics, what they do, how they do it, and particularly, how they affect organizational outcomes.[1] The executives who are the subjects of strategic leadership research can be individuals (e.g., CEOs or division general managers), groups (top management teams), or other governance bodies (e.g., boards of directors).

We use the term "strategic leadership" because it connotes management of an overall enterprise, not just a small unit; and it implies substantive decision-making responsibilities. As will be seen, we are centrally concerned with why executives make the strategic choices they do. We do not rule out the interpersonal and inspirational aspects of leadership; but unlike some theorists, we do not insist on their presence to invoke the word *leadership* (Kotter 1988; Kets de Vries 1994). If not so cumbersome, we could use less value-laden words, such as *headship* or *executiveship*.

We share with other strategy scholars an abiding interest in comprehending the factors that lead to superior organizational performance. And, like many of our colleagues, we believe that performance is determined in great part by the strategic choices and other major organizational decisions made within the firm.

However, from where does the company's strategy come? Is it imposed by external norms and conventions? Is it generated by formula, such as SWOT analysis (strengths, weaknesses, opportunities, and threats) or Porter's (1980) five-forces analysis? Is it an incremental variation of the company's prior strategy? (Quinn 1980). (Which in turn raises the question, from where did *that* strategy come?) Sometimes the answers to these questions are yes. Imitation, inertia, and careful, objective decision making have all been documented as sources of strategic profiles. But as the Borden example indicates, along with a wealth of research and everyday observation, strategy and other major organizational choices are made by humans, primarily top executives, who act on the basis of their idiosyncratic experiences, motives, and dispositions. If we want to understand strategy, we must understand strategists.

In the face of the complex, multitudinous, and ambiguous information that typifies the top management task, no two strategists will identify the same array of options for the firm; they will rarely prefer the same options; they almost certainly will not implement them identically. Biases, egos, aptitudes, experiences, and other human factors in the executive ranks greatly affect what happens to companies. This is not to say that managers are weak or sinister, only that they are human and limited.

The distinguished organizational theorist James Thompson wrote of the role of "the variable human" in influencing organizational action (1967, 101). This is exactly the perspective we take, arguing that senior executives vary, and thus so do their choices. Executives vary in their experiences, capabilities, values, and personalities; these differences in turn cause executives to differ in their awareness and interpretation of strategic stimuli, their aspiration levels, their beliefs about causation, even their beliefs about what it is they are trying to accomplish and how urgent it is. It follows that executives will differ in their behaviors and choices. The organization becomes "a reflection of its top managers" (Hambrick and Mason 1984).

However, a behavioral theory of senior leadership extends beyond an interest in the cognitions of individual executives because strategic management is fundamentally a social and political activity. Decision makers are informed, influenced, and sometimes constrained by others, both inside and outside the organization. For this reason, we have an interest in senior-level management groups (commonly called top management teams), in the roles and influence of boards of directors, and in the effects of industry norms and models on top executive decisions. Our perspective on strategic leadership resides at the intersection of cognitive, social, and political concepts.

In short, we are interested in the human element in strategic choice and organizational performance. By focusing on senior executives, however, we do not wish to be seen as glorifying them. In fact, executives are important to a complete theory of strategic management precisely because of their limitations—the biases, filters, and varying motives they bring to their decisions and indecisions.

Moreover, by focusing on top executives, we do not mean to imply that all strategic choices are generated at the apex of the organization. Strategies come from the top, but they also bubble up and accrete from below (Bower 1970; Burgelman 1983). Typically, however, the types and magnitudes of strategic initiatives advanced by the operating levels of the organization are determined by the staffing, structural, and incentive decisions made by top executives. Even though they do not control all decision outcomes, upper-level executives have a predominant influence on what happens to the organization. No other small population in the organization typically has nearly as much effect on the form and fate of the enterprise.

ACADEMIC ATTENTION TO EXECUTIVES: AN HISTORICAL VIEW

Scholarly interest in top executives has ebbed and flowed, in the extreme, over the past fifty years. At one point, senior managers were an integral part of major theories of organization (Barnard 1938; Selznick 1957; Chandler 1962). In the field of strategy, top executives were once seen as central determiners of the direction of the firm. For example, the Harvard model (Learned, Christensen, and Andrews 1961; Andrews 1971), which served as principal guide for business policy thinkers in the 1960s and 1970s, emphasized the personal role of senior executives in shaping their firms. Consider these quotes from Andrews:

> Executives in charge of company destinies do not look exclusively at what a company might do and can do. [They] sometimes seem heavily influenced by what they personally *want* to do. (p. 104)

> We will be able to understand the strategic decision better if we admit rather than resist the dimension of preference. (p. 105)

> Strategy is a human construction. . . . (p. 107)

In the Harvard model, the individuals at the top of the enterprise were seen as pivotal for understanding what happens to the enterprise.

But then organizations were disembodied, or perhaps "beheaded," by many in the academic community. Among organizational theorists, essentially mechanical models came to the fore. An organization's structure was seen as determined by such factors as environment, technology, and size (e.g., Hage and Aiken 1969; Hickson, Pugh, and Pheysey 1969; Blau 1970). There were imperatives facing organizations, not choices to be made.

On the heels of the deterministic view came population ecology. Here, the focus was on explaining the birth, growth, and death of organizations. In the ecologist's framework, the environment was the centerpiece, containing resources and favoring certain organizational forms. Organizational variation was largely random, accidental, or rooted in history, not willfully achieved (Hannan and Freeman 1977; Aldrich 1979). In fact, these theorists saw organizations as generally inertial, hemmed in by external and internal constraints, and not readily amenable to the influences of leadership.

Even the field of strategy, despite its long tradition of a managerial perspective, lost sight of senior executives in the late 1970s and early 1980s. In the influential 1979 volume edited by Schendel and Hofer, to which many of the leading figures in the field contributed pieces and in which the field of "business policy" was reanointed as "strategic management," attention to the role of senior executives was nearly absent. Instead, a focus on "techno-economic" frameworks was ushered in. Strategy scholars became preoccupied with product life cycles, portfolio matrices, industry and competitor analysis, market shares, experience curves, and generic strategies (e.g., Porter 1980). To some extent, this movement toward relatively quantifiable and concisely modeled conceptions of strategy was probably due to the yearning of strategy scholars to demonstrate that their domain was as analytically rigorous as any other. The fuzziness and multidimensional nature of executive behavior was best left behind or set aside for others to assess.

The countertrend, toward renewed interest in top managers, can be traced as a two-step process. First came John Child's (1972) influential article on "strategic choice." Not content with organization theorists' deterministic conceptions of organizational forms, Child wrote:

> . . . many available contributions to a theory of organizational structure do not incorporate the direct source of variation in formal structural arrangements, namely the strategic decisions of those who have the power of structural initiation . . .

> . . . when incorporating strategic choice in a theory of organization, one is recognizing the operation of an essentially political process in which constraints and opportunities are functions of the power exercised by decision makers. . . . (1972,16)

As an organization theorist, Child was interested primarily in improved understanding of organization structure (as the above quotes indicate). However, he adopted the term "strategic choice" to refer to any willful action of major significance for the organization—not only decisions about structure, but also about goals, technology, and human resources.

As an antidote to the prevailing mechanical view of organizational functioning, Child's paper captured a great deal of interest from academics. However, it did not directly form the basis for a new direction in empirical research. This may be due to Child's equivocality as to *who* makes strategic choices in organizations. Invoking Cyert and March's (1963) concept of the "dominant coalition," Child argued that strategic choice is exercised by whomever has power in a given organization at a given time but that the identity of these parties cannot be generally specified. The dominant coalition could be some combination of board members, executives, investors, technical employees, union leaders, or others. Under such a view, scholars could not reliably target a fixed locus of strategic choice in a cross-section of organizations; hence, systematic research based on Child's ideas was somewhat stymied.

Then came a sudden willingness to focus specifically on top executives as the primary shapers of strategic direction. In 1982, Kotter wrote *The General Managers*, a book on the key challenges of senior management positions in which he posited how differences in managers' behaviors may be traceable to differences in their personal and background characteristics.[2] In 1984, Hambrick and Mason presented a more formalized theory, the "upper echelons" perspective, proposing that senior executives make strategic choices on the basis of their cognitions and values and that the organization becomes a reflection of its top managers. In the same year, Gupta and Govindarajan (1984) conducted a systematic study of division general managers, finding that their business units performed well to the extent that the managers' experiences and personalities aligned with the critical requirements posed by the chosen strategy of the business. At the same time, several other influential works on top executives appeared (e.g., Donaldson and Lorsch 1983; Meindl, Ehrlich, and Dukerich 1985; Miller, Kets de Vries and Toulouse, 1982; Wagner, Pfeffer, and O'Reilly 1984).

After that, the floodgates were open. Hundreds of academic and applied articles, books, and monographs on top executives and their organizations have been written in the past ten years. It is now rare to pick up any issue of a major management or strategy journal and not find at least one article dealing with top executives.

That the fields of organization theory and strategy would return to a focus on top executives was perhaps inevitable, since the few people at the top of an enterprise have a major influence—through decisions and indecision, boldness and timidity—on its form and fate. If scholars wish to understand why organizations do the things they do and why they perform the way they do, then top managers must be a central part of any explanatory theory.

This book is meant to serve two purposes. The first is to take stock, assess, and integrate the now huge body of literature on top executives. As we shall see, the last ten years of explosive growth of this topic have not yielded a particularly orderly, cumulative, or concise set of findings. In fact, the literature on top executives is immensely diverse in methods and perspectives, and often inconsistent in results. Our aim is to help the reader navigate and make sense of this profuse domain.

Our second objective is to go well beyond what is already known and set forth new frameworks, perspectives, testable propositions, and methodological recommendations for the study of top executives. In places, our ideas are clearly speculative, meant to stimulate debate and systematic test. The book is intended to provide a new platform for theory and research on strategic leadership—coalescing what is already known, identifying the high priorities for what next needs to be known, and proposing how scholars might fruitfully conduct their inquiries.

THE LOCUS OF STRATEGIC LEADERSHIP: WHOM TO STUDY?

Research on strategic leadership can be conducted at multiple levels of analysis. The prevailing conception of leadership entails a focus on the individual executive. In contemporary organizations, this would particularly mean chief executive officers (CEOs) and business unit heads. However, strategic leadership can also be considered at the group level. This might mean the small group of top executives, usually called the "top management team" (TMT). Other governance bodies, particularly boards of directors, are also within the scope of strategic leadership.

Chief Executive Officers

The chief executive officer is the executive who has overall responsibility for the conduct and performance of an entire organization, not just a subunit. The CEO designation has gained widespread use since about 1970, as a result of the need to draw distinctions among various senior executive positions in today's elaborate corporate structures. For example, sometimes a chief operating officer (COO), responsible for internal operational affairs, is among the executives who report to a CEO, who in turn is responsible for integrating internal and external, longer-term issues, such as acquisitions, government relations, and investor relations.

In publicly traded corporations, often the chairperson of the board of directors is also the CEO, while the president (if such a title even exists) is the COO. In other cases (particularly European companies), the chairperson is not an executive officer at all but rather an external overseer, while the president, the senior-ranking employed manager, is the CEO. Other variations exist as well. Further complicating the scholar's task of identifying the CEO of a company is that the label may not be explicitly bestowed on anyone. Still, theorists and other observers of organizations are drawn to the idea that some one person has overall responsibility for the management of an enterprise and that, in turn, that person's characteristics and actions are of consequence to the organization and its stakeholders.

Business Unit Heads

With the advent and growth of the diversified firm and the accompanying structure of divisionalization, multiple general management positions have been created in most large companies (Chandler 1962; Rumelt 1974). Managers holding these posts do not have the scope of responsibility of CEO positions; however, they often oversee very large organizations, have considerable autonomy, and sometimes are even bestowed such titles as president, managing director, or even CEO of their respective business units.

The opportunity and need to focus on business unit managers are great, if for no other reason than so many of them exist in contemporary divisionalized firms and it is at their level that many strategic initiatives are formulated and executed. As we shall see, some of the most important contributors to the study of strategic leadership have focused on the level of the business general manager (e.g., Gupta and Govindarajan 1984). However, such research has so far been very sparse, probably due to the difficulty of obtaining data, as compared to data on CEOs and others at the corporate level.

Top Management Teams

The term "top management team" has been adopted by strategic leadership theorists to refer to the relatively small group of most influential executives at the apex of an organization—usually the CEO (or general manager) and those who report directly to him or her. The term does not necessarily imply a formalized management-by-committee arrangement, but rather simply the constellation of, say, the top three to ten executives.

A scholarly interest in top management teams emerged in the early 1980s and has been pronounced ever since. Realizing that top management typically is a shared activity, researchers have moved beyond an examination of singular leaders to a wider focus on the top leadership group.

In articulating their "upper echelons theory," Hambrick and Mason (1984) gave this example of how an understanding of overall team characteristics can greatly enhance the researcher's ability to predict or explain a chosen strategy:

... assume that two firms each have chief executives whose primary functional backgrounds are in production. In Firm A, three of four other key executives also rose primarily through production-oriented careers even though they are now serving in nonproduction or generalist roles. In Firm B, the mix of executive backgrounds is more balanced and typical—one from production, one from sales, one from engineering, and one from accounting. Knowledge about the central tendencies of the entire top management teams improves one's confidence in any predictions about the firms' strategies.(p. 196)

Our ability to predict that Firm B would pursue a strategy emphasizing production capabilities would be much stronger than any prediction we could generate about Firm A. Indeed, the limited empirical evidence as to whether the top executive alone or the entire top management team is a better predictor of organizational outcomes clearly supports the conclusion that the full team has the greater explanatory power (Hage and Dewar 1973; Tushman, Virany, and Romanelli 1985; Finkelstein 1988).

Boards of Directors

Finally, boards of directors are within the purview of strategic leadership theory. While not charged with the routine administration of the firm, boards are responsible for reviewing major policy choices. As we shall see, boards vary widely in the degree to which they involve themselves in strategic choices, but it is now well known that board characteristics affect such fundamental choices as acquisitions, diversification, divestitures, research and development spending, executive compensation, and, of course, CEO dismissal (Helmich 1980; Hill and Snell 1988; Haunschild 1993; Lambert, Larcker, and Weigelt 1993).

With the increasing call for board activism (Lorsch 1989; Magnet 1993), the influence of boards over organizational outcomes will only grow. Perhaps best thought of as "supra-TMTs," boards are an important target for strategic leadership research.

ADDITIONAL MATTERS OF SCOPE

Thus, in terms of whom in the organization is of interest, we cast our net widely: CEOs, division managers, top management teams, and boards of directors. In some other ways, however, we restrict our scope and intent.

First, the book has a theoretical, predictive, explanatory focus: How can executive characteristics and behaviors be used to explain variance in organizational outcomes? Prescription will not be ignored, but it will be secondary. Until the basic phenomena can be understood and explained, prescription is premature. We believe this is why the normative literature on leadership has resulted in so much confusion and skepticism (Kets de Vries 1994).

Second, and correspondingly, the book is meant primarily for students of organizations—those who strive to assess and understand the phenomena of strategic leadership. We will discuss the evolution of theories, the fine points of research designs, and empirical research results. We aim primarily to stimulate and guide future thinking and research on this important topic.

Beyond students and scholars, yet another group may derive very practical benefits from the book—those who are responsible for evaluating, selecting, motivating, and developing senior executives. Professionals involved in executive search, compensation, appraisal and staffing, as well as board members who must evaluate top executive performance and prospects, will find here a considerable foundation on which they might create their tools and perspectives.

Overview of the Book

This book synthesizes what is known about strategic leadership and suggests new research directions. Although each chapter focuses on a relatively well-defined aspect of strategic leadership, many of these topics are interconnected. Where we placed a particular research contribution in the text depended on our assessment of where it could provide the most meaning to readers. In striving for a synthesis of strategic leadership research, our approach has the effect of creating a set of overlaying research domains that build upon, as well as inform, previous chapters. As we suggest new frameworks and propositions to help guide future research, we will rely on a key underlying theme of the book—that the intersection of cognitive, social, and political perspectives greatly informs strategic leadership.

Our discussion of strategic leadership begins in Chapter 2 with an examination of a fundamental assumption of the entire book—that top managers do indeed have an important impact on organizational outcomes. The question of "Do top executives matter?" has a long history and a widely varying set of answers. At its core lies the debate between deterministic theories of environmental constraint and strategic choice perspectives on executive action. As we argue, definitively resolving this debate is virtually impossible, since both sides rely on such fundamental phenomena as constraint and choice. It is hard to imagine an organization not subject to both of these effects. For this reason, the concept of managerial discretion is offered as a bridge between opposing camps, an attempt to step back and recognize that managerial impact on organizational outcomes is subject to the interplay of both constraint and choice; this interplay is itself driven by a set of knowable and measurable factors that are central to research on strategic leadership.

Chapters 3 and 4 focus on executive effects on organizational outcomes, developing the idea that an executive's "orientation," a complex set of psychological and observable characteristics, gives rise to his or her perceptions and choices. Building on classic work by the "Carnegie School," we suggest a model of human limits on strategic choice that has clear implications for how organizational outcomes are often a reflection of top executive orientations.

Chapter 3 focuses specifically on psychological attributes of executives: executive values, cognitive models, and other elements of personality. We discuss the major dimensions of executive psychology and develop a new set of propositions that link these dimensions to executive actions.

Chapter 4 then emphasizes the role of executive experiences. By this we mean the wide set of experiences executives bring to their positions, as embodied by such characteristics as tenure, functional background, and education. Research on demographic characteristics and organizational outcomes is abundant, and this chapter tries to make sense of what is known and not known about these relationships. In addition, a major goal of this chapter is to help move this research toward a potentially more promising and intriguing line of inquiry that breaks away from more established patterns. Hence, this chapter offers suggestions for examining a broader set of executive experiences and executive populations than have traditionally been studied and calls for more attention to developing executive typologies. Perhaps most important, we build on work in social psychology (Snyder and Ickes 1985) to develop a model of when the associations between executive characteristics and organizational outcomes will be great or small.

In Chapter 5, we broaden the unit of analysis from individual executives to top management teams. However, as we discuss, shifting from a focus on individuals to a focus on groups is more than just a change in unit of analysis. Conceptually, top management teams are more than simply collections of individual executives, and one of the goals of this chapter is to indicate why. We argue that top management teams affect organizational outcomes not solely because of the collection of executive orientations that are prevalent among senior executives (although this is important), but also because the interrelationships among managers at the top have their own unique implications for organizations. Chief among these interrelationships are the distribution of power among top managers and the heterogeneity of executive orientations, topics on which we develop new ideas and suggest promising analytical and research directions.

Chapters 6, 7, and 8 each focus on one specific area of strategic leadership: executive turnover and succession, board-management relations, and executive compensation, respectively. These chapters build on the earlier ones in many ways, but they also are relatively self-contained, each addressing a set of issues that are well defined in the literature. As a result, each of these chapters draws upon a wide base of research, often from related fields, such as organizational sociology, managerial economics, and finance. Our goal has not been to conduct exhaustive literature reviews; rather, it has been to develop frameworks in each chapter that parsimoniously capture existing literature and suggest a set of important, unresolved research questions.

Chapter 6 synthesizes what is known about executive turnover and succession, presenting a model of the succession process that analytically distinguishes among the precipitating context for succession, the actual event and process, successor characteristics, and the effects of succession. This framework gives rise to the four fundamental research questions addressed in the chapter: Will succession occur? How will succession occur? Who will get picked? and What will the consequences be? We develop some new ideas in response to each of these questions. Executive successions are complex and informationally rich events. As a result, many of the issues discussed in other chapters are useful in understanding succession.

Chapter 7 shifts the locus of strategic leadership from top executives to the board of directors. In so doing, it enables an integration of board and executive perspectives on corporate governance and highlights how boards are in some ways "supra-top management teams." Once again, we develop a framework to help clarify and reconcile existing research, and we suggest promising lines of inquiry. This chapter focuses on three major research questions: What are the determinants of board characteristics? What determines the vigilance and behavior of boards? and How do boards affect organizational choices, strategy, and performance? Varying amounts of work have addressed each of these issues, but we believe our tripartite focus highlights much of what is essential about boards from a strategic leadership perspective. Indeed, we use these research questions as a springboard to develop a set of propositions that encapsulate much of what we still need to learn about boards.

Chapter 8 builds directly on the previous chapter, since executive compensation is closely related to the activities of boards of directors. Consistent with the themes of the book, however, we go beyond only considering boards in the compensation-setting process. We set forth a broader examination of how economic, social-psychological, and political perspectives help explain both the determinants and consequences of executive compensation. This broader view is valuable because, once again, it allows for both synthesis and analysis of a large and eclectic body of research. A further contribution of this chapter is in its formal consideration of both individual executive compensation and the distribution of pay within top management teams. This latter issue has the potential to become a central thrust in future research on executive compensation but thus far has been barely addressed. Overall, this chapter suggests numerous new lines of inquiry for scholars interested in executive compensation.

In contrast to the topic-focused nature of earlier chapters, Chapter 9 presents a comprehensive analysis of contemporary research on strategic leadership. Drawing upon both survey and archival data sources, we identify the leading contributions to research on strategic leadership since 1980. We then analyze this work through a variety of conceptual and methodological lenses. Our goal is to gain an appreciation for what has been done in the strategic leadership area, as well as to highlight the critical voids—what has not been done, and hence, what the major research opportunities are in this domain.

While Chapter 9 partitions and disaggregates research on strategic leadership, Chapter 10 does the reverse, focusing on synthesis, on pulling it all together. The chapter builds on all the earlier ones that examined specific research topics within strategic leadership. Our approach is to apply the full scope of our ideas on strategic leadership, chapter by chapter, to a discussion of the case of William Agee, a highly visible and controversial CEO—first at Bendix, later at Morrison Knudsen. The examination of the Agee story illustrates the analytic, explanatory power in focusing on senior executives as a way to understand organizational outcomes.

In sum, the book is optimistic, portraying strategic leadership as a stream of research within strategic management that will help provide a fundamental understanding of how and why organizations make their choices. It is clear that there still is very much more we need to know. This challenge poses a great opportunity, for the better our understanding of strategic leadership, the more we will know about the essence of strategy, about how organizations undertake strategies and perform the way they do.

NOTES

1. We use the terms "executive" and "top manager" interchangeably.
2. Mintzberg's book, *The Nature of Managerial Work* (1973), predated Kotter's by almost a decade. Even though it was widely noted and admired, Mintzberg's book did not spawn a new major stream of empirical research.

Do Top Executives Matter?

Those of us who teach in business schools rarely ponder the question, "Do managers matter?" Were we to do so, we would have to deal with unsettling questions about the basic worthwhileness of our work, as well as the scruples of taking our students' time and money to help them become "better managers." Perhaps we all implicitly have considered the issue of whether managers have much effect on organizational outcomes and arrived at a reassuringly affirmative answer. After all, we are surrounded daily with news about executive brilliance and ineptitude, about CEOs saving companies and ruining companies, about shareholders and boards replacing ineffective top executives with promising new talent. "Of course, managers matter," we say to ourselves.

However, not all who have looked at the issue carefully agree. In fact, there is a school of thought, supported by some evidence, that top managers in general do not have much effect on organizational outcomes. Before proceeding too far with a book on strategic leadership, we have to confront this fundamental issue.

Such is the purpose of this chapter. We start with a discussion of what it is top executives do, tracing a relatively well developed literature on executive roles, responsibilities, and arenas of action. We then turn to the central debate, first reviewing the arguments and evidence of those who are skeptical about managerial effects, then the perspective of those who argue that top managers have considerable influence on their organizations. Our resolution of the debate is not to pick one view as correct, but rather to propose a middle ground: sometimes managers matter a great deal, sometimes not at all, and usually it is somewhere in between. "Managerial discretion," or latitude of action, is the theoretical fulcrum we propose as a way of reconciling the two opposing camps. We then discuss the tendency for society to overattribute organizational outcomes to top executives, creating heroes and villains in the process and generally complicating the task of objectively tracing managerial impacts. We close the chapter with an inventory of research priorities.

WHAT DO TOP EXECUTIVES DO?

The head of an enterprise, say a CEO or a division president, has numerous roles to fulfill, not all of which square with typical images of top executives at work. Classic conceptions of the CEO depict a big person behind a big desk engaged in big actions: planning, organizing, coordinating, commanding, and controlling (Fayol 1950). Even loftier imagery is provided by Barnard (1938) and Selznick (1957), who emphasized the top executive's job as defining institutional mission and goals, maintaining institutional integrity, and obtaining cooperation from organizational members. Adding further to the picture of the remoteness of the CEO job was the post–World War II proliferation of models for rational decision making for the most complex of issues: for example, operations research, formal long-range planning, and portfolio analysis. The joint emergence of computer technology and the professionalization of management led to a belief, or heightened an existing one, that CEOs were, first and foremost, careful and comprehensive deciders of major courses of action.

It is precisely because of these entrenched ideologies about and images of top executives that Henry Mintzberg's book, *The Nature of Managerial Work* (1973), was so startling and important. Mintzberg studied the minute-by-minute activities of five experienced CEOs, each for a week. What he found was that CEOs are *not* buffered from daily minutiae and crises, they do *not* engage in much reflective planning, and decision making is but a

Drawing by Ziegler; © 1979 *The New Yorker* Magazine, Inc.

modest portion of what they do. Instead, CEOs were found to work at a hectic and unrelenting pace on a wide array of tasks; their activity is characterized by brevity, fragmentation, and interruption; they gravitate toward the current and well-specified and away from the distant and vague; they are attracted to and place credence in oral media; and they spend a great deal of time interacting—talking, cajoling, soothing, selling, listening, and nodding—with a wide array of parties inside and outside the organization.

On the basis of his data, Mintzberg distilled a set of ten managerial roles that he placed in three broad categories: interpersonal (figurehead, leader, and liaison), informational (monitor, disseminator, and spokesperson), and decisional (entrepreneur, disturbance handler, resource allocator, and negotiator). Figure 2-1 presents a summary of Mintzberg's executive roles.

Some studies have found that Mintzberg's roles are sometimes difficult to distinguish when observing discrete managerial activities (McCall and Segrist 1980). Other studies (typically examining various types of managers, not just CEOs) confirm the behaviors Mintzberg observed but argue that the roles can be further distilled, possibly down to as few as six: leader, spokesperson, resource allocator, entrepreneur, environmental monitor, and liaison (Tsui 1984). Kotter's (1982) in-depth research on fifteen

FIGURE 2-1   **Summary of Mintzberg's Executive Roles**

Role	Definition
Interpersonal	
Figurehead	Symbolic head; obligated to perform a number of routine duties of a legal or social nature.
Leader	Responsible for the motivation and activation of subordinates and for staffing, training, and associated duties.
Liaison	Maintains self-developed network of outside contacts and informers who provide favors and information.
Informational	
Monitor	Seeks and receives a wide variety of special information (much of it current) to develop a thorough understanding of the organization and the environment; emerges as the nerve center of internal and external information of the organization.
Disseminator	Transmits information received from outsiders or from subordinates to members of the organization. Some information is factual, while some involves the interpretation and integration of diverse value positions of organizational influences.
Spokesperson	Transmits information to outsiders on the organization's plans, policies, actions, results, and so on; serves as an expert on the organization's industry.
Decisional	
Entrepreneur	Searches the organization and its environment for opportunities and initiates "improvement projects" to bring about changes; supervises the design of certain projects as well.
Disturbance handler	Responsible for corrective action when the organization faces important, unexpected disturbances.
Resource allocator	Responsible for the allocation of organizational resources of all kinds—in effect, the making or approval of all significant organizational decisions.
Negotiator	Responsible for representing the organization during major negotiations with others.

SOURCE: Adapted from Mintzberg (1973) and Pavett and Lau (1982, 9).

general managers confirmed Mintzberg's general portrayal of managerial work but concluded that it could be distilled even further: short- and long-term agenda setting, internal and external network building, and getting the network to implement the agenda. None of these later studies is at odds with Mintzberg. When combined with yet other inquiries and models, they all indicate some basic dimensions of the top executive's job, which we now discuss.

Basic Dimensions of the Job

External and Internal Activities. Top executives operate at the boundary between the external environment and their organization (Thompson 1967). They gather information from outside, and they convey information, impressions, and reassurances to the outside. They alert insiders about external news and developments. They take actions to align the organization with the current and expected external environment (technology, market trends, regulatory forces, and competitors' initiatives); at times they try to modify the environment (through lobbying, trade associations, consortia, and joint ventures).

Strategy Formulation, Implementation, and Context Creation. Top executives may orchestrate the formulation of company strategy, including the choices of which products and markets to emphasize, how to outdo competitors, how fast to grow, and so on (Ansoff 1965; Porter 1980). Top executives also have a role in strategy implementation—allocating resources, establishing policies and programs, and developing an organization that is aligned with the strategic thrusts of the firm (Chandler 1962; Galbraith and Kazanjian 1986; Quinn 1980). And top executives create a context—through staffing, reward and measurement systems, culture and style—that influences the strategic choices made by the managers and technical specialists throughout the organization who are most familiar with the marketplace, technologies, and competitors (Bower 1970; Burgelman 1983).

Substance and Symbols. When we think of executive action, we usually gravitate to the substantive: acquiring or divesting a business, increasing a research and development (R&D) budget, opening a new factory, forming a task force to launch a total quality program, and so on. However, executives also operate in the world of symbols. A symbol is something that has meaning beyond its inherent substance. By virtue of where top executives are in the organization, their actions often convey extra meaning (Pfeffer 1983). Some top executive actions are expressly symbolic, such as hosting a farewell dinner for a much-loved employee, holding a recognition ceremony to honor some extraordinary achievement, or personally appearing in the company's advertisements. However, to some extent, all executive actions carry added meaning, or what might be called "symbolic fallout," conveying surplus messages to observers who are trying to detect the executive's intentions, values, predispositions, and where he or she is headed. For example, decisions to promote one person but not another, to close one plant but not another, or to have an important meeting in one location but not another all convey meaning beyond their inherent substance to parties inside and possibly even outside the organization. In fact, some have said that the top executive's most important task is to establish and convey an "organizational meaning" (Barnard 1938).

Thus, top executives are engaged, at least potentially, in a wide array of roles, responsibilities, and activities. We say "potentially" because which roles are emphasized varies immensely among executives. For example, the CEO of a publicly held corporation may engage in many more external activities (with security analysts, external board members, business journalists, and so on) than the CEO of a privately held company. The CEO of a company engaged in a turnaround effort will focus on different matters than the CEO of a company with abundant slack resources. In fact, Mintzberg (1973) laid out a series of descriptive hypotheses about how several contingency factors cause variation in managerial work. These contingency factors include environmental, organizational, situational, and individual factors, such as the executive's personality. We know of no studies that have attempted to directly test Mintzberg's hypotheses; however, as we will see throughout this book, numerous studies have documented the tendency for executives' own attributes (their experiences, education, functional background, personality, and so on) to affect their behaviors and choices.

That top executives would act on the basis of their own predispositions is fully understandable. Senior managers are embedded in ambiguity, complexity, and information overload. They encounter far more stimuli than they can comprehend; and those stimuli are typically vague, ill-formed, and contradictory (March and Simon 1958). Thus, the top executive faces the classic case of what the renowned psychologist Walter Mischel (1968) calls a "weak situation," that is, one in which the characteristics of the situation are not clear-cut enough to dictate a course of action. In such circumstances, the decision maker's personal frame of reference, not the objective characteristics of the situation, becomes the basis for action.

Precisely because of the multiplicity of executive roles, activities, and courses of action, along with the ambiguity and overload of the information confronting executives, it is critically important to study the effects of different executives on the form and fate of their organizations. Ultimately, executives' experiences, interpretations, and preferences greatly affect what happens to companies.

Do Managers Matter? A Doubtful View

As intuitively reasonable as it may seem, the idea that top executives hold great sway over organizational outcomes is not universally held. Some theorists have set forth cogent arguments about the strict limits within which executives operate. And empirical evidence has been presented that, at least on its face, suggests that top executives have far less effect than other factors on organizations.

Population ecologists particularly have argued that organizations—and their top managers—are largely inertial, hemmed in by environmental and organizational constraints. Hannan and Freeman (1977), for example, noted several internal constraints on managerial action: fixed investment in specialized assets, restricted information flows, internal political constraints, and entrenched norms and cultures. Similarly, they identified some significant external constraints: legal and fiscal barriers to entry and exit from markets, restricted access to external information, and legitimacy constraints.

Institutional theorists have argued that legitimacy constraints on organizations are particularly confining (e.g., DiMaggio and Powell 1983). Under great pressure to appear "normal" and rational, organizations must adopt numerous conventions that pull them into conformity with external expectations. Moreover, in the face of uncertainty, managers may be compelled to conclude that the least risky course of action is to imitate the choices of their counterparts (particularly the more successful ones) in other organizations. So, a process of "mimetic isomorphism" leads to remarkable homogeneity, particularly within an industry (Spender 1989; Hambrick, Geletkanycz, and Fredrickson 1993).

An additional reason proposed for why managers may account for little variance in organizational outcomes is that managers as a group are exceedingly homogeneous (March and March 1977), that is, there is not much variance in the independent variable. Certainly, on the surface, CEOs are not a diverse lot. In America's Fortune 500 companies, almost all CEOs are white men, age 50 to 65, who have college degrees and significant big-company experience (*Business Week* 1993). In some countries, the pathways to large company presidencies are even more restricted, often requiring graduation from one of a small set of elite universities (e.g., Whitehill 1991). If top executives are drawn from a very narrow pool and then subjected to a long period of common socialization, they likely will not exhibit much independence of thought and action.

Thus, for reasons of substantive constraint, institutional pressures for conformity and imitation, and extreme homogeneity of the top executive population, some have argued that managers do not matter. And at least two well-known empirical studies seem to point to that conclusion.

The most commonly cited evidence of minimal executive effects is Lieberson and O'Connor's (1972) study of top executives in large corporations.

Using an analysis of variance procedure on a sample of 167 companies over a twenty-year period, the authors statistically isolated the portion of company performance (as measured by sales, profits, and return on sales) that could be attributed to the top executive in place in a given year. After the authors controlled for the year, industry, and specific company, leadership explained only between 6.5 and 14.5 percent of variance in the three performance measures examined. Lieberson and O'Connor concluded: "In short, all three performance variables are affected by forces beyond a leader's immediate control. . ." (page 121).

The second work often cited as evidence of negligible managerial effects is Salancik and Pfeffer's (1977) study of city mayors. Examining data on thirty U.S. cities over a seventeen-year period, the authors employed analysis similar to Lieberson and O'Connor's. However, instead of explaining variance in organizational performance, Salancik and Pfeffer sought to explain variance in city expenditures in eight different budget categories. As did Lieberson and O'Connor, they inserted control variables, for city and year, before assessing the amount of variance explained by the mayor. They found that the mayor accounted for 5 to 15 percent of variance in the expenditure categories. And, like Lieberson and O'Connor, they concluded a confined role for leaders: "Leadership in organizations operates within constraints deriving from internal structural and procedural factors and from external demands on the organization" (page 492).

So, on the one hand, reasonable logic and large-sample data provide a basis for believing that top executives do not matter very much. On the other hand, a great deal of everyday observation, as well as other systematic studies, point to the opposite conclusion.

Do Managers Matter? A Positive View

Some companies do not change much over time. But many do, and at the hands of their top executives. Consider these firms: Dial, the soap and consumer products company (formerly Greyhound, the bus line); Travelers, the financial services company (formerly named Primerica, and before that, American Can, a container company); and Trinova, a maker of metal and plastic industrial products (formerly Libby-Owens-Ford, the glass company). Within the last few years, these companies have completely ceased or divested all operations in their original lines of business. Today, their founders would not recognize them, nor would their CEOs in 1970 or possibly even in 1980. These companies are fundamentally different because of choices made by top executives.

Executives in other companies make different kinds of choices. Sometimes, as with the companies listed above, the choices are bold and quantum; sometimes they are incremental; sometimes they maintain the status quo; and sometimes they are not choices at all, but rather a failure to generate and consider choices. But managers act. As we shall argue throughout this book, they act on the basis of their own highly idiosyncratic experiences, repertoires, aspirations, knowledge of alternatives, and values.

Problems with Lieberson and O'Connor's Study. Before presenting affirmative evidence about managerial effects, we wish to return to Lieberson and O'Connor's (1972) oft-cited finding that top executives account for little variance in organizational performance. Their study, as influential as it is, had several methodological and analytic problems, *all* of which biased the results against observing managerial effects.

The most widely noted criticism of Lieberson and O'Connor deals with their choice of performance measures (Hambrick and Mason 1984; Romanelli and Tushman 1988). Two of their three performance measures—sales and earnings—are primarily indicators of the firm's size. In their data analysis, the authors sought first to explain variance by using three independent variables: year, industry, and company. Not surprisingly, these variables were exceedingly strong predictors of sales and earnings, with explained variance as high as 97 percent. (If we know that a company is in the steel industry, and specifically it is U.S. Steel in the year 1950, our ability to estimate the company's sales level will be relatively high.) Then, and only then, was the analysis rerun with leadership—represented by a dummy variable for each of the individual CEOs—included to determine how much additional variance could be explained. Since by this point almost all variance has been explained, the apparent added effect of leadership was nil. When Weiner and Mahoney (1981) replicated Lieberson and O'Connor's study, they allowed the leadership variable to enter the analysis at the same stage as the other variables and found that leadership, or "stewardship," accounted for 44 percent of the variance in profitability of major firms.

Other problems bias Lieberson and O'Connor's study as well. First, they designated a new leader whenever a new president *or* board chairperson was appointed, without any attempt to identify the CEO *per se*. But if a chairperson (who also is CEO) names a new president, there, in fact, has not been a change in CEO; if the president serves as the CEO and there is a change in the chairperson, there has not been a change in CEO; or if a chairperson relinquishes the CEO duties to an incumbent president, there is a change in CEO even though the two parties have not changed. In American companies, these are all common possibilities. Hence, Lieberson and O'Connor's method for assigning specific CEOs to particular periods of time must have contained considerable error, making doubtful any attempts to associate specific CEOs with specific performance levels.

Next, Lieberson and O'Connor specifically excluded from their sample any industries heavily populated with diverse firms, as well as any firms that engaged in major mergers or acquisitions during the period of the study. However, altering a firm's portfolio of businesses—through diversification, acquisitions, and divestitures—is *the primary way* for an executive to have an immediate quantum effect on the form and fate of the firm. By excluding such cases, Lieberson and O'Connor tightly restricted their sample to more incremental strategies and, not surprisingly, an apparently lessened executive effect.

Our point is not to dismiss the Lieberson and O'Connor study. The authors had good reasons for the research design choices they made. However, their choices consistently biased their findings away from observing managerial influence on corporate outcomes. Hence, their study provides far less than the definitive word on the matter.

Evidence of Executive Effects.   Beyond abundant anecdotal evidence that top executives can substantially alter organizations (e.g., Tichy and Devanna 1986a; Tichy and Sherman 1993), numerous large-sample studies point to executive effects as well. Some of those studies, such as Weiner and Mahoney (1981), have been directly aimed at demonstrating the limitations of Lieberson and O'Connor's (1972) study. Other works have gone beyond methodological refinements, introducing important theoretical perspectives. For example, Smith, Carson, and Alexander (1984) used a sample of Methodist ministers to demonstrate that leaders who had been very effective in prior assignments tended to deliver higher performance in their current assignments (measured by church attendance and financial statistics) than leaders who had been previously less effective. In their view, a measure of managerial quality enhances the ability to predict managerial effectiveness. Similarly, Pfeffer and Davis-Blake (1986) found that the prior records of professional basketball coaches helped predict their performance in new coaching assignments.

Numerous other studies have examined and found significant associations between executive attributes or succession and organizational performance. A few examples will serve to illustrate this abundant stream of research. Virany and Tushman (1986), for example, found that the senior managers of better-performing microcomputer firms had significant previous experience in the industry and tended to include the firm's founder. Gupta and Govindarajan (1984) found that different types of general manager expertise were associated with business performance, depending on the strategy being pursued by the business. Murray (1989), from a sample of twenty-six oil companies, found that top management teams composed of members of diverse tenures outperformed those with more homogeneous tenures. Haleblian and Finkelstein (1993) studied a sample of computer and natural gas companies and found that the size of the top management team was positively associated with company performance, while a measure of CEO dominance was negatively associated with performance.

Not all research on top executives has sought to examine direct effects on organizational performance. Some investigators have focused on understanding how top management characteristics are associated with strategies and structures selected. For example, Hage and Dewar (1973) found that the values held by top management teams affected their organizations' subsequent degree of innovation. Miller and Droge (1986) found that chief executive personality influenced the structure of the organization. And Helmich and Brown (1972) found that whether a new chief executive comes from inside or outside the organization affects how much organizational change will occur early in his or her tenure.

These are just a minor sampling of the evidence that managers have influence on their organizations' profiles and performance. We do not wish to imply that such influence is total or easy to exercise, but it exists.

Moreover, we do not seek to extol the virtues of top managers. Executives are worth studying as much for their limitations as for their achievements. In fact, population ecologists may have erroneously stated their initial case against managerial effects because they required any such effects to be positive. This quote illustrates the ecologists' early view of the adaptation, or strategic choice, perspective:

> According to the adaptation perspective, subunits of the organization, usually managers or dominant coalitions, scan the *relevant* environment for opportunities and threats, formulate strategic responses, and adjust organizational structure *appropriately* (emphasis added). (Hannan and Freeman 1977, 929)

Such an interpretation omits the possibility that managers scan the *irrelevant* environment and formulate responses *inappropriately*. Population ecologists tend to equate deteriorating organizational performance with an absence of managerial effect, when what they may be observing is simply unwise or unlucky choices on the part of managers. Part of the problem may be terminology. Ecologists use interchangeably the terms *adaptation* and *strategic choice* to describe the model that rivals theirs. Because *adaptation* clearly connotes success in adjusting to the environment, it may be that in observing that organizations regularly fail, the ecologists assume that organizations do not adapt and, beyond that, that strategic choices are not made.

Later work by population ecologists envisioned a more significant role for top executives in influencing organizational outcomes (e.g., Hannan and Freeman 1984). In fact, some empirical research by ecologists has explicitly examined the effects of executive departures on survival rates of organizations (Carroll 1984; Haveman 1993). Such could not have been considered under the earliest formulations of the ecological perspective.

Managerial Discretion

So, do managers matter a great deal, all the time? No, the amount of leeway available to senior executives, even CEOs, varies widely. In an effort to bridge opposing views about how much effect top executives have on organizational outcomes, Hambrick and Finkelstein (1987) introduced and elaborated on the concept of executive discretion, or latitude of action. Depending on how much discretion exists, an organization's form and fate may lie totally outside the control of its top managers, completely within their control, or, more typically, somewhere in between.

For discretion to exist, an executive must have, and be aware of, multiple possible courses of action. As such, discretion is not absolute. It stems from contextual forces, but it also is derived from within the executive. Stated another way, one executive might create or detect alternative courses of action in a given situation, while another in the same situation might not be aware of such alternatives. Thus, as we discuss below, an executive's discretion is in part a function of his or her own characteristics, especially cognitive limits.

Moreover, an executive's discretion is rarely explicitly defined. Executives typically do not know exactly what actions might be allowed by powerful parties. So, they operate on the basis of rough estimates of the extent of their discretion, sometimes floating trial balloons to test the boundaries; occasionally they even overstep those boundaries, only *then* to be sanctioned severely by governing or powerful stakeholders.

A CEO's degree of discretion does not occur by happenstance. It is derived from three sets of factors: environmental, organizational, and individual managerial characteristics. So, as stated by Hambrick and Finkelstein (1987, 379):

> . . . a chief executive's latitude of action is a function of (1) the degree to which the environment allows variety and change, (2) the degree to which the organization itself is amenable to an array of possible actions and empowers the chief executive to formulate and execute those actions, and (3) the degree to which the chief executive personally is able to envision or create multiple courses of action.

As Figure 2-2 indicates, Hambrick and Finkelstein posited some specific determinants of discretion within each of these three spheres. We now
discuss those.

Environmental Sources.   The characteristics of the firm's task environment greatly affects the level of executive discretion and, in turn, how much
influence managers have on organizational outcomes. Let us return briefly
to Lieberson and O'Connor's study, which, as discussed above, is primarily
known for demonstrating minimal managerial effects. A less-noted finding
from their study is that managerial effects on corporate performance differ

FIGURE 2–2   **The Forces Affecting Chief Executive Discretion**

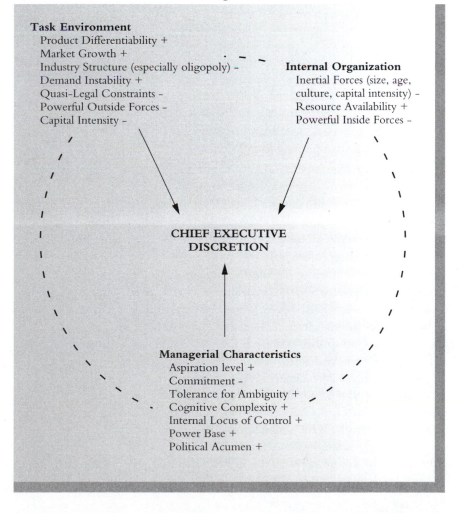

Task Environment
  Product Differentiability +
  Market Growth +
  Industry Structure (especially oligopoly) –
  Demand Instability +
  Quasi-Legal Constraints –
  Powerful Outside Forces –
  Capital Intensity –

Internal Organization
  Inertial Forces (size, age,
  culture, capital intensity) –
  Resource Availability +
  Powerful Inside Forces –

**CHIEF EXECUTIVE
DISCRETION**

Managerial Characteristics
  Aspiration level +
  Commitment –
  Tolerance for Ambiguity +
  Cognitive Complexity +
  Internal Locus of Control +
  Power Base +
  Political Acumen +

substantially across industries. Firms in the publishing and soaps/toiletries industries had the greatest amount of variance in profit margins explained by executive leadership, while firms in the clay products and shipbuilding industries had the least. Hambrick and Finkelstein (1987) attempted to explain and extend these results by arguing that the former industries provided far more executive discretion than the latter and that, in general, environments confer discretion to the extent that (1) there is a relative absence of clear means-ends linkages, that is, where a wide range of options can meet stakeholders' nominal tests of plausibility; and (2) there is an absence of direct and concentrated constraints.

In turn, Hambrick and Finkelstein set forth the following industry determinants of executive discretion:

- product differentiability
- market growth
- demand instability
- low capital intensity
- monopolistic and purely competitive industry structures (as opposed to oligopolies)
- absence of legal and quasi-legal constraints (e.g., regulation)
- absence of powerful outside forces (e.g., large, concentrated customers, suppliers, funding sources)

Preliminary attempts to identify high- and low-discretion industries, for purposes of empirical inquiry, relied primarily on qualitative application of Hambrick and Finkelstein's ideas. For instance, Finkelstein and Hambrick (1990) examined in the aggregate the indicators of product differentiability, market growth, and so forth of sixteen major industries to select the computer, chemical, and natural-gas distribution industries as high-, medium-, and low-discretion environments, respectively. Similarly, Hambrick, Geletkanycz, and Fredrickson (1993) used qualitative, gestalt judgments to assign foods/beverages, computing equipment, and scientific/measuring equipment as high-discretion industries and public utilities and telecommunications services as low-discretion, citing the wide differences between the two sets of industries in terms of differentiability, capital intensity, degree of regulation, and growth rates.

Only recently have more rigorous and exhaustive approaches been undertaken. Haleblian and Finkelstein (1993) used archival indicators of advertising intensity, R&D intensity, market growth, and degree of regulation to create an overall index of discretion in the computer and natural gas industries. The components of the index were highly internally consistent, and the index score differed widely between the two industries.

Hambrick and Abrahamson (1995) used a panel of academic experts to rate the overall amount of managerial discretion in seventeen industries. They found a very high degree of reliability between raters and, moreover, a high degree of agreement with the ratings of security analysts who specialized in each of the seventeen industries. Hambrick and Abrahamson then examined the associations between the panelists' ratings and actual objective characteristics of industry discretion (from Compustat data), as originally set forth by Hambrick and Finkelstein. Using regression analysis, they were able to estimate the implicit weights the panelists attached to specific industry characteristics (e.g., market growth) in rating overall discretion. The authors then applied these weightings of industry characteristics to determine the overall amount of discretion of fifty-three additional industries. Figure 2-3 lists, in rank order of discretion, the seventeen indus-

FIGURE 2-3 **Ratings of Managerial Discretion in Seventy Industries**

Industry Name	Standard Industrial Code	Discretion Score
Computer and software wholesaling	5045	6.89
Computer communication equipment	3576	6.72
Electromedical Apparatus	3845	6.72
Computer storage devices	3572	6.62
Perfume, cosmetic, toilet preparations	2844	6.60
Catalog, mail-order houses	5961	6.44
Medical laboratories	8071	6.43
*Computer programming	7372	6.38
In vitro, in vivo diagnostics	2835	6.36
Help supply services	7363	6.16
*Motion picture production	7313	6.08
Photographic equipment and supplies	3861	5.99
*Computer equipment	3570	5.77
Telephone and telegraph apparatus	3661	5.70
Variety stores	5331	5.66
*Engineering/scientific instruments	3826	5.63
*Games and toys	3944	5.55
Computer integrated system design	7373	5.55
*Pharmaceuticals	2834	5.54
*Surgical/medical instruments	3841	5.42
Women's; misses, junior's outerwear	2330	5.32
Eating places	5812	5.22
Miscellaneous amusement and recreation services	7990	5.21
Industrial measurement instruments	3823	5.19
Motor vehicles and car bodies	3711	5.18
*Radio/TV communication equipment	3663	5.17
Real estate investment trusts	6798	5.15
Orthopedic, prosthetic, surgical appliances	3842	5.07

Industry Name	Standard Industrial Code	Discretion Score
State commercial banks	6022	5.06
Newspaper publishing	2711	5.06
Personal credit institutions	6141	5.04
Chemicals and allied products	2800	5.02
★Book publishing	2731	4.92
Search and navigation systems	3812	4.91
National commercial banks	6021	4.87
Family clothing stores	5651	4.79
Drug and proprietary stores	5912	4.78
Women's clothing stores	5621	4.75
Department stores	5311	4.75
Electric lighting, wiring equipment	3640	4.73
Television broadcast stations	4833	4.72
Men's, youth, boy's furnishings	2320	4.72
Groceries and related products—wholesale	5140	4.71
Converted paper, paperboard (except boxes)	2670	4.68
Hotels, motels, tourist courts	7011	4.67
Hazardous waste management	4955	4.65
★Semiconductors	3674	4.61
Insurance agents, brokers, and service	6411	4.54
Paper mills	2621	4.46
Engineering services	8711	4.46
Water transportation	4400	4.34
★Instruments to measure electricity	3825	4.33
Grocery stores	5411	4.32
Savings institutions, federally chartered	6035	4.32
★Security brokers	6211	4.27
Natural gas distribution	4924	4.05
Commercial printing	2750	4.03
Motor vehicle parts and accessories	3714	3.92
Air conditioning, heating, refrigeration equipment	3585	3.80
Phone communication (except radiotelephone)	4813	3.72
Railroads, line–haul operating	4011	3.51
Drilling oil and gas wells	1381	3.41
★Certified air transportation	4512	3.23
Petroleum refining	2911	3.07
Water supply	4941	3.04
★Trucking (except local)	4213	2.72
★Gold and silver ores	1040	2.42
★Petroleum/natural gas production	1311	2.33
Electric services	4911	2.25
★Blast furnices/steel mills	3312	2.08
Natural gas transmission	4922	2.01

SOURCE: From Hambrick and Abrahamson (1995).

★These seventeen industries were included in the set rated by academic experts and security analysts; multivariate analysis of objective industry characteristics provides the basis for rating the other fifty-three industries.

tries used for establishing the weights and the other fifty-three. As can be seen, such industries as computer programming, perfumes and cosmetics, and motion picture production receive very high discretion scores. Such industries as natural gas transmission, electric services, and water supply were rated as very low discretion.

It is possible that environmental factors have brought about a general expansion of managerial discretion over the past several years. Beyond the obvious trend of deregulation in many countries, more options simply exist on the organizational landscape. Companies can select unique combinations of businesses to be active in; they can be fully active in a business or partly active through joint ventures or other alliances; they can select among myriad geographic locales for producing their products and still others for selling them; they can use full-time, relatively permanent employees or contingent, temporary workers. In short, societal and economic trends, as well as organizational innovations, have expanded the choices for senior executives, perhaps well beyond what existed when Lieberson and O'Connor (1972) did their study pointing to limited managerial effects.

Organizational Sources. In addition to environmental factors, the organization may have characteristics that enhance or, conversely, limit the chief executive's discretion. These include inertial forces, such as organizational size, age, a strong culture, and capital intensity, all of which limit executive latitude. Large, mature organizations with very entrenched cultures, such as IBM, Philips, Sears, and GE, are not easily changed. Their top executives operate under severe inertial constraints.

Also affecting executive discretion is the amount of resources available to the organization and internal political conditions (as determined by the distribution of ownership, board composition and loyalties, and internal power concentrations). For example, executives have far more discretion when ownership is widely dispersed than when one or a few owners own concentrated blocks (McEachern 1975; Hambrick and Finkelstein 1995). A CEO who is also chairperson of the board has more discretion than a CEO who does not hold both posts (especially when the chairperson is the prior CEO and is strongly committed to established policies). In short, characteristics of the organization greatly affect how much latitude top executives have over directions and policy.

Individual Sources. Finally, as noted above, discretion is derived in part from the executive him- or herself. By virtue of their personal characteristics, chief executives differ in the degree to which they generate and are aware of multiple courses of action. Some executives see alternatives that others do not. Some executives, because of their own persuasive and political skills, can consider options that others cannot. Hambrick and Finkelstein (1987) posited the following as more specific individual attributes affecting discretion: aspiration level, tolerance of ambiguity, cognitive complexity, locus of control, power base, and political acumen.

So far, researchers have not empirically examined these individual-level bases of discretion. However, this is a critically important arena for investigation, since the creation of discretion may be the crucial ingredient in executive capability:

> . . . managerial quality could be defined in part as the ability to perceive, create and enact discretion. Managerial excellence is a function of sheer awareness of options. Although it is an open (and researchable) issue, we suspect that managerial performance is more a matter of generating options than of selecting among them. Namely, among a given set of options, to most knowledgeable executives one will typically tend to stand out as the best. Thus, the opportunity for managerial contribution lies in improving on the list. (Hambrick and Finkelstein 1987, 374)

That is, to some extent, executives create their own discretion. Effective managers find and create options that others do not have. They may do this through creativity and insight, political acumen, persistence, or sheer will. Managers, even in a given situation, are not uniformly hemmed in.

Effects of Discretion.   Executive discretion can be expected to affect a variety of phenomena of interest to organizational scholars. For example, Hambrick and Finkelstein (1987) argued that in situations of low discretion, the following could be expected: older CEOs promoted from within (to fulfill largely figurehead roles), low executive compensation, little use of incentive executive compensation, low administrative intensity, low involuntary turnover of CEOs, stable strategy, and changes in organizational performance tied closely to changes in the task environment. Situations of high discretion would tend to result in opposite effects.

As important, however, discretion serves to attenuate the relationship between executive characteristics (values, experiences, and so on) and organizational outcomes. Namely, if high discretion exists, executive orientations become reflected in organizational outcomes; if low discretion exists, they do not. On this matter, research support is clear and consistent. For example, Finkelstein and Hambrick (1990) found that executive tenure was positively related to strategic persistence and strategic conformity to industry norms (reflecting presumably risk-averse and imitative tendencies of long-tenure executives) in high–discretion industries but not in low–discretion industries. The authors also found that when the organization allowed top managers significant latitude—as indicated by abundant slack or small company size—the firm's strategic choices were more likely to reflect the tenure of the top executives than when slack was limited or the company was large.

Additional research, while not specifically invoking the concept of discretion, provides further evidence in line with Hambrick and Finkelstein's suppositions. For example, Miller, Kets de Vries, and Toulouse (1982) found that CEO locus of control was strongly associated with organizational strategy and structure in small firms but not in large firms. The authors wrote, ". . . these [small firms] might be more easily dominated than large ones, which, all things being equal, are more difficult to control" (page 249). In the same vein, Reinganum (1985) found evidence that the stock market distinguishes between high- and low-discretion situations. On the announcement of CEO succession, stock prices rise abnormally, but only for small companies and when the predecessor CEO is totally departing the firm, these being conditions in which a new CEO can have an enhanced effect.

Several pieces of evidence support Hambrick and Finkelstein's ideas that discretion affects executive compensation arrangements, with executives in low-discretion situations receiving relatively low levels of pay and little incentive pay. Rajagopalan and Finkelstein (1992) studied the electric utility industry from 1978 to 1987, a period of steadily increasing deregulation and hence, increasing discretion. They found that executive compensation (for the CEO and top team) and the use of performance-contingent compensation increased over time as environmental discretion increased.

Other studies, while not explicitly investigating managerial discretion, have yielded corroborative findings. For example, a study by Kerr and Kren (1992), while not labeling firms as high or low on discretion, found that such indicators of discretion as R&D and advertising intensity strengthened the association between CEO pay and performance. Other studies further support the effects of discretion on executive compensation. Balkin and Gomez-Mejia (1987) found that high-technology firms, which tend to be characterized by greater levels of discretion (Hambrick and Abrahamson 1995), use incentive pay plans more than other firms do. And Napier and Smith (1987) found that the proportion of corporate managers' incentive pay was significantly greater in more diversified (and hence, higher discretion) firms. Further, Jensen and Murphy (1990) found that the relative amount of incentive compensation for CEOs was much greater in small firms than in large firms, prompting the authors to conclude: "Higher pay-performance sensitivities for small firms could reflect that CEOs are more influential in smaller companies" (page 260).

Recent work has suggested that executives may be aware, even if implicitly, of how much discretion they possess and that this shapes their cognitive processing. For example, in a large-sample study, Hambrick, Geletkanycz and Fredrickson (1993) found that in high-discretion industries, a firm's current level of performance was positively related to top executive commitment to the status quo (the belief that the organization's strategy and leadership characteristics in the future should remain as they are). This included, of course, the tendency for executives in poor-performing firms to believe that their firms should change. However, in low-discretion industries, no such association was found, leading the authors to state (page 406):

> . . . for the executive in a low-discretion situation, there is not a strong connec-tion between current performance and a belief in the correctness of current organizational strategy and leadership profiles. In this instance, performance, be it high or low, emanates largely from uncontrollables—the environment, the organization's confining history, etc.

It is an open and interesting question as to whether executives modify their beliefs about the potency of executive action after sustained exposure to a high- or low-discretion situation, or whether managers with certain types of beliefs and personalities (say, in terms of locus of control) are drawn to high- and low-discretion settings.

In general, executive discretion is an important construct for helping to bridge the debate about the influence of executives on organizational out-comes. Moreover, discretion may be a conceptual lever for improving our understanding of such matters as executive compensation, executive dis-missal, organizational inertia, and executive personality.

The Managerial Mystique

No discussion of the question of whether managers matter would be com-plete without addressing the unequivocal human tendency to believe that they matter. People seek to have heroes and villains as a way to explain organizational and institutional successes and failures. Through the ages, people have blamed kings for droughts, prime ministers for poor econom-ic conditions, and baseball managers for losing seasons. Humans gravitate to human explanations for noteworthy events or trends.

The work of James Meindl and his associates has been particularly instrumental in enhancing our understanding of "the romance of leadership." In one paper, Meindl, Ehrlich, and Dukerich (1985) argue that leadership is a "perception" that allows people to make sense out of organizationally relevant phenomenon. The authors examine the idea that attributions to leaders will be greatest when organizational performance is extreme—either very good or very bad. Their evidence, drawn from multiple methods and levels of analysis, is not definitive but clearly intriguing. They find that business press headlines refer to a company's leadership in direct proportion to the company's performance: the better the performance, the more attention is showered on leaders. At a more macro level, the authors find that the number of doctoral dissertations written on leadership subjects increases in bad economic times ("Where's the leadership to take care of this mess?") and that the number of articles in the business press dealing with leadership increases in good economic times ("Hurray for all this great leadership!"). (The difference between the pattern for dissertations and the press perhaps says something about the cynical lenses of academics.) Finally, in a series of laboratory studies, Meindl and his associates found that subjects, after reading a vignette, were relatively likely to ascribe extreme performance—either good or bad—to the leader of a business; more moderate or neutral performance was less likely to be attributed to the leader.

In a follow-up study, Chen and Meindl (1991) examined the role of the press in bestowing heroic and villainous status on leaders. Tracking the press acounts of the rise and fall of Donald Burr and People Express airline, the authors found that the press endowed Burr's ascendancy with a host of flattering images, then created a new set of images of Burr to account for the company's collapse—all the while striving to demonstrate a consistency in the two distinct sets of portrayals. This project, and the research stream it represents, highlights the tendency of people—exacerbated by the press—to attribute organizational outcomes to senior leaders.

Executives also generate their own attributions about their effects on their organizations. Here, the data are clear and quite consistent with the human need to manage impressions. Executives tend to take credit for favorable outcomes and blame external forces for unfavorable outcomes. The predominant research method for detecting this pattern is content analysis of the letters to shareholders in annual reports (Bettman and Weitz 1983; Abrahamson and Park 1994). One such project captures in its title the essence of the phenomenon: "Strategy and the Weather." In it, Bowman (1976) found that food companies that performed poorly very often blamed the weather and accompanying crop conditions, whereas food companies that performed well (and presumably faced the same weather) made no mention of the weather but instead pointed to the wisdom of their strategic choices.

The attributions made about executive influences on organizations are exceedingly interesting in their own right. Of course, these attributions also pose complications for the researcher who is interested in trying to objectively detect executive effects.

SUMMARY AND FUTURE RESEARCH

This chapter leads to a set of interconnected summary statements:

1. A senior executive operates in a wide array of spheres, encompassing substance and symbols, decisional and interpersonal roles, and external and internal activities.
2. Hence, there are numerous avenues by which a top executive can influence organizational outcomes. Moreover, situated where they are (i.e., at the top), top executives would seem to have the power to make things happen.
3. However, some research has concluded that top managers, including CEOs, do not have a strong effect on organizational performance. And although reservations can be raised about the analytic aspects of those studies, they cannot be entirely dismissed. Constraints on executives do exist, more so in some instances than in others.
4. Executives sometimes have very little latitude of action, sometimes a great deal, and usually somewhere in between. Executive discretion is the concept that allows us to describe and understand how much leeway exists. Discretion stems from factors in the environment, the organization, and the executive him- or herself.
5. Even though executives rarely have full say over what happens to their organizations, people tend to attribute extreme outcomes to leadership. This gives rise to a romance of leadership—heroes, villains, and scapegoats. Executives themselves further complicate the observer's ability to assign outcomes to leadership behaviors by consistently taking credit for favorable outcomes and pointing to "uncontrollable factors" for unfavorable outcomes.

Considerable research is still needed on the most basic elements of what managers do and whether they matter. This need is particularly great since so much idealized imagery, prescriptive folklore, and naive attributions exist about top executives. Careful examination of executives' roles and activities is warranted. Mintzberg (1973) and Kotter (1982) created a foundation for dissecting and classifying managerial roles, but too little research has extended these ideas. Particularly needed is an examination of the factors that affect an executive's involvement in various roles (external versus internal, decisional versus informational, and so on). Explanations based on environmental, organizational, temporal, and individual factors may allow important advances in understanding managerial work and even in generating prescriptions about "fitting" managers to specific circumstances. We would particularly encourage research on the symbolic aspects of top executive work. We are convinced that this is an important side of executive behavior, yet very few systematic or generalizable insights about executive symbolism have been generated.

Executive discretion also will be a fruitful target for research. Considerable work is needed in understanding the determinants of discretion. We particularly encourage examination of how organizational and individual characteristics affect the top executive's latitude of action, to complement the bit of progress made in understanding environmental sources of discretion (Hambrick and Abrahamson 1995).

Great opportunity also exists for research on the consequences of discretion. Some work has indicated that discretion affects executive compensation arrangements, but even here more needs to be known. Other possible consequences of discretion—including executive profiles, turnover rates, executive mobility and careers, administrative intensity, and executive personality—have gone unexplored. Discretion, we believe, will be an important theoretical fulcrum for understanding these and other important organizational phenomena.

Finally, one of the most promising areas of research will be executive images and attributions. How an executive is perceived obviously affects his or her own professional capital, but it also affects the firm's legitimacy and its ability to attract support from stakeholders. Executives no doubt engage in impression management to improve their images; however, the press and other external information conduits (such as executive search firms and business associations) also greatly influence how an executive is perceived. It may be that managerial attributions vary widely by national culture, with individualist countries such as the United States imbuing more of a managerial mystique than do countries with collectivist cultures, such as Finland and Japan. We anticipate that executive reputations, stigma, prestige, and attributions will be prominent constructs in some of the most interesting research on top management over the next several years.

THREE

INDIVIDUAL BASES OF EXECUTIVE ACTION

op executives operate in a world of ambiguity and complexity. Unlike convenient business school case studies, in which all the "relevant facts" are packed into twenty-five pages, real strategic situations lack structure; the identification and diagnosis of problems are open to varying interpretations, and potentially pertinent information is often far-flung, elusive, cryptic, even contradictory. At odds with most strategy frameworks in textbooks, top executives do not deal in a world of tidily packaged, verifiable external and internal phenomena. Even if they were to conduct in-depth comprehensive analysis, they would often arrive at widely differing conclusions because strategic situations are not knowable, they are only interpretable.

Consider, for instance, the myriad projections, estimates, and interpretations that entered into the 1994 bidding war between QVC and Viacom to acquire Paramount. The bids kept growing until finally Viacom won with a bid that was well above Paramount's market value before the frenzy started, greatly lowering Viacom's own stock price in the process. The two bidding companies purportedly had some ideas about the imminent convergence of various media, programming, and telecommunications activities. (Many observers also contend that QVC's chairman, Barry Diller, was motivated greatly by a desire to give Paramount's CEO, Martin Davis, his comeuppance for once having fired Diller from an executive position.)

Presumably, there were other media companies, just as well-heeled as QVC or Viacom, that could have entered the fray but decided that such combinations are not necessary or not even sensible, at least not at the prices that emerged. Obviously, someone was wrong—either the reluctant bystanders, QVC for not bidding more, or Viacom for bidding so much. The actual payoffs in the years ahead for all these parties depend on dozens or even hundreds of possible future events or trends—few of which can be estimated with any precision. No one knows what will happen, but that does not stop strategic decision makers from estimating or assuming what will happen, having strong preferences for some options and objectives over others, and making choices.

Strategic decisions thus clearly represent what psychologist Walter Mischel (1977) calls a "weak situation," one in which available stimuli are many, complex, and ambiguous. In such situations, the choices of decision makers vary widely and cannot be predicted by the stimuli themselves. Thus, decision makers inject a great deal of themselves into such choices.

Such a view is consistent with the logic of the Carnegie School of decision theory, which is in turn a central underpinning of our own point of view. According to Carnegie theorists, complex choices are largely determined by behavioral factors, rather than by calculations of optimal actions (March and Simon 1958; Cyert and March 1963). In their view, bounded rationality, multiple and sometimes incompatible goals, myriad options, and varying aspiration levels all serve to limit the extent to which complex decisions can be made on a techno-economic basis. Instead, complex choices are a result of human limits and biases. This is not to say that strategic decision makers are capricious or whimsical but simply that they act on the basis of what they know, believe, perceive, and want. And these can vary widely from strategist to strategist.

A MODEL OF HUMAN LIMITS
ON STRATEGIC CHOICE

If bounded rationality characterizes executive decision making, then it is important to understand how this "boundedness" occurs. How is it that executives come to perceive only a limited portion of all potentially relevant information, often attach peculiar interpretations to that, and assign idiosyncratic weights to different possible outcomes?

Our model for portraying this process is shown in Figure 3–1. At the left-hand side is the "strategic situation"—the myriad events and trends inside and outside the organization. Toward the right-hand side are "strategic choices" (decisions to diversify, enter into a joint venture, introduce a new profit-sharing system, and so on). We use the term "strategic choice" in the same way as Child (1972) did, to encompass choices made formally and informally, inaction as well as action, major administrative choices (such as decisions about staffing, rewards, and so on), and product or market and competitive actions usually associated with the term "strategy." Even further to the right is organizational performance.

The centerpiece of the model, however, is the executive and the process by which he or she arrives at a "construed reality" of the strategic situation and what ought to be done about it. We conceive of an "executive's orientation," consisting of an interwoven set of psychological characteristics and observable experiences, such as formal education and functional background (Finkelstein 1988). This executive orientation, then, serves as the basis on which the executive interprets the strategic situation and decides on a course of action. So, standing between the "objective" strategic situation and actual choices are human factors: "Biases, blinders, egos, aptitudes, experiences, fatigue, and other human factors in the executive ranks greatly affect what happens to companies" (Hambrick 1989, 5).

The Filtering Process

The logic of bounded rationality hinges on the premise that top executives are confronted with far more stimuli—from both within and outside the organization—than they can possibly fully comprehend and that those stimuli are often ambiguous, complex, and even contradictory. Accordingly, in arriving at their own rendition of a strategic situation, or "construed reality" (Sutton 1987), executives distill and interpret available information. This occurs through a three-stage filtering process—limited field of vision, selective perception, and interpretation—as depicted in Figure 3–1.

Limited Field of Vision.   As a first step in the filtering process, an executive will be exposed to only a subset of all stimuli. As Simon (1945) termed it, each decision maker has a limited and specific "focus of attention." Researchers of environmental scanning have found that executives vary widely in how much they scan, as well as their use of different sources for learning about external events or trends (Aguilar 1967; Kefalas and

FIGURE 3–1   Strategic Choice Under Bounded Rationality: The Executive's Construed Reality

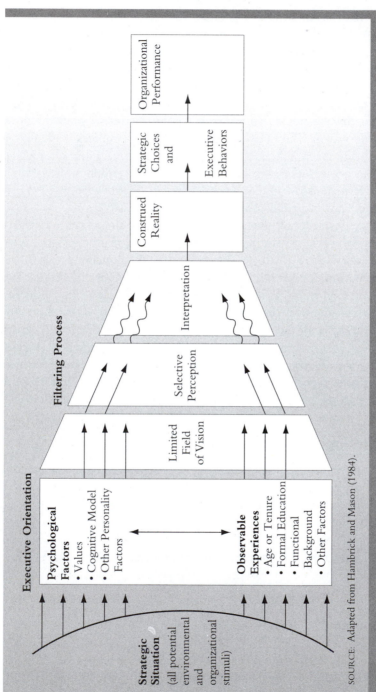

SOURCE: Adapted from Hambrick and Mason (1984).

Schoderbeck 1973; Hambrick 1982). For example, while some executives expend great effort reading formal reports from external consultants and research organizations, others rely more on informal interactions to learn about environmental forces. Executives also differ widely in terms of which environmental sectors they most attend to, for example, market, competitive, regulatory, and international sectors. Research on environmental scanning supports the conclusion that a given executive cannot scan everything that might be pertinent (Aguilar 1967; Hambrick 1981a; Daft, Sormunen, and Parks 1988; Waller, Huber and Glick in press).

Moreover, research on internal organization processes suggests that top executives may not even fully stay abreast of events and conditions in their own organizations. Strategic projects can be initiated (Bower 1970; Burgelman 1983), worker morale can deteriorate greatly, illegal behavior can occur (Micelli and Near 1994), all without a top executive's knowledge.[1] Obviously, an executive's field of vision is proportionately more limited in a large, complex organization than in a small, simple one.

An executive's network of contacts is a primary determinant of his or her field of vision (Chattopadhyay, et al., in press). Most senior executives have significant networks through which they both receive and disseminate information (Mintzberg 1973; Kotter 1982). However, these executive networks vary widely and can create significant differences in senior executives' fields of vision. For example, a new CEO recruited from outside the firm will tend not to have the same internal network as a CEO promoted from within (Gabarro 1987). An executive who is actively involved in industry trade associations has a network different from an executive who is not (Geletkanycz 1994). And an executive who sits on other companies' boards has an expanded field of vision by virtue of those associations (Lorsch 1989).

To sum up, an executive cannot be looking in every direction or listening for every possible piece of news.

Selective Perception.   Further filtering occurs because an executive only selectively perceives a portion of the stimuli within his or her field of vision.[2] Think, for example, of the executive who reads a consultant's report on technological trends in the industry. The executive's eyes may gaze upon every page (actually unlikely), but chances are, he or she will not read or comprehend every word. For one thing, the executive's grasp of and interest in technological issues will affect how much of the report "gets through." But other factors will matter as well: the executive's general regard for the consulting firm, whether the executive likes the editorial style and layout of the report, whether the passages in the report are consistent with what he or she has heard or read elsewhere, and so on. The same filtering process may occur when the executive sits through a long meeting of presentations by subordinates or has a conversation with a supplier. Not all of the information within the executive's field of vision will register equally: some will be vivid, meaningful, and engaging; some will slide into the executive's subconscious; and some will escape the executive's attention entirely.

Starbuck and Milliken (1988) refer to this as the process of "noticing" and argue that noticing is a complex function of what is familiar and unfamiliar to the decision maker. On the one hand, people become relatively insensitive to familiar stimuli; on the other hand, with experience, people are able to notice the slightest perturbation in familiar stimuli. Not enough research has been done on executive "noticing" to be able to reconcile these complex phenomena. However, it is clear that strategists only see a portion of what they are watching, and they hear only a portion of what they are listening to.

Interpretation.   As a third step in the sequential filtering process, the executive interprets or attaches meaning to stimuli. This step, directly or indirectly, has been the object of most research on executive perception. Managers have been studied for whether they interpret certain stimuli as opportunities or as threats (e.g., Dutton and Jackson 1987); for how they categorize or group stimuli (e.g., Day and Lord 1992); for how they use available stimuli to draw conclusions or inferences (e.g., Milliken 1990); and other interpretive processes. Starbuck and Milliken (1988) refer to this stage as "sensemaking," arguing that it is has various aspects: "comprehending, understanding, explaining, extrapolating, and predicting . . . ."

As an example of how executives can attach their own interpretations to information, Milliken (1990) found that college executives varied widely in drawing implications from a well-publicized and verifiable external trend, the imminent shrinking of the eighteen- to twenty-two-year-old population in the United States. Some executives saw this trend as a grave threat, others expressed little concern, and some even asserted that the trend would not occur. (Experts rated the probability of occurrence at 100 per cent.) Beyond their varying interpretations of the trend itself, the executives differed even more widely in their judgments about how their institutions should respond to the trend.

The three-stage information filtering process is made analytically tractable by thinking of it as a strictly sequential process: field of vision, selective perception, and interpretation (as portrayed in Figure 3–1). However, the three stages of the process may interact in nonsequential ways. For instance, if an executive comprehends and is engaged by a very high proportion of the information coming from a specific information source, he or she is even more likely to rely on that source in the future. In such a case, selective perception affects field of vision. Other iterative links in this filtering process can be anticipated as well.[3]

As a result of the filtering process we have described, an executive's ultimate perception of the strategic situation, or "construed reality" (what Weick (1969) might term "enacted environment"), may bear little correspondence to the objective "facts" (even if those could be ascertained).[4] And, more important, one executive's construed reality can be quite different from another's:

> In the face of the ambiguity and massive bombardment of information that typifies the top management task, no two strategists will necessarily identify the same array of options; if they were to pick the same major options, they almost certainly would not implement them identically. (Hambrick 1987, 88)

Such a contention is useful, as far as it goes. However, we seek fuller explanation and prediction, because if executives filter stimuli randomly, we do not have much of a theory.

It is the "executive's orientation," an interwoven set of psychological and observable characteristics, that engages the filtering process, in turn giving rise to construed reality and strategic choices, and ultimately affecting organizational performance. These orienting characteristics are the givens that an executive brings to an administrative situation (March and Simon 1958). If we wish to understand the strategic choices and performance of organizations—the right-hand side of Figure 3–1—we must examine and understand their top executives.

Executive Orientation—An Overview

Two major classes of personal characteristics constitute an executive's "orientation." First are psychological properties, such as values, cognitive model, and other elements of personality. These qualities provide a basis on which the executive filters and interprets stimuli, and they dispose the executive toward certain choices. For example, Miller and Droge (1986) found that CEOs in a sample of companies differed significantly in their need for achievement, an element of personality. The greater the CEO's need for achievement, the greater the organization's structural centralization and formalization, reflecting, the authors thought, the high achiever's strong desires to personally monitor and control all company actions and take credit for company successes.

The second set of characteristics comprising an executive's orientation are those observable dimensions of the person's experiences. Such variables as functional background, company tenure, and formal education have been prominent in studies of senior executives in recent years. For example, a well-known finding from several studies is that executives tend to make more and bigger strategic changes early in their tenures than they do later on; moreover, new executives from outside the firm make more changes than those promoted from within (Helmich and Brown 1972; Gabarro 1987; Baumrin 1990; Hambrick and Fukutomi 1991).

Researchers who use executive experiences to explain executive behaviors sometimes make assertions about psychological characteristics that are being proxied by the experiences. For instance, in the research just mentioned, the mechanism causing so much strategic change early in an executive's tenure (and less later on) could be the new executive's open-mindedness, eagerness to demonstrate efficacy, lack of entrenched relationships, or simply emotional (and possibly physical) energy. However, in the cited studies, these psychological qualities went unexamined, so the actual operative mechanism behind a robust and interesting relationship remains a "black box."

Psychological constructs have the advantage of conceptual clarity and, perhaps more important, provide a pointed causal link to the executive behaviors or choices being explained. And it is certainly better to have an explanation for a relationship than to simply demonstrate its existence (Lawrence 1991).

However, the use of psychological constructs poses major limitations for researchers of senior executives (Finkelstein 1988). First, top executives are often reluctant to submit to batteries of psychological tests. In our experience, the larger and more visible the company, the greater the reluctance. Thus, it is not surprising that most studies of psychological characteristics of top executives are based on samples from small and medium-sized firms or nonprofit organizations. Second, if the researcher is interested in studying the effects of executive psychological characteristics on subsequent strategic choices, and perhaps even on further subsequent performance, any psychological data gathered must "await," possibly for two years or more, the strategic and performance measures being explained. The elapsed time and expense of such a research program can be considerable. Finally, some psychological constructs have the drawback of doubtful validity when applied to senior executives. For example, recent debates have focused on whether the conventional scales for gauging personality dimensions are too general and detached from executive issues to be useful for studying top managers (Boone and De Brabander 1993; Hodgkinson 1993).

Measures of executive experiences pose the obverse strengths and weaknesses. Experience data are abundant for various types of companies, over long timeframes, and even for different countries (Wiersema and Bird 1993). Such data are also relatively reliable. For instance, an executive's tenure in the firm is open to essentially no measurement error; an executive's primary functional background is open to little error and can be coded reliably (Barbosa 1985). In this vein, Pfeffer argued for the use of experience, or demographic, variables:

> It is possible for demography to do a better job at explaining variation in the dependent variables than measures of the presumed intervening constructs, for the reason that many of the intervening constructs are mental processes . . . that are more difficult to access and reliably measure. (1983, 351)

Obviously, the chief drawback of demographic data is the "black box" problem. When a relationship between an executive's experiences and an organizational outcome is observed, the nagging question is always "Why?" Sometimes the researcher will attempt to logically justify what the experience variable is tapping. For instance, Finkelstein and Hambrick (1990) used prior literature to argue that executive tenure in the firm is a proxy for an executive's commitment to the status quo, risk aversion, and narrowness of information sources used. However, without data on these three possible operative mechanisms, there is no way of knowing which of them (or in what proportions) actually affected the relationships the authors observed between executive tenure and strategic persistence.

Hambrick and Mason also acknowledged this problem:

> Demographic indicators may contain more noise than purer psychological measures. For example, a person's educational background may serve as a muddied indicator of socioeconomic background, motivation, cognitive style, risk propensity, and other underlying traits. (1984, 196)

However, executive psychological characteristics and experiences probably are mutually dependent through two-way causality. As is often asserted, experiences affect psychological characteristics. For example, long tenure in the firm may induce a commitment to the status quo. However, fundamental psychological qualities can also substantially affect an executive's experiences. For example, risk-averse individuals may tend not to change employers often and hence have long tenures; similarly, individuals with different cognitive styles may vary in how much formal education they pursue as well as in their choices of curricula.

So, as we show in Figure 3–1, executive psychological and experience characteristics cannot reliably be put one before the other. They affect each other, and far more research needs to examine the associations between executive experience and psychological characteristics. If strong, recurring patterns are observed, it may even be possible to develop a useful typology of executive profiles, with each type consisting of a combination of experiences and psychological attributes.

The question is not which of these two approaches to gauging executive characteristics—experience or psychological—better provides an understanding of the effects of executives on their organizations. Ultimately, the two approaches will be used in concert.

The remainder of this chapter focuses on executive psychological factors and their influences on strategic choice. Chapter 4 will examine the burgeoning literature on executive experiences, or demographics.

PSYCHOLOGICAL CHARACTERISTICS AS BASES FOR EXECUTIVE ACTION

Psychologists have numerous ways of characterizing people and their minds. The work on executive psychology, however, has focused primarily on three broad fronts: executive values, cognitive models, and other elements of personality. In this section, we examine some of the major ideas and findings regarding these three elements of executive psychology, defining each concept, discussing some of its major dimensions, and describing its theorized or demonstrated links to executive actions.

Executive Values[5]

Top managers vary in what they want—for themselves, their organizations, their employees, and society; that is, executives vary in their values and act accordingly. In fact, values may greatly determine other executive psychological characteristics, including cognitions; therefore, we consider them first.

Rokeach defined values as follows:

[T]o say that a person "has a value" is to say that he has an enduring belief that a specific mode of conduct or end-state of existence is personally and socially preferable to alternative modes of conduct or end-states of existence. (1973, 159–60)

Hofstede's (1980) definition is very similar: "a broad tendency to prefer certain states of affairs over others" (p. 19). Hambrick and Brandon's (1988) definition, which we adopt, is a minor modification of those of

Rokeach and Hofstede: *a broad and relatively enduring preference for some state of affairs.*

Most theorists allow for both personal and social values. Personal values are conceptions of what the individual aspires to (e.g., prestige, family security, wealth, wisdom). Social values have to do with what the person finds desirable in others or in the broader social system (e.g., rationality, honesty, courage, world peace). Additionally, values can be either instrumental or terminal, dealing either with means (e.g., courage, honesty) or ends (e.g., equality, self-respect).

As each value is learned or modified, it becomes integrated into an overall values system in which each value has its own place, perhaps of high or low priority. For instance, managers typically confront situations in which they cannot satisfy all their values. They may have to choose between behaving compassionately or behaving competently; they may have to choose between their own job security and stockholder wealth maximization, and so on. Their hierarchy of values drive these choices.

Values are relatively enduring, thus standing in contrast to ephemeral attitudes or emotions. However, values are not entirely fixed over a person's adult life. Rokeach commented on a theoretical conception that allows for both stability and change in a person's value system:

> It is stable enough to reflect the fact of sameness and continuity of a unique personality socialized within a given culture and society, yet unstable enough to permit rearrangements of value priorities as a result of changes in culture, society, and personal experience. (1973,11)

Origins of Values.   Values only exist in a social context; one can speak of "values" only in maturing or mature individuals who have been regularly exposed to models, rules, and sanctions of a social system. The social system exists in several layers—national culture, regional society, family, and employing organizations—all exerting influence on a person's values.

The influence of national culture in shaping values of executives has been heavily examined. Studies by Bendix (1956), Sutton, Harris, Kaysen, and Tobin (1956), and Chatov (1973) all concluded that the values that business executives bring to their tasks are largely due to a national system of beliefs. England (1975) found that national origin accounted for 30 to 45 percent of the variations in executive values. Hofstede (1980) similarly documented the strong role of national culture in accounting for values of employees, including managers, in an international company.

Other layers of the social system operate as well. Cohort history, and particularly the occurrence of wars, depressions, disasters, or major social movements, can sharply affect the values of a body of individuals in a society (e.g., Kluckhohn 1951; Jacob, Flink, and Shuchman 1962; Schmidt and Posner 1983). In addition, family influences, such as class, race, and religious upbringing, are all strongly associated with value variations (Rokeach 1969a, 1969b; Rokeach and Parker 1970).

At the occupational level, a self-selection process occurs, such that individuals entering a certain line of work tend to have values that differ from the population as a whole (Allport, Vernon, and Lindzen 1970; Rawls and Nelson 1975). Selection and socialization processes continue to operate after entry to an occupation. To the extent that the occupation has a codified body of standards and norms that are repeatedly reinforced, members can be expected to strengthen their values (e.g., Blau and McKinley 1979; Cafferata 1979). For individuals who are highly successful within their occupations, their initial values are further reinforced (Mortimer and Lorence 1979).

The employing organization also exerts its own pressure on values. Organizations convey something of themselves in attracting employment candidates and, in turn, seek to hire individuals whose values "fit" the setting. After entry, socialization occurs (Feldman 1981), further shaping the values of members (Pfeffer 1981a; Louis, Posner, and Powell 1983). The longer a member stays in the organization, the more his or her values will resemble those preferred by the organization (Wiener 1982). Members who achieve extraordinary success by abiding by and transmitting organizational values—such as executives—will particularly embrace those values.

In sum, senior executives can be expected to have relatively entrenched value sets. Their extended exposure to value-shaping stimuli, their self-selection into settings compatible with their values, and the reinforcement they have received through their successes all give rise to a well-defined value profile.

Values Dimensions.   Theorists have set forth many value dimensions—far too many to fully reconcile or employ. Adding to the frustration is that none of the major theorists has pointedly addressed how or why their own value typologies differ from the others. In an attempt to overcome this disjointedness, Hambrick and Brandon (1988) attempted a systematic consolidation of four prominent values schemes—those of Allport, Vernon, and Lindzey (1970), Rokeach (1973), England (1967), and Hofstede (1980).

Table 3–1 shows the results of Hambrick and Brandon's integration of these values frameworks. As can be seen, the vast majority of all the values dimensions set forth in the four schemes can be distilled into six constructs of central importance to students of executive behavior. As named and defined by Hambrick and Brandon (1988), these six robust dimensions are:

Collectivism: to value the wholeness of humankind and of social systems; regard and respect for all people

Duty: to value the integrity of reciprocal relationships; obligation and loyalty

Rationality: to value fact-based, emotion-free decisions and actions

Novelty: to value change, the new, the different

Materialism: to value wealth and tangible possessions

Power: to value control of situations and people

Hambrick and Brandon's distillation encompasses the vast majority of the values dimensions proposed by four sets of prominent theorists, thus providing a set of six "core" values dimensions tapped by these major frameworks. This synthesis is not exhaustive, however, since some of the theorists' dimensions were unique, with no counterparts in the other schemes and thus fell outside of Hambrick and Brandon's consolidation.[6] However, in general, the integration by Hambrick and Brandon greatly reduces the disjointedness of the earlier schemes and should be of help in conducting theory development and research on executive values.

Effects on Choices.   Despite the abundant literature on executive values, little theory or research has been set forth on how values are converted into action. With limited exceptions (e.g., England 1967), the few investigators who have explored the association between managerial values and actions have been primarily interested in cross-sectionally documenting that such a link might exist, rather than the process by which it occurs (e.g., Guth and Taguiri 1965; Farris 1973; England 1973a; Lee 1975).

Following England (1967), we believe that executive values affect choices in two ways. First, there may be a direct influence, as when an executive selects a course of action strictly because of value preferences. The person may fully comprehend the facts on all sides of an issue, and select the course of action that suits his or her values. England (1967) refers to this direct influence of values on action as "behavior channelling." When this occurs, the "filtering process" shown in Figure 3–1 is skirted or immaterial.

Far more common, we believe, are the indirect influences that values have on executive actions. In this indirect mode, values work through the perceptual filtering process. Values affect the executive's field of vision—the intensity with which new information will be sought, the media that will be used, and so on. Moreover, values affect selective perception in interpretation: The manager "sees what he wants to see," "hears what she wants to hear" (Weick 1979b). This well-known process, called "perceptual

TABLE 3-1 A Distilled Set of Six Significant Executive Value Dimensions

Executive Value Dimension	Allport, Vernon, and Lindzey (1970)	Analogues in Other Value Schemes		
		Rokeach (1973)[1]	England (1967)[2]	Hofstede (1980)
Collectivism	Social	Personal versus Social World at peace National security Equality	Social Equality Social welfare Liberalism Equality Compassion Employee welfare	Individualism (–)
Duty		Inner versus Other-Directed Obedient Polite Helpful Clean	Personal Loyalty Loyalty Trust Obedience Honor Dignity	
Rationality	Theoretical	Competence versus Morality Intellectual Logical Capable	Irrational Behavior (–) Conflict Emotions Prejudice	Masculinity

TABLE 3–1 A Distilled Set of Six Significant Executive Value Dimensions, *continued*

Analogues in Other Value Schemes

Executive Value Dimension	Allport, Vernon, and Lindzey (1970)	Rokeach (1973)[1]	England (1967)[2]	Hofstede (1980)
Novelty			Entrepreneurialism Change Risk Competition	Uncertainty Avoidance (–)
Materialism	Economic	Delayed versus Immediate Gratification Pleasure A comfortable life An exciting life	Extrinsic Rewards Money Property	
Power	Political		Personal Influence Prestige Power Influence	Power Distance

SOURCE: Hambrick and Brandon (1988).

1. Listed are factor names and component elements from a factor analysis of Rokeach's items conducted by Howard, Shudo, and Umeshima (1983), on samples of American and Japanese executives.

2. Listed are factor names and component elements from a factor analysis of England's items conducted by Whitely and England (1980) on a sample of executives from several companies.

screening" by England, has been documented by numerous psychologists but primarily derives from early work by Postman, Bruner and Mc-Ginnies (1948).

Clearly, this process of perceptual screening invokes our over-arching model of how executive orientations ultimately become reflected in strategic choices (Figure 3–1): The conversion occurs through the sequential filtering process of field of vision, selective perception, and interpretation. This gives rise to four major propositions:

PROPOSITION 3–1A
Executives' values affect their field of vision.
Example: Exectives who highly value collectivism are directly exposed to more information from individuals of low hierarchical rank in their organizations than are executives without such values.

PROPOSITION 3–1B
Executives' values affect their selective perception of information.
Example: Executives who highly value collectivism notice are aware of a greater proportion of the information they are exposed to from low-rank individuals than are executives without such values.

PROPOSITION 3–1C
Executives' values affect their interpretation of information.
Example: Executives who highly value collectivism place more credence in information from low-rank individuals than executives without such values.

One can similarly anticipate how other values drive the filtering and interpretation process. And, when combined with the more direct effects of behavior channeling, the following overarching proposition can be reliably set forth:

PROPOSITION 3–1D
Executives' values are reflected in the choices they make.

Executive values is an open field for research. Even though values are undoubtedly important factors in executive choice, they have not been the focus of much systematic study. As the citation dates in this section indicate, the topic of executive values has been relatively dormant for the last twenty years. Six avenues of inquiry would seem particularly important and promising.

First, we need much more examination of the factors shaping executive values. What are the relative influences of professional and organization factors, as opposed to early upbringing and family factors? To what extent do institutional forces in a society exert homogenizing influences on executive values? And what causes executives' values to change?

Second, and related to the first, is the need to study executive values from the perspective of agency theory. According to agency theory, executives are not supposed to pursue *their* values; they are supposed to pursue *shareholders'* values, that is, wealth maximization (Jensen and Meckling 1976). Monitoring systems, executive compensation schemes, and even the corporate takeover market are all meant to be devices for reining in executives' pursuit of their own, sometimes self-seeking, agendas (Eisenhardt 1989a; Walsh and Seward 1990). What influence do these devices have on executive values? Do they drive out executives with certain values? Do they cause executives to change their values, to simply submerge their values, only to exert them in other, nonbusiness arenas? Or do values-dampening mechanisms create a counterproductive tension, prompting executives to pursue strategies they fundamentally do not prefer? For instance, what are the implications when a company led by an owner-founder who has strong noneconomic values becomes a publicly traded corporation subject to the disciplines of Wall Street? A reconciliation of agency theory and executive values is greatly needed.

Third is a need for greater understanding of the links between values and cognition. How do executives screen and interpret information so that their conclusions suit their values? Essentially no research has been done on the associations between executive values and information processing, and this should be a high priority. For instance, do executives who highly value rationality strive consciously to not allow their other values to affect their screening and interpretation of information?

Fourth, researchers need to examine how executive values and specific situations interact to affect choice. Executives who highly value collectivism, for instance, may tend to respond very differently to major choices about organizational decentralization, involvement in trade associations, and corporate philanthropy—all of which would seem on the surface to follow from a collectivist orientation. Unfortunately, to the extent that values and situations combine in highly specific ways to affect executive choice, the search for a parsimonious typology of values will be elusive; and, in fact, "attitudes" would then seem a more appropriate term than "values."

Fifth is the need to study the links between executive values and corporate goal setting. Organizations vary widely in the performance measures used to chart progress—some focusing on growth, some on market share, some on profitability, some on cash flow, still others on stock price. Moreover, organizations vary widely in the height of the goals they set— some seeking incremental improvements, some more substantial advances, still others have aspirations widely different from what they are currently achieving. Executive values must play an important role in the goal-setting process, but so far, this has not been examined.

Finally, researchers need to study the broad associations between exec-. utive values and organizational characteristics. Do executives in different industries and types of companies differ in their values? Do executives, as Hage and Dewar (1973) found, tend to select strategies in line with their values? Hambrick and Brandon (1988) developed an inventory of over thirty relatively testable hypotheses of links between executive values and organization characteristics. For example, they hypothesized that executives who highly value novelty will adopt organizational structures that are highly ambiguous (e.g., matrix structures) and will engage in relatively frequent reorganizations. These hypotheses, and numerous others that could be generated, might form the basis for future empirical work.

The basic concept that executive values are reflected in strategic choices was once a central element in prevailing models of strategy. For example, one of the early chapters in Andrews's (1971) classic treatise on strategy is entitled, "The Company and Its Strategists: Relating Economic Strategy and Personal Values"; it is full of case examples of executives favoring certain courses of action because of value preferences. Guth and Taguiri (1965) and Shirley (1975) similarly described case studies of executive values playing crucial roles in setting corporate strategy. Several studies relying strictly on survey methods or laboratory tasks have yielded indications of links between values and business choices (e.g., Farris 1973; England 1973a). The most compelling study, by Hage and Dewar (1973), found that the top executives of social service agencies who valued change were associated with subsequent high levels of program innovation in their agencies.

For the most part, however, systematic evidence of the links between executive values and strategic choice is limited. To conduct such research, scholars face the challenge of developing and administering valid instruments to gauge executive values. However, the payoffs from such inquiries may be considerable, because values very likely affect executive information processing and strategic choices (including approaches to strategy formulation and implementation and, executive style), as well as organizational performance.

Cognitive Model

Ever since March and Simon's (1958) explication of bounded rationality, scholars have been interested in cognitive limits and biases in strategic decision making. Recently, interest in managerial cognition has grown explosively, with books (Srivastava and Associates 1983; Sims and Gioia 1986; Huff 1990), extensive reviews (Walsh 1995), special issues of major journals (e.g., *Organization Science*, August 1994), and a new cognition interest group in the large scholarly society, the Academy of Management, all attesting to intellectual activity in this important domain.

Theory and research on executive cognition is too extensive in volume and scope to be adequately summarized here. At the heart of this literature, however, is the concept that every manager is endowed (or burdened) with a cognitive model that determines whether and how new stimuli will be noticed, encoded, and acted on. These cognitive models have been variously referred to as cognitive maps (Axelrod 1976; Weick and Bougon 1986), world views (Starbuck and Hedberg 1977; Mason and Mitroff 1981), "mindscapes" (Maruyama 1982), and other, often lyrical, terms.

Here, we will discuss three chief elements of an executive's cognitive model. Ranging from the most basic and disaggregated to the most complex and interwoven, the three are:

1. Cognitive content
2. Cognitive structure
3. Cognitive style

As we shall see, these elements of cognition affect each other, even determine each other, so the dividing lines among them are not precise. Still, they allow a useful conceptual disentangling of some complex phenomena.

Cognitive Content. At the most basic level, an executive's cognitive model consists of the things he or she knows, assumes, and believes. Consider the array of items that executives can possibly carry in their heads, creating a foundation for more elaborate information processing and strategic choice. An executive's cognitive content, stemming from personal and professional experiences, can include recollection of vivid events, such as an economic depression, a business bankruptcy, or a dishonest customer. It can include familiarity with management tools or concepts, such as sophisticated financial statement analysis, Porter's five-forces industry analysis, or psychographic market segmentation. Cognitive content can include simple first-hand knowledge about other people, what they know, and how to reach them. For instance, an executive who is on a first-name basis with senior Pentagon officials or knows a variety of influential investment bankers has cognitive content that others may not have. Of course, cognitive content also consists of simple facts, data, and perceptions.

March and Simon (1958) described the cognitive givens an executive brings to an administrative situation as consisting of his or her knowledge or assumptions about future events, alternatives, and consequences attached to alternatives. However, as our discussion indicates, an executive's cognitive content extends well beyond what was envisioned by March and Simon.

What an executive knows—or does not know—forms the basis by which new information is noticed and interpreted. An executive's existing knowledge provides a platform from which additional knowledge is sought, comprehended, and interpreted. Returning again to the sequential model of perceptual filtering and interpretation, we set forth propositions:

PROPOSITION 3-2A

Executives' cognitive content affects their field of vision.

Example: Executives who have in-depth familiarity with advanced technology seek out more information about technology than executives without such familiarity.[7]

PROPOSITION 3-2B

Executives' cognitive content affects their selective perception of information.

Example: Executives who have in-depth familiarity with advanced technology notice and are aware of a greater proportion of the technology information to which they are exposed than executives without such familiarity.

PROPOSITION 3-2C

Executives' cognitive content affects their interpretation of information.

Example: Executives who have in-depth familiarity with advanced technology require fewer pieces of information to form an opinion about a technological trend or development than executives without such familiarity.

PROPOSITION 3-2D

Executives' cognitive content is reflected in the choices they make.

Example: Executives who have in-depth familiarity with advanced technology make earlier and larger investments in new technologies than do executives without such familiarity.

Perhaps because cognitive content is the most disaggregated way of considering what is in a decision maker's mind and implies no particular priorities or complex associations, researchers of managerial cognitions have paid relatively little attention to it. We believe this is a mistake, because basic cognitive content is at the core of more sophisticated conceptions of managerial thinking. Researchers have focused instead on the more elaborate and analytically intriguing areas of cognitive structure and cognitive style.

Cognitive Structure.   If cognitive content is the basic raw material for executive knowledge, then cognitive structure is how the content is arranged, connected, or situated in the executive's mind. The term "causal map" is widely used among cognition theorists (Axelrod 1976; Huff 1990), clearly connoting a spatial and topographical feature of thinking.

Isenberg (1984) referred to "terrain structures," or an individual's conceptions of where things—organizational resources, customers, competitors, subunits, and so on—are located, either relative to each other or to some set of dimensions. An executive may cognitively differentiate between entities, considering them very dissimilar, or mentally juxtapose entities, in a belief that they are similar or even of a kind. As an illustration, Isenberg (1984) asked senior executives in three companies to rate the overall similarity of all pairwise combinations of the subunits of their organizations. He then used multidimensional scaling (MDS) (a useful analytic method for gauging cognitive structures) to reveal each executive's mental map of his or her organization. Figure 3–2 shows the "terrain structure" of the CEO of a metals corporation, Metals International, in three-dimensional space (the dimensions labeled by the researcher). As the figure shows, the CEO considered the primary fabrication (A) and mining operations (B, partly hidden by A in the figure) as very similar to each other but very different from the executive committee (D), the overall corporation (G), and the corporate staff (I, partly blocked by G). The public affairs committee (E) was seen by the CEO as quite distinct from any other part of the company.

Isenberg did not attempt to relate these CEOs' cognitive maps to the CEOs' backgrounds or to organizational characteristics, such as power distribution, strategy, succession patterns, and so on. However, these and numerous other research avenues could be pursued through the use of such cognitive mapping of organizational characteristics and should be a high priority for future investigations (Huff 1990).

Another stream of research has focused on executives' mental maps of their competitors. For instance, Gripsrud and Gronhaug (1985) found that the managers of retailing firms typically perceived only a small portion of all the other stores in their markets to be their competitors. The managers

FIGURE 3-2 **A CEO's Cognitive Structure of the Company:
Metals International, Inc.**

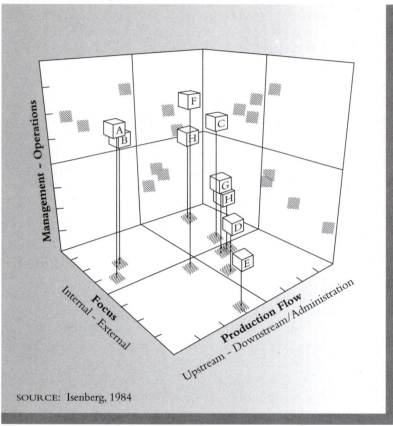

SOURCE: Isenberg, 1984

tended to see stores that were larger and geographically close to them as competitors and ignored other stores, some of which were actually direct rivals. Similarly, Reger and Huff (1993) examined how managers cognitively distinguished strategic groups in the Chicago banking market. They found that most managers agreed on the categorization of many of the banks but differed widely in their assignment of others. The authors did not speculate about the determinants of each manager's own conception of the competitive arena, but their study clearly indicates that competitor identification and assessment is open to varying interpretations. If strategic choices hinge on competitive dynamics (Porter 1980; Chen and MacMillan 1992) and if executives arrive at their own highly personalized assessments of competitors (Zahra and Chaples 1993), then an understanding of how those assessments are derived would be of major practical significance.

In addition to simple associations, an executive's cognitive structure also consists of myriad inferences, guiding the person from one observation to another. An executive could draw interpersonal inferences: "If emotional, infer friendliness; if blunt, infer trustworthiness" (Isenberg 1981). The executive can draw inferences about things in the organization: "Marketing managers tend to produce over-optimistic forecasts"; "middle managers are more resistant to change than any other group in the organization." And, of course, executives carry a host of inferences about external factors: "The Japanese never actually say no"; "small advertising agencies are more creative than large ones."[8]

Beyond inferences, or beliefs about simple co-variation, are an executive's beliefs about causality. For instance, an executive might have strong beliefs about employee stock ownership enhancing productivity or about increased R&D spending enhancing innovation. In a classic article, Hall (1976) used patterns of resource allocation at the *Saturday Evening Post* to infer the causal maps of top executives during that magazine's death spiral. More recently, Narayanan and Fahey (1990), used content analysis of annual reports and trade journal articles to extract the causal maps of executives at Admiral Corporation over the last fifteen years of the television manufacturer's life. For instance, the authors used available data to construct the Admiral executives' causal map for the years 1964 to 1966, as shown in Figure 3–3. According to the schematic, the executives seemed preoccupied with the effects of the macroenvironment on the company's performance but did not perceive much connection between their more proximate environment—their competitors, customers, imports, and so on—and what was happening to their firm.

By this point, it should be clear that an executive's cognitive structure is a highly personalized interpretation of reality, not necessarily aligning with objective conditions. Moreover, one's cognitive structure can become self-fulfilling and self-reinforcing (Weick 1983). In some cases, elements of this structure are so well established and unshakable that contrary data are overlooked or, if noticed, severely discounted. Thus, we propose:

PROPOSITION 3–3A

Executives' cognitive structures affect their field of vision.

Example: Executives who cognitively differentiate widely between customers use a wider array of sources for staying abreast of customer behaviors and preferences than executives with more homogenized cognitive maps of customers.

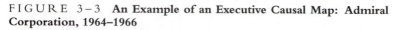

FIGURE 3-3 **An Example of an Executive Causal Map: Admiral Corporation, 1964–1966**

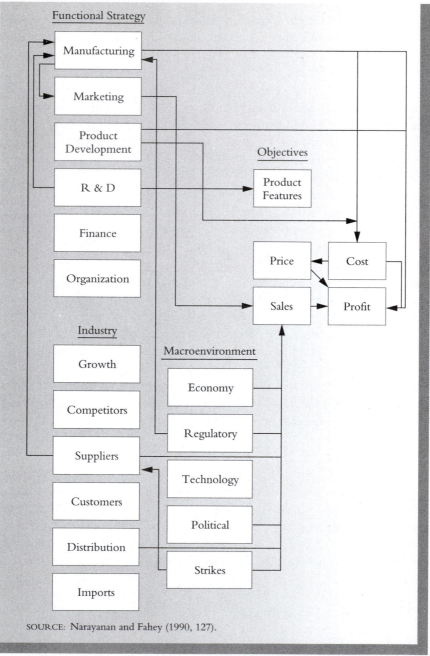

SOURCE: Narayanan and Fahey (1990, 127).

PROPOSITION 3–3B

Executives' cognitive structures affect their selective perception of information.

Example: Executives who cognitively differentiate widely between customers notice and are aware of more extreme and unusual customer requirements than are executives with more homogenized maps.

PROPOSITION 3–3C

Executives' cognitive structures affect their interpretation of information.

Example: Executives who cognitively differentiate widely between customers are more likely to see extreme or unusual customer requirements as both legitimate and an opportunity than are executives with more homogenized cognitive maps of their customers.

PROPOSITION 3–3D

Executives' cognitive structures are reflected in the choices they make.

Example: Executives who cognitively differentiate widely between customers develop more customized offerings and highly segmented strategies than do executives with more homogeneous maps.

Evidence that executives' cognitive structures will be reflected in their strategic choices is not abundant but has been observed in some studies. Fiol (1989) used textual analysis of CEOs' letters to shareholders to investigate whether revealed beliefs about the strength of organizational boundaries were related to the company's joint venture activity. In the ten chemical companies studied, she found that companies led by executives who indicated a perception of strong internal boundaries (demarcations between subunits and hierarchical layers) and weak external boundaries (imaginary dividing lines between the organizations and their environments) engaged in the most joint ventures. Day and Lord (1992) found that the cognitive structures of executives in machine tool companies were related to their organizations' strategies. In particular, executives who drew the finest distinctions between different types of strategic problems (in an experimental setting) were those whose firms had the widest arrays of product or service offerings. Whether these cognitively complex executives had chosen complex business strategies or their cognitions had been influenced by their strategies cannot be determined from the data. Allowing more confidence about causality, Thomas, Clark, and Gioia (1993) found in their study of a large sample of hospitals that the CEO's labeling of strategic issues as controllable (in a survey questionnaire) was positively related to subsequent product or service changes actually made by the hospital. Thus, the executives engaged in innovation and expansionary endeavors to the extent that their cognitive structures contained the belief that managerial actions could surmount, seize, or exploit strategic issues faced by their hospitals.

Finally, Priem (1994) had thirty-three CEOs of manufacturing firms complete a judgment task that required them to reveal their beliefs (or cognitive structures) about the optimal alignments among strategy, structure, and environment. Then, comparing these beliefs to the classic contingency prescriptions in the organizational literature, Priem found that firms whose CEOs had beliefs that closely adhered to customary prescriptions outperformed those firms whose CEOs had beliefs that differed from the normative ideals. This study is important for its careful, direct assessment of managerial judgment and its demonstrated explicit links to organizational policies and performance. This and the other studies we have noted provide consistent, but still sparse, indication that executives' knowledge structures affect their strategic choices.

Cognitive Style.   "Numbers just don't speak to me. And, frankly, I'm not wild about conversing with them." This quote, from the CEO of a medium-size fashion apparel company, is emblematic of the distinct cognitive styles of executives. Cognitive style refers to how a person's mind works—how he or she gathers and processes information. Barnard (1938, 302) was among the first to address different types of executive thought processes, saying that "mental processes consist of two groups which I shall call 'non-logical' and 'logical.' " By "logical," Barnard meant conscious thought that can be expressed in words or symbols—often called "reasoning." By "non-logical", he meant intuition, instinct, or tacit judgment. In Barnard's view, an effective executive has an abundance of both types of cognitive capabilities and can draw on either mode as the situation requires.

However, as the quote from the apparel company CEO suggests, it is not always that easy. Executives may differ widely in their cognitive styles and sometimes lack the "multidexterity" that Barnard envisioned. For instance, Mintzberg asked:

> Why is it that some of the most creative thinkers cannot comprehend a balance sheet, and that some accountants have no sense of product development? (1976,49)

Mintzberg's answer, based on a wealth of research in psychology and medicine, was that managers may differ in their cognitive styles due to biological factors, particularly in the relative strength or dominance of the two hemispheres of the brain. He contended that individuals with dominant left hemispheres—the locus of logic, linear thinking, and intellectual order—may make good *planners*. Conversely, those with dominant right hemispheres—the source of holistic information processing, imagination, and visual imagery—may make good *managers*.

Another conceptual approach to considering cognitive style (and not unrelated to the hemispheric model) draws from the work of Carl Jung, one of psychology's classic theorists (summarized in Taggart and Robey 1981; Myers 1982; Hurst, Rush, and White 1989). Jung's theory identifies two dimensions of cognitive style: perception (gathering information) and judgment (processing information). Perception occurs by either *sensation* (S) (physical stimuli taken in by the five senses) or *intuition* (N) (discerning patterns, gaps, or relationships among stimuli). Judgment, or information processing and evaluation, occurs either through *thinking* (T) (linking ideas using logic and notions of cause and effect) or *feeling* (F) (basing evaluation on personal and group values). Pairing each mode of perception with a mode of judgment yields four basic cognitive styles, as arrayed in Figure 3–4.

Drawing from several researchers' portrayals of the four types of cognitive styles, Figure 3–4 describes accompanying tendencies and informational orientation in terms of amount of scanning, media used for scanning, and cognitive structure. We go further, attaching labels to describe the archetypical manager in each cell: administrator, strategist, coach, and visionary.

For instance, the ST, or administrator, tends to be fact-oriented, impersonal, practical, and orderly. This person engages in a great deal of scanning, placing heavy reliance on written, formal information sources. His or her cognitive structure tends to correspond to empirical reality, comprehending *what is*, but not *what will be* or *what might be*. The other three types bear their own orientations.

Some of the most interesting research on Jungian types, as applied to top executives, has been done by Nutt. In one study (Nutt 1986a), executives were asked to indicate their readiness to accept several briefly described capital investment proposals. Those executives with an ST profile adopted the fewest proposals, showing a general aversion to action and also rating the proposals as highly risky, often noting the sketchiness or incompleteness of the project descriptions. SF executives were most inclined to adopt the projects and rated them as relatively low-risk. The other two types, the NT and NF executives, were in between the extremes.

In a later project, Nutt (1993) incorporated the idea that some executives have flexible, "multidextrous" decision styles, not always adhering to only one Jungian type. In turn, he found that executives with multiple, hybrid orientations, when faced with several hypothetical capital investment proposals that varied in how they were described, were willing to

FIGURE 3-4   **Four Types of Cognitive Styles: Four Types of Executives**

	Mode of Perception	
	Sensation (S)	Intuition (N)
Feeling (F)	*SF : Coach* Tend to be: • fact-oriented • personal • friendly • spontaneous Informational Orientation • much scanning • heavy reliance on oral, informal media • cognitive structure corresponds to empirical reality	*NF : Visionary* Tends to be: • possibilities-oriented • personal • enthusiastic • insightful Information Orientation • little scanning • reliance primarily on oral, informal media • cognitive structure is idiosyncratic; little correspondence to empirical reality
Mode of Judgment **Thinking (T)**	*ST : Administrator* Tends to be: • fact-oriented • impersonal • practical • orderly Informational Orientation • much scanning • heavy reliance on written, formal media • cognitive structure corresponds to empirical reality	*NT : Strategist* Tends to be: • possibilities-oriented • impersonal • ingenious • integrative Informational Orientation • little scanning • reliance primarily on written, formal media • cognitive structure is idiosyncratic; little correspondence to empirical reality

SOURCE: Adapted from Keirsey and Bates (1978); Taggart and Robey (1981); Myers (1982); Hurst, Rush, and White (1989).

adopt more of them (and rated them as less risky) than were executives with only a single Jungian orientation.

Nutt's work is among the relatively little empirical research that has been done on the cognitive styles of senior executives. Thus, our portrayals (and those of many other writers on the Jungian framework as applied to executives) are incomplete and speculative. However, it is reasonable to conclude from related research that executives may differ significantly in how they obtain and process information, greatly affecting their filtering and interpretive processes and ultimately influencing their strategic choices. Thus:

PROPOSITION 3–4A

Executives' cognitive styles affect their field of vision.

Example: Executives whose perceptions are based primarily on sensation (Jung's S's) scan more historical, verifiable data (and less future-oriented, speculative data) than do executives whose perceptions are based primarily on intuition (N's).

PROPOSITION 3–4B

Executives' cognitive styles affect their selective perception of information.

Example: S-type executives notice and are aware of proportionately more historical, verifiable data (and less future-oriented, speculative data) than are N-type executives.

PROPOSITION 3–4C

Executives' cognitive styles affect their interpretation of information.

Example: S-type executives place greater credence in the relevance of historical, verifiable data (and less credence in future-oriented, speculative data) than do N-type executives.

PROPOSITION 3–4D

Executives' cognitive styles are reflected in the choices they make.

Example: S-type executives tend to pursue more incremental, imitative strategies than N-type executives (who pursue more radical, innovative strategies).

Another way of viewing cognitive style is through the construct called "cognitive complexity," or the individual's ability to draw mental distinctions among objects (Schneier 1979). Long used in organizational behavior research, cognitive complexity has been incorporated in some recent research on executives. Hitt and Tyler (1991) found that cognitive complexity was not associated with executives' decision models in evaluating acquisition candidates. However, Wally and Baum (1994) did find that a factor comprised of cognitive complexity and amount of education was strongly positively related to the pace at which executives evaluated acquisition candidates.

In sum, all three facets of executive cognitions we have discussed—cognitive content, structure, and style—play important roles in triggering and shaping the executive's attention to and filtering of new information. The currently burgeoning interest in managerial cognitions is highly warranted and should lead to important new insights about the forming of strategic choices.

Future Directions.   Research on executive cognitive models might beneficially proceed along several lines. First, as we called for in future research on values, substantial work needs to be done on the antecedents, or determinants, of managers' cognitive models. The distinct influences of different types of experiences in shaping cognitions need to be understood. There is particularly a great need and opportunity to understand the role of social and professional networks in shaping executives' cognitive models (Galaskiewicz and Burt 1991; Burt 1992; Geletkanycz 1994). Second, and related to the first line of research, is the need to examine the linkages among cognitive content, structure, and style. These three elements of cognition must substantially affect each other—with cognitive style constraining the executive's acquisition of new content, new cognitive content giving rise to modified cognitive structure, and so on. Theorists need to understand the associations among these elements of cognition.

The third and fourth ideas have to do with research methods for studying executive cognitions. We believe the use of highly strutured complex simulations holds great promise for tapping managers' cognitions. A "bounded rationality game"—in which participants have access to far more information than they can actually absorb, must operate under time and resource constraints in accessing information, and have to make various strategic choices—particularly could be an important device for systematically examining the determinants, as well as the consequences, of cognitive models.

Fourth, research on managerial cognitions must move toward methods of greater reliability and replicability. An immersion into the current literature confronts one with innumerable subjective renditions of managerial thinking as adduced by the researchers. Granted, every research method inserts the investigator's own biases into the investigation, but with strictly qualitative, anecdotal descriptions, one cannot begin to discern how much researcher "spin" exists. We are tolerant of and encourage a wide array of methodological approaches, but in the area of managerial cognition, the pendulum has swung too far to the qualitative. Thus, we recommend the following: simulations, such as proposed above; other exercises in experimental settings; highly structured, replicable content analysis of speeches, letters to shareholders, and so on; and batteries of paper-and-pencil tests.

Finally, researchers of executive cognitions need to focus more on the implications of those cognitions for strategic choices or executive behaviors. While the need to delve into the cognitions themselves is great, the real significance of executive cognitions lies in their consequences. So, beyond describing cognitive models, investigators need to establish connections to choices, behaviors, and perhaps even organizational performance.

Other Personality Factors

Beyond executive values and executive cognitions, various other facets of personality have been examined by scholars of top management. For example, Kets de Vries and Miller (1984) drew on psychoanalytic theory, arguing that some CEOs (like other individuals) hold various neuroses and these neuroses can give rise to predictable organizational dysfunctions. The compulsive CEO begets an organization driven by rules, an inward focus, and an incremental, risk-averse strategy. Other CEO neuroses, such as paranoia and depression, similarly give rise to corresponding organizational pathologies.

In a less clinical vein, Gupta and Govindarajan (1984) examined executives' willingness to take risks, finding that this personality factor was more conducive to organizational performance for businesses trying to build their market share than for those trying to generate earnings while maintaining their market share. Additional personality factors, including need for achievement (Miller and Droge 1986), tolerance for risk (Wally and Baum 1994), and tolerance for ambiguity (Gupta and Govindarajan 1984), have also been the focus of research on senior executives.

However, two specific streams of research on executive personality have been particularly pronounced, and to fail to single them out for attention would be a glaring omission. These areas of research deal with personality characteristics associated with charisma and executive locus of control.

Personality and Charisma. A massive literature has examined the personality characteristics associated with charisma (summarized and extended in Conger and Kanungo 1988). We say "associated with charisma" because the recent and prevailing view is that charisma is not itself a personality trait but rather a relationship between a leader and subordinates, often enabled or enhanced by the leader's personality (House, Spangler, and Woycke 1991). Thus, charisma is affected by personality but is not in itself a personality type.

The particular kinds of follower responses constituting a charismatic relationship include: performance beyond expectations (Bass 1985); changes in the fundamental values of followers (Etzioni 1975); devotion, loyalty, and reverence toward the leader (House 1977); a sense of excitement and enthusiasm (Weber 1946; Bass 1985); and a willingness on the part of subordinates to sacrifice their own personal interests for the sake of a collective goal (House 1977).

What are the leader personality qualities that tend to evoke such responses from followers? Bass (1985) inventoried the following: self-confidence, self-determination, insight into needs and values of their followers, and the ability to enhance or enflame those needs and values through persuasive words and actions. Conger and Kanungo (1988) also included high activity level, confidence, commitment, and need for power as leader characteristics typified in the charismatic influence process.

As one might expect, the portrayal of charisma is not always positive. In fact, Conger (1990) has written eloquently about the "dark side" of charisma, noting the devastation from the likes of Stalin, Hitler, and Jim Jones, the religious leader who precipitated a mass suicide of his followers in Guyana.

However, charisma is usually spoken of in favorable terms, and certainly abundant anecdotal evidence suggests the sometimes remarkable achievements of organizations under charisma-prone leaders (see Bass 1985; Tichy and Devanna 1986a; Conger and Kanungo 1988). A recent large-scale study by Agle and Sonnenfeld (1994) provides some systematic evidence of favorable organizational outcomes from charisma. Surveying top executives about the characteristics of their CEOs (and finding strong consistency among raters in their descriptions), the authors established a strong association between numerous charismatic behaviors and three diverse measures of company performance—as rated by executives, profitability, and stock returns. This is a comprehensive study, and while it does not address the underlying personality factors associated with charisma, it still helps greatly in reaffirming the importance of this leadership syndrome.

In an elaborate study of U.S. presidents, that employed extensive public accounts and historians' analyses, House, Spangler and Woycke (1991) drew upon the work of McClelland and associates (e.g., McClelland and Boyatzis 1982) to empirically examine the personality qualities associated with charisma. They found that charisma was 1) positively related to the president's need for power, 2) negatively related to the need for personal achievement, and 3) positively related to activity inhibition (a measure of the extent to which the executive uses power to achieve institutional rather than strictly personal goals). In this study, charisma was found to be positively associated with five diverse measures of presidential performance, encompassing international, economic, and social spheres. The authors' interpretations of these results were that: 1) a need for power is a prerequisite to developing the strong persuasive abilities that accompany charisma; and 2) charisma-prone executives have a genuine desire for institutional and collective achievement, rather than personal achievement.

The House and associates' study is instructive for at least two reasons. First, it represents a most impressive effort to bring rigor to an examination of very intangible (and often quite fuzzy) aspects of leadership. The authors drew from a wide array of data sources, demonstrated their reliability, and included appropriate controls. This is an admirable effort, representing where more research on senior leadership should be headed.

Second, this study, as well as the Agle and Sonnenfeld (1994) study and, all other research on charisma (and "transformational leadership"), highlights that executives do not affect their organizations only through their strategic choices. They also have impact through their influence over others in the organization, who in turn put forth effort and make major choices affecting the organization's performance (Bower 1970). Thus, it is appropriate that our conception of executive activity, as first discussed in Chapter 2 and portrayed toward the right-hand side of Figure 3-1 in this chapter, extends beyond the decisional domain of "Strategic Choice" to include "Executive Behaviors." Day in-day out, seemingly minute actions by executives can have a major effect on organizational functioning and performance.

The effects of the charismatic executive on followers, however, may extend to strategic choice processes as well. Particularly to the extent that the charismatic executive possesses and exhibits moral righteousness (House 1977) and extreme self-confidence (Bass 1985) and followers place blind faith in the leader and tend to suspend their disbelief in contrary perspectives, the following can be posited:

PROPOSITION 3-5A
Personality characteristics associated with charisma affect executives' field of vision.
Example: Executives with personalities that evoke charisma receive more filtered and distilled information from their subordinates than do executives without such personalities.

PROPOSITION 3-5B
Personality characteristics associated with charisma affect executives' selective perception of information.
Example: Executives with personalities that evoke charisma notice and are aware of proportionately less information that conflicts with their articulated vision than do executives without such personalities.

PROPOSITION 3-5C
Personality characteristics associated with charisma affect executives' interpretation of information.
Example: Executives with personalities that evoke charisma place less credence in information unsupportive of their vision than do executives without such personality characteristics.

PROPOSITION 3–5D

Personality characteristics associated with charisma are reflected in executives' strategic choices.

Example: Executives with personalities that evoke charisma are more persistent in their pursuit of a chosen strategy (even in the face of disconfirming evidence) than are executives without such personality characteristics.

With regard to the final proposition, it is worth noting that personality characteristics could have a significant effect on the well-known behavioral phenomenon of escalating commitment to a course of action, in a way that researchers have not considered (Staw 1976; Rubin and Brockner 1975). One of the determinants of commitment is the degree to which the decision maker has publicly declared his or her intentions. To the extent that the charisma-prone executive has a grand vision and articulates that vision—both of which are well-known accompaniments of charisma—he or she heightens the likelihood of escalating commitment to a course of action. One of the most widely documented ill-fated military escalations, the U.S. involvement in Vietnam, occurred primarily during the tenure of the president scoring among the highest on the charisma score in the House, Spangler, Woycke study—Lyndon B. Johnson.

Locus of Control.   Another executive personality variable examined in several studies is locus of control (Anderson 1977; Miller, Kets de Vries, and Toulouse 1982; Miller and Toulouse 1986a; Begley and Boyd 1987; Boone and De Brabander 1993). Rotter's (1966) conception of internal versus external orientations has been used in most of this research. "Internal" individuals believe that events in their lives are within their control. "Externals" believe that events in their lives are outside their control, stemming from fate, luck, or destiny. As managers, externals could be expected to be passive, reactive, and not innovative. In pressurized or turbulent environments, these qualities would lead to poor organizational peformance.

In fact, researchers have found evidence that groups led by internals perform better than those led by externals (Anderson and Schneier 1978), and that internal managers are more task-oriented and perform better in stressful situations than externals (Anderson 1977; Anderson, Hellriegel, and Slocum 1977).

In the literature examining locus of control of top executives, similarly beneficial effects from "internal" (not to be confused with internally appointed) CEOs have been consistently observed. Miller and Toulouse (1986a, 1986b) found that CEOs with internal locus of control were associated with high organizational performance. Two additional studies reported a relationship between internal locus of control of managers and the success and survival rate of small firms and new ventures (Brockhaus 1980; Van de Ven, Hudson, and Schroeder 1984).

However, the study by Miller, Kets de Vries, and Toulouse (1982) has been the most widely noted examination of executive locus of control. With a sample of Canadian top executives, they found that firms led by internals were more innovative and more likely to be in dynamic environments than were firms led by externals. The authors conclude, "Managers who believe that their destiny lies in their own hands are more likely to try to control it actively" (p. 245).

In a supplementary analysis, the authors found that the associations between executive locus of control and organizational innovation and environental dynamism were far stronger in cases of long CEO tenures than of short ones, causing the researchers to further conclude that executive personality shapes strategy, rather than strategy and environment affecting the types of individuals who become top executives of specific firms.

Here, though, we must anticipate two-way causality. If an environment confers relatively little executive discretion, or latitude of action, it is unlikely that an "internal" individual will be drawn to the firm or climb to executive ranks within it (Hambrick and Finkelstein 1987). Rather, externals would self-select themselves into such settings, would be comfortable, and would persist. As externals, they would engage in minimal innovation, suiting the confining, low-discretion environment.

Thus, causality may be not just two-way but "circular," as shown in Figure 3-5. A high-discretion situation (conferred through environmental and organizational factors) tends to attract and select a top executive with an internal locus of control, who then engages in considerable strategic action and innovation. If the actions yield high performance, then even more discretion is created (Hambrick and Finkelstein 1987), the executive's sense of efficacy has been enhanced (Weick 1983), and the cycle is reinforced. If this loop is somehow arrested (for instance, the environment changes from high-discretion to low-discretion, or despite the company's innovation efforts, performance is impaired by exogenous shocks), then a whole new cycle could be initiated, but with different characteristics: low discretion, an executive with an external locus of control, little innovation, poor performance, a perception in turn of even less discretion, and so on.

In a related vein, it may strike some as implausible that an "external"— someone who sees events as outside their control—could even rise to a top management position at all. After all, executive selection processes would seem to strongly favor "take-charge" types, such that managers would seem

FIGURE 3-5   **A Self-Reinforcing Cycle of Executive Efficacy**

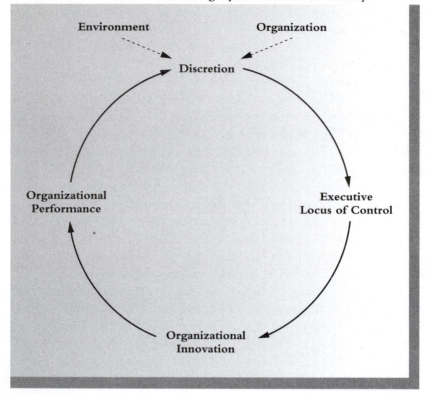

to be at some disadvantage in mid-career advancement tournaments if they act as if the fate of their operation is outside their influence. Still, all available studies of the locus of control of top executives find a range of scores on this personality variable (although skewed toward an internal orientation), suggesting that a wide array of contexts and advancement conduits exist so as to allow considerable diversity in executive profiles.[9]

The concept of executive locus of control allows some very direct links to be drawn back to our model of the sequential filtering process by which executives arrive at their construed reality:

PROPOSITION 3-6A

Executives' locus of control affects their field of vision.

Example: Executives with an internal locus of control ("internals") devote more effort to environmental scanning, using a wider array of sources, than do executives with an external locus of control ("externals").

PROPOSITION 3–6B

Executives' locus of control affects their selective perception of information.

Example: "Internal" executives notice and are aware of a greater proportion of the information they scan than are "external" executives.

PROPOSITION 3–6C

Executives' locus of control affects their interpretation of information.

Example: "Internal" executives are more likely to consider environmental trends as "opportunities or threats requiring action" than are externals.

PROPOSITION 3–6D

Executives' locus of control is reflected in their strategic choices.

Example: Organizations led by "internals" are more innovative, more adaptive to the environment, and have higher performance than are organizations led by "externals."

While already of demonstrated relevance to executive leadership, locus of control is only one vantage on managerial personality. We encourage theory and research on other personality dimensions as well—particularly tolerance for risk, tolerance for ambiguity, introversion versus extroversion, and self-monitoring. These dimensions, along with those personality qualities asociated with charisma, may play important roles in an eventually complete conceptualization of executive behavior and strategic choice.

SUMMARY

In this chapter we have had two aims. The first was to present our core model of how and why executives will differ in their strategic choices. We have argued that executives confront a multitude of typically ambiguous information and that their orientations—both experiences and psychological factors—greatly determine which of the information will be comprehended and how it will be interpreted. Thus, decision makers act on the basis of highly filtered, personalized, idiosyncratic understandings of their situations, options, and potential effects of options.

Our second aim has been to elaborate on one-half of the concept of executive orientation: psychological factors. Here we have discussed the role of executive values, cognitive models, and two other personality factors—

locus of control and charisma—that have been the subjects of considerable theory and research. These psychological characteristics have considerable influence on the executive's eventual construed reality and, in turn, on strategic choices and organizational performance. We now turn to the second major element of executive orientation, the executive's experiences.

NOTES

1. It is important to note that some information restriction is due to social structures and organizational characteristics, not merely to the executive's own human limits; the context may not be inclined to provide an executive with all potentially pertinent information. To address this issue would entail a discussion more on organization design than on executive behavior. In line with our theory, we would expect that executives would seek to modify information flows as a function of their own biases and dispositions.

2. One of the first and best known references to "selective perception" was by Dearborn and Simon (1958). However, they used the term to refer to the interpretive act, the third phase in our sequential information processing model. "Selective perception" is an expression that seems apt for conveying incomplete noticing, a concept not considered by Dearborn and Simon.

3. See Dutton, Fahey, and Narayanan (1983) for a thoughtful discussion of iterative information processing by strategists.

4. See Corner, Kinicki, and Keats (1994) for sequential information processing model analogous to ours. Their stages are: attention, encoding, storage/retrieval, decision, and action.

5. This section is adapted from Hambrick and Brandon (1988).

6. These unique values constructs were as follows:
   Allport, Vernon, and Lindzey (1970): religious, aesthetic
   Rokeach (1973) (factor analyzed by Howard, Shudor, and Umeshima 1983):
      enlarger versus enfolder (loving, honest, mature love, family, security)
      self-directed versus outward-oriented (world of beauty, cheerful, broadminded)
   England (1967) (factor analyzed by Whitely and England 1980):
      subordinate employees (e.g. blue-collar workers, laborers, craftspeople)
      organizational effectiveness (organizational stability, effectiveness)
      personal assertiveness (autonomy, force, aggressiveness)
      organizational ownership (stockholders, owners)
      personal competence (skill, ability)

7. A case can be made for exactly the opposite—that executives strive to overcome informational deficienceis by more intensive scanning of those domains. For instance, upon becoming CEO of Apple Computers, John Sculley reputedly spent months trying to learn everything he could about computer technology. For the most part, however, we expect executives to gravitate to the familiar and comfortable.

8. As discussed earlier, cognitive structure, including inferences, are shaped in part by values. Thus, the inference "The Japanese never actually say no" may arise through an amalgamation of concrete experiences, vague impressions, and

deeply held values. Inferences and other discrete elements of cognitive structure could legitimately be referred to as attitudes or beliefs.

9. A recent debate has emerged over whether Rotter's (1966) original scale is sufficiently germane to executives. Hodgkinson (1992) advocates a more specific scale, measuring "strategic control expectancies." A critique by Boone and De Brabander (1993) argues that Hodgkinson's scale taps the executive's perceptions of his or her strategic situation instead of tapping personality and that Rotter's scale is in fact suitable for research on executives.

FOUR

EXECUTIVE EXPERIENCES AND STRATEGIC CHOICE

A 1985 case study on Louis Gerstner, then head of the travel-related businesses at American Express, described his strategic initiatives and leadership style, including his tendency to meet with employees several levels below him, his emphasis on creating bundled products that exploited the full range of businesses he oversaw, and his tilting of executive compensation criteria toward overall company performance and away from strictly individual performance (Kao 1985). This way of managing met with great success for American Express and for Gerstner. He went on to be the CEO of RJR Nabisco for several years and then, in the most publicized corporate executive search ever conducted, won the top job at IBM. How is he approaching things at IBM? A 1994 article has a familiar ring: Gerstner is striving to "integrate" IBM's products, he has linked more than half the pay of 150 senior executives to overall company performance, and he is establishing "informal networks of communication with employees further down in the company" (Lohr 1994). Ten years later, in a strikingly different industry, a completely different business situation, Lou Gerstner is understandably doing what worked so well for him once before.

To some extent, all of us—including senior executives—exist in a web of our own personal and professional experiences. We may try to be open-minded, detached, and thorough; but we are confined greatly by what we already know and believe, by what we have already experienced. Particularly in complex situations, decision makers rely on the familiar, often drawing on approaches that have worked well in the past (Cyert and March 1963). Experiences serve to shape values and cognitive models in ways that may substantially affect decision making and behavior (Hitt and Tyler 1991). If so, then demographic or background factors, reflective of an executive's experiences, should be associated with strategic choices.

The past ten years have witnessed an explosion of research on the relationships between executive background characteristics and organizational outcomes. The vast majority of this research has pursued the general logic that observable experiences of executives shape their cognitions and values and hence are reflected in their strategic choices. A smaller stream of research has posited the reverse causality—that certain strategic conditions give rise to particular types of executive characteristics, due to intentional or emergent alignment of executive qualities with strategic requirements. A third research focus has been essentially a hybrid of the other two, pursuing the idea that different strategic conditions favor different types of executive qualities and that the organization will perform well to the extent that its executives have those characteristics.

Research on executive background characteristics, typically focusing on demographic characteristics, has yielded numerous significant findings; some of these results, as will be discussed below, recur in multiple studies. Thus, using observable executive experiences in organizational research appears to be a promising line of inquiry.

Various executive experiences have been examined for their associations with organizational outcomes, such as strategy and performance. However, three sets of executive background characteristics account for the vast majority of inquiries: executive tenure, functional experiences (marketing, finance, and so on), and formal education. In this section, we will review and integrate the studies that have examined these three sets of executive characteristics. For each, we will discuss three types of observed associations. The first is the link to executive psychological constructs and perceptions. Such a review helps to establish the most fundamental implications of executive experiences. However, because most studies of executive experiences have treated psychological processes as a "black box," we will have relatively little to report here; thus, at times we will supplement research on senior executives with studies of links between demographics and psychological properties in other populations. Second, we will summarize the links to organizational strategy and conduct. This is where most upper-echelons research has focused, in line with the general concept that executives' experiences are reflected in their strategic choices. The third set of results includes those examining the links between executive characteristics and organizational performance. In some cases, these are direct; more often, they are contingent, with the association between characteristics and performance depending on specific contextual conditions.

Executive experiences influence strategic choices through the same three-stage information filtering process presented in Figure 3-1. To be sure, numerous propositions could be set forth as to how experiences, considered as demographic characteristics, affect an executive's field of vision, selective perception, and interpretation of strategic stimuli. For instance, we can expect that executives with long tenures in their organizations receive a greater proportion of their information from internal sources than do executives with short tenures (Aguilar 1967). As a further example, executives whose primary functional experiences are in marketing and sales can be expected to attach more marketing and sales implications to strategic stimuli than executives with other functional backgrounds. The list of promising propositions for links between executive experiences and the filtering process is so extensive that, for the sake of space, we do not formally present them. Instead, we limit our propositions to those dealing with links between experiences and either psychological characteristics or organizational strategy and performance.

EXECUTIVE TENURE

Research and theory on executive tenure has clustered generally around one major idea: long-tenured executives tend not to make strategic changes in their organizations. In fact, there is considerable evidence of this important phenomenon. However, as simple and stark as this conclusion is, the processes by which it occurs, and even the concept of executive tenure itself, warrant elaboration.

Executive tenure has been conceived in various ways: tenure in the position (e.g., Hambrick and Fukutomi 1991; Miller 1991); tenure in the organization (e.g., Thomas, Litschert, and Ramaswamy 1991); and tenure in the industry (Hambrick, Geletkanycz, and Fredrickson 1993).[1] Obviously, these three types of tenure co-vary and are even definitionally nested, since all time spent in the position is also spent in the organization and in the industry, and all time spent in the organization is also spent in the industry. Still, each type of tenure can be considered separately.

Tenure and Executive Psychology

Unfortunately, relatively little empirical research has examined the psychological accompaniments of executive tenure. Some evidence is available, however, and theorists have set forth extensive arguments about the tendencies for executive mind-sets and orientations to evolve over time.

Attention to the significance of tenure in the position is relatively recent. Hambrick and Fukutomi (1991) drew on widespread but fragmentary literature to develop a comprehensive model of the "seasons of a CEO's tenure." They argued that during an executive's time in office, critical trends tend to occur on five fronts. We will summarize their arguments (Table 4-1) and formalize them as propositions.

Under pressure to quickly demonstrate their efficacy, and usually with a directional mandate from their board, CEOs start their jobs with relatively strong commitment to their paradigms (implicit mental models of priorities, options, and causal relations). After early success and gaining a foothold, CEOs may have a brief period in which they experiment and are more open-minded. However, they soon tend to commit psychologically to whatever approach has been most comfortable and effective. Then, with each passing year in the position, the CEO's commitment to his or her paradigm increases, bringing a heightened sense of correctness in established ways of operating and viewing the world. In describing the same phenomena, Miller (1991) referred to the "overconfidence" that accompanies executive tenure. Thus,

PROPOSITION 4-1A

After an initial period of strong commitment to their paradigms, often followed by a brief period of cognitive flexibility, executives' commitment to their paradigms increases steadily during their time in office.

Second, as a CEO's tenure advances, the sources of his or her information become increasingly narrow and restricted, and the information is more finely filtered and distilled. This occurs because of habituation, the establishment of informational routines, the cultivation of trusted sources,

TABLE 4-1 **The Five Seasons of a CEO's Tenure**

Critical CEO Characteristics	1 Response to Mandate	2 Experimentation	3 Selection of an Enduring Theme	4 Convergence	5 Dysfunction
Commitment to a Paradigm	Moderately strong	Could be strong or weak	Moderately strong	Strong; increasing	Very strong
Task Knowledge	Low but rapidly increasing	Moderate; somewhat increasing	High; slightly increasing	High; slightly increasing	High; slightly increasing
Information Diversity	Many sources; unfiltered	Many sources but increasingly filtered	Fewer sources; moderately filtered	Few sources; highly filtered	Very few sources; highly filtered
Task Interest	High	High	Moderately high	Moderately high but diminishing	Moderately low and diminishing
Power	Low; increasing	Moderate; increasing	Moderate; increasing	Strong; increasing	Very strong; increasing
Overall Pattern	Legitimacy-building. Actions strongly consistent with CEO's background and mandate	Repertoire expansion. Has political foothold. Tries new things	Selects what has worked best so far, what is most comfortable. May revert to initial repertoire	All actions reinforce and bolster the theme. Primarily incremental change	Relatively few actions at all. Outside interests increase
General Duration (Years)	1-2	1-2	1-2	3-5	All remaining years

SOURCE: Adapted from Hambrick and Fukutomi (1991).

and the tendency for those sources to cater to the executive's information preferences. For example, Aguilar (1967) found that new general managers tended to rely about equally on external and internal sources of information about the business environment; but, as they developed more reliable internal networks, the managers greatly reduced their use of external information sources. In the same vein, Tushman and Romanelli (1985) and Miller (1991) argued that the amount and quality of information gathering and analysis may decline with tenure. Thus,

PROPOSITION 4–1B

As their tenures advance, executives tend to receive narrower and more finely filtered information.

Third, executives evolve in their level of task knowledge. An executive appointed from inside the firm may not have the same knowledge deficit as an executive appointed from the outside, but in general, any executive new in a position confronts some unfamiliar elements (in terms of facts, trends, contacts, and so on). However, the executive's task knowledge increases rapidly at first but then advances only very gradually.

PROPOSITION 4–1C

As their tenures advance, executives acquire more task knowledge—at first rapidly and then more slowly.

Fourth, Hambrick and Fukutomi (1991) argued that executives are not immune from the tedium that comes with repetition and relative mastery of any type of work. Executive positions may involve relatively great novelty and challenge, but they also have substantial elements of sameness and routine (reviewing budgets and capital requests, making plant visits, preparing for board meetings, and so on). After doing these tasks numerous times, the executive may feel less of a challenge in the position and experience (perhaps unknowingly) a dulled acuity.

PROPOSITION 4–1D

Executives start their positions with a high degree of task interest, which starts declining after several years.

Fifth, and finally, in the Hambrick and Fukutomi framework, it is expected that an executive's (particularly a CEO's) power increases with tenure. This can occur through co-optation of the board (since the CEO often has a major role in board appointments), the development of a patriarchal aura, or the accumulation of shareholdings. Miller (1991) referred similarly to the "autonomy" that comes with executive tenure.

PROPOSITION 4–1E

As executives' tenures advance, their power increases.

Taken together, these trends create discernible phases or seasons within an executive's tenure in a position, giving rise to distinct patterns of executive attention, behavior, and ultimately performance. Table 4-1 shows how the five trends are delineated across the seasons posited by Hambrick and Fukutomi. Although grounded in prior theory and evidence, and very similar to Miller's logic in claiming that CEOs become "stale in the saddle," many aspects of the Hambrick and Fukutomi seasons model still await test. However, the most basic implication—that executives tend to become inertial as their tenures mount—is consistent with available psychological and organizational evidence.

Theorists also have posited that tenure in the organization affects an executive's cognitions. Organizational tenure is thought to be associated with rigidity and commitment to established policies and practices (March and March 1977; Katz 1982). Tenure causes the executive to have a great stake in the status quo, since his or her competences have been deemed valuable for the firm's *current* configuration. Organizational tenure also may restrict information processing through the executive establishment of routine, familiar information sources, and development of predictable repertoires for dealing with information (Katz 1982; Miller 1991).

In an empirical study, Hambrick, Geletkanycz, and Fredrickson (1993) examined the correlates of executive commitment to the status quo (CSQ)—that is, the executive's belief in the enduring correctness of current organizational policies and profiles. In their large sample of senior executives, the authors found that the executive's tenure in the organization had a significant positive effect on CSQ.

PROPOSITION 4–2

The longer an executive's tenure in the organization, the greater his or her commitment to the status quo.

However, in the study by Hambrick and associates, the effect of tenure in the industry on CSQ was even more pronounced. The authors interpreted their finding as testimony to the strength of industry conventions, "recipes," and "common bodies of knowledge" (Hambrick 1982; Spender 1989), concluding:

Membership in an industry inserts a person into a social setting in which actions, contexts, and outcomes are subjected to a shared interpretation (Burrell and Morgan 1979). Those individuals who have participated in this 'social construction of reality' for the longest time are most convinced of its correctness. In fact, they may have difficulty even conceiving of alternative logics . . . . (p. 412)

Other investigators have studied critical transitions in the airline, banking, and steel industries, concluding that in each of these, a well-developed "industry knowledge" had been established that long-tenured executives had great difficulty transcending (Marcus and Goodman 1986; Goodman 1988; Newell 1989).[2]

PROPOSITION 4–3

The longer an executive's tenure in the industry, the greater his or her commitment to the status quo.

Finally, we may anticipate that tenure in each layer of a social system— in a position, in an organization, and in an industry—adds in its own way to the informational constriction and social-psychological "embeddedness" of an executive (Granovetter 1985). Therefore, we posit:

PROPOSITION 4–4

Tenure in the position, in the organization, and in the industry have independent and additive effects on an executive's commitment to the status quo. Executives with long tenures of all three types are most committed to the status quo.

Organizational Strategy

Studies examining the associations between executive tenure and organizational strategies have been quite consistent in their findings. The first robust conclusion is that top executive tenure is inversely related to organizational change. In an in-depth study, Gabarro (1987) found that almost all the actions taken by new general managers occur in the first two and one-half years in office. After that is a period of "refinement," in which only a few changes are made by the managers, primarily to fine-tune the organization. Figure 4-1 portrays how Gabarro's managers varied their intensity of change efforts over their first three years in office.

Evidence of the inhibiting effect of company tenure on strategic change also was set forth by Wiersema and Bantel (1992).[3] In their study

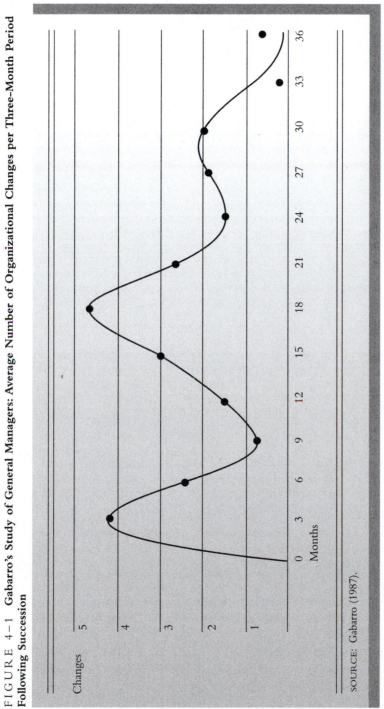

FIGURE 4–1 Gabarro's Study of General Managers: Average Number of Organizational Changes per Three-Month Period Following Succession

SOURCE: Gabarro (1987).

of eighty-seven firms, they found that top executive tenure was negatively related to change in company diversification strategy over the subsequent three-year period. They concluded that executives with short tenures, particularly new executives from the outside, are more likely to view the firm as a blank slate that can take on many possible forms. Long-tenured executives, conversely, were seen as more encumbered by the history and current configuration of the company.

Additional evidence that executive tenure reduces strategic change was offered by Finkelstein and Hambrick (1990). In a study of one hundred companies in three industries, the authors found that the company tenure of the top executives was highly positively related to strategic persistence, or absence of strategic change, over the ensuing year. This relationship was monotonic—every increase in tenure brought an even higher level of strategic persistence—over the full range of tenure values; that is, the statistical association was not due simply to radical changes brought on by new managers recruited from the outside. The authors also found that executive tenure was positively related to strategic conformity, or the company's adherence to the general strategic tendencies of the industry. The authors posited a logic for the effect of company tenure on conformity:

> [Executives] with short tenures have fresh, diverse information and are willing to take risks, often departing widely from industry conventions. As tenure increases, perceptions become very restricted and risk taking is avoided. The lowest-risk thing to do is to follow the general tendency of mainstream competitors. (488)

Finally, in a study of U.S. railroads, Grimm and Smith (1991) found that the tenure of top executives in the railroad industry was inversely related to the degree that their firms changed strategies after deregulation. In line with Hambrick, Geletkanycz, and Fredrickson (1993), they found that industry tenure had an even greater effect on strategic inertia than did company tenure.

PROPOSITION 4–5

The longer an executive's tenure (in the position, the organization, or the industry), the less the strategic change that ensues in the organization.

PROPOSITION 4–6

The longer an executive's tenure (in the position, the organization, or the industry), the greater the organizations's strategy conforms to industry averages.

Evidence suggests that top executive tenure has an effect not only on strategic persistence and strategic conformity, but also on the specific type of strategy pursued. At least two studies have found that long-tenured executives tend to pursue what Miles and Snow (1978) called "Defender" strategies (emphasizing stability and efficiency), whereas short-tenure executives are more likely to pursue "Prospector" strategies (emphasizing product or market innovation). One of these studies, by Chaganti and Sambharya (1987), examined the top executive characteristics and company strategies of the three major tobacco companies headquartered in the United States. The other study, by Thomas, Litschert, and Ramaswamy (1991), was based on a sample of 224 firms in the electronic computing industry. Both sets of authors argued that long tenures lead to an "internal" focus, making product or market innovation relatively unlikely.

PROPOSITION 4-7

The longer an executive's tenure, the greater the organization's strategy emphasizes stability and efficiency, rather than product or market innovation.

Tenure and Performance

If executive tenure affects strategy, it must also affect performance. The study by Finkelstein and Hambrick (1990) illustrates this parallel effect. Recall their finding that executive tenure is positively associated with strategic conformity to average industry tendencies, reflecting, the authors argued, low-risk imitative tendencies by long-tenured management groups. Finkelstein and Hambrick also found a positive association between executive tenure and performance conformity to industry averages: The longer the tenures of top executives, the more the performance of their companies (measured as an index of return on sales, return on equity, and market or book value of owners' equity) aligned with the average performance of their industries. Thus, imitative strategies give rise to neutral levels of performance.

PROPOSITION 4-8

The longer an executive's tenure, the more the organization's performance conforms to industry averages.

Miller's (1991) research additionally sheds light on how CEO tenure may affect organizational performance. In a study of ninety-five Canadian companies, he found that the alignments between environmental and organizational characteristics, as classically prescribed by contingency theory (e.g., Burns and Stalker 1961; Lawrence and Lorsch 1967), indeed existed for companies whose CEOs had tenures of less than ten years; however, the alignments did not exist for long-tenure CEOs. Moreover, the greater the mis-alignment between environmental and organizational characteristics, the worse the company's performance. Miller concluded that long-tenure CEOs become "stale in the saddle"—committed to the status quo, risk-averse, and insulated from fresh, accurate information—and their companies suffer for it. This view, highly consistent with the seasons model posited by Hambrick and Fukutomi (1991), suggests this proposition:

PROPOSITION 4–9

Organizations led by CEOs with very long tenures (say, beyond ten years) do not perform as well as they performed in the earlier years of the CEOs' tenures.

Some researchers who have explored the effects of executive tenure on organizational performance have avoided trying to demonstrate any universal, blanket patterns. Instead, they have adopted contingency views, in line with Hambrick and Mason's (1984) contention that long executive tenures will be helpful to company performance under some conditions and harmful under others. In such a test, Norburn and Birley (1988) found that executive tenures were positively associated with company performance (growth and profitability) in stable industries but negatively associated with performance in turbulent industries. This symmetrical pattern was observed for three types of executive tenure—in the job, in the company, and in the career (essentially capturing age). These results corroborate the commonsense idea that stable industry conditions favor experience and well-developed repertoires, whereas dynamic and discontinuous industry conditions favor freshness and open-mindedness.

PROPOSITION 4–10

Long executive tenure is more positively (or less negatively) associated with organizational performance in stable industries than in turbulent industries.

The relative advantages of long executive tenure may depend not only on the requirements of the external environment but also on those imposed by the firm's chosen strategy. It is in this vein that Thomas, Litschert, and Ramaswamy (1991) conducted their study. Beyond their finding that Prospector companies in the computer industry had executives with shorter organizational tenures than did Defender companies, they also found that the highest performing Prospectors and Defenders differed similarly in their executive tenures. In their most compelling test, the authors found that high company performance accrued to those firms whose executive tenures most closely conformed to the "ideal" for their strategic type. This study takes the perspective that top executives are responsible for implementing a chosen strategy. If the strategy requires product or market innovation, then short executive tenures—presumably conferring freshness, open-mindedness, and an external focus—are advantageous. If the strategy is one of stability and efficiency-seeking, longer tenures and their benefits of internal experience, are called for. Thus,

PROPOSITION 4–11

Long executive tenure is more positively (or less negatively) associated with organizational performance in Defenders than in Prospectors.

It is clear that executive tenure may have far-ranging implications for organizational functioning and fates. Figure 4-2, in an abbreviated form of Figure 3-1, summarizes some of the major findings regarding executive tenure.

So far, the effects of tenure are not yet well understood, and there is particularly a need to separately examine the influence of tenure in the position, in the organization, and in the industry. Our strong belief is that each of these forms of longevity has its own effects on executive mind-sets, strategic choice, and performance.

FUNCTIONAL BACKGROUND

Consultants and academics long have exhorted companies to expose their managers to multiple functions, both because it would enhance their breadth of perspective in their current assignments and because such a policy would yield broader-gauged top-level executives (Ouchi and Jaeger 1978; Raskas and Hambrick 1992). To be sure, some top executives have significant experiences in multiple functions. However, many have spent the greater part of their careers in one primary functional area, such as marketing, finance, or engineering.

It is reasonable to expect that an executive's functional experiences provide a lens through which he or she sees business problems and solutions in general (Dearborn and Simon 1958). A correspondence between functional experiences, psychological tendencies, and strategic choices

FIGURE 4–2 Executive Tenure: Some Observed Associations

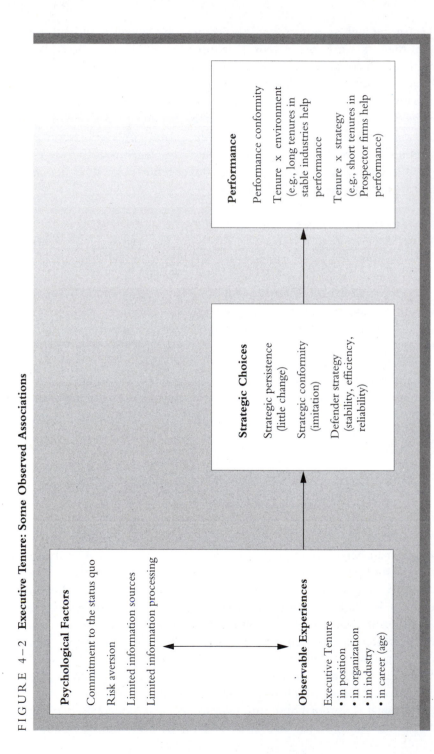

Psychological Factors

Commitment to the status quo

Risk aversion

Limited information sources

Limited information processing

Observable Experiences

Executive Tenure
• in position
• in organization
• in industry
• in career (age)

Strategic Choices

Strategic persistence (little change)

Strategic conformity (imitation)

Defender strategy (stability, efficiency, reliability)

Performance

Performance conformity

Tenure x environment (e.g., long tenures in stable industries help performance)

Tenure x strategy (e.g., short tenures in Prospector firms help performance) could occur through at least three mechanisms. First, individuals may be drawn to functional areas that suit their personalities or aptitudes (e.g., Schein 1968). At the start of their careers, individuals in different functions already have different cognitive models and values. Second, with the passage of time and the accumulation of successes in a functional area, an individual becomes more and more socialized and inculcated with the mode of thinking and acting that is typical for that professional area (Blau and McKinley 1979; Mortimer and Lorence 1979). And third, even when individuals are operating outside their functional areas, say in eventual general management positions, they still gravitate toward perceiving problems in familiar terms, generating and preferring familiar solutions (March and Simon 1958). In fact, it was from a belief in the orienting and filtering effects of functional experiences that Dearborn and Simon (1958) did their seminal study that ultimately led to today's widespread interest in the effects of executive backgrounds on decision making.

Executive Psychology and Perceptions

Dearborn and Simon (1958) argued that exposure to the goals and reinforcements of a particular functional area will cause managers to attend to certain information in a complex business situation and, in turn, to interpret that information in terms that suit their functional expertise. To test these ideas, Dearborn and Simon had twenty-three middle managers from a single company read a ten thousand-word business case that presented a large number of facts with virtually no structure or interpretation. The managers were then asked to identify the major problem facing the company. As the researchers expected, the managers tended to gravitate to interpretations that mirrored their functional backgrounds. For example, sales executives mentioned more sales-related problems than did executives from other functional areas. However, a careful reading of the results in an appendix leads one to conclude that Dearborn and Simon's findings are only suggestive, not definitive. There were not wholesale differences between functions, although some evidence of functional bias in interpreting business problems was observed.

Almost thirty years later, Walsh (1986) conducted an elaborate replication and extension of Dearborn and Simon's study. He had 121 participants enrolled in an executive MBA program do two tasks: 1) read a thousand-word business case and identify the major problems faced by the company, and 2) sort cards with business terms into piles to reveal underlying cognitive structures. Walsh hypothesized that the participants' handling of these tasks would reflect their functional backgrounds, but this was not at all borne out. No discernible functional biases were revealed in either of these information-processing endeavors.

Why did Dearborn and Simon find functional biases (albeit, of a limited nature) and Walsh observe none? We wish to posit several reasons, beyond minor methodological issues, that address the basic significance of an executive's functional background.

First, consider the basic differences between the mid-1950s and the mid-1980s, the eras in which the two studies were conducted. In the mid-1950s, there was not a pervasive concept of general management in America. All but a few companies had only one general manager, the CEO. There were relatively few MBA programs, a handful of popular business magazines, very few executive seminars, and certainly no best-selling books on managing. By the mid-1980s, all managers in business were bombarded with information and insights beyond their primary professional area. Most major companies had numerous general management and quasi-general management positions. MBAs, trained primarily for breadth, were in profusion. Executive seminars abounded. Books by Peters and Waterman (1982) and Iacocca (1984) had led a series of best-sellers on general management that pulled many business people beyond their parochial zones.[4] Moreover, many corporations had adopted programs to expose promising managers to diverse experiences. In short, by the 1980s, managers may have been genuinely less confined by their functional backgrounds than were their predecessors in the 1950s. We can expect that the broad cultural milieu may affect the degree of cognitive parochialism of managers in general.

PROPOSITION 4-12

The greater the emphasis on general management in the broader cultural milieu, the weaker the relationship between executives' functional backgrounds and their interpretation of strategic stimuli.

It is noteworthy that Dearborn and Simon's subjects were participants in a short company training program, whereas Walsh's subjects were enrolled in a two-year executive MBA program. We may expect that Walsh's subjects were amidst intensive socialization into a multifunctional perspective; they had self-selected themselves into this quite extensive experience; and since companies customarily pay tuition for such programs, their supervisors probably selected them on the basis of their promotability and potential for general management positions. Therefore, Walsh's participants may have been far less functionally bounded than their peers who were not enrolled in such a program and certainly less bounded than Dearborn and Simon's subjects.

PROPOSITION 4–13

The more formal education they have in management, the weaker the relationship between executives' functional backgrounds and their interpretations of strategic stimuli.

The third point of reconciliation, seemingly minor, may be the one of greatest theoretical significance. Consider the fact that the case Walsh had his subjects read was one-thousand words long (three pages) and he gave them twenty-five minutes to study it. This would not seem to be an instance of information overload in which the manager would have to engage in mental shortcuts or fall back on the familiar. Rather, the manager could be very thorough and deliberate, quite readily assessing all available information. Namely, the task may not have met the conditions envisioned by the Carnegie School when they developed the concept of bounded rationality. In comparison, Dearborn and Simon's case was ten thousand words long, and the chances of complete mastery of the material and surmounting of cognitive biases seem far lower. That is, functional background—or any biasing experience—has its greatest effect on interpretation and choice when the manager 1) faces an abundance of complex, ambiguous information and 2) has to deal with the information under urgency or other forms of pressure. When these conditions exist, executives can be expected to scan, selectively perceive, and interpret strategic stimuli in line with their functional experiences.

PROPOSITION 4–14

The more ambiguous and multitudinous strategic stimuli are, the stronger the relationship between executives' functional experiences and their interpretation of the stimuli.

PROPOSITION 4–15

The less time executives have to consider strategic stimuli, the stronger the relationship between executives' functional experiences and their interpretation of the stimuli.

Our own view is that actual strategic situations faced by senior executives typically contain a great deal of ambiguity, information overload, and urgency. In turn, executives will manifest functional biases (as well as other types of dispositions) in their choices, and such biases are a promising and important target for research.

As already noted, some managers may have more than one area of functional experience. So, researchers may need to use more fine-grained approaches for eliciting and gauging functional backgrounds than assigning just one per person. In this vein, Gupta and Govindarajan (1984) measured the overall number of years general managers had spent in the specific functional area of marketing and sales, finding it to be positively related to the managers' tolerance for ambiguity. This is in line with common conceptions of marketing and sales managers having to deal with more exogenous, uncontrollable factors than do managers in other, more internally oriented functional areas, such as operations or accounting.

However, Gupta and Govindarajan found no association between functional background and the manager's risk-taking propensity. Earlier, Vroom and Pahl (1971) had observed the same lack of association. And, more recently, Hitt and Tyler (1991), using elaborate cluster analysis of executives' functional experiences, also found no strong relationships between any of the clusters and a survey measure of risk propensity. Thus, the implications of functional experiences may be limited to fewer psychological constructs than might logically be anticipated. And, as our reconciliation of Dearborn and Simon (1958) and Walsh (1986) indicates, even the most direct implications of functional experience are complex and depend on various moderating forces.

Links to Strategy and Performance

Inquiries into the effects of executive functional background on organizational profiles have centered on two classes of organizational strategy. The first is the company's competitive strategy in its major line of business, or its business strategy. The second is the company's diversification profile, or its corporate strategy. In each of these streams, some recurring and intuitively reasonable patterns emerge.

Competitive strategies can take many forms, but the typologies of Miles and Snow (1978) and Porter (1980) have been instrumental in identifying some major classes of strategic profiles. Research on executive functional backgrounds and business strategy have particularly applied the Miles and Snow typology. In their study of major tobacco companies, Chaganti and Sambharya (1987) found that the top executive ranks of the Prospector company they examined (Philip Morris) differed from those of the Analyzer (R. J. Reynolds) and Defender (American Brands) companies. Specifically, the Prospector had proportionately more executives with marketing and R&D backgrounds and fewer with finance backgrounds. Thomas, Litschert and Ramaswamy (1991) examined the functional backgrounds of the CEOs of computer companies and found similar results. Of the Prospector companies studied, 77 percent of their CEOs had experience primarily in "output-oriented" functions (i.e., marketing, sales, and R&D), as compared to only 10 percent of the CEOs in the Defender companies. Conversely, 90 percent of the Defenders' CEOs were primarily from "throughput-oriented functions" (manufacturing, accounting, finance, administration), compared to 23 percent of the Prospector CEOs.

PROPOSITION 4–16

Executives with primary experiences in output functions tend to pursue Prospector strategies. Executives with primary experiences in throughput functions tend to pursue Defender strategies.

Beyond the descriptive tendency for executives to pursue competitive strategies in line with their own functional capabilities and dispositions is the possibility that they are wise to do so. There may be performance advantages in having a fit between executive functional expertise and strategy. The little bit of available evidence supports this idea. For instance, Thomas, Litschert, and Ramaswamy found that the best-performing Prospectors had CEOs with output-oriented functional backgrounds, the best-performing Defenders had CEOs with throughput-oriented backgrounds, and, most noteworthy of all, firms tended to perform less well when they had CEOs that did not fit their strategy.

PROPOSITION 4–17

Firms pursuing Prospector strategies perform well to the extent their top executives have experience in output functions. Firms pursuing Defender strategies perform well to the extent their top executives have experience in throughput functions.

At least two other studies have found performance advantages stemming from an alignment of executive functional background and competitive strategy. Gupta and Govindarajan (1984) found that business units pursuing "build" strategies (involving aggressive market share quests) performed better to the extent that their general managers had experience in marketing and sales; there was no such association in businesses pursuing "hold" or "harvest" strategies, in which operational and financial competences are presumably more valuable. (Gupta and Govindarajan did not collect data on operational and financial functional experience, so it is not known whether such experience would in fact be beneficial for "hold" or "harvest" missions. We would anticipate that this would be the case.)

Barbosa (1985) found further evidence that business innovation is enhanced by certain functional capabilities among top executives. In a large-scale study of the forest products industry, he found that the conversion of product innovation efforts (R&D spending and staffing levels) into actual product innovations (patents, sales from new products, and so on) was strongly related to the degree of marketing experience among the company's top executives. He concluded that a marketing orientation among top executives confers more of a customer-based, creative, expansionist capability in the firm, which serves to enhance the yield from innovation efforts.

The second major research stream dealing with executive functional backgrounds and strategy has focused particularly on the company's diversification strategy. The chief line of argument has been that companies without operational connections among their business units (at the extreme, mere holding companies) would be likely to have top executives with financial, legal, and administrative backgrounds, while companies with more substantive interdependencies would be led by executives with experience in more "core" functions, such as marketing and sales, R&D, and operations. Song (1982) found support for this idea, observing that firms that were diversifying primarily through acquisitions were relatively likely to have CEOs with financial and legal backgrounds, while companies diversifying through internal, organic extensions were more likely to have CEOs with core function experience (in operations, R&D, and marketing and sales).

Michel and Hambrick (1992) extended these ideas in a somewhat more fine-grained way, arguing that top executives would have core function experiences in direct proportion to the amount of strategic interdependence existing among their major lines of business. Building upon Rumelt's (1974) framework, they posited that four categories of diversified firms lie on a continuum ranging from very low to very high strategic interdependence: unrelated, related in a loosely linked way, related in a tightly constrained way, and vertically integrated. They found, in line with their hypothesis, that the proportions of senior executives with primarily core function experience were as follows:

unrelated	18%
related–linked	27
related–constrained	35
vertically integrated	44

This pattern was highly statistically significant.

However, pursuing the concept that companies perform better to the degree that executive backgrounds fit the firm's chosen strategy, Michel and

Hambrick found results quite contradictory to their expectations. For the unrelated firms, profitability was positively related to core function expertise; for the vertically integrated firms, profitability was negatively related to such expertise. The authors concluded that the actual executive profiles of these two types of diversification strategies, as reported above, may have been counterproductive:

> . . . the average unrelated firm may have had managers with less core function expertise than was optimal . . . [they] may have had critical voids in operating knowledge, impairing their ability to evaluate division requests, performance patterns, and acquisition candidates beyond the most superficial financial and administrative levels.

> . . . [the high percentage of executives with core function expertise in the vertically integrated firms may have been similarly counterproductive.] . . . these firms may have benefitted from more objective, staff-analytic executives who were not overly committed to a specific business or way of operating. (p.32)

Hayes and Abernathy (1980), in their influential article, "Managing Our Way to Economic Decline," were among the first to raise the idea that functional capabilities of senior executives would significantly affect the health of companies. They envisioned a universal effect—that executives with experience in core functions will produce superior returns. So far, the most direct tests of this supposition, particularly by Michel and Hambrick, provide no support for it. As yet, we know of no evidence of a generally advantageous functional profile for top executives. Instead, the external environment and the company's chosen strategy create a context in which certain functional orientations may have distinct but conditional benefits.

Figure 4-3 summarizes some of the observed associations among executive functional experiences, psychological factors, strategic choices, and organizational performance.

FORMAL EDUCATION

Since top executives typically are many years beyond their formal education, it may seem unlikely that their educational experiences would affect their current strategic choices and behaviors. Yet a significant body of research suggests that the schooling of senior managers is reflected in the characteristics of their organizations.

A substantial literature in developmental psychology and higher education exists regarding the effects of education on individual values and

FIGURE 4–3 **Executive Functional Background: Some Observed Associations**

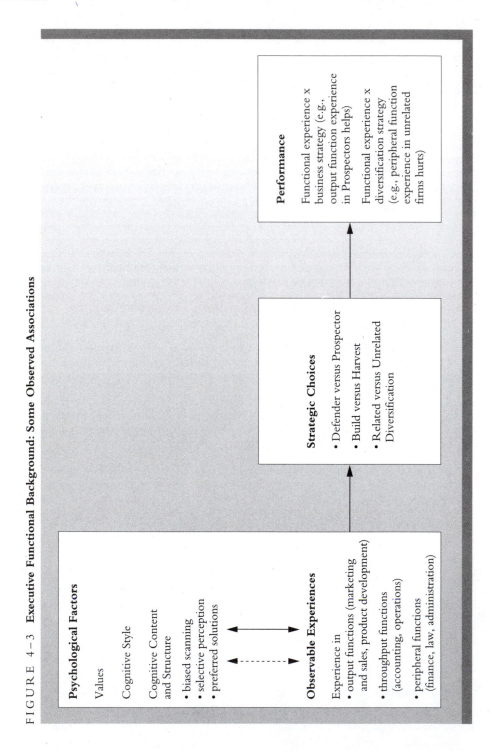

cognitions, as well as on the types of individuals who self-select themselves into certain educational experiences (e.g., Smart and Pascarella 1986; Byrne 1984; Cherrington, Condie, and England 1979; Schein 1968; Altmeyer 1966). However, very little research has examined associations specifically between education and executive psychological constructs. One possibility is that education confers, or is at least associated with, intellectual dexterity. In a survey study of 106 CEOs, Wally and Baum (1994) found a very strong correlation between amount of formal education and a measure of cognitive complexity, or the ability to discern patterns and distinguish among objects. Hitt and Tyler (1991) found a weaker but still positive link, thus suggesting this relationship:

PROPOSITION 4–18

An executive's amount of formal education is positively associated with cognitive complexity.

Further in line with the premise that formal education reflects an individual's cognitive ability, particularly open-mindedness, researchers have found that education is associated with receptivity to innovation (Becker 1970a; Becker 1970b; Rogers and Shoemaker 1971). Moreover, evidence consistently has indicated a positive link between the education level of senior executives and the amount of innovation in their organizations. Kimberly and Evanisko (1981) were among the first to document this pattern, finding that the amount of formal education of hospital chief administrators was positively associated with the adoption of both technological and administrative innovations in hospitals. Similar positive associations between executive education levels and organization innovation have been observed in samples of commercial banks (Bantel and Jackson 1989), forest product companies (Barbosa 1985), and computer companies (Thomas, Litschert, and Ramaswamy 1991). Relatedly, Norburn and Birley (1988) found that amount of education of top executives was positively associated with company growth in three of five industries studied. Finally, Wiersema and Bantel (1992) found that education levels of top executives were positively associated with strategic portfolio changes in a large sample of diversified firms. Thus, the effects of executive education levels on organizational innovation, change, and growth are widely documented.

Hambrick and Mason (1984) cautioned that any observed associations between education and innovation may be due to an unobserved spurious effect from executive age. There has been a marked, steady tendency toward increased education levels of executives over the past thirty or forty years, and young executives tend to be more highly educated than their older colleagues and predecessors. However, at least three of the studies cited above have used multivariate analysis, while controlling for age, and they still find significant effects stemming from education (Barbosa 1985; Bantel and Jackson 1989; Wiersema and Bantel 1992). Another possible confounding factor—the inevitable correlation between the amount of innovation in an industry and the amount of education—can similarly be set aside because almost all studies cited have controlled for industry effects. Hence, the association between the level of education of senior executives and the amount of innovation and change in their organizations appears to be robust and stable.

PROPOSITION 4-19

The greater the amount of formal education of top executives, the more innovative their organizations.

The effects of education level on organizational performance, however, are not as widely observed or clear-cut. Of course, one can conceive of growth as a performance indicator, in which case executive education levels seem to have a salutary effect (Norburn and Birley 1988). However, effects on profitability and shareholder returns have barely been examined. Here, we must reasonably expect contingency effects: high levels of formal education are more conducive to organizational performance in some environments, and in pursuit of some strategies, than in others. Once again, the contingency model tested by Thomas, Litschert, and Ramaswamy (1991) is instructive. They not only found that the CEOs of Prospector firms were more highly educated than the CEOs of Defender firms, but also that the best performing firms of each type also differed similarly; firms did less well to the extent that their CEOs had profiles differing from the "ideal" for their type. Thus, some competitive and marketplace conditions call for more formal education—and concomitant open-mindedness, information processing abilities, and cognitive flexibility—than do other settings.

PROPOSITION 4-20

The amount of formal education of executives is more positively associated with organizational performance for Prospectors than for Defenders.

In addition to examining the organizational implications of the amount of education of executives, some limited research has focused on particular curricula or fields of study. The two chief premises of this line of inquiry are that 1) individuals with certain dispositions, aptitudes, and cognitive styles tend to pursue certain compatible educational curricula, and 2) educational curricula differ in the influences they exert on individuals

(Hitt and Tyler 1991). As might be expected, there particularly has been an interest in investigating the organizational implications of having senior executives with formal education in business administration, particularly in MBA programs. Still, just a few such studies have been conducted, with somewhat disparate results.

We will briefly summarize three studies and then propose a possible reconciling theme. Kimberly and Evanisko (1981), in addition to examining overall amount of education, also explored whether hospital administrators educated specifically in administration would be associated with organizational innovation. They found no such relationship: executives educated formally in fields of administration were associated with no more or less innovation than those with formal education in other fields. (As noted above, formal education, in general, was positively associated with innovation.) Grimm and Smith (1991), on the other hand, did find that U.S. railroads that changed their strategies after deregulation were more likely to have MBAs among their senior executives than were the railroads that did not change their strategies. Finally, in a study of high-technology firms, Hambrick, Black, and Fredrickson (1992) found companies led by CEOs with MBA degrees were more profitable than those without such CEOs. The authors argued that executives with MBAs tend to confer formalization and control on organizations; in high-technology companies, which can tend toward chaos, these are valuable capabilities.

Thus, from these three studies, we might conclude:

1. MBA-educated executives are not associated with any more innovation than executives with equivalent formal education in other areas.
2. When a clear-cut, unambiguous environmental shift occurs, companies led by MBA-educated executives are relatively likely to respond.
3. MBA-educated executives inject control into an organization.

We believe these findings can be reconciled by a line of argument set forth by Hambrick and Mason:

> the analytic techniques learned in an MBA program are geared primarily to avoiding high losses or mistakes . . . business schools are not particularly well inclined to develop innovative or risk-taking tendencies . . . people who are drawn to business schools . . . tend to be "organizers and rationalizers." (1984, 201)

This leads us to restate one of Hambrick and Mason's propositions that, although so far untested, is a promising and intriguing way to think about formal education in business (p. 201):

PROPOSITION 4-21

Firms whose managers have had little formal management education show greater variation from industry performance averages than firms whose managers are highly educated in management.

In short, we anticipate that executives' formal education in business is associated with "alert moderation"—strategies responsive to clear-cut trends in the environment but relatively conformist, tightly controlled, and yielding moderate performance levels. Why might these patterns occur? Because 1) individuals who enroll in MBA programs are, by predisposition, generally risk-averse and conventional, 2) MBA curricula reinforce and enhance risk-aversion and mainstream mind-sets, and 3) executives with MBAs are more likely to be in the social and business elite (Useem and Karabel 1986), in which conformity and conventionality are facilitated and enhanced.[5]

Indeed, it may be that having an MBA draws one into the business mainstream but that having an *elite* MBA particularly facilitates exposure to the inner circle of business activity. This was the concept explored by Palmer, Jennings, and Zhou (1993), who found that companies with CEOs who had MBAs from a small set of elite schools were relatively likely to adopt the multidivisional corporate form (M-form). The authors viewed the M-form as an administrative innovation that diffused through leading-edge social networks of business executives. The executives with elite MBAs created and propagated the convention of the M-form organization.

This line of thought about the effects of MBA education is strictly speculative but clearly intriguing and, we believe, reasonable. There is widespread interest, and at the same time cynicism, about the effects of MBA programs on the health and vitality of corporations. Focusing on the executives who have graduated from such programs, and comparing their strategic actions and performance to those who have not, is one potentially powerful way of advancing this debate. Attention to the overall amount of education and even the educational institutions of executives (Useem and Karabel 1986; D'Aveni 1990) may yield important insights into the origins of strategic choice and performance.

Figure 4-4 summarizes some observed and hypothesized associations among formal education of executives, psychological factors, strategic choice, and organizational performance. As with executive tenure and functional backgrounds, we can say that some important patterns have been established but that their subtleties and the operative mechanisms through which they occur remain important targets for future study.

FIGURE 4–4 Executive Formal Education: Some Observed and Hypothesized Associations

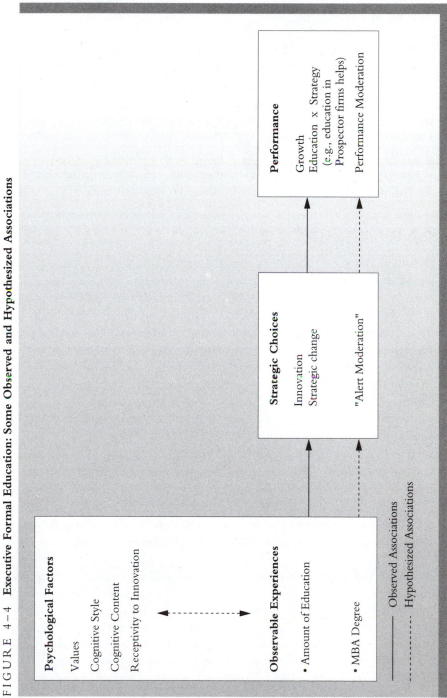

FUTURE DIRECTIONS

The fundamental idea that executive dispositions become reflected in organizational outcomes is clearly bearing fruit. The past ten years have seen a steady accumulation of evidence that the psychological and background characteristics of senior managers affect the choices they make, or at least that executive and organizational characteristics co-vary. However, we are far from definitive conclusions; considerably more research on these issues is needed. Here, we will identify several high priorities, focusing first on specific thrusts we see as promising and then describing an integrated new perspective that warrants great attention.

Promising Avenues of Research

Additional executive background factors.   Beyond the demographic variables that have been the primary focus of upper-echelons research so far—primarily executive tenure, functional background, and formal education—lies the need to examine other background characteristics that may have important bearing on organizational outcomes. Given the trends underway in many societies, particularly in the United States, it may be promising to examine executive gender, ethnic background, and national origin as factors that influence psychological constructs, strategy, and organizational performance. Historically, so few women and people of color or other nationalities have been among the top executive ranks of U.S. companies that such studies would have been impossible. But the proportions of such executives are growing, notably among mid-sized and smaller companies (a population of firms we will return to momentarily), and such inquiries are not only now possible but also exceedingly timely. To be sure, theory and research on matters of gender, ethnicity, and national origin have abounded in recent years, but the focus has been on general populations or low- or mid-level managerial ranks and not yet on senior executives.

A search for executive types.   The academic field of strategy has benefited immensely from the development of several robust, powerful strategy typologies. The classification systems set forth by Rumelt (1974), Miles and Snow (1978), and Porter (1980) have been particularly useful in allowing strategy researchers to move away from having to examine one strategy variable at a time. Similar typologies of senior level executives are urgently needed if the field of strategic leadership is going to achieve any theoretical parsimony and predictive power.

Typologies rest on the premise that phenomena of interest do not occur in endless combinations, at least not with equal likelihoods (Hambrick 1984). Certainly this premise is valid for a population of senior executives. We can reasonably expect that certain combinations of psychological and experience characteristics exist disproportionately among executives. If these pronounced executive profiles could be identified, research and theory-building regarding executive effects on organizations could advance greatly.

In the early 1980s, some executive typological schemes were set forth. For example, Wissema, Van Der Pol, and Messer (1980) described six types of managers (e.g., "Pioneer," "Administrator," "Economizer") and proposed their appropriateness for different strategic circumstances. Leontiades (1982) articulated a different typology, yet, as with the work of Wissema and associates, there was no significant grounding or empirical test of the framework.

A more recent attempt, grounded in a quantitative analysis of twenty-seven published cases on executive behavior, extracted four major, recurring "leadership patterns": entrepreneurial, bureaucratic, political, and professional (Shrivastava and Nachman 1989). This is directionally what we would encourage. However, instead of using data on executive behaviors to create the taxonomy or typology, we would go one step back in the causal chain and use data on the fundamental characteristics of the executives themselves (such as their risk orientation, cognitive style, values, tenure in their company, functional background).

To develop such a taxonomy will require far-ranging data on a sizable cross-section of senior executives. Such an undertaking may be possible only for certain research groups that have in-depth, psychometric access to large numbers of executives from diverse settings. The Center for Creative Leadership and major university executive programs are sites where such research could be done. Until we have the analytic parsimony provided by typologies, we must resign ourselves to relatively piecemeal and fragmentary examinations of executive characteristics.

Beyond the Fortune 500. The vast preponderance of upper-echelons research, using demographic factors, has examined executive effects in the biggest publicly traded corporations. To some extent, this is understandable because data on these companies are relatively abundant and the companies are economically noteworthy. However, by focusing on such large, visible corporations, researchers introduce an important bias and, unwittingly, probably greatly restrict the likelihood of observing strong executive influences on organizational outcomes.

First, as we discussed in Chapter 2, executives in large, long-lived companies do not have as much discretion as executives in smaller or younger companies. In this vein, Finkelstein and Hambrick (1990) found that the observed relationship between top executive tenure and strategic persistence and conformity was far stronger for smaller firms in their sample than for the larger firms. Researchers can benefit from explicitly including discretion-determining factors in their theoretical and empirical designs. At a minimum, they must be aware that very large, mature companies generally confer relatively little managerial discretion.

In addition, however, we believe that institutional pressures greatly homogenize the perspectives and outlooks of senior executives in the largest companies, such that there may be relatively little variance in their cognitions and values. Large companies tend disproportionately to be located in large commercial centers (such as New York, Los Angeles, or Chicago), their executives interact a great deal (through board affiliations, business associations (e.g., the Business Roundtable and philanthropic and civic endeavors), and these companies are the chief subjects of the business press and prominent security analysts. All of these factors place great pressure on the top executives to think and act in certain ways, through forces of social contamination, mimetic behavior, and external norms (DiMaggio and Powell 1983). These companies are least likely to be reflections of the dispositions and qualities of their top executives.

In our experience, executive orientations much more strongly manifest themselves in mid-sized and smaller companies located far away from major commercial centers and in industries that are not closely followed by the business press or the financial establishment. Executives in such companies are more likely to be outside the central network of managerial norms and influences that serves to homogenize the dispositions of executives in Fortune 500 companies.

Causality.   One cannot possibly read this chapter on executive and organizational co-variation without wondering about the direction of causality. Do executives make strategic choices in line with their own experiences and biases, as posited by upper-echelons theory? Or do organizational contexts give rise to the selection and perpetuation of certain executive profiles? Over time, a reinforcing spiral probably occurs (Miles and Snow 1978): managers select strategies that mirror their beliefs and preferences, successors are selected according to how much their qualities suit the strategy, and so on.

To date, relatively few upper-echelons studies have been designed in a way as to allow convincing conclusions about causality. This must be a high priority going forward. This can be accomplished through careful research designs and data analysis. Longitudinal designs using cross-lagged correlations, change scores (or first-difference scores), controls for prior states, and simultaneous equation modeling are among the means researchers must adopt if they are to shed clearer light on the degree to which executive characteristics give rise to organizational characteristics, as opposed to the reverse.

A New Perspective: The Factors Affecting the Predictive Strength of Executive Characteristics

The central idea of this chapter, indeed of the entire book, is that executives make choices on the basis of their own highly personalized interpretations of problems, options, and outcomes—and hence, that the organization becomes a reflection of its top managers. Readers familiar with the social psychology literature will recognize in this line of argument our emphasis on individual "dispositions" as predictors of behavior. So, too, will these readers recognize that many social psychologists place far greater weight on situational factors in affecting human behavior. Indeed during the late–middle part of this century, the dispositional paradigm was in utterly low repute, regarded as somewhat atheoretical and, in any event, simply not yielding very strong predictions of human behavior.

In recent years, however, social psychologists have focused more on the middle ground—an "interactionist" perspective, in which dispositional and situational factors operate in tandem to determine behaviors (Weiss and Adler 1984; Snyder and Ickes 1985). The role of individual dispositions has been rehabilitated somewhat, and now the critical question addressed by many social psychologists is not whether one view or the other is correct, but rather, when is each more correct? This perspective stems from Kurt Lewin's seminal proposition that "[e]very psychological event depends upon the state of the person and at the same time on the environment, although their relative importance is different in different cases" (1936, 12).

One of the major breakthroughs in identifying the circumstances under which dispositional or situational factors prevail as predictors of behavior was Mischel's concept of "situational strength" (1968). However, other factors that affect the predictive strength of situational versus dispositional characteristics also have been examined by scholars interested in this debate. Indeed, in an exhaustive review of the "interactional" framework, Snyder and Ickes (1985) proposed that the relative predictive strengths of dispositional and situational factors in social behavior hinge on these matters:

- Which traits (dispositional characteristics)?
- Which behaviors?
- Which people?
- Which situations?

If strategic leadership scholars are similarly interested in comprehending the conditions under which executive characteristics are most predictive of strategic choices, more attention must be paid to the questions raised by Snyder and Ickes. So far, the only significant attempt to adopt the interactionist perspective in research on executive leadership is the concept of executive discretion, or latitude of action, discussed at length in Chapter 2. However, we believe Snyder and Ickes's analysis (1985) provides an excellent point of departure for considering a wider set of forces that will affect the ability of strategic leadership researchers to obtain significant predictive strength from executive characteristics. Our purpose in proposing these factors is not so that researchers may "stack the deck," always examining conditions that favor the effects of executive characteristics, but rather so that scholars may finally start to understand the subtleties of executive effects on organizations.

In addressing Snyder and Ickes's questions in the context of strategic leadership research, we focus predominantly on executive demographic factors as possible predictors of executive choices and organizational outcomes, both because demographic factors have a prominent, promising place in research on executives and because these factors are not directly addressed by Snyder and Ickes. The line of argument also applies to the use of psychological constructs as predictors of behavior, which was the domain that Snyder and Ickes addressed. We must acknowledge that much of our discussion is speculative, because as just noted, very little executive leadership research or theory has adopted the interactionist model.

Which traits?   Social psychologists have found that some individual traits, as measured by psychological instruments, are more predictive of behaviors than are others and particularly that some traits are manifested more consistently than others. The same can be expected for executive demographic characteristics: Some may provide stronger predictions of strategic choices than others. Take the case of an executive's tenure in an industry. It is reasonable to expect that tenure in a highly concentrated, homogeneous industry would be more strongly associated with commitment to the status quo and strategic conformity to industry norms than would tenure spent in a more heterogeneous and dispersed industry. Two reasons could account for this. First, the homogeneous industry has a strong, shared conventional wisdom and widely held "recipes" (Huff 1982; Spender 1989) that become part of the entrenched belief system of executives who have been a part of the industry for a long time. Second, and following directly from the first reason, executive tenure in the homogeneous industry is simply a more reliable proxy, a more telling indicator, of executive experiences than time spent in a more diffuse industry.

Similar differences between other demographic experiences can be expected. For example, tenure spent in an organization with a strong culture will be more predictive of executive psychology and behavior than tenure spent in an organization with a weak culture. As for functional experience, it may be that certain functions have very strong professional norms and shared values, serving to homogenize the outlooks and predispositions of individuals who have been members of those functions. In contrast, other functions may exert far less socialization and homogenization. For instance, it may be that long experience in accounting is more predictive of executive outlook and behavior than, say, experience in marketing. Gupta and Govindarajan (1984) found that the number of years that general managers had spent in marketing and sales was marginally positively related to executive tolerance for ambiguity. It may be that if they had measured years spent in some other function, say accounting, they would have observed far stronger relationships (although, with accounting, possibly a negative sign). Differences might also be expected between various types of educational experiences. In short, the ability to predict executive choices from background characteristics may vary widely, depending on the specific background factor being considered.

Which behaviors?   Not all behaviors are equally amenable to prediction and certainly not from a given executive characteristic. As Snyder and Ickes (1985) discussed, aggregations of acts are easier to predict than are single acts. This, of course, is a fundamental axiom of construct reliability. However, it was a focus on single acts in experimental settings that contributed to social psychologists' early conclusions that dispositions do not account for much variance in these acts. As soon as the experimenters moved to the examination of multiple or aggregated tasks, they encountered greater predictive strength primarily because of increased reliability of the criterion measure (summarized in Snyder and Ickes 1985).

For the most part, researchers of executive leadership tend to focus on aggregated acts, or outcomes. For instance, diversification strategy, levels of innovation, even R&D spending all represent numerous managerial choices. However, researchers can be occasionally tempted to study single decisions or acts; when they do so, they must anticipate reduced predictive power. For instance, studies attempting to predict discrete choices—for example, whether a firm will make an acquisition or not, whether a firm will pay greenmail or not, or who a CEO will pick as his or her successor—may face long odds in terms of the likelihood of generating strong results.

A behavior is also predictable from an executive characteristic to the extent that the behavior is "prototypical" of what the trait is theoretically expected to engender. For example, it would be tempting to consider CEO experience in R&D as generally predictive of organizational innovation. However, it may be that an executive's experience in R&D is a strong predictor of R&D spending, only a moderate predictor of adoption of other firms' innovations, and a very poor predictor of adoption of administrative innovations. Each of these organizational characteristics—tapping different elements of innovation—vary widely in how prototypical or central they are to the executive orientation engendered by R&D experience.

Which people?   Are there some executives who vividly and regularly manifest their background characteristics in their actions and others who simply do not? If so, can we analytically distinguish between them? Snyder and Ickes, in addressing this issue for social psychological research in general, invoked the concept of "self-monitoring," or the tendency to comprehend and regulate one's behavior in the context of specific situational cues. High self-monitors, Snyder and Ickes argued, are responsive to the specific context; low self-monitors act more on the basis of their values, personality, and inherent beliefs.

We can reasonably expect that executives, too, vary in their self-monitoring tendencies and that this will cause differences in the degree to which their personal dispositions appear in their decisions. For example, a low self-monitor CEO may be inclined to favor in the resource allocation process the functional area in which he or she rose. This is a phenomenon observed in many companies and reflects the logic from the upper-echelons perspective. However, high self-monitor CEOs may comprehend not only their tendency to look favorably on the old home function, but also that to do so exposes them to complaints about favoritism; in such cases, the home function may not receive more resources than the others (and in extreme acts of self-monitoring, the home function might receive less than the other functions!).

Executives might also vary in how much they value rationality and fact-based decision making, such that they differ in how much their *other* biases and dispositions affect their choices. In their discussion of executive values, Hambrick and Brandon (1988) posited that the strong believer in rationality strives to gather and evaluate facts, perhaps taking in a wide array of viewpoints, and thus may be relatively unlikely to act primarily on the basis of personal experience and preference. Although executives as a whole may tend to place a high value on rationality, they almost certainly are not uniform in this regard. Through this variable, self-monitoring, and yet other unspecified factors, we may have a way of understanding why the experiences of some executives are more strongly reflected in their strategic choices than are those of others.

Which situations?   It is with the type of situation that social psychologists have been able to alter greatly the amount of variance in behaviors due to dispositional factors. Mischel's (1968) distinction between strong and weak situations is seminal in this regard, with far more dispositional effects observed when the situation is "weak," that is, ambiguous. It is in part because strategic situations faced by senior executives are generally weak— complex, ambiguous, with many interpretations and information overload—that research regarding executive effects on organizations has consistently yielded significant results and is a promising avenue of inquiry. However, even strategic situations may vary widely in how strong or weak they are, and researchers should be aware of this, both for reasons of theory and research design.

A weak situation is unstructured and without clear means-ends causal connections, and it is here that executive effects will be most pronounced. For instance, choices made in a very heterogeneous industry, in which firms pursue widely differing strategies, will be more reflective of executive characteristics than choices made in a homogeneous industry. In the latter, the "correct pathway" to organizational effectiveness is apparent, even if only by convention (Thompson 1967).

Similarly, strategic issues that lack precedence or clear models are more likely to be resolved on the basis of executive disposition than are issues for which clear models or strong institutional forces exist. In this vein, Johnson and Johnson's handling of its tragic Tylenol tampering episode in the early 1980s was probably due, in great part, to values and experiences of the company's senior executives. However, they received so many plaudits for their actions, from so many quarters, that their actions become a compelling model for executives in any company that might face a product tampering or defect problem. The problem now lacks ambiguity: there now exists a clear-cut solution to any life-threatening product-defect problem that is pursued by executives who have widely varying backgrounds and personalities.

More broadly, however, we must return to the concept of discretion as a pivotal way of viewing strategic situations. In a high-discretion situation— one in which the environment and organization confer wide latitude of action—executive characteristics are likely to be reflected in organizational choices. In situations of low discretion—in which there are constraining forces or simply strong convictions about means-ends connections—executive dispositions do not correspond much with strategic choices.

The study of strategic leadership will advance not simply by searching for evidences of executive effects on organizations, but rather by isolating the conditions under which those effects are great or small. In doing so, researchers will not only aid each other in terms of theory refinement and establishing appropriate research designs; they also will contribute to eventual practical implications in the arenas of executive selection, succession, evaluation, and rewards.

NOTES

1. Executive age, or "tenure in life," has also been the subject of some research. Because of mandatory retirement provisions for officers of most major companies, executives over 65 are relatively rare. Hence, age ranges are severely truncated, and such measures may be capturing tenure-based phenomena more than age-based phenomena. Nonetheless, research has extended Vroom and Pahl's (1971) observation that managerial age is negatively associated with risk-taking, finding that executive age is negatively associated with 1) product or market innovation strategies (Thomas, Litschert, and Ramaswamy 1991), 2) strategic change following industry deregulation (Grimm and Smith 1991), and 3) change in diversification profiles (Wiersema and Bantel 1992). Thus, available evidence on executive age conforms to the same gereral pattern obtained when the focus is executive tenure.

2. Some companies are active in multiple industries, and of course some executives move from industry to industry. Under these conditions, industry effects on executive commitment to the status quo will be muted.

3. This study and several others we review in this section are based on average demographic characteristics of top management teams, not just of individual executives. As a group average, such a characteristic can be thought to tap the collective "mind" or cognition of the top managers, whereas measures of dispersion or heterogeneity would be suggestive of group process and rightly discussed in Chapter 5, on TMTs.

4. Nohria and Berkley (1994) provide intriguing data on the further proliferation of a "managerial culture" in America, citing astronomic growth between 1982 and 1992 in numbers of business schools, MBAs granted, management consultants, corporate expenditures on training, business stories in the media, and business books.

5. It is interesting to consider the possibility that business schools differ systematically in the types of students they attract. For example, fundamentally different types of individuals may enroll at Harvard than at Chicago; and innovative schools that emphasize creativity and entrepreneurship may attract students who differ widely from the average MBA candidate.

Top Management Teams: Group Bases of Executive Action

Although the pyramid headed by an all-powerful indi-
vidual has been a symbol of organizations, such
omnipotence is possible only in simple situations where
perfected technologies and bland task environments
make computational decision processes feasible. Where
technology is incomplete or the task environment hetero-
geneous, the judgmental decision strategy is required
and control is vested in a dominant coalition.
(Thompson 1967, 143)

One of the most enduring ideas in organization theory is that environments impose constraints on individuals (Lawrence and Lorsch 1967), making it exceedingly difficult for any one person, even a chief executive officer, to control all aspects of organizational life. The conditions for omnipotence noted by Thompson (1967) are rare, for they imply the absence of decision-making uncertainty. Rather, given the great ambiguity and complexity inherent to strategic decision making (Mintzberg 1973), the formation of a coalition of individuals seems a more plausible outcome. As a result, when modeling how strategic leaders make strategic decisions, we must be "left with something more complicated than an individual entrepreneur" (Cyert and March 1963, 30).

The idea that it is valuable, in both a conceptual and predictive sense, to study groups of top managers rather than just CEOs is powerful. We see four main advantages. First, as an aggregation of individuals, organizations have multiple goals that are often in conflict (Cyert and March 1963; Weick 1979a). The existence of these multiple goals, and hence multiple preferences, at the top of organizational hierarchies is likely to affect how organizations strive toward organizational outcomes, as well as the characteristics of those outcomes. Second, descriptions of the strategic decision-making process typically emphasize the relevance of stages, sequences, and processes that involve a group of top managers interacting toward desired ends (Pettigrew 1973; Mintzberg, Raisinghani and Theoret, 1976; Nutt 1984). Indeed, the top management team (TMT) is at the strategic apex of an organization (Mintzberg 1979); it is the executive body most responsible for strategic decision making and, by extension, such fundamental organizational outcomes as firm strategy, structure, and performance. Third, to the extent individual top managers affect organizational outcomes, predictive ability is enhanced when a group of top managers is considered (Hambrick and Mason 1984). Fourth, the interactions among top managers create outcomes of interest to strategists, such as power distributions, decision processes and integration, and fragmentation within top managerial groups. So, whether one refers to groups of top managers as dominant coalitions (Cyert and March 1963; Bourgeois 1980), "inner circles" (Thompson 1967; Finkelstein 1992), top management groups (Hambrick 1994), or top management teams (Bourgeois 1980; Hambrick and Mason 1984), there is much to gain from focusing on the constellation of executives at the top of organizations.

The study of top management teams[1] in organizations must necessarily involve consideration of the strategic decision-making process and the role TMTs play in it. Focusing on a group of individuals at the top creates both opportunity and obligation to examine how they interact in the process of performing a key component of their jobs: the making of strategic decisions. Although CEOs play a particularly important role in the strategic decision-making process (a subject that we discuss below), we believe a more tenable assumption is that there is a group of executives at the top who are potentially influential. However, we need not rely on assertion to support this point; rather, it may make more sense to actually consider the relative power of individual executives in the strategic decision-making process. As Finkelstein has argued:

> Power is . . . central to research on top management teams. In fact, the choice of unit of analysis in research on top managers and the issue of managerial power are two sides of the same coin. That is, adoption of a unit of analysis rests on an implicit assumption about the distribution of power among top managers. For example, in an organization in which the CEO wields dominant power, studying only the CEO may provide sufficient information with which to test propositions. However, in organizations in which power is less polarized, consideration of a coalition of top managers is necessary to fully capture the range of managerial orientations prevailing. Hence, consideration of the distribution of power among top managers seems an essential ingredient for research on top management teams. (1992, 505)

In addition, abundant evidence exists that studying TMTs, rather than CEOs alone, provides better predictions of organizational outcomes (Hage and Dewar 1973; Tushman, Virany, and Romanelli 1985; Finkelstein 1988; Ancona 1990; O'Reilly, Snyder, and Boothe 1993). For example, in a series of tests of upper–echelons hypotheses, Finkelstein (1988) reported stronger results at the TMT than at the CEO level of analysis in 81 percent of all regressions. Yet, we believe that understanding the distribution of power within TMTs is important not only because it provides a rationale for studying them, but also because its effects are pervasive throughout the strategic decision–making process. Hence, this chapter focuses on TMTs in the context of the strategic decision–making process and models the interactions among TMT members as a central construct in that process.

Defined in this way, TMTs present many possible research questions. TMTs are not only a central component in the strategic decision–making process; they may also be viewed as a basic organizational attribute, worthy of explanation in their own right. This dual emphasis, implying concern for both the antecedents and consequences of TMTs and their role in strategic decision making, is adopted in this chapter.

An important matter of scope, however, requires clarification. The strategic decision–making literature is vast and involves numerous sets of relationships among determinants, decision-specific factors, process characteristics, process outcomes, and consequences (Eisenhardt and Zbaracki 1992; Rajagopalan, Rasheed, and Datta 1993). It is clearly beyond the scope of this chapter to fully address each facet of the strategic decision–making process. Rather, our interest is in the role of TMTs in strategic decision making and, even more specifically, the nature and effects of social relations among top team members as they develop strategies for their organizations.

Below we define what we mean by "top management team" and further clarify the scope of our interest in top teams and strategic decision making.

DEFINING TOP MANAGEMENT TEAMS

Although the term "top management team" is now widely used, it is not uncommon for related research to emphasize different aspects of what is, in essence, a multidimensional construct. A top management team has three central conceptual elements: composition, structure, and process. First, composition refers to the collective characteristics of top team members, such as their values, cognitive bases, and experiences. Although these characteristics can be considered in terms of both the central tendency of the team and the heterogeneity of the team, in this chapter we focus solely on the latter.[2] In addition, and consistent with Chapters 3 and 4, our conceptualization of TMT heterogeneity encompasses both personality factors (values, beliefs, cognitions) and aspects of executive experience (age, tenure, functional background, education).

Second, the structure of a top team is defined by the roles of members and the relationships among those roles. Central to this definition is the role interdependence of team members, an important construct that may have significant consequences for how strategic decisions are made (Michel and Hambrick 1992). We define role interdependence as the degree to which the performance of the firm depends on resource sharing and coordination within the TMT. For example, a TMT consisting of heads of functional areas typically has more role interdependence than one made up of heads of independent business units or regional operations. Beyond the nature of executive roles, the actual size of a team is also a fundamental aspect of structure (Merton 1968; Keck 1990). Thus, we define TMT size as the number of top executives with active responsibility for the overall direction of the organization.

The third major conceptual element of a TMT is its processes. By processes, we mean in particular the nature of interaction among top managers as they engage in strategic decision making. While many potential dimensions of process could be studied, we focus our attention on two: social integration and consensus. Social integration is defined as "the attraction to the group, satisfaction with other members of the group, and social interaction among the group members" (O'Reilly, Caldwell, and Barnett 1989, 22) and is one of the most studied of process constructs. Consensus within a TMT is "the agreement of all parties to a group decision" (Dess and Origer 1987, 313).

All three conceptual elements—composition, structure, and process—are related to the social makeup and interactions of the top team in the process of making strategic decisions. Strategic decisions are not made in a vacuum; rather, they involve multiple top managers interacting in several places over some length of time. The nature of these interactions and their effects on both strategic decision making and organizational outcomes are of central importance. Beyond the complex set of interactions at the top, strategic decision making is also heavily influenced by activities in the organization and its environment. Hence, we are also interested in the contextual conditions that give rise to particular TMT configurations.

We believe these issues can be best understood by adopting the framework shown in Figure 5–1. At the center of this framework is the TMT, characterized in terms of a series of conceptual constructs that define what goes on at the top: heterogeneity (TMT composition), role interdependence and team size (TMT structure), and social integration and consensus (TMT process). We focus on these constructs, in particular, because they are central to both strategic decision making and social relations within TMTs and they have been the subject of considerable theoretical interest among scholars for some time. While other aspects of TMTs are certainly important and worthy of study, the goals of this chapter call for this relatively circumscribed scope.

The framework we developed suggests how each of these facets of TMTs are interrelated. The model also encompasses the effects of contextual conditions on TMTs. These contextual factors include environment, organization, and even (and especially) the CEO. Finally, Figure 5–1 shows how TMTs are associated with the strategic decision-making process and the organizational outcomes that arise from this process. A primary goal of this framework is to highlight three key research questions on TMTs: 1) What is the nature of interaction within TMTs? 2) How do contextual conditions affect TMTs? and 3) What are the consequences of TMTs for both strategic decision making and organizational outcomes? These questions define the scope of the major sections of this chapter.

TMT Interaction and Strategic Decision Making

There is a long history of work in social psychology on the composition of groups and the nature of their interactions (Jackson 1992). For the most part, this research has been conducted on ad hoc "groups" (via lab experiments on college students) or on lower-level employee work groups.

FIGURE 5–1   A Model of Top Management Teams

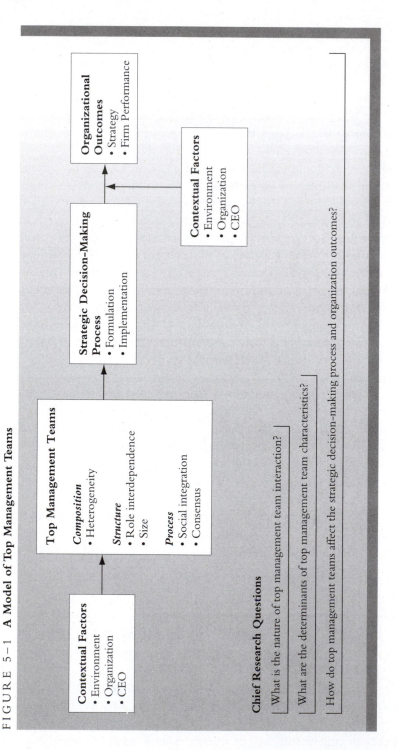

Contextual Factors
• Environment
• Organization
• CEO

Top Management Teams

Composition
• Heterogeneity

Structure
• Role interdependence
• Size

Process
• Social integration
• Consensus

Strategic Decision-Making Process
• Formulation
• Implementation

Contextual Factors
• Environment
• Organization
• CEO

Organizational Outcomes
• Strategy
• Firm Performance

Chief Research Questions

What is the nature of top management team interaction?

What are the determinants of top management team characteristics?

How do top management teams affect the strategic decision-making process and organization outcomes?

Much less common are studies of groups of top managers (exceptions include Glick, Miller, and Huber 1993; O'Reilly, Snyder, and Boothe 1993; Smith, et al. 1994). However, the dynamics of TMT interaction affect the extent of social integration and consensus, both of which have been conceptually but seldom empirically linked to a wide set of organizational outcomes (e.g., Wiersema and Bantel 1992). Rather, "the logic in these studies has been that team demography influences team processes . . . , and these processes, in turn, affect organizational outcomes" (Smith et al. 1994).

A large number of potential intervening processes exist between TMT composition and organizational outcomes. For example, the strategic decision-making process has many steps, including generation and evaluation of alternatives, selection, implementation, and evaluation. Before a decision can affect organizational outcomes, it must go through each of these stages—with TMT members interacting throughout. An impressive body of work documents linkages between TMTs and outcomes. Our goal in this section is to shed light on some of the intervening processes that define the "black box" in much of this work. We do so by considering interrelationships among TMT composition, structure, and process and by focusing on how these factors affect the strategic decision-making process.

It is at once problematic and self-evident that top management "teams" are really top management "groups." It is problematic because virtually all published research on the constellation of executives at the top characterizes these managers as a team in spite of the fact that they may not be cohesive or cooperative. For example, consider how the executive vice-president of marketing in a large firm described his team:

> Team? How do you define 'team'? When I think of a team, I think of interaction, a lot of give-and-take, and shared purpose. In our company, we're a collection of strong players, but hardly a 'team.' We rarely meet as a team—rarely see each other, in fact. We don't particularly share the same views. I wouldn't say we actually work at cross-purposes, but a lot of self-centered behavior occurs. Where's the 'team' in all this? (Hambrick 1994, 172)

It is also self-evident that TMTs are really top management groups because virtually all of the underlying theoretical support for proposed relationships on TMTs is based on research on work groups in social psychology. As Jackson notes, "Most of the relevant studies have been conducted by psychologists interested in understanding group processes and group performance. After fifty years of psychological research on groups, a large body of findings has accumulated" (1992, 354). Several important consequences follow: 1) definitions of top management teams or groups need to make clear which executives are included and why; 2) the importance of power dynamics among the group of executives at the top becomes more central; and 3) relationships among different facets of TMTs need to be empirically investigated. We elaborate on each of these points below.

Who Is in the Top Group?

Who actually constitutes the TMT[3] is an important issue because of the surprisingly wide set of operational definitions used in the literature. In addition, TMT size is increasingly being modeled as a meaningful construct in empirical work (e.g., Haleblian and Finkelstein 1993).

There is general agreement that the top management team sits at the strategic apex of an organization. Hence, by definition, a TMT is the group of top executives with "overall responsibility for the organization" (Mintzberg 1979, 24). As simple as this definition appears, there is no consensus among researchers conducting empirical work on TMTs regarding an appropriate operational definition, and definitional concerns have been largely ignored in published research. Among the different measures used to identify TMT members are: 1) all managers identified by the CEO as belonging to the TMT (e.g., Bantel and Jackson 1989; Glick, Miller, and Huber 1993; O'Reilly, Snyder, and Boothe 1993; Smith et al. 1994; Sutcliffe 1994); 2) inside board members (e.g., Finkelstein and Hambrick 1990; Haleblian and Finkelstein 1993); 3) all managers at the vice-president level and higher (e.g., Wagner, Pfeffer, and O'Reilly 1984; Hambrick and D'Aveni 1992; Michel and Hambrick 1992; Keck and Tushman 1993); 4) the two highest executive levels (e.g., Wiersema and Bantel 1992); and 5) all founders of the organization (Eisenhardt and Schoonhoven 1990).

On an *a priori* basis, it is not possible to unequivocally favor one definition over another.[4] Rather, the definition used should correspond to the research questions that guide a particular study (O'Reilly, Snyder, and Boothe 1993). For example, it is not appropriate for most studies to define TMTs in terms of founders, but that is a suitable definition for the purpose of studying entrepreneurial startup firms (Eisenhardt and Schoonhoven 1990).

Also, there is a need for investigation of the sensitivity of findings to different operationalizations of TMTs. The ability to gradually develop more generalizable theory on strategic leadership may be enhanced if results are found to differ systematically according to TMT definition. For example, in a study of TMT demography and organization innovation, Flatt (1992) compared results using alternative definitions of the TMT and found that they differed significantly. To some extent, such a sensitivity analysis is possible in many studies because developing more restrictive definitions of a TMT in a given data set is often feasible. Stronger theory may arise from this type of analysis, for it could enable greater understanding of which executives are influential in a particular setting. More generally, the definition of a TMT in an empirical project may be a variable worthy of study. Not only does this suggest that future work pay careful attention to operational issues, it also suggests that some meta-analysis of TMT research that measures the effects of alternative TMT definitions may be warranted. A more fine-grained understanding of TMTs may be possible from such an investigation.

Considerable exploratory work is warranted. For example, the appropriate definition of a TMT may depend on the strategic issue under consideration, with a somewhat different set of top managers involved depending on the issue (Dutton, Fahey, and Narayanan 1983). Such a "strategic issue processing" perspective assumes that the top decision-making body is not constant and implies that the appropriate definition of a TMT is that set of executives who are most active on a particular issue (Jackson 1992). While not without problems (Hambrick 1992), this perspective offers an alternative conceptualization of TMTs that envisions fluctuating boundaries of the top team.

Power Dynamics at the Top

One answer to the "Who constitutes the TMT?" question is those executives with the greatest power to affect the overall strategic direction of an organization. This is precisely the point made by Finkelstein (1992), when he argued that the distribution of power among top executives is not necessarily equal and that a consideration of power differences may go a long way toward better predictions of TMT effects. Hence, it may make sense to evaluate the power of a wide set of top managers and then focus on the subset that appears most influential. This is no different than Thompson's (1967) notion of the inner circle—the group of individuals with greatest decision-making power in an organization.

One piece of related evidence offers some support for this approach. In a study of 102 companies, Finkelstein (1988) asked top managers to rate the influence of themselves and others within their firms on specific strategic decisions. The group of top managers whose power was rated included the five most highly paid executives in the firm. Using these data, it was possible to compare the relative power of members of this executive cadre. Data were collected on a total of 444 top managers, consisting of 283 inside board members and 161 executives who held other top managerial positions but did not sit on the board. The average rating of managerial power for board members was 13.99,[5] while the average score for "nonboard" executives was 9.80, with the difference statistically significant at $p < .001$.

Even when CEOs were excluded from the analysis (and power scores for board members dropped to 12.00), the difference remained significant ($p < .001$). Hence, top managers identified a significant gap between the power of inside board members and other executives, providing support for the use of inside board members as an operational definition of TMT. More generally, some of the sensitivity analysis recommended earlier may be more feasible in studies that collect data on managerial power. In addition, using such data facilitates an empirically based determination of who constitutes the top team.

Beyond identifying TMT members, research on the distribution of power among top managers is important for several reasons. First, and perhaps foremost, power is central to strategic choice (Child 1972; Finkelstein 1992). It is generally well-established that strategic decisions are unstructured and ambiguous (Mintzberg, Raisinghani, and Theoret 1976) and, hence, invite the use of power (Mintzberg 1983). Numerous examples exist of the important role of power in the strategic decision-making process (Allison 1971; Carter 1971; Pettigrew 1973; Hinings et al. 1974; Miles and Cameron 1982; Eisenhardt and Bourgeois 1988). Second, and as we discussed earlier, the distribution of power within TMTs affects which executives are influential and, as a result, the impact of executive experiences and personality on organizational outcomes (Finkelstein 1992). Finally, studying top managerial power makes clear that TMTs are really groups of individuals—each with their own goals and preferences—and are not necessarily cooperative teams with unitary goals and preferences (Cyert and March 1963).

It is this issue of focusing on the dynamics of TMTs to which we now turn our attention. In particular, we consider how TMT composition, structure, and process are interconnected and how the distribution of power within TMTs affects these important facets of executive interaction.

The Nature of Interaction Within TMTs

Figure 5–2 elaborates on Figure 5–1 by depicting several relationships among TMT composition, structure, and process. In this section, we develop the rationale for the associations proposed by drawing on work in social psychology, organizational demography, and strategic management. Because almost all of the relevant research comes from conceptual articles or empirical studies using samples of people who are not executives, these ideas constitute unfinished business for a research agenda on strategic leadership.

To help understand how senior executives interact as a group, it is useful to carefully consider one of the most studied facets of TMTs—demo-

FIGURE 5-2   **Top Management Team Interaction**

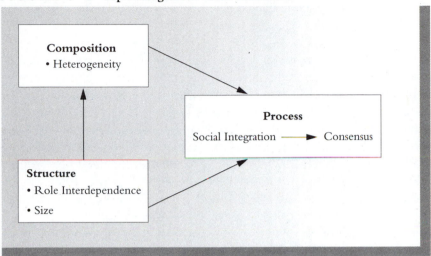

graphic heterogeneity. Referring to the extent to which TMT members have had a wide variety of experiences, demographic heterogeneity is one of the most studied characteristic of TMTs but still among the most ambiguous. Its popularity among researchers is owed to a fair degree to the accessibility, objectivity, and reliability of demographic data (Hambrick and Mason 1984), but critics have questioned the underlying meaning of that data (e.g., Smith et al. 1994).

Much of the confusion surrounding demographic heterogeneity relates to its implications for social integration and cognitive heterogeneity within TMTs. At one level, demographic heterogeneity may be seen as a proxy for cognitive heterogeneity (Hambrick and Mason 1984), representing innovativeness (Bantel and Jackson 1989; Murray 1989), problem-solving abilities (Nemeth 1986; Hurst, Rush, and White, 1989), creativity (Triandis, Hall, and Ewen 1965; Shaw 1981; Wanous and Youtz 1986; Bantel and Jackson 1989), diversity of information sources and perspectives (Jackson 1992; Wiersema and Bantel 1992; Sutcliffe 1994), openness to change (Katz 1982; Dutton and Duncan 1987; Virany, Tushman, and Romanelli 1992; Glick, Miller, and Huber 1993), and a willingness to challenge and be challenged (Hoffman and Maier 1961; Sorenson 1968; Janis 1972; Gladstein 1984; Eisenhardt and Schoonhoven 1990). Although these positive effects are typically associated with superior group, and by implication superior organizational performance, for now we restrict ourselves to a straightforward summary proposition:

PROPOSITION 5-1A

The greater the demographic heterogeneity within TMTs, the greater the cognitive heterogeneity within TMTs.

Alternatively, there is also considerable support for the idea that demographic heterogeneity reduces social integration within TMTs (and by implication group and organizational performance) by increasing conflict (Schmidt 1974; Reed 1978; Pfeffer 1981a; Deutsch 1985; Nemeth and Staw 1989; O'Reilly, Snyder, and Boothe 1993) and coordination costs (Pfeffer 1983; Smith et al. 1994) and by reducing communication frequency (Roberts and O'Reilly 1979; McCain, O'Reilly, and Pfeffer 1983; Wagner, Pfeffer, and O'Reilly 1984; O'Reilly, Caldwell, and Barnett 1989; Zenger and Lawrence 1989; Stasser 1993), as well as group identification and cohesiveness (Lott and Lott 1965; Zander 1977; Ancona and Caldwell 1992; Michel and Hambrick 1992). Nevertheless, in spite of the strength of these arguments, empirical investigations among TMTs have yet to establish this finding consistently. (For instance, research by O'Reilly, Snyder, and Boothe [1993] is supportive; Glick, Miller, and Huber [1993] reports mixed results; and Smith et al. [1994] is not supportive). Thus, this question remains an open one:

PROPOSITION 5-1B

The greater the demographic heterogeneity within TMTs, the less the degree of social integration within TMTs.

The opposite predictions for cognitive heterogeneity and social integration imply that they should be negatively associated as well. Indeed, social integration is facilitated when group members are more similar (Byrne 1961; Pfeffer 1981a), while many of the effects of demographic heterogeneity, such as greater diversity of perspectives and willingness to challenge others (Eisenhardt and Schoonhoven 1990; Glick, Miller, and Huber 1993), can create conflict that detracts from team cohesiveness and social integration. Hence, we propose the following:

PROPOSITION 5-1C

The greater the cognitive heterogeneity within TMTs, the less the degree of social integration within TMTs.

Demographic (and cognitive) homogeneity and social integration may increase TMT consensus. Homogeneous teams develop greater cohesive-

"Gentlemen, let us pool our expertise."

SOURCE: Stan Hunt; © 1975 The New Yorker Magazine, Inc.

ness over time (Pfeffer 1983), which promotes greater agreement about the organization and its goals (Tushman and Romanelli 1985). Hence, consensus is formed, as TMT members are able to coalesce around a shared understanding of what the organization seeks to accomplish (Dutton and Duncan 1987; Wiersema and Bantel 1992). To the extent that TMT homogeneity promotes a "dominant logic" (Prahalad and Bettis 1986) among a group of top managers, consensus is more likely (Dess and Keats 1987) (see cartoon). Shared understandings are also engendered through cooperation, frequent communication, and group identification, all of which are attributes of socially integrated groups (Lott and Lott 1965; O'Reilly, Caldwell, and Barnett 1989). Finally, TMT heterogeneity may weaken consensus on goals and perceptions (Cyert and March 1963; Grinyer and Norburn 1975; Bettenhausen and Murnighan 1985; Bourgeois 1985; Priem 1990; Amason and Schweiger 1992). In all, TMT consensus is expected to be positively related to TMT homogeneity and integration.[6]

PROPOSITION 5-1D

The greater the heterogeneity within TMTs, the less the degree of consensus within TMTs.

PROPOSITION 5-1E

The greater the social integration within TMTs, the greater the degree of consensus within TMTs.

The number of individuals within a TMT (its size) is also expected to affect cognitive heterogeneity, social integration, and consensus for many of the same reasons already enunciated. To some extent, this may be definitional, because the larger the team, the stronger the likelihood that executives will be demographically heterogeneous (Haleblian and Finkelstein 1993). Nevertheless, we can add two more rationales: 1) larger groups have greater capabilities and resources upon which to rely in the strategy-making process (Hambrick and D'Aveni 1992; Haleblian and Finkelstein 1993), increasing the variety of perspectives they can bring to a problem and thus promoting greater cognitive heterogeneity but less consensus at the top; and 2) larger groups create coordination and communication problems that smaller groups do not have (Blau 1970; Shaw and Harkey 1976), curtailing member cohesiveness, cooperation (Wagner 1995), social integration (Shaw 1981), and consensus (Shull, Delbecq, and Cummings 1970).

PROPOSITION 5-1F

The larger the size of TMTs, the greater the degree of cognitive heterogeneity within TMTs.

PROPOSITION 5-1G

The larger the size of TMTs, the less the degree of social integration within TMTs.

PROPOSITION 5-1H

The larger the size of TMTs, the less the degree of consensus within TMTs.

Although we draw on research in social psychology to develop propositions on the interrelationships among TMT characteristics, there are important differences between TMTs and other groups. Indeed, one of the problems in interpreting the meaning of TMT heterogeneity is that researchers tend not to explicitly consider how top management groups are different from other groups (upon which much of the supporting literature on TMT heterogeneity typically cited is based).[7] Perhaps of greatest importance is the role of power in TMTs (Keck 1990; Finkelstein 1992; O'Reilly, Snyder, and Boothe 1993). As opposed to typical work groups, one of the major functions of TMTs is to direct the behavior of others, an activity that both generates and uses power for each executive. In addition, top managers are expected to have a fundamental impact on organizations (Mintzberg 1979), but without the power to make decisions and direct others, they are unable to do so. Hence, it seems particularly important to incorporate power in models of TMT interaction. Nevertheless, such a focus is rare in the literature to date.

One of the most promising efforts along these lines has been the work of Eisenhardt and Bourgeois (1988). Through interviews and surveys, these authors investigated the "politics of strategic decision making" in eight microcomputer companies, developing a series of propositions on power and politics within TMTs. For example, they linked power and politics to TMT centralization, coalition formation, and demography. Unfortunately, their ideas have yet to be formally studied in any large-scale empirical investigation.

We suggest a different perspective on power in TMTs that builds on research by Finkelstein (1992). He suggested that research on TMTs requires a "recognition of the role of power in strategic choice and a means of incorporating power" if stronger predictions of executive effects are to be found (Finkelstein 1992, 532). The basic logic of this approach can be applied to TMT interaction. For example, the effects of TMT heterogeneity on TMT process should be stronger when the relative power of each top manager is taken into consideration. In a typical test of TMT heterogeneity, the dispersion of an attribute among different executives (such as tenure or tolerance for ambiguity) is calculated for the overall group. The impact of each executive on the top team is considered equal to that of any other executive, when in fact this very likely would not be the case (Mintzberg 1979; Finkelstein 1992). Because CEOs are generally more influential than others, an accurate assessment of the real level of heterogeneity in a TMT should take this into consideration. In other cases, managers with particular expertise, prestige, or ownership position may be more powerful (Finkelstein 1992). Hence, if only one or two executives hold all the power, taking the coefficient of variation of tenure within a TMT and suggesting that this accurately assesses the heterogeneity of that team along this dimension is potentially misleading. The most powerful managers have the greatest impact on strategic choices (Child 1972), thus it seems important to factor this into the analysis of TMT interaction.

One way to do this is to measure the relative power of each member of a TMT and adjust the demographic or cognitive makeup of the team by weighting each executive's tenure or tolerance for ambiguity by his or her power before computing heterogeneity measures. Such an analysis would yield more precise (and accurate) measures of heterogeneity and perhaps help establish more consistent and stronger relationships between TMT composition, structure, and process than has been evident in the literature to date. The following proposition is representative:

PROPOSITION 5-11

The effects of TMT heterogeneity on other characteristics of TMTs are stronger when the relative power of each member of the TMT is factored into the computation of heterogeneity.

In summary, significant interrelationships exist among the major facets of TMT interaction. Although they are sometimes recognized in the literature, we believe it is important to make these associations explicit. We have suggested several basic propositions that, with a few exceptions, have not been directly tested in an empirical setting. In addition, the idea that power is central to processes within a TMT is generally accepted but has seen only limited application in published research (e.g., Eisenhardt and Bourgeois 1988). Armed with this understanding of the nature of TMT interaction, we are now in a position to analyze both the determinants and consequences of TMTs. We turn first to the contextual conditions that help explain TMT characteristics.

DETERMINANTS OF TOP MANAGEMENT TEAM CHARACTERISTICS

Contextual conditions that arise from environmental, organizational, and CEO factors may have pervasive effects on TMTs. The proposition that top managerial characteristics and actions are greatly affected by these forces is not a new one (e.g., Hambrick and Finkelstein 1987); yet adequate research attention has not been devoted to it. In fact, there appears to be a real "need to treat team characteristics as a dependent variable—why do teams look the way they do?" (Pettigrew 1992, 176). Thus, in this section, we develop propositions on how contextual conditions affect TMTs. Although research on the major contextual conditions we focus on is abundant, relatively little of this work has been specifically directed toward TMTs.

Environment

An organization's environment constrains and shapes activities and behaviors within the boundaries of the firm (Duncan 1972; Aldrich 1979; Dess and Beard 1984). Research has indicated the pervasiveness of environmental effects by showing how they affect such major facets of organizational life as strategy (Porter 1980; Miller, Droge, and Toulouse 1988), structure (Lawrence and Lorsch 1967; Keats and Hitt 1988), organizational processes (Rajagopalan and Finkelstein 1992), and firm performance (Hannan and Freeman 1977). Although few studies have directly examined how TMTs are shaped by environmental influences, environmental effects likely are important here as well. To help guide our discussion, we consider three fundamental dimensions of the environment: complexity, instability, and munificence (Dess and Beard 1984). Environmental complexity refers to the number of environmental factors that impinge on an organization (Thompson 1967); environmental instability is defined by the rate of change in these factors (Thompson 1967); and environmental munificence refers to the extent to which the environment supports sustained growth (Starbuck 1976). We now consider the effects of each of these dimensions on TMTs.

Environmental complexity.   Organizations in complex environments are typically confronted with conflicting demands from multiple constituencies (Thompson 1967). Managing each of these stakeholders may require a different set of skills or competencies that force organizations to develop greater structural differentiation to cope (Pfeffer and Salancik 1978). As Gupta effectively asserts by citing Lawrence and Lorsch (1967) and Arrow (1974), "The more diverse an organization's environment, the more necessary it becomes to have a differentiated top management team in order to appropriately monitor the diversity of the environment" (1988,160). Indeed, environmental complexity has often been operationalized as heterogeneity in the environment (e.g., Dess and Beard 1984; Keats and Hitt 1988).

Although these ideas have been subject to only limited empirical investigation (Wiersema and Bantel 1993), they seem worth pursuing. Firms in complex environments often face ill-defined and novel problem-solving situations, suggesting that larger, more heterogeneous TMTs may be more common under these conditions (Janis 1972). Such teams have a broader range of skills represented among its members (Steiner 1972), are more likely to develop diverse interpretations and perspectives (Wanous and Youtz 1986), and tend to engender more debate and questioning among team members (Hoffman and Maier 1961). In simpler, less complex environments, such heterogeneity is not required and indeed may be dysfunctional to the extent that it promotes poor communication (Zenger and Lawrence 1989), and conflict (Ebadi and Utterback 1984). In addition, as Thompson (1967) has argued, to the degree that environmental complexity creates additional challenges for top management, the dominant coalition will be larger. As a result, we offer the following propositions:

PROPOSITION 5-2A
The more complex the environment, the greater the heterogeneity within TMTs.

PROPOSITION 5-2B
The more complex the environment, the larger the size of TMTs.

A related argument can be offered for role interdependence. Environmental complexity promotes greater differentiation within the top team and reduces the opportunity for executives to interact, share resources, and operate in a cohesive manner. The greater environmental demands characteristic of this setting force greater task specialization and make coordination more difficult (Mintzberg 1979). While these circumstances may call for greater integration (Lawrence and Lorsch 1967), the demands on top team members from environmental constituencies may make such integration difficult to achieve. As Galbraith (1973) has argued, complexity forces greater specialization and decentralization, reducing opportunities for coordination and increasing both the number of individuals involved in decision making and their decision-making independence.

PROPOSITION 5-2C
The more complex the environment, the less the role interdependence within TMTs.

Finally, environmental complexity is expected to have a direct effect on TMT social integration and consensus. Arguing that environmental complexity requires greater division of labor, which in turn increases differences within TMTs in interpersonal orientation and time orientation (Lawrence and Lorsch 1967), Dess and Origer suggest that "such divergence in perspectives makes consensus on the strategic direction of the firm difficult"

(1987, 326). The same logic also suggests that environmental complexity reduces social integration by forcing TMTs to attend to multiple stimuli and demands that highlight differences within the top team. At the same time, the added demands of complex environments also reduce opportunities for team-building and cohesion. Consistent with Bourgeois's (1980) contention that complexity promotes conflict and with Dess and Origer (1987), we expect the following:

PROPOSITION 5–2D

The more complex the environment, the less the degree of social integration within TMTs.

PROPOSITION 5–2E

The more complex the environment, the less the degree of consensus within TMTs.

Environmental instability. Environments vary in the degree to which they are characterized by unpredictability and unexpected change (Mintzberg 1979). Such environmental instability can have a dramatic impact on how organizations are structured and operate (Duncan 1972) and, of primary importance here, on the nature of TMT composition, structure, and even process. Environmental instability may refer to the "steady-state" rate of change in environmental factors affecting organizations (Thompson 1967) or to the extent of discontinuous change in the environment (Tushman and Romanelli 1985). Using either definition, not many studies have probed the effects of environmental instability on TMTs. Nevertheless, as we discuss below, important relationships may exist.

In a manner analogous to our argument above on environmental complexity, environmental instability may affect TMT heterogeneity and size. Such environments increase the variation and fragmentation of managerial work (Mintzberg 1973), enlarging the information-processing demands on the top team (Daft, Sormunen, and Parks 1988). As Galbraith argued, "The greater the task uncertainty, the greater the amount of information that must be processed among decision makers during task execution" (1973, 4). The greater information-processing requirements characteristic of unstable environments have two effects on top teams: greater heterogeneity and greater size. Both effects arise from the need for TMTs to increase the quantity and range of 1) information absorbed and recalled, 2) perspectives brought to bear on a problem, and 3) potential solutions considered (Hoffman and Maier 1961; Harrison 1975; Shaw 1981) as environments become more unstable. Hence, the greater information-processing capabilities of larger and more heterogeneous teams (e.g., Steiner 1972) are needed to help firms adapt to the greater information-processing requirements of unstable environments (Haleblian and Finkelstein 1993).

PROPOSITION 5-3A
The more unstable the environment, the greater the heterogeneity within TMTs.

PROPOSITION 5-3B
The more unstable the environment, the larger the size of TMTs.

Environmental instability may affect other aspects of TMTs as well. Challenging environments create huge demands on TMT members to cope with external requirements (Pfeffer and Salancik 1978). As with complex environments, when environmental instability is high, TMTs face greater information-processing and decision-making demands (Kotter 1982) and greater time pressures to reach decisions (Eisenhardt 1989b). The result is less opportunity for role interdependence and, by implication, less social integration. We would also expect TMT consensus to be more difficult to attain, because instability and change promote multiple perspectives (Khandalla 1977) and uncertainty about both means-ends relationships and outcome preferences (Thompson 1967). The resulting diversity of opinions creates conflict and makes consensus elusive. In contrast, higher levels of consensus may be relatively achievable in stable environments (Priem 1990).

PROPOSITION 5-3C
The more unstable the environment, the less the degree of role interdependence within TMTs.

PROPOSITION 5-3D
The more unstable the environment, the less the degree of social integration within TMTs.

PROPOSITION 5-3E
The more unstable the environment, the less the degree of consensus within TMTs.

These arguments are expected to hold when environments change more dramatically as well. For example, technological discontinuities

(Tushman and Anderson 1986), changing competitive conditions, and regulatory changes (Miles and Cameron 1982) are all expected to affect TMTs. As Keck and Tushman noted, "Organizations in jolted environments may require substantially altered executive teams to allow firms to develop the competencies and internal processes that will make it possible for them to cope with altered competitive requirements" (1993, 1317). In the interests of space, however, we only offer an illustrative proposition for environmental discontinuities, rather than repeating each proposition just presented.

PROPOSITION 5–3F

Environmental discontinuities increase the degree of heterogeneity within TMTs.

Environmental munificence.   Munificent environments help buffer organizations from external threats and enable them to accumulate slack resources (Cyert and March 1963). In addition, munificence confers on organizations flexibility and growth opportunities (Aldrich 1979). To a considerable extent, the general lack of external threat allows TMTs to operate with less constraint than otherwise might exist. As a result, predicting the consequential effects on TMTs is difficult. For example, on the one hand, TMT consensus may be greater in munificent environments because the generally nonthreatening conditions facilitate agreement and cooperation. On the other hand, because environmental munificence offers TMTs a wider breadth of choices on how to compete, there is room for more diversity of opinion and, hence, disagreement (Dess and Origer 1987).

The only proposition we offer here relates to TMT size. As noted, greater organization slack often accompanies environmental munificence, creating a "problem" of how to use it. Williamson (1963) has suggested that firms with slack resources tend to hire more staff than needed—especially at the executive level. This argument is analogous to a more recent one by Jensen (1986), who held that top managers with "free cash flow" may have an incentive to engage in such nonprofit-maximizing behavior as empire-building. In contrast, firms in more stringent industries often focus on cost containment (Hofer 1975), including reducing executive and other staff. Hence, environmental munificence may have a direct effect on TMT size (Keats and Hitt 1988; Bantel and Finkelstein 1995).

PROPOSITION 5–4

The more munificent the environment, the larger the size of TMTs.

Organization

Numerous aspects of organizations may affect TMTs. As with environment, however, the empirical work on this question has been quite limited. As a result, we will focus on only two characteristics of organizations—its strategy and its performance—in developing propositions on the determinants of TMT composition, structure, and process. Firm strategy and performance are emphasized here because they 1) are central to the study of strategic leadership, 2) are fundamental organizational attributes of interest to a wide set of scholars, and 3) appear particularly promising as antecedents to TMTs. This latter concern is important given our interest in encouraging future investigations of the relationships we discuss.

Strategy.   Of all potential antecedents of TMT characteristics, the strategy of a firm may be the most important, yet equivocal, factor. On the one hand, according to the old maxim that "structure follows strategy" (Chandler 1962), organizational characteristics such as the TMT should be at least partially a function of the organization's strategy. For example, Porter argued that his "generic strategies [implied] differing organizational arrangements, control procedures, and incentive systems" (1980, 40), all of which affect the TMT. Hence, the effects of strategy on TMTs may be pervasive. On the other hand, as we discussed in Chapter 4, organizations and the strategies they follow may be a reflection of their top managers (Hambrick and Mason 1984). Thus, disentangling causal direction in these relationships seems to be a fundamental requirement for future work.

A firm's corporate strategy, defining the mix of businesses in which the firm competes, may have important implications for TMTs. Michel and Hambrick (1992) tested a series of hypotheses linking corporate strategy with TMT characteristics by developing theory on how the interdependence of a firm's diversification posture called for greater social cohesion and a larger knowledge base among top managers. They arrayed the interdependence of diversification postures from low to high in the following order: unrelated, related-linked, related-constrained, and vertically integrated.

The same logic can be used to make predictions about TMT composition, structure, and process. For example, in firms with highly interdependent diversification postures, such as those that are vertically integrated, "there is need for abundant interunit negotiation, compromise, and collaboration. This process is greatly aided if corporate managers have a well-developed rapport and a common outlook and language" (Michel and Hambrick 1992, 17). As a result, firms with highly interdependent operations should have TMTs with the following characteristics: low heterogeneity, high social integration, and high consensus. Role interdependence within TMTs is almost definitionally related to the interdependence of diversification postures as well. The following propositions summarize this discussion:

PROPOSITION 5–5A

The greater the interdependence of a firm's diversification posture, the less the heterogeneity within its TMT.

PROPOSITION 5–5B

The greater the interdependence of a firm's diversification posture, the greater the degree of role interdependence within its TMT.

PROPOSITION 5–5C

The greater the interdependence of a firm's diversification posture, the greater the degree of social integration within its TMT.

PROPOSITION 5–5D

The greater the interdependence of a firm's diversification posture, the greater the degree of consensus within its TMT.

One final proposition concerns team size. Managing firms with unrelated diversification postures has been likened to managing a financial portfolio (Berg 1969; Rumelt 1974). Top teams are more concerned with buying and selling businesses than with actively managing the operations of each business. Because the task of operating each business is decentralized to general managers at the divisional level, the corporate offices of highly diversified firms tend to be quite small (Pitts 1980). In contrast, corporate management in firms with more interdependent diversification postures may be larger because they "typically retain responsibility for overall product-market strategy and initiate investment projects (Ackerman 1970)" (Michel and Hambrick 1992, 12). These firms tend to rely on strategic controls instead of financial controls (Hoskisson and Hitt 1988; Hoskisson and Hitt 1994) and promote coordination among business units by use of specialized incentives based on corporate as well as divisional performance (Hoskisson, Hitt, and Hill 1993). The ability to enact strategic controls, as well as to effectively manage the greater information-processing demands that arise from corporate-based incentives, add complexity and, hence, staffing needs to the corporate office. Therefore, we propose the following:

PROPOSITION 5–5E

The greater the interdependence of the diversification posture, the larger the size of TMTs.

A firm's competitive, or business, strategy is also likely to affect the composition, structure, and process of its TMT. While the notion that TMTs can affect strategic outcomes is now well-accepted in the literature, there have been no empirical investigations of the strategic antecedents of TMTs. To help structure our discussion, we contrast how the strategies of Prospector (growth, innovation, and the search for new opportunities) and Defender (cost control, stability, and efficiency) firms call for different TMT characteristics (Miles and Snow 1978).

Compared to Prospectors, the greater stability in Defender firms suggests that they face fewer strategic contingencies (Hambrick 1981b) and do not require larger, more differentiated TMTs. Firms following Defender strategies generally exhibit lower growth, constraining internal labor markets by limiting promotion opportunities for top managers (Pfeffer 1983). Prospectors are not only more growth-oriented, they are also more innovative and forward-looking.

These differences between Prospectors and Defenders have several implications for TMTs. First, it is likely that TMTs will be smaller and less heterogeneous in Defenders, given the importance of maintaining existing domains. As Miles and Snow note, "It is more advantageous for the dominant coalition to know the strengths and capacities of 'our company' than it is for them to know the trends and developments in 'our industry'" (1978, 42). Such internally focused TMTs do not require the same breadth and diversity that TMTs with Prospector strategies might need.

Second, top management teams in Prospector firms need to be receptive to change and innovation—searching for new opportunities may require new perspectives and approaches that are more likely to exist when TMTs are heterogeneous (Wiersema and Bantel 1992). In contrast, TMTs in firms with Defender strategies have already coalesced around a specific product-market and a narrow range of competitive weapons to defend their firm's position in that product-market. What's more, Defenders face much less uncertainty (Miles and Snow 1978). Hence, TMTs with Defender strategies are more likely to have similar mind-sets, exhibit greater cohesiveness, and develop congruent beliefs about their firm and how it operates, making it easier for them to reach agreement (Dutton and Duncan 1987). Indeed, both means-ends relationships and desired outcomes are fixed to a much greater extent in these firms.

PROPOSITION 5–6A

Firms pursuing Defender strategies exhibit less TMT heterogeneity than do Prospector firms.

PROPOSITION 5–6B

Firms pursuing Defender strategies have fewer members in their TMTs than do Prospector firms.

PROPOSITION 5–6C

Firms pursuing Defender strategies exhibit more social integration within their TMTs than do Prospector firms.

PROPOSITION 5–6D

Firms pursuing Defender strategies exhibit more consensus within their TMTs than do Prospector firms.

A final characteristic of a firm's strategy considered here is the extent to which it is relatively constant or changing. Strategic change creates ripple effects throughout an organization, including within the TMT (Wiersema and Bantel 1992; Keck and Tushman 1993). Changes in firm strategy often disrupt existing ways of doing business, involve shifts to new domains or new tactics within the same domain, and create new power bases within the firm (Starbuck, Greve, and Hedberg 1978; Tushman and Romanelli 1985). These changes have significant ramifications for the functioning of the TMT. Established communication patterns (Zenger and Lawrence 1989), knowledge structures (Gersick and Hackman 1990), needed competencies and processes (Ancona 1990), and patterns of interaction (O'Reilly, Caldwell, and Barnett 1989) all shift. To the extent that the strategic changes are severe, threatening the integrity of the organization or the positions of top managers, constriction of power and control may also result (Staw, Sandelands, and Dutton 1981). Under these conditions, we would expect to see several changes in the TMT: greater heterogeneity and size to try to cope with the changes; less role interdependence as it becomes more difficult for top managers to coordinate activities, at least in the short term; less social integration as a consequence of disrupted patterns of interaction; and greater difficulty in reaching consensus because the rules of the game are in flux.

PROPOSITION 5–7A

The greater the amount of strategic change, the greater the heterogeneity within TMTs.

PROPOSITION 5–7B

The greater the amount of strategic change, the less the degree of role interdependence within TMTs.

PROPOSITION 5-7C

The greater the amount of strategic change, the larger the size of TMTs.

PROPOSITION 5-7D

The greater the amount of strategic change, the less the degree of social integration within TMTs.

PROPOSITION 5-7E

The greater the amount of strategic change, the less the degree of consensus within TMTs.

Organization performance.   The effects of few organizational attributes are as immediately felt as those of performance. These effects are observed by numerous stakeholders, both within and outside of an organization, leading one to expect that organization performance may have important consequences on TMTs as well. Nevertheless, as was the case for the other contextual conditions that give rise to different TMT configurations of composition, structure, and process, empirical work is lacking. Hence, in this section, we build on theories of threat rigidity and organization slack to help develop some testable propositions on the relationship between organization performance and TMTs.

High-performing firms are characterized by excess organization slack and, by extension, a multitude of strategic options (Miles and Cameron 1982). Organization slack is defined as "the difference between the resources of the organization and the combination of demands made on it" (Cohen, March, and Olsen 1972, 12). In a sense, performance and slack create additional opportunities that might be foreclosed in firms with less abundant resources. For example, decisions to enter new markets or develop new products are possible only when adequate resources exist. When resource constraints are tighter, fewer options exist, and the organization must be more reactive than proactive in dealing with environmental and strategic contingencies (Pfeffer and Salancik 1978). What is more, when performance is very poor, organizations tend to constrict control at the top, restricting intragroup information flows and promoting dissension (Staw, Sandelands, and Dutton 1981).

These effects have several important consequences for TMTs. Specifically, since high-performing firms have abundant slack and opportunity, while low-performing firms are constrained and constricted, we expect a curvilinear relationship between organization performance and several attributes of TMTs. For example, TMTs are larger in both the highest performers (because their excess slack facilitates expenditures on staff [Williamson 1963]) and lowest performers (because centralized control at the top creates a need for additional senior executives to take over responsibilities that were previously delegated).[8]

PROPOSITION 5–8A

Under conditions of very low and very high organization performance, TMT size is larger; when organization performance is at a moderate level, TMTs have fewer members.

The same effects of very high and very low organization performance are expected to affect several other dimensions of TMTs: role interdependence, social integration, and consensus. As we have described, resources are so plentiful in very high–performing firms that TMTs do not have to deal with trade-offs, elaborate coordination, or efforts to optimize. Under these conditions, TMT members need not engage in intensive interchange, because abundant slack allows "the unchecked pursuit of subunit goals" (Bourgeois 1981, 33). Moreover, the TMTs of successful firms, because of their very success, may become less interactive and collaborative over time as the resource constraints that forced careful orchestration and attention to external contingencies dissipate (Hambrick 1995). Hence, we would expect less emphasis on role interdependence, a breakdown of social integration, and more disagreement on means and ends.

These same TMT effects occur in organizations whose performance is dire. A dominant individual or inner circle at the top takes charge, forcing changes without the same degree of collaboration and consultation that may have previously existed (Staw, Sandelands, and Dutton 1981). Time pressures force immediate actions, reducing role interdependence, and conflict and self-seeking behavior abound (Eisenhardt and Bourgeois 1988). It is only when firm performance is not at an extreme that social interactions within TMTs can be emphasized. Thus, we offer the following propositions:

PROPOSITION 5–8B

Under conditions of very low and very high organization performance, role interdependence within TMTs is low; when organization performance is at a moderate level, role interdependence is greatest.

PROPOSITION 5–8C

Under conditions of very low and very high organization performance, social integration within TMTs is low; when organization performance is at a moderate level, social integration is greatest.

PROPOSITION 5-8D

Under conditions of very low and very high organization performance, consensus within TMTs is low; when organization performance is at a moderate level, consensus is greatest.

CEO

Chief executive officers play a major role in the composition and functioning of TMTs. CEOs are central members of the TMT (Jackson 1992)
who have a disproportionate impact on team characteristics and outcomes
(Finkelstein 1992). Although the importance of CEO characteristics and
behaviors to TMTs seems almost self-evident (Hambrick 1994), studies
investigating the nature of this relationship are rare. Thus, it seems important to examine how a CEO's influence permeates TMTs, the topic to
which we now turn.

We will consider the impact of CEOs in two related ways. First, extending Hambrick and Mason's (1984) core idea that organizations are a reflection of their senior executives, it seems sensible to consider the degree to
which TMT composition, structure, and process reflect CEO preferences.
Hence, it may be that CEO characteristics affect TMTs as much as they do
strategies and performance.[9] Second, CEO power is variable and is likely to
affect TMTs (Finkelstein 1992; Hambrick and D'Aveni 1992; Jackson 1992).
Research on CEO power or dominance is not plentiful, and the little that
has been done has not focused on its effects on TMTs. Thus, there are
important reasons to examine how CEO dominance affects TMTs.[10]

A multitude of CEO characteristics and their effects on TMTs can be
considered. In the interests of space, however, we only examine "CEO
openness"—a composite of such facets of CEO personality as awareness of
multiple perspectives, valuing discourse and debate, and openness to new
ideas. Such CEOs are not so committed to a paradigm that alternative perspectives on strategic problems are foreclosed; rather, they are willing to try
new approaches (Hambrick and Fukutomi 1991). CEO openness may be
gauged by an array of characteristics, including a broad educational background, a higher level of education, newness to the organization, and a high
variety of work experience, such as in multiple functional areas and industries. CEOs with this type of background are more likely to value diversity of opinion for the intellectual discourse it promotes as much as for the
more varied range of ideas generated.

Some related support exists for these ideas: highly educated CEOs, particularly those with MBAs, promote administrative complexity and sophistication (Hambrick and Mason 1984), as well as innovativeness (Kimberly
and Evanisko 1981; Bantel and Jackson 1989)—both of which may lead to

inclusion and diversity (Bantel and Jackson 1989). For example, to the extent that large TMTs have greater information-processing and decision-making capabilities than small teams (Eisenhardt and Schoonhoven 1990; Haleblian and Finkelstein 1993), a wider set of opinions can be heard.

CEO openness may also be enhanced when the CEO is new to the organization. CEOs selected from outside the firm are not as beholden to the status quo and often bring new perspectives to the organization (Dalton and Kesner 1985). In addition, outsiders tend to replace more members of the TMT within their first two years in office than CEOs promoted from within (Helmich and Brown 1972; Gabarro 1987). These changes are consistent with the idea that CEO openness, as gauged by newness to the organization, promotes TMT heterogeneity (Keck and Tushman 1993).

PROPOSITION 5-9A

The greater the level of CEO openness, the greater the heterogeneity within TMTs.

PROPOSITION 5-9B

The greater the level of CEO openness, the larger the size of TMTs.

The effects of CEO openness are not expected to remain constant over time. Although CEO interest in discussion and debate promotes heterogeneity and inclusiveness, we expect that these effects will dissipate over time. Gradually, CEOs develop routinized procedures (Tushman and Romanelli 1985; Keck and Tushman 1993), stronger opinions on appropriate strategies and how to achieve them (Gabarro 1987), greater interest in perpetuating their power (Pfeffer 1981a; Finkelstein and Hambrick 1989), and more concern for their legacy (Westphal and Zajac 1995). Whether referred to as "commitment to a paradigm" (Hambrick and Fukutomi 1991), "stale in the saddle" (Miller 1991), or "entrenchment" (Fama and Jensen 1983), even long-tenured CEOs from diverse backgrounds become less responsive to diverse perspectives (Katz 1982; Hambrick, Geletkancyz, and Fredrickson 1993). Long tenure not only attenuates the effects of CEO openness, it also reduces TMT heterogeneity directly because shared understandings about decision making and strategy become progressively more refined and similar over time (Pfeffer and Salancik 1978; Kiesler and Sproull 1982; Fredrickson and Iaquinto 1989; Keck and Tushman 1993).[11]

PROPOSITION 5-9C

The longer a CEO's tenure, the weaker the relationships between CEO openness and TMT heterogeneity and size.

PROPOSITION 5-9D

The longer a CEO's tenure, the less the heterogeneity within TMTs.

The second important characteristic of a CEO is his or her power within the TMT. With few exceptions (Hambrick 1981; Eisenhardt and Bourgeois 1988; Finkelstein 1992), the distribution of power among senior executives has not been the subject of in-depth investigation. As we argued earlier, however, understanding who has power and who does not within the TMT seems essential for developing more complete models of strategic decision making. Our interest here is in how CEO dominance affects TMTs, specifically their heterogeneity and consensus.

Responsibility for selecting a top team generally resides with the CEO (Kotter 1982). Nevertheless, his or her ability to make such selections without constraint depends to some extent on other stakeholders, such as the board of directors (Lorsch 1989), organizations and individuals on which a firm is dependent (Pfeffer and Salancik 1978), and even other top managers (Finkelstein 1988). Thus, the more powerful or dominant the CEO, the greater his or her influence on the executive selection process. Dominant CEOs are likely to select top managers who are similar to themselves. This belief is predicated on three related arguments: 1) individuals tend to prefer others who are similar to themselves (Byrne 1971); 2) individuals may derive self-esteem by belonging to a group of similar individuals (Tsui, Egan, and O'Reilly 1992); and 3) by selecting individuals with similar perspectives, CEOs can consolidate power at the top (Westphal and Zajac 1995).

PROPOSITION 5-10A

The greater the CEO dominance, the less the heterogeneity within TMTs.

Although CEO dominance is expected to reduce heterogeneity within the top team, it is likely that the actual size of the team may grow. Several writers have noted the tendency for powerful individuals to add staff and personnel in an attempt to build a protective core around their positions (Williamson 1963; Whistler, et al. 1967; Mintzberg 1983). The more powerful the CEO, the greater the ability to institutionalize power within the organization (Pfeffer 1981a). The net effect of such empire-building is a larger TMT.

PROPOSITION 5-10B

The greater the CEO dominance, the larger the size of TMTs.

Finally, CEO dominance may also reduce the degree of consensus achieved in reaching strategic decisions. For example, Eisenhardt and

Bourgeois (1988) found that power centralization (a notion akin to CEO dominance) was associated with a higher degree of political activity within TMTs. Where CEOs were less dominant, there was greater sharing of information, and the decision process was described as "consensus style" (p. 749). Eisenhardt and Bourgeois's description of strategic decision making at Alpha, one of the companies they studied, is informative:

> The CEO (the president) was described as a "parent" and "benevolent dictator." His power score was 9.6, tied for highest in our cases. The next most powerful executive at Alpha scored only 5.8. The strategic decision we studied corroborated those data. For example, the VP sales said of the decision process: "The decision was a Don Rogers edict—not a vote." The president agreed: "I made the decision myself, despite the objections of everyone. I said 'the hell with it, let's go with the PC interface.' " (1988, 748–49)

PROPOSITION 5–10C

The greater the CEO dominance, the less the degree of consensus within TMTs.

To conclude, this section has elaborated a model of the determinants of TMT characteristics. This model is based on the idea that the context within which a TMT operates significantly influences its composition, structure, and process. We focused on such important antecedents as environment, organization, and the central player within the top team, the chief executive. Although our model is not meant to be exhaustive (other factors may also contribute to an explanation of TMTs), it is an important first step toward opening up our investigative lenses to issues surrounding how a TMT comes to take on certain characteristics. An emphasis on antecedents is important not only because of the greater understanding of TMTs it affords, but also because of its implications for what TMTs actually do. That is, much of the interest in TMTs apparent in the literature is driven by a desire to learn more about how TMTs are involved in strategic decision making and how this involvement translates into actions that help determine organizational strategy and performance. It is to these issues we now turn.

CONSEQUENCES OF TMT INTERACTION

Empirical research on TMTs and organizational outcomes has increased dramatically in the last several years, much of it focusing on the effects of demographic characteristics. In this section, we review this research to assess what progress has been made and to suggest some new lines of inquiry. Although some studies have examined multiple organizational outcomes, we organize this discussion by the dependent variables of strategic decision-making process, strategic choices and changes, and firm performance.[12]

Consequences of TMTs on Strategic Decision Making

Research on strategic decision making is abundant. Numerous attributes of this process can be studied, including decision speed (Eisenhardt 1989a), comprehensiveness (Fredrickson 1984), analytical techniques (Schweiger, Sandberg, and Rechner 1989), urgency (Pinfield 1986), complexity (Astley, et al. 1982), political activity (Welsh and Slusher 1986; Eisenhardt and Bourgeois 1988), and extent of subunit involvement (Duhaime and Baird 1987) (see Rajagopalan, Rasheed, and Datta [1993] for a review). Here, we develop propositions that relate the major facets of TMTs examined in this chapter with the strategic decision-making process.

The strategic decision-making process is often depicted as a series of stages, beginning with the generation of alternative strategic choices, and moving through evaluation of those alternatives, strategic choice, implementation, and, finally, evaluation (Ansoff 1965; Hofer and Schendel 1978). Although there are important differences across each stage, strategists for some time have adopted the analytical convention of viewing the process in terms of formulation and implementation (e.g., Andrews 1971). The strategy formulation process involves the generation and evaluation of alternatives, and the choice, while strategy implementation encompasses the implementation and evaluation of that choice. While this bifurcation of the strategic decision-making process is somewhat artificial (Mintzberg 1978), it serves a valuable purpose in facilitating the more pointed consideration of potential relationships with TMT dynamics that we will now consider.

Strategy formulation requires an analysis of 1) external threats and opportunities, especially with respect to the competitive environment (Andrews 1971; Porter 1980) and 2) internal strengths and weaknesses within and across functional areas (Prahalad and Hamel 1990). The alternatives that arise from this analysis are assessed and debated before settling on a satisficing solution (Cyert and March 1963). Top management team members are active throughout this process, in part through direct participation and in part by setting agendas (Kotter 1982), by delegating to others (Mintzberg 1983), and by signaling ideas and preferences (Pfeffer and Salancik 1978).

Our review of related research suggests that TMTs with certain characteristics, such as large size and heterogeneity, are likely to generate more alternatives, evaluate those alternatives along more dimensions, and, as a consequence, make higher-quality decisions than TMTs without these attributes. As we argued earlier, heterogeneous teams are more innovative, have greater problem-solving skills, and employ multiple perspectives (e.g., Bantel and Jackson 1989), all of which should increase the number and variety of alternatives under consideration. In addition, they can rely on their heterogeneous backgrounds to gather information from different internal and external contacts (Jackson 1992), something that is much less likely in homogeneous teams. Moreover, evaluation of alternatives should be comprehensive, given the propensity and willingness of heterogeneous team members to challenge and debate each other (e.g., Gladstein 1984; Schweiger, Sandberg, and Rechner 1989). To the extent that decision quality depends on analytical effectiveness, the resulting strategic choices may prove superior (Hoffman 1959; Filley, House, and Kerr 1976; Shaw 1981; McGrath 1984).

In contrast, social integration within TMTs may have the opposite effect. Socially integrated teams value cooperation, are more cohesive, and are motivated by a desire to maintain cordial relations among members (O'Reilly, Caldwell, and Barnett 1989). What is more, highly cohesive groups tend to exert more pressure for conformity than less cohesive groups (Hackman 1976). For example, Lott and Lott (1965) found that cohesiveness was highly correlated with pressures for attitudinal conformity. In TMTs, this emphasis on cooperation and conformity may limit the quality of both alternative generation and evaluation.

PROPOSITION 5–11A

The quality of strategic decisions (as defined by the generation of multiple feasible alternatives and the comprehensive evaluation of those alternatives) is positively associated with TMT heterogeneity and size and negatively associated with social integration within TMTs.

Strategy implementation involves mobilizing the resources needed to ensure that the strategic initiatives selected are appropriately executed. The implementation process typically requires significant integration of people and resources, takes considerable time, and depends on the cooperation of numerous individuals both in and out of the TMT (Galbraith and Kazanjian 1986). Effectively implementing strategic decisions is challenging because executives who find particular changes threatening or objectionable often have numerous opportunities to disrupt the process (Bardach 1977; Guth and MacMillan 1986). As a result, it becomes important to gain their acceptance and commitment to a strategic decision (Dess 1987; Nutt

1987), especially in light of evidence that direct intervention, persuasion, and participation implementation tactics are superior to the use of edicts (Nutt 1986b).

The implications of these arguments for TMTs are twofold. First, as we have seen, some evidence suggests that heterogeneous teams engender conflict (O'Reilly, Snyder, and Boothe 1993). Indeed, many of the positive features of heterogeneous TMTs, such as debate, multiple perspectives, and confrontation, also have negative side effects, including dissatisfaction and dissensus (Schweiger, Sandberg, and Rechner 1989; Priem 1990). These problems are particularly important for implementation because "successful installation . . . often depends on obtaining the involvement, cooperation, endorsement, or consent" (Nutt 1989, 145) of managers. When team members disagree with a decision, implementation becomes problematic (Hitt and Tyler 1991). Thus, "the ultimate value of high-quality decisions depends to a great extent on the willingness of managers to cooperate in implementing those decisions (Maier 1970; Guth and MacMillan 1986; Woolridge and Floyd 1990)" (Korsgaard, Schweiger, and Sapienza 1995, 60).

If heterogeneity is disadvantageous for strategy implementation, social integration and consensus should be beneficial. We have already emphasized that social integration is associated with cooperation, frequent communication, and group identification (O'Reilly, Caldwell, and Barnett 1989), all of which may facilitate the implementation process (Guth and MacMillan 1986). And TMT consensus tends to engender greater feelings of satisfaction with the decision-making process, promoting decision acceptance and commitment (Dess 1987; Fredrickson and Iaquinto 1989; Isabella and Waddock 1994). Hence, we propose:

PROPOSITION 5–11B
The effectiveness of the strategy implementation process is positively associated with social integration and consensus within TMTs and negatively associated with TMT heterogeneity and size.

Consequences of TMTs on Strategy

If TMT composition, structure, and process affect strategic decision making, they also likely will affect the types of strategic choices made. Over the last few years, a series of studies on this very point have examined organizational innovativeness, interdependence of diversification posture, and strategic change. Table 5–1 summarizes these works (as well as others that included measures of firm performance as dependent variables). The findings reported in these studies generally have been inconsistent.

TABLE 5-1 Research on TMT Effects on Strategic Choices and Firm Performance

Study	Theoretical Link	Dependent Variables	Independent Variables	Results		Sample
Bantel and Jackson 1989	Cognitive diversity	Innovativeness	Age heterogeneity	n.s. (not significant)		199 banks
			Firm tenure heterogeneity	n.s.		
			Educational specialization heterogeneity	n.s.		
			Dominant functional heterogeneity	+		
			Team size	n.s.		
Murray 1989	"Clannishness"	(1) Short-term firm performance		(1)	(2)	84 firms in the oil and food industries between 1967 and 1981
		(2) Long-term firm performance	(A) Temporal heterogeneity	n.s.	+	
			(B) Occupational heterogeneity	mixed	n.s.	
			Industry rivalry			
			x (A)	n.s.	n.s.	
			x (B)	n.s.	mixed	
			Industry change			
			x (A)	n.s.	mixed	
			x (B)	n.s.	n.s.	
O'Reilly and Flatt 1989	Social integration	(1) Organization innovation		(1)	(2)	40 firms in 4 industries in 1983
		(2) Return on equity	(A) Firm tenure heterogeneity	mixed	n.s.	
			(B) Age heterogeneity	mixed	n.s.	
			Team size			
			Industry			
			x (1)	n.s.		
			x (2)	n.s.		

TABLE 5-1 Research on TMT Effects on Strategic Choices and Firm Performance, *continued*

Study	Theoretical Link	Dependent Variables	Independent Variables	Results	Sample
Eisenhardt and Schoonhoven 1990	Speed in decision making; Constructive conflict; Specialization in decision making	Growth among new firms	(1) Previous joint work experience	mixed	92 new semiconductor firms founded between 1978 and 1985
			(2) Industry tenure heterogeneity	+	
			(3) Team size	+	
			(4) Index of (1),(2), and (3)	+	
			(5) Growth-stage market	+	
			Firm age x (1)	n.s.	
			x (2)	n.s.	
			x (3)	+	
			x (4)	+	
			x (5)	+	
Hambrick and D'Aveni 1992	Social structure; Team resources	Bankruptcy	Firm tenure heterogeneity	mixed	57 matched pairs of large bankrupts and survivors between 1972 and 1982
			CEO dominance	mixed	
			Team size	mixed	
Michel and Hambrick 1992	Social cohesion; Knowledge base	Interdependence of diversification posture	(1) TMT tenure homogeneity	–	134 Fortune 500 firms between 1971 and 1974
			(2) Dominant functional homogeneity	n.s.	
			(3) Average number of interunit moves	n.s.	

TABLE 5-1 **Research on TMT Effects on Strategic Choices and Firm Performance,** *continued*

Study	Theoretical Link	Dependent Variables	Independent Variables	Results	Sample
Wiersema and Bantel 1992	Diversity of information sources and perspectives; Creative-innovative decision making	Return on Assets	Interdependence of diversification posture x (1) x (2) x (3) Age heterogeneity Organizational tenure heterogeneity Executive tenure heterogeneity Educational specialization heterogeneity Team size	 n.s. n.s. n.s. n.s. n.s. n.s. + n.s.	87 Fortune 500 firms between 1980 and 1983
Glick, Miller, and Huber 1993	Creativity and change; Social cohesion	(1) Preference diversity (2) Belief diversity (3) Comprehensiveness (4) Communication effectiveness (5) Cohesion (6) Open systems effectiveness (7) Profitability	Functional diversity Age diversity Firm tenure diversity TMT tenure diversity	(1) (2) (3) (4) (5) (6) (7) n.s. mixed n.s. n.s. n.s. n.s. n.s. n.s. mixed n.s. n.s. n.s. + n.s. n.s. n.s. n.s. n.s. n.s. n.s. n.s. n.s. n.s. n.s. n.s. n.s. n.s. +	78 business units or firms

TABLE 5-1 Research on TMT Effects on Strategic Choices and Firm Performance, *continued*

Study	Theoretical Link	Dependent Variables	Independent Variables	Results					Sample
				(1)	(2)	(3)	(4)	(5)	
Haleblian and Finkelstein 1993	Information-processing capabilities	Firm performance	Environmental turbulence	−					47 firms in the computer and natural gas industries between 1978 and 1982
			x CEO dominance x Team size	+					
O'Reilly, Snyder, and Boothe 1993	Cooperation	(1) TMT interaction (2) Adaptive organization change (3) Responsibility organization change	Tenure heterogeneity	−	−	n.s.			24 firms in the electronics industry
			Team size	n.s.	mixed	n.s.			
			TMT interaction	n.s.	—	—			
Smith et al. 1994	Social integration Informal communication Communication frequency	(1) Return on Investment (2) Sales growth (3) Social integration (4) Informal communication (5) Communication frequency	Tenure heterogeneity	−	n.s.	n.s.	−	n.s.	53 small technology-based firms
			Education heterogeneity	+	+	n.s.	n.s.	n.s.	
			Dominant functional heterogeneity	n.s.	n.s.	n.s.	n.s.	n.s.	
			Team size	n.s.	n.s.	n.s.	—	n.s.	
			Social integration	+	+				
			Communication frequency	−	−				
			Informal communication	n.s.	—				

152

TABLE 5-1 Research on TMT Effects on Strategic Choices and Firm Performance, *continued*

Study	Theoretical Link	Dependent Variables	Independent Variables	Results		Sample
Sutcliffe 1994	Information diversity	Accuracy of TMT's perception of (1) environmental instability (2) environmental munificence	Functional diversity Team size	(1) n.s. n.s.	(2) − n.s.	65 single-business firms

NOTE: Only findings related to "group" diversity or interaction are included in this table. Significant results (denoted by + or −) were based on $p < .05$ or better.

Two studies have been conducted on the associations among demographic heterogeneity,[13] team size, and organizational innovation. Arguing that demographic heterogeneity proxied for cognitive heterogeneity within a TMT, Bantel and Jackson (1989) found that functional heterogeneity was positively associated with administrative innovation in a sample of 199 banks in the Midwest. However, the heterogeneity of team members along other demographic dimensions, such as age, tenure, and educational specialization, did not significantly predict administrative innovations. All four heterogeneity measures were also unrelated to technical innovation.

In the other study on innovation, O'Reilly and Flatt (1989) used multiple measures of organization innovation (i.e., the score from a *Fortune* magazine survey on innovation and a metric based on articles in *F&S Predicasts*), as well as of both age and tenure heterogeneity (coefficient of variation and standard deviation), to test related hypotheses. Overall, results were mixed, with some measures of age and tenure heterogeneity being negatively associated with one of the innovation measures. Of the eight different models tested, three yielded negative and significant results, indicating that homogeneous TMTs were more innovative in these cases.

No consistent pattern of results arises across the two studies. Of the sixteen different models tested across articles, one indicated that heterogeneity was a positive predictor of innovation and three suggested the opposite.[14] There were significant differences in the methods employed: Bantel and Jackson (1989) defined a TMT in terms of the number of individuals listed by the CEO in a survey, while O'Reilly and Flatt (1989) counted the number of vice-presidents. These design choices will have an impact on measures of heterogeneity. Both studies also used different operationalizations of innovation.

A third study of the effects of TMT heterogeneity, this time with the interdependence of diversification posture as the dependent variable, also yielded mixed results. Michel and Hambrick (1982) sampled 134 Fortune 500 firms from the original Rumelt (1974) study and found that, contrary to expectations, TMT tenure homogeneity was negatively associated with an ordinal scale of diversification posture interdependence (1 equaled unrelated; 4 equaled vertically integrated). Dominant functional homogeneity, however, was not significantly related to strategy.

Although there are differences across studies, the inconsistent results apparent in the three articles reviewed are troubling. One explanation may be that attempts to relate TMT heterogeneity and strategic choices directly are assuming a connection that is more distant than commonly recognized. In this chapter, we argued that demographic heterogeneity is associated with cognitive heterogeneity, both of which increase the number of

strategic alternatives considered by a TMT and the quality of the evaluation of those alternatives. Rigorous strategy formulation, in turn, is expected to lead to higher quality decisions. Using this logic to predict strategic
outcomes is subject to three potential drawbacks.

First, and as is the case for predictions based on the central tendencies
of TMTs, there are several logical stages between TMT composition and
strategic choice that can disrupt or attenuate expected associations. For
example, the strategic decision-making process is complex and ambiguous,
numerous contextual conditions can affect the process through which
strategic choices are selected and implemented, and many of these same
contextual factors are often direct determinants of strategic choices as well.
Hence, while TMTs undoubtedly affect strategic outcomes, our ability to
empirically detect this relationship may be limited.

Second, the logical sequence we outlined above does not link TMT
heterogeneity to strategic choices as much as it relates heterogeneity to the
quality of strategic decisions. There is a big difference between predicting
rigorous strategy formulation and predicting specific strategic outcomes,
which suggests that measures of cognitive heterogeneity should not be any
better predictors of strategy, since heterogeneity—whether measured
demographically or cognitively—is potentially far-removed from specific
strategic outcomes.

Finally, there is a point that is seldom noted in the literature but may
be quite telling. Logically, a significant difference exists between how TMT
heterogeneity and TMT average tendencies are expected to affect strategy.
Because the extent to which a TMT is characterized by a particular com-
positional attribute defines its orientation or preference set (Finkelstein
1988), this concept can more easily be translated into specific strategic outcomes than is true for TMT heterogeneity. For example, TMTs dominated by executives with sales and marketing experience will see, perceive, and
interpret information in such a way that they will be more likely to prefer
such strategies as product innovation and differentiation (Hambrick and
Mason 1984). In contrast, and as we have seen, TMT heterogeneity affects
the *process* of making strategic decisions much more than it does the *content*
of those strategies. Hence, we should not necessarily expect heterogeneity
to have a direct impact on strategy content.

These difficulties in studying the strategic effects of TMT heterogeneity are only partially ameliorated in studies of strategic change. However, the
two studies conducted to date have employed virtually opposing theoretical
rationales. Wiersema and Bantel (1992) argued that demographically heterogeneous TMTs will be more creative and will be able to rely on a wider
set of information sources and perspectives during the decision-making

process than more homogeneous TMTs. As a result, they will be more open to change. In addition, although these authors did not make this argument, it stands to reason that TMT heterogeneity should enhance the variety of strategic alternatives considered and the degree to which they are rigorously evaluated, increasing the likelihood that new strategic initiatives will be suggested. In contrast, O'Reilly, Snyder, and Boothe (1993) argued that TMT homogeneity promotes the cooperation that is needed to implement strategic changes. Hence, Wiersema and Bantel (1992) predicted a positive association and O'Reilly, Snyder, and Boothe (1993) a negative association between TMT heterogeneity and change.

Our analysis of TMTs and strategic decision making produces more equivocal expectations: that is, if TMT heterogeneity increases the breadth of strategy formulation (Proposition 5–11a) but detracts from the implementation process (Proposition 5–11b), the resulting extent of strategic change observed is uncertain.[15] The findings of these two studies are consistent with this interpretation. Wiersema and Bantel (1992) reported that one of four demographic measures of heterogeneity (educational specialization) was positively associated with change, while O'Reilly, Snyder, and Boothe (1993) found that TMT tenure heterogeneity was negatively associated with one of two measures of change. O'Reilly, Snyder, and Boothe (1993) also reported that a perceptual measure of TMT cooperation or consensus was not associated with organization change but negatively related to political change.

In all, the findings we summarize here suggest that direct relationships between TMT heterogeneity and strategic choices are unlikely to be robust. Rather, it may be that TMT heterogeneity and social integration interact during strategic decision making, potentially affecting how the formulation and implementation processes come out. As a result, it seems important to study the relationships among TMT heterogeneity, social integration, and strategic decision making as a first step before attempting to predict strategic outcomes.

Consequences of TMTs on Firm Performance

Given some of the problems in empirically establishing linkages between TMT interaction processes and strategic choices, it would not be surprising if studies of the association between the distributional properties of TMTs and firm performance were even more problematic. To some extent, this is reflected in the often inconsistent findings that emerge from this work. In contrast to studies of strategic outcomes, however, several of the projects predicting firm performance have also incorporated contingency factors, such as industry change or turbulence, that have the potential to strengthen results. Although this work also has inconsistencies, it offers the potential for redirecting research on the consequences of TMTs on firm performance in the future.

In one of the first studies to examine these issues, Murray (1989) collected longitudinal data on TMT temporal heterogeneity (an index of age and tenure heterogeneity, and mean tenure in the firm [loading negatively]) and "occupational" heterogeneity (an index of two measures of functional heterogeneity) in eighty-four firms in the oil and food industries. He predicted that heterogeneous TMTs would do worse in the short run because they often disrupt established norms and procedures that promote efficiency but better in the long-term because of their superior adaptability. In a series of regressions, Murray (1989) reported that 1) temporal heterogeneity was positively associated with long-term performance (in two of four regressions), while occupational heterogeneity was not, and 2) occupational heterogeneity was negatively associated with short-term performance (in one of four models), while temporal heterogeneity was not. Of the sixteen regressions conducted, results were consistent with expectations three times.

The pattern of results reported by Murray (1989) provides only the most limited support for the effects of TMT heterogeneity on firm performance. However, this study is commendable for its consideration of multiple industries, independent measures of industry change and rivalry, multiple measures of firm performance, and especially for its attempt to develop more complex theory that appreciates some of the subtleties of TMTs. Nevertheless, one tentative conclusion that emerges from this work (as well as from three other studies examining related ideas [O'Reilly and Flatt 1989; Hambrick and D'Aveni 1992; Glick, Miller, and Huber 1993]) is that the distributional properties of TMTs will not be predictive of firm performance in all circumstances[16]

Of the other studies published on TMTs and firm performance, contingency factors were explicitly (Michel and Hambrick 1992; Haleblian and Finkelstein 1993) or implicitly (Eisenhardt and Schoonhoven 1990; Smith et al. 1994) incorporated. In Michel and Hambrick (1992), the only study in this group to model strategy as a contingency factor, the interdependence of a firm's diversification posture did not moderate the TMT heterogeneity-firm performance relationship. However, Haleblian and Finkelstein's (1993) study of forty-seven firms in the computer and natural gas distribution industries found that environmental turbulence moderated the association between firm performance and both team size and CEO dominance. Specifically, they found that firms with larger teams and less dominant CEOs did better in turbulent environments, ostensibly because such TMTs had superior information-processing capabilities.

Finally, two studies examined TMT characteristics and firm performance in rapidly changing, or "high-velocity," industries. Arguing that larger and more heterogeneous TMTs engaged in more constructive conflict (Eisenhardt and Schoonhoven 1990) and exhibited less social integration (Smith et al. 1994), these studies found a positive association between several measures of TMT heterogeneity and firm performance. Although not all associations were consistently positive, the overall pattern from these studies quite strongly indicates support for the authors' ideas.

In summary, while an empirical record on the association between TMT heterogeneity and firm performance has been established, it appears from this work that we are unlikely to uncover a strong direct relationship between the heterogeneity of TMTs and the success of the firms they manage. Nevertheless, the positive effects of TMT heterogeneity on firm performance in "high velocity" or turbulent environments in several of these studies may help point the way to a clearer understanding of what heterogeneity among top managers really means. Recall our earlier discussion of how TMT heterogeneity promotes a more rigorous strategy formulation process by increasing the number of feasible strategic alternatives under consideration and the quality of their evaluation. In fast-changing, dynamic environments, managerial work becomes more fragmented (Mintzberg 1973), information-processing requirements increase, and new opportunities and crises necessitate greater adaptive capabilities (Galbraith 1973)—all of which place a higher premium on the generation of multiple and novel solutions. It is precisely in the most unstable environments that TMT heterogeneity is most important.

In contrast, consider Haleblian and Finkelstein's (1993, 847) description of stable environments:

> Information processing requirements are not as intense in stable environments (Ancona 1990). For example, Kotter found that top managerial information and decision making requirements in stable environments were "more standardized and routine" than in turbulent environments (1982, 29). Stable environments tend to attenuate learning requirements (Tushman and Keck 1990), making problem solving more systematic than it is in turbulent environments (Eisenhardt 1989).

Under conditions of stability, we might expect strategy implementation to be more salient than strategy formulation, because the strategic challenge is less in developing new ideas than it is in preserving established procedures (Tushman and Romanelli 1985). As we discussed earlier, TMT cooperation and stability become more important when environments are more stable (Nutt 1987), suggesting that integrated TMTs may be preferred. Hence, in stable environments, TMT social integration, rather than heterogeneity, may be related to firm performance. The following two propositions summarize these arguments:

PROPOSITION 5-12A

The more unstable the environment, the stronger the relationship between TMT heterogeneity and firm performance.

PROPOSITION 5-12B

The more unstable the environment, the weaker the relationship between TMT social integration and firm performance.

Beyond the moderating role of organizational environments, other contingency factors may help explain how and when TMT heterogeneity affects firm performance. For example, the contextual conditions that give rise to different configurations of TMTs may themselves often operate as moderating forces on firm performance. The propositions on environmental instability above are cases in point. Earlier in this chapter, we argued that TMT heterogeneity is greater in unstable environments, to a large extent because such environments impose demands on how organizations should structure their TMTs. An implicit assumption in Proposition 5-3a was that organizations would respond to these environmental requirements in a variety of ways because these responses would enhance their position and performance. Thus, to the extent that organizations are responsive to environmental demands, firm performance should be greater. Restating this logic in terms of Proposition 5-3a suggests that firms promoting TMT demographic heterogeneity in unstable environments should do better, a prediction represented by Proposition 5-12a. Hence, an extension of the "fit" or alignment argument implicit in Proposition 5-3a gives rise to the contingency-based Proposition 5-12a.

While we will forgo translating each of the propositions predicting TMT characteristics to propositions predicting firm performance, such propositions do represent viable and interesting research questions that have relatively strong support in the literature, as we have documented. There may be other relevant contextual factors worthy of study as well.

We need more complex frameworks of TMTs that recognize the role of senior executives in strategic decision making, along with the moderating role of such important contextual influences as the environment, the organization, and the CEO. In addition, much more work is needed on such basic aspects of TMTs as their boundaries and determinants. This chapter offers one model of these phenomena that we believe is particularly promising for future research.

NOTES

1. We refer to the group of executives at the top of an organization as a "team" only for ease of presentation; we agree with Hambrick (1994) that this constellation of executives may not necessarily behave in a "teamlike" fashion. Indeed, as we discuss below, the nature of the interactions among top managers comprising a team is a variable that can be studied in its own right.

2. In Chapters 3 and 4, we described both the personality characteristics and experiences of executives. Although much of that discussion is relevant to a group of executives as well, it will not be repeated here. Nevertheless, it is important to keep in mind that mean levels of psychological and demographic attributes of top management are consequential (e.g., Hage and Dewar 1973; Finkelstein and Hambrick 1990).

3. We continue to use the "TMT" label after calling for greater attention to the "group" nature of top executive interaction simply for ease of reference and continuity and because essentially all of the research we review in this chapter also adopts this nomenclature.

4. It is critical to control for industry, however, because institutional arrangements within industries often affect structural arrangements, such as the hierarchy of positions at the top (DiMaggio and Powell 1983). For example, the number of vice-presidents differs across industries, as does its meaning. There are many more vice-presidents in firms in the investment banking industry than in other industries, but all are not influential in strategic decision making. As a result, definitions of TMT that are based on hierarchical position may be problematic in cross-industry studies.

5. Respondents were asked to rate managerial power for three different strategic decisions (major resource allocations, organizational redesign, and domain changes), with each measured on a seven-point scale (from "no influence" to "total influence"). The reported rating of managerial power is the sum of the scores for each of the three strategic decisions.

6. Although some may suggest that role interdependence is related to TMT consensus, we have purposely refrained from arguing for such an association. When TMT roles are interdependent, there is a greater need for cooperation and resource sharing among senior executives. Nevertheless, a need for such activities does not necessarily translate into actual behavior, so it is not clear whether interdependent TMTs really do cooperate. By the same token, the relationship between role interdependence and social integration is imprecise, because it cannot necessarily be assumed that interdependent TMTs are cohesive (Schmidt and Kochan 1972).

7. A different problem sometimes noted, stemming from the paucity of studies directly examining the association between TMT demography and TMT interaction processes, is that demographic and process constructs may not actually be directly related. While this critique is no different than the one we

addressed in Chapter 4 on the validity of demographic data, the lack of empirical work linking demography and process is problematic.

8. Hambrick and D'Aveni, however, found in their study of bankrupts and survivors that in the year before bankruptcy, "the actual size of the bankrupt teams shrank appreciably" (1992, 1462).

9. Actually, we would expect CEO effects on TMTs to be more readily discernible empirically because CEOs can change the makeup of their team more easily than they can the organization's strategy and performance.

10. We define CEO dominance as the power of the CEO relative to the rest of the TMT (Hambrick and D'Aveni 1992; Haleblian and Finkelstein 1993).

11. Although we do not do so in the context of a chapter on TMTs, it is also possible to offer a proposition on the negative association between CEO openness and CEO tenure.

12. Research has also been conducted on the association between TMTs and executive turnover (e.g., Wagner, Pfeffer, and O'Reilly 1984; Jackson et al. 1991; Wiersema and Bantel 1993; Wiersema and Bird 1993), as we discuss in Chapter 6.

13. Almost all of this work has focused on demographic heterogeneity as the independent variable.

14. Both studies included team size as a control variable but reported no significant associations with dependent variables.

15. The operational definitions and methods of identifying change in the two studies are also very different and could account for some of the inconsistent results.

16. Neither Hambrick and Mason (1984) nor Pfeffer (1983) suggests direct associations between demographic heterogeneity and organization performance.

SIX

CHANGES AT THE TOP: EXECUTIVE TURNOVER AND SUCCESSION

The replacement of one leader by another has been a matter of fascination and drama through the ages. Executive succession evokes a political picture, with the continuity or disruption of regimes at stake and the creation of clear winners and losers. Turnover at the top instills hope, fear, or simply anxiety in organizational members and other stakeholders. It comes as little surprise, then, that executive succession has been the subject of a huge volume of research, which has grown exponentially along with other research on top executives over the past fifteen years.

At the core of research on succession has been the goal of answering the "so what?" question: As a practical matter, what are the implications or consequences of executive succession? Some researchers have asked the stark question, Does executive succession help or hurt organizational performance? But even when the question is asked with more subtlety, it quickly becomes clear that one cannot comprehend the consequences of succession in a vacuum. What occurs after new leaders take charge depends on a wide array of factors, ranging from the conditions surrounding the predecessor's departure, the process by which the successor was named, and, of course, the characteristics and actions of the successor (Guest 1962; Gordon and Rosen 1981; Hambrick and Fukutomi 1991).

In fact, we believe that the effects of executive succession, along with other important phenomena associated with top management turnover, can be framed and best understood by adopting the framework shown as Figure 6-1. At the start of the succession framework is the precipitating context, or the conditions that influence and surround the departure of the predecessor. These contextual factors include: 1) the performance of the organization, 2) agency conditions (including ownership and board factors), 3) other organizational characteristics (such as size, structure, strategy), 4) external conditions, and 5) the characteristics of the predecessor (including background, tenure, power, and personality).

This precipitating context, in turn, affects whether (or when) succession will occur and the process by which it will unfold—the succession event and process. Next, on the basis of the precipitating context and succession process, one is in a position to explain or understand the successor characteristics (e.g., insider versus outsider and similarity to predecessor).

Finally, one can examine the effects of succession. Here, areas of interest include the successor's behaviors, organizational changes, organizational performance, and the reactions of stakeholders (including investors).

Figure 6-1 is not only a useful conceptual framework for building specific predictive models of succession phenomena.[1] It also provides a basis for organizing the vast wealth of literature on executive succession according to these major overarching questions:

1. Will succession occur?
2. How will it occur? That is, by what process?
3. Who will be selected?
4. What will the consequences be?

These questions form the basis for the major sections of this chapter. Some sections are longer than others because of widely varying amounts of relevant research and theory. Our focus is primarily on succession of the chief executive, because that position has been the target of almost all research on executive succession. However, many of the concepts and findings also have relevance for succession or turnover in other executive positions, such

FIGURE 6-1 **Executive Succession: A Conceptual Framework**

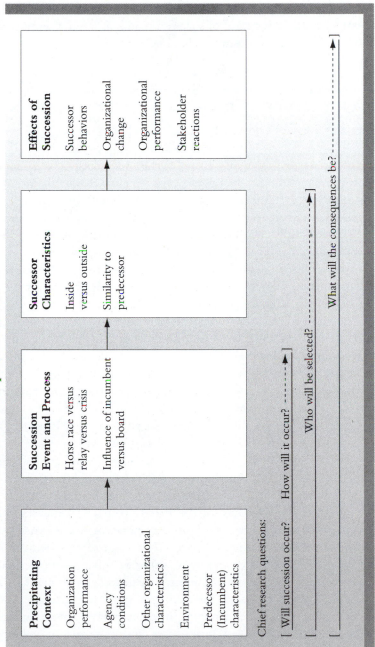

Precipitating Context	**Succession Event and Process**	**Successor Characteristics**	**Effects of Succession**
Organization performance	Horse race versus relay versus crisis	Inside versus outside	Successor behaviors
Agency conditions	Influence of incumbent versus board	Similarity to predecessor	Organizational change
Other organizational characteristics			Organizational performance
Environment			Stakeholder reactions
Predecessor (Incumbent) characteristics			

Chief research questions:

[Will succession occur?

[How will it occur? -------]

[Who will be selected? ----------------------]

[What will the consequences be? -------------------------]

as division general managers. We also include a section on turnover within top management teams, a variation of succession and an interesting research focus that has gathered momentum in recent years.

WILL SUCCESSION OCCUR? DETERMINANTS OF TOP EXECUTIVE DEPARTURE

Executive departures come in several forms, including death, illness, mandatory retirement, early retirement for personal reasons, leaving for an executive position in another company, and dismissal. From a theoretical standpoint, these departure routes are not equally interesting. Death and illness are least interesting for organizational scholars, reflecting choices on no one's part and probably accounting for under 5 percent of all CEO exits from office (Vancil 1987). Early retirements and departures to join other companies, ostensibly voluntary exits, have not been singled out for study but should be. Such voluntary departures do not occur randomly, and it would be interesting to know if certain organizational circumstances are associated with them. For instance, as we discuss in the chapter on executive compensation, it may be that executives are inclined to depart voluntarily to the degree that their pay is lower than their peers' in comparable firms. Executives may leave due to fatigue or lack of enjoyment, perhaps stemming from performance pressures, conflict with large shareholders or board members, or a stressful competitive environment. If so, voluntary departure might be predicted by the same factors that predict CEO dismissal.

In this vein, it is important to point out that some "voluntary" departures are not truly voluntary, but rather occur at the strong encouragement or insistence of the board. Moreover, to the extent that the departing CEO is influenced by his or her forecast of the firm's prospects, it may be that voluntary departures tend to precede significant performance downturns.

The most common circumstance for CEO departure is mandatory retirement. (In the United States and many other countries, senior executives are exempt from legislation prohibiting mandatory retirement.) On the surface, it would not seem very interesting to study the antecedents of departures occurring under mandatory retirement policies, because these exits are due to institutionalized procedures and not out of volition. However, attention should be paid to the factors associated with adoption of mandatory retirement provisions for senior executives. Not all firms have such policies, and their adoption may stem from very important institutional, agency, and organizational life cycle forces. In fact, the adoption of mandatory retirement provisions for senior officers could signal a fundamental shift within a firm regarding beliefs about executive entrenchment, staffing, and organizational adaptation.

Perhaps even more important, mandatory retirement provisions are sometimes—we believe increasingly—abrogated when a particularly influential CEO convinces the board that he or she should stay beyond the legislated date. Recent visible cases include Harry Gray at United Technologies, Richard Gelb at Bristol-Myers Squibb, Roy Vagelos at Merck, and Roberto Goizueta at Coca-Cola. It could be interesting to study the conditions that give rise to such abrupt cancellation of company strictures, as well as the effects of lingering CEOs—say, on the retention and motivation of other senior executives and on stock market reactions.

Finally, we have CEO dismissals, theoretically the most interesting of the CEO exits and certainly the most studied. Dismissals can only be understood through a complex and far-ranging set of organizational factors (Fredrickson, Hambrick, and Baumrin 1988). It is not clear how many CEOs are dismissed, but most accounts suggest a range of 10 to 20 percent (Herman 1981; James and Soref 1981; Vancil 1987; Boeker 1992). Because CEO dismissals have been the explicit or implicit focus of most research on executive departure, our discussion of precipitating factors is primarily oriented toward their explanation. In some places, we depart from the focus on dismissal to reconcile with phenomena of overall turnover.

The methods for detecting dismissals have varied widely, reflecting the fact that forced departures are often euphemistically presented to the public. Some researchers have relied on departure before age sixty-five (the typical mandatory retirement age in large American firms) as signaling dismissal (Vancil 1987; Puffer and Weintrop 1991). Some have relied on press accounts, in some cases triangulating across multiple accounts of a departure (James and Soref 1981). Perhaps the most ingenious and reliable approach was Boeker's (1992) use of the detailed records of two major market research firms in the semiconductor industry to identify CEO dismissals in that industry. A major challenge in studying dismissals is to identify them correctly. An unappealing alternative, requiring no judgments, is to simply aggregate all CEO departures. However, this introduces a great deal of noise to the sampling procedure, because the majority of executive departures are not dismissals or even resignations under pressure.

Organizational Performance

Why do CEOs lose their jobs? The most obvious answer is, *because their organizations are performing poorly*. On this matter, the research is abundantly clear: poor organizational performance tends to precede executive departure. Some of these studies have focused specifically on the CEO and some on a broader set of top executives. Some studies have attempted to identify the effects of performance on dismissals in particular, while some have examined the effects on executive turnover in general, envisioning a combination of dismissals, voluntary "escapes," and executive fatigue in the face of poor performance. Essentially all the studies have sufficiently arranged the chronology of their data to allow the conclusion that the poor performance *precedes* the departures (As we shall see, this becomes more problematic when considering research on the *effects* of executive departures.)

However, even though a general relationship exists between poor performance and executive departure, the various studies are somewhat disjointed, because of their widely differing samples (ranging from large conglomerates to semiconductor firms to baseball teams) and measures of performance. One major series of studies, among the earliest to systematically study succession, found that the won–lost records of sports teams are associated with general manager turnover (Grusky 1963; Gamson and Scotch 1964; Allen, Panian and Lotz 1979). Some studies have documented the effects of poor stock returns on executive departure (Benston 1985; Coughlan and Schmidt 1985; Warner, Watts, and Wruck 1988). Others have relied on profitability measures as predictors of executive departure (McEachern 1975; Salancik and Pfeffer 1977; James and Soref 1981; Wagner, Pfeffer, and O'Reilly 1984; Harrison, Torres, and Kukalis 1988). In his study of CEO dismissals in semiconductor firms, Boeker (1992) used sales growth as the performance measure because many of the companies in the sample were relatively young and still building their strategic positions; for them, profitability would not have been a relevant indicator (also, since many were privately held, stock return data, which might have been relevant, were not available). Finally, in an intriguing paper, Puffer and Weintrop (1991) found that CEO dismissal was more tied to the gap between security analysts' expectations and actual company earnings than to the absolute level of stock market or accounting performance of the company.

Overall, the pattern of poor performance preceding CEO executive departure is robust, recurring in sample after sample and across various performance measures. However, the explantory power of this pattern is not particularly strong. That is, organizational performance, while statistically associated with executive departure, does not explain a great deal of variance in departure rates. In the above-cited studies, the variance explained by performance was always below 50 percent and typically in the range of 10 to 20 percent. In this vein, many of us can think of CEOs who have been dismissed when their organizations were performing well and others who have held onto their jobs through years of poor performance.

To some extent, researchers might explain more variance in executive departure by examining the various forms of disappointing performance. Aside from considering multiple performance metrics (say, profitability, stock returns, and sales growth), researchers should examine each metric from different vantages: its level, its trend, its persistence, and its deviation from expectations. This raises the question: What is most likely to get CEOs fired—low performance, persistently low performance, steadily deteriorating performance, or, as Puffer and Weintrop (1991) found, unexpectedly low performance? It would be interesting to assess the relative influence of these various performance shortfalls on executive departure; it might also be useful to develop a summative index of *overall* performance (comprised of various elements) as a basis for predicting departure.

At a minimum, various performance measures may have different triggering effects on CEO departure, depending on the context. For example, profits might be the salient performance indicator for large, mature firms, but sales growth may provide the basis for executive retention versus departure in small, high-technology firms (Boeker 1992); or profits may be associated with executive departure for one type of ownership configuration, but stock returns may be a stronger determinant of departure under another ownership configuration (Salancik and Pfeffer 1980). As these examples suggest, and as the modest degree of variance explained by performance clearly indicates, the researcher who seeks to accurately predict executive departure will need to look beyond performance to other precipitating factors. Among the most promising of these factors are the agency conditions existing in the firm.

Agency Conditions

Since Berle and Means (1932) documented the increasing separation of ownership and managerial control of large American corporations, theorists have been interested in the implications of varying relationships between owners (or principals) and managers (or agents). Agency theory has many facets (Jensen and Meckling 1976; Eisenhardt 1989a), with clear implications for executive retention versus departure.

One series of studies examined whether CEO tenure depends on the ownership configuration of the firm. McEachern (1977) found that the tenures of owner-managers (with at least 4 percent of stock) were substantially greater than those of other CEOs. In an elaboration on McEachern's work, Salancik and Pfeffer (1980) sought to determine whether the association between company performance and CEO tenure varied, depending on ownership profile. They found that in owner-managed companies, no association existed between performance and tenure; in "externally controlled" firms, in which at least one nonmanager held a concentrated amount of stock, a positive association existed between profitability and tenure; and in "management-controlled" firms, in which shares were widely dispersed with no single major owner, stockholder returns were found to be positively associated with tenure. Allen and Panian (1982), in a closely related study, found that in firms in which a family owned 5 percent or more, CEOs who were not members of that family had 1) shorter tenures and 2) tenures more closely tied to performance than did CEOs who were members of the controlling family or where there was no such controlling interest. Thus, across these projects, there is evidence that ownership configuration affects executive tenures, with owner-managers, not surprisingly, somewhat sheltered from the disciplinary consequences of poor performance.

A potential problem arises, however, in focusing on the CEO's tenure as an indicator for whether he or she is buffered from dismissal, as has been the logic in the three above-cited studies. Tenure represents *all* the years that the CEO has been in office, which in turn is a function of how long he or she is allowed to stay, as well as *how early he or she started the job*. Because owner-managers are relatively likely to have been founders or members of founding families, they probably become CEOs at younger ages than CEOs who are not major owners. Therefore, the long tenures of owner-managers may be due as much to their early starting dates as to their relative immunity from dismissal.

Fortunately, at least two studies have examined dismissals specifically, so we have some opportunity to observe the disciplining of CEOs under differing ownership contexts. James and Soref (1981), as noted earlier, found that poor profitability was associated with dismissal. However, contrary to their expectations, they found no significant differences in the effects of poor performance on dismissal for different ownership situations, even with several established ownership classification schemes. Their sample was limited, however, (only sixteen firings), so their results are only suggestive.

Boeker's (1992) sample was more substantial (67 semiconductor firms over a 22-year period, with 115 CEO dismissals), and his results conform to what would be expected from agency theory. He found that CEOs' stockholdings were negatively related to dismissal in general, as well as in cases of poor performance. Moreover, in cases of poor performance, the more widely dispersed the ownership, the lower the likelihood of CEO dismissal. Thus, across various studies, it appears that owner-managers are relatively buffered from dismissal. Similarly, widely dispersed ownership can also protect the CEO from dismissal, even in the face of poor performance. A CEO is most vulnerable where stock is highly concentrated in one or a few nonmanager owners.

Agency theory also allows predictions of dismissal based on board composition. Here, too, the data provide a consistent picture. Salancik and Pfeffer (1981) established the general finding that the greater the percentage of board members who are insiders, that is, officers largely beholden to the CEO, the longer the tenure of the CEO. Weisbach (1988) similarly found the relationship between performance and executive tenure held only in companies whose boards were dominated by outsiders. Finally, Boeker (1992) found that in situations of low performance, the percent of insiders on the board was negatively related to dismissal.

In sum, agency conditions—as manifested in ownership profile or board composition—have distinct effects on executive departure. The greater the CEO's control—through his or her own stockholdings, through the absence of a major vigilant owner, or a small outsider contingent on the board—the lower the likelihood of dismissal even when performance is poor.

Other Organizational Characteristics

Beyond its agency conditions, other characteristics of the organization may also affect the likelihood of executive succession. Organizational size has particularly been examined in this regard. Grusky (1961) compared the largest twenty-six and the smallest twenty-seven Fortune 500 companies in the early 1960s and found that the larger companies experienced more frequent executive successions. Grusky's interpretation was that larger firms are more institutionalized and can experience CEO succession without great disruption; hence, they may be relatively likely to have mandatory retirement provisions to make room for other qualified executives to advance and a willingness to dismiss the CEO if performance falters. It is important to note that Grusky's sample, encompassing the top and bottom of the Fortune 500, is very restricted in the range of company sizes; namely, no truly *small* companies were included.

Attempts to corroborate Grusky's finding have yielded mixed results. James and Soref (1981) found that the larger firms in their sample were more likely to fire their CEOs than were the smaller firms. However, in their studies of CEO dismissal, Puffer and Weintrop (1991) and Boeker (1992) found no effects from organizational size.

Our own interpretation is that size will tend to be positively associated with overall CEO *turnover* rates, but primarily because CEOs in large companies are appointed to their jobs at more advanced ages (Vancil 1987) and those companies are relatively likely to have mandatory CEO retirement. In line with Grusky's logic, these characteristics exist because of the bureaucratization and institutional forces in large firms. However, it is doubtful that bureaucratization engenders a higher rate of CEO dismissals in large firms.

If anything, the boards of large companies may be reluctant to dismiss their CEOs because of the unfavorable media attention that attends to such acts and because, generally speaking, the pool of eligible replacement candidates may be very limited. Large firms require CEOs who have experience and stature commensurate with the firms' size and stature. Hence, while dozens of candidates may be nominally eligible to be CEO of a small company in an industry, exceedingly few hold appropriate credentials to be considered as CEO for the largest firm in an industry.

In short, we do not believe that the final work on organizational size and CEO succession has been written. Our best estimate of what will be found can be expressed as two propositions:

PROPOSITION 6-1

Large firms have more frequent CEO turnover than small firms (primarily due to advanced age at time of appointment and mandatory retirement provisions).

PROPOSITION 6-2

Small firms are more likely to dismiss their CEOs than large firms (after controlling for performance, ownership profile, and so on).

Another organizational characteristic not yet examined by researchers may have an important effect on CEO departure rates, including dismissals. We speak of the structure of the firm, particularly whether it consists of divisions (the "M-form" of Williamson [1975]) or not. Essentially, a divisional structure creates multiple general management positions that enhance training for, and observation of, potential CEO skills. In contrast to a functionally organized firm, in which no executive other than the CEO has experience in running an entire business, the firm with a divisional structure (which may also have a layer of group executives responsible for multiple divisions) has a ready pool of potential internal CEO candidates. We expect that such firms will have relatively high rates of CEO turnover, because their supply of internal talent not only warrants mandatory CEO retirement provisions to make room for advancement of others, but also provides ready replacements for faltering CEOs. Thus:

PROPOSITION 6-3

Firms with a divisional structure have higher CEO turnover rates than functionally organized firms.

Environment

Factors external to the firm, particularly industry characteristics, may also influence rates of CEO successions. While almost no empirical research has examined such relationships, they have been briefly discussed by theorists. One line of thought is that CEO succession rates vary with the industry's age or stage of development. However, the influence of these factors may affect overall executive turnover rates and dismissals in opposing ways. First, firms in young, high-growth industries will tend to have young executives (Harris 1979). Therefore, succession due to mandatory retirement, death, and illness should be less frequent in young industries than in mature industries. However, the ambiguity of means-ends relationships is greater in young industries than in more mature ones (Pfeffer and Moore 1980), causing uncertainty and, in turn, strong causal attributions about the effectiveness of organizational leaders (Meindl, Ehrlich, and Dukerich 1985; Hambrick and Finkelstein 1987). When firms in young industries do not perform well, the leader is likely to be seen as the source of the problem and replaced. When firms in more mature industries do not perform well, observers are more likely to attribute the problem to industry conditions, instead of company executives. Therefore:

PROPOSITION 6-4

Dismissals in young, growing industries are more common than in mature industries.

The number of firms in an industry may be another characteristic affecting executive turnover. Fredrickson, Hambrick, and Baumrin (1988) asserted that the larger the number of firms, the greater the potential supply of eligible candidates for a CEO job. To the extent that succession decisions are influenced by the availability of feasible candidates and that experience in the industry is judged an important criterion for selection,[2] the number of firms in the industry may indeed affect rates of succession.

PROPOSITION 6-5

The greater the number of firms in an industry, the greater the CEO turnover rate.

In general, the influences of environmental factors on executive turnover, largely overlooked in research to date, should be a high priority for investigation.

Predecessor (Incumbent) Characteristics

Finally, the characteristics of the incumbent CEO must be considered for their possible influence on successions. We have already discussed how the CEO's own stockholdings tend to protect him or her from dismissal, but other forms of power could achieve the same end. These bases of power could include the executive's tenure (Hambrick and Fukutomi 1991; Ocasio 1994), achievement of a patriarchal aura (Vancil 1987), simultaneously holding the boardchair and the CEO position (Finkelstein and D'Aveni 1994), as well as other forms of power well established in the literature (Finkelstein 1992). In fact, the CEO's power may be not only a basis for avoiding dismissal, but also the dominant factor in the waiving of mandatory CEO retirement provisions.

Elements of the CEO's personality also can be expected to affect his or her propensity to stay in, or depart from, the job. In an in-depth analysis of CEO departure patterns, Sonnenfeld (1988) found that some executives cling tenaciously to the job, because they have a "heroic self-concept." Sonnenfeld did not specify the personality constructs that may constitute this syndrome, but narcissism, need for power, and even neurotic delusions of grandeur may be among a psychologist's conceptual explanations (McClelland 1975; Zaleznik and Kets de Vries 1975; Kets de Vries and Miller 1984; House, Spangler, and Woycke 1991).

In sum, the likelihood of CEO succession depends on a wide range of precipitating factors. The organization's performance may be the most important element in a succession model, but it by no means acts alone. The agency conditions in the firm, other organizational characteristics, the external environment, and the characteristics of the incumbent (particularly his or her power and personality) are all needed to achieve strong predictions of executive departures. These same precipitating factors influence the succession process, to which we now turn.

WHAT WILL BE THE DYNAMICS OF THE SUCCESSION PROCESS?

Some CEO successions are messy, noisy, and traumatic for the organization and the individual contenders. Other successions seem like nonevents, barely noticeable or noteworthy. Unfortunately, little research has been done on succession processes. The explanation for this lack of research is readily apparent. In contrast to more publicly traceable aspects of succession, an examination of processes typically requires access to highly sensitive deliberations and events inside the organization. The most comprehensive analysis of succession processes was undertaken by Vancil (1987), whose book title, *Passing the Baton*, reveals his own preference for smooth, orderly transitions. However, his research, based on in-depth interviews with CEOs and board members, describes an array of succession profiles.

Types of Successions

At one extreme, and most "healthy" in Vancil's eyes is the "relay race" (p. 13). With this approach, an heir apparent is selected well before the incumbent's departure, typically elevated to a clear "number two" status in the organizational hierarchy (usually with the title of president or chief operating officer), and readied for the transition to the CEO slot (Figure 6–2a). This approach is orderly and emphasizes continuity.

An alternative succession process is the "horse race." With this approach, two or more executives are placed in competition with each other for the top job (Figure 6–2b). Sometimes a horse race is run very explicitly, with contenders clearly designated and the entire organization and even the media watching intently. Such was the case with two widely noted succession horse races in the early 1980s—the contests to succeed Walter Wriston at Citibank (won by John Reed) and Reginald Jones at General Electric (Jack Welch). However, sometimes a horse race is more discreet, with the contenders told they are in the race but no public acknowledgment made of the contest. In some cases, the contestants may not be told expressly that a race is on or that they are in it. Such ambiguity allows flexibility, perhaps minimizes heated rivalry and acrimony, and even injects into the process a further test of ambition and astuteness.

Sometimes a horse race precedes a relay, with contestants vying for the heir apparent slot (Figure 6–2c). Indeed, it could be argued that until an heir apparent is designated, an implicit horse race is underway, as ambitious executives vie to improve their chances for later in the tournament (Lazear and Rosen 1981).

Finally, there are crisis successions in which there is no designated heir apparent (Figure 6-2d). These may include cases of illness or death or, more commonly, the abrupt dismissal of the incumbent.

The factors that determine which of these succession processes will occur have received almost no attention. Various forces enter in, including, in the case of crises, essentially stochastic or random factors. We focus specifically on the factors that might give rise to an explicit horse race as opposed to a relay.

FIGURE 6–2 **Some Major Types of Succession Processes**

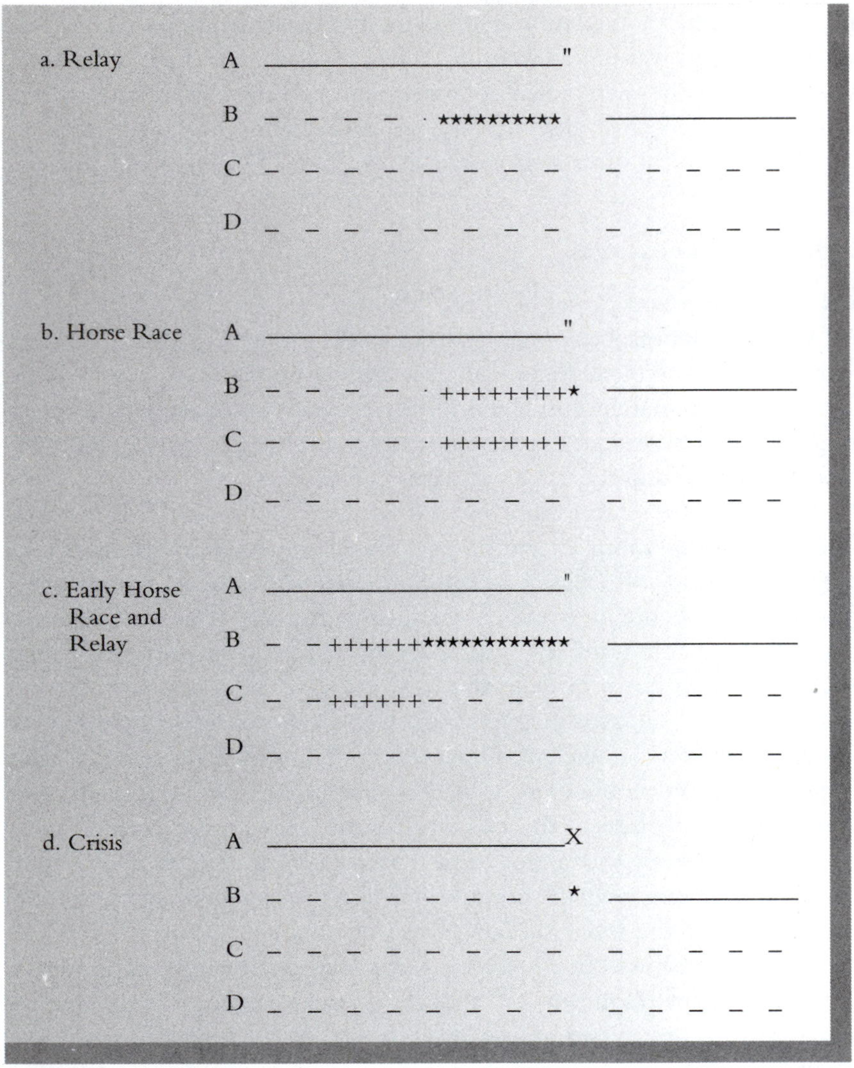

a. Relay

A _____ "

B – – – – · ✦✦✦✦✦✦✦✦✦✦ _____

C – – – – – – – – – – – – – –

D – – – – – – – – – – – – – –

b. Horse Race

A _____ "

B – – – – · ++++++++★ _____

C – – – – · ++++++++ – – – – –

D – – – – – – – – – – – – – –

c. Early Horse Race and Relay

A _____ "

B – – ++++++✦✦✦✦✦✦✦✦✦✦ _____

C – – ++++++– – – – – – – – – –

D – – – – – – – – – – – – – –

d. Crisis

A _____ X

B – – – – – – – – –★ _____

C – – – – – – – – – – – – – –

D – – – – – – – – – – – – – –

A, B, C, D	: Executives
_____	: Service as CEO
"	: Expected departure date
X	: Abrupt departure
– – –	: Service as TMT member with no designation as succession contender
+++++++	: Defined or signaled as succession contender
✦✦✦✦✦✦✦✦	: Defined or signaled as heir apparent

First, the horse race requires multiple viable contestants. At the most basic level, it needs two or more executives who are the "right age," that is, who could serve at least several years if they won the contest. Executives over sixty rarely are considered as CEO candidates (especially in companies with mandatory executive retirement at age sixty-five), thus limiting the field or even the potential for a horse race. Beyond executive age are more systematic forces favoring one succession mode or another. We expect the following:

PROPOSITION 6–6

A horse race succession is more likely than a relay if:
1. the company has a divisional (M-form) organization with multiple general management positions as CEO proving grounds;
2. the largest operating units are of roughly equal size; and
3. more than one of the largest operating units are relatively high-performing.

These conditions give rise to multiple eligible contenders, each of whom feel that they should be carefully and thoroughly considered for the CEO job. The likelihood of a horse race also increases if the company does not have an entrenched tradition of a COO position, a typical stepping-stone in a relay.

Conversely, a relay is most likely in firms that have an institutionalized COO position, that are functionally organized, or have one subunit that exceeds all others in size, strategic centrality, or performance. In such firms, there is a clear stepping-stone for one executive to the top job.

Finally, firms may differ systematically in *how early* they designate their heir apparents (either via an early horse race or relay hand-off). In conditions of turbulence and instability, the firms benefit from delaying their choice of CEO as long as possible, so they can apply the most current criteria in their selection. Conversely, in more stable situations, the needed qualifications of the next CEO can be anticipated further in advance, and little is gained in postponing the designation. Thus:

PROPOSITION 6–7

The more stable the industry and the more stable the firm's performance, the earlier an heir apparent is selected—either through a relay or an early horse race. If the environment or strategic situation is turbulent, decision makers are relatively likely to postpone their choice for new CEO, so they can be relatively sure of emerging requirements for leadership qualifications.

Influence of the Incumbent Versus the Board

The task of selecting a new CEO is expressly bestowed on the board of directors (Vancil 1987; Lorsch 1989), and some theorists have concluded that it is the only task the board can credibly or effectively perform (Mizruchi 1983). Trends in board reform and investor activism in the last several years have probably led to more diligence and thoroughness by boards in selecting CEOs. However, it is widely believed that incumbent CEOs still often have a dominant role in the selection of their successors, frequently specifying both the process and the result.

In a classic article, Levinson (1974) implored CEOs: "Don't Choose Your Own Successor," arguing that incumbents lack objectivity about the new talents most needed and the abilities various candidates possess. However, many incumbents have clear favorites among their lieutenants and sometimes make promises, even if implicit, to specific candidates about eventual elevation. At a minimum, most CEOs have the human desire to further extend their impact on the organization through a hand-picked successor. In fact, incumbent CEOs can be expected to influence the succession process to the fullest extent allowed by the board.

Thus, the succession process can be incumbent-driven, board-driven, or somewhere in between (what Vancil [1987] refers to as "partnership"). Zald (1965) provides an in-depth portrayal of such a shared "partnership" succession process in a community service organization. In this particular case, the incumbent executive shaped the process, but the board made the actual choice, picking one of two clear internal candidates. A careful reading of Zald's case study makes it clear that the board selected the candidate who aligned more with the incumbent's ideology, even though that candidate was initially far less well known by the board than the other candidate. It was through shaping the process, and particularly by creating forums for extended board exposure to the two candidates, that the incumbent succeeded in turning the long-shot contender into a winner.

Zald (1965) offers a useful inventory of factors that enhanced the influence of the incumbent in the succession process he studied. Drawing on Zald's factors but extending them with some additional items, we set forth the following propositions:

PROPOSITION 6-8

The incumbent CEO will have influence in the succession decision to the extent that:

1. the organization's current performance is strong;
2. the incumbent has had a long tenure;

3. the board has had little first-hand exposure to the senior executives who are eligible succession contenders (This could be the case when numerous board members are relatively new, when the succession contenders are relatively new to the company, and when the succession contenders are not board members.);
4. agency conditions serve to weaken the influence of the board. Such conditions include:
   a. widely dispersed shares with no single major owner (other than possibly the incumbent CEO);
   b. board members own few shares;
   c. the CEO also serves as board chairman; and
   d. board members were selected or appointed by the incumbent CEO.

In essence, then, the same forces that lessen the likelihood that an incumbent CEO will be dismissed (as discussed earlier in this chapter) also buoy the incumbent's influence in the appointment of a successor. It is a matter of CEO power versus board power.

Most broadly, though, the succession process greatly affects the succession outcome.

WHO WILL BE SELECTED?

The selection of a new top executive is widely thought to be an important opportunity for the organization to adapt to the shifting requirements of its environment. Research at the aggregate level has found that some correspondence, in fact, exists between external conditions and the characteristics of CEOs. For example, Fligstein (1987) traced the increasing proportion of CEOs with finance backgrounds to American antitrust laws that promoted corporate diversification—a strategy favoring financial rather than operating competencies. Hambrick, Black, and Fredrickson (1992) found that CEOs in high-technology industries tended to be younger and have shorter tenures, more technical education, and more R&D experience than CEOs in low-technology industries.

Similarly, researchers have found that executive characteristics tend to align with the context created by the organization. For example, Drazin and Kazanjian (1993) found that technology-based firms in the growth phases of their life cycle tended to have CEOs with technology expertise, whereas in later, more mature stages, CEOs with financial, administrative, and marketing backgrounds were more common. Pfeffer and Salancik (1978) laid out additional examples of alignments between critical contingencies faced by organizations and the characteristics of their CEOs.

Numerous normative models have been set forth, arguing for the need to match managerial characteristics with the specific demands of the job (Wissema and Van der Pol 1980; Szilagyi and Schweiger 1984; Gupta 1986). Executive search firms also have their own frameworks and logics for specifying ideal executive characteristics needed for certain types of situations.

Our interest in this chapter is more specific. We are less interested in the general covariation of contextual conditions and executive characteristics than we are in the question of who will be selected as the new executive in a given situation. By focusing specifically on succession events, we can achieve an understanding of the underlying process by which aggregate covariation patterns occur. And by focusing specifically on succession events, we can examine how various precipitating forces give rise to selection outcomes.

The preponderance of empirical research on CEO selection outcomes has focused on explaining when an "outsider" will be chosen as the new leader. We examine this interesting issue in depth but argue for a new way of conceiving of "outsiderness." We then posit that the choice of an insider versus outsider as CEO is only one variation of the broader issue of how much continuity to seek in executive staffing.

Insider Versus Outsider Selection

The selection of a new CEO from outside an organization, occurring only in a minority of cases for business firms, is usually seen as a stark indicator that the board of directors wants change. Conversely, the choice of an insider signals the board's desire for more continuity and maintenance of current strategic thrusts.

Role of Performance.   Thus, the most obvious potential predictor of whether a new CEO will come from the outside is the performance of the organization in the period before the succession. Of the several studies examining this issue, most have found that presuccession performance was lower in cases where an outsider was appointed than when an insider was appointed. This pattern has been observed in samples of baseball teams (Allen, Panian, and Lotz 1979) and semiconductor firms (Boeker and Goodstein 1993) and in a cross-section of large companies in various industries (Cannella and Lubatkin 1993).

While Dalton and Kesner (1985) found no association between prior performance and selection of an outsider CEO, their sample was appreciably smaller than those in the other studies noted here. Also, unlike the other studies, Dalton and Kesner examined performance (profitability and stock price) without adjusting for industry averages, thus making it difficult to interpret this study's results. Our general conclusion is that outsiders tend to be brought into low-performance situations.

However, even in the studies in which poor performance and outsider selection were associated, the link was far from complete. The amount of variance explained by performance was under 20 percent in Boeker and Goodstein's study and under 10 percent in Cannella and Lubatkin's study. In the Allen, Panian, and Lotz (1979) study, the winning percentages of the baseball teams selecting inside versus outside managers, differed negligibly (49.6 percent versus 46.6 percent)—graphic evidence that low performance alone does not account for the insider versus outsider choice.

Social and Political Factors.   Social and political factors also must enter in. The choice of an outsider to be the new CEO is a highly charged decision. It represents a repudiation of the incumbent's strategic direction, or at least of his or her staffing capabilities; it violates implicit deals with potential inside successors; and it stymies other executives who would have advanced with the ascendance of an insider (Cannella and Lubatkin 1993). Since outside succession is an extraordinary event for business firms, additional conditions must exist for the board to turn outside for a new leader. Poor performance alone is not enough.

Recent studies have focused on these conditions, particularly political and agency factors, in predicting outside succession. Boeker and Goodstein (1993) found, for instance, that the greater the proportion of insiders on the board and the greater the ownership concentration among the board insiders, the less likely a new CEO would come from the outside. Cannella and Lubatkin (1993) found that when the incumbent CEO also was the board chair, the likelihood of outside succession was diminished. These findings clearly signal the ability of agency and political factors, particularly the strength of insiders, to affect the insider versus outsider choice. Other measures of agency conditions, such as overall ownership concentration, percentage of institutional holdings, percentage of the board appointed during the tenure of the incumbent, and the stockholdings of the incumbent, should be included in future studies.

The Common Origins of CEO Dismissal and Outside Succession.
Indeed, the decision to hire an outsider CEO emanates largely from the same forces that give rise to CEO dismissal. This is not to say that dismissal always leads to outside appointment; they covary, but not totally (Cannella and Lubatkin 1993). Rather, the two actions depend on essentially the same

forces, representing the board's activism in the face of disappointment with the current regime. Thus, with some modification, we would expect that a strong model for predicting dismissal would also be a strong model for predicting outside succession.

Let us draw on the comprehensive framework for predicting dismissals set forth by Fredrickson, Hambrick, and Baumrin (1988), as summarized in Table 6–1. Poor performance is a precipitating force behind both the CEO dismissal and the outsider selection decisions. As discussed earlier in the section on dismissal, a challenge for researchers is to think broadly and carefully about how they conceive of poor performance (level, trend, and persistence; profits, growth, stock price, and analyst expectations; industry norms; and so on). It is likely that the most potent performance metric for predicting dismissal will also have greatest strength for predicting outside CEO selection.

TABLE 6-1   **Commonality in the Major Factors for Predicting CEO Dismissal and Selection of an Outsider**

Predictive Construct	CEO Dismissal	Selection of Outsider
Current or Recent Organizational Performance	Poor performance increases the likelihood of dismissal and the appointment of an outsider.	
Board's Expectations or Attributions	If the board has very high performance expectations or considers current management to blame for poor performance, the likelihood of dismissal and outsider selection is increased.	
Board's Allegiances and Values	If the board's allegiances are totally to shareholders and not to incumbent management, the likelihood of dismissal and outsider selection is increased.	
Incumbent CEO's Power	If the incumbent CEO has great power, relative to the board, the likelihood of dismissal and outside selection is diminished.	
Availability of Alternative Candidates	Availability of qualified external candidates increases the likelihood of dismissal and outside selection.	
	Availability of qualified internal candidates increases the likelihood of dismissal.	Availability of qualified internal candidates decreases the likelihood of outside selection.

SOURCE: Adapted from Fredrickson, Hambrick, and Baumrin (1988)

Table 6–1 suggests that essentially all the additional predictive constructs exert similar forces on the dismissal and outside selection decisions. These constructs include the board's expectations and attributions, the board's allegiances and values, the incumbent CEO's power, and availability of qualified external candidates. The one exception—the one factor that leads to differing predictions—is the availability of internal candidates: existence of qualified insiders may edge a board toward a dismissal, but the internal pool would also facilitate an inside appointment.

The central thrust of this discussion of CEO dismissal and outside selection is that they cohere and are two manifestations of largely the same syndrome: a board or other decision-making body striving to break the organization away from the current leadership regime and, as important, visibly demonstrating to stakeholders that they are doing so. In this regard, it should be clear that both dismissal and outside selection have great symbolic significance: They are cleansing rituals, scapegoating, and emphatic demonstrations by the board that the past is past (Gamson and Scotch 1964).

Of course, not all outsider selection decisions rest on political forces, nor do they necessarily require poor performance. Some organizations, by their very nature, have few individuals prepared for or interested in being CEO. These would include universities, hospitals, and sports teams. In such industries, CEO candidates move from organization to organization, generally trying to trade up to more prestige or income. The strong norm in these industries is outside replacement, and insiders are rarely considered.

Some boards select outsiders in anticipation of the need for very different leadership expertise but before performance deteriorates. An example would be the decision in 1994 by the board of the large pharmaceutical firm Merck to hire Raymond Gilmartin from the outside, in anticipation of the intense competitive pressures that will face drug companies with the consolidation and rationalization of the health industry. Such proactive outside appointments are relatively rare; again, an outside appointment is extremely jarring and traumatic. However, it is reasonable to expect that the selection of an outsider CEO is more likely in an industry on the verge of, or in the midst of, a major discontinuity (e.g., deregulation or a major technology shift) than in a more stable one. We encourage an examination of inside versus outside succession patterns in different industries.

An "Outsiderness" Continuum.   We believe, however, that the biggest breakthroughs in the study of inside versus outside succession will come from a new conception of "outsiderness." In essentially all prior studies, inside versus outside succession has been determined in strictly binary terms: the new CEO either was previously employed in the top management ranks of the company or was not.[3] This is a very limiting approach, at odds with the reality that there are degrees of "outsiderness." For instance, a new CEO hired directly from outside the company is more of an outsider than a new CEO who has three years of tenure with the company. However, that new CEO with three years' tenure is very much an outsider compared to one who has 25 years'.

Let us step back and consider why we should be interested in inside versus outside succession in the first place. As discussed earlier, an outside succession will occur to the degree that the board seeks a shift away from the prior leadership regime. Specifically, the board may expect that an outsider will be 1) cognitively open-minded, with low commitment to the status quo, able to envision and consider new courses of action, and 2) socially and interpersonally unencumbered, with fewer attachments to internal executives, and hence able to make major staffing changes. Moreover, the mere act of appointing an outsider is meant to send signals 3) internally that change is coming and 4) externally that the board has taken an extraordinary measure to break with the past. All of these aims can be considered in scalar, continuous terms; and different degrees of "outsiderness" may achieve different amounts of these desired objectives.

Figure 6–3 presents a continuum of CEOs from extreme insider to extreme outsider. The extreme insider (with over fifteen years in the firm) is the norm in large business firms (Vancil 1987). Next is the executive with medium tenure in the firm (say, five to fifteen years). Then comes the executive who has long or medium tenure but has recently risen very quickly or is otherwise seen as a "maverick" or a member of the "new generation." Prominent examples of this type would be William Anderson, who was appointed CEO at NCR Corporation in the early 1970's, after having been head of the firm's small Japanese subsidiary and never having worked at company headquarters (Meyer and Starbuck 1992), and Jack Welch, whose elevation to CEO of General Electric was preceded by a meteoric rise through several layers and over hundreds of other GE executives (Tichy and Sherman 1993). An appropriate operationalization of the "quick rise" concept might use the number of years the executive has been a company officer as a percentage of his or her company tenure.

Next on the continuum comes the executive with a short tenure (say, one to five years) in the firm (including someone brought in expressly to be the next CEO). Under most prior studies, these executives would be treated as insiders, even though compared to CEO norms they are quite new to the company. The next gradation is one that seems to be occurring with greater frequency in American business—the appointment of an outside board member to be the new CEO. Typically a former CEO at another company, this individual is only a "quasi-outsider," because he or she

FIGURE 6-3 A Continuum of New CEO "Outsiderness" and Expected Accompaniments

Expected Tendencies

Origin of New CEO	Cognitive Openness to Change	Social/ Interpersonal Openness to Change	Internal Signal of Change	External Signal of Change
Extreme Insider				
Long tenure in firm (more than 15 years)	+	+	+	+
Medium tenure in firm (5 to 15 years)	++	++	++	++
"Maverick" or quick rise in firm (with long or medium tenure)	+++	++	+++	++
Short tenure in firm (1 to 5 years)	+++	+++	++++	++
Outside director	+++	+++	++++	+++
New hire from same industry	++++	+++++	+++++	++++
New hire from related industry	+++++	+++++	+++++	+++++
New hire from unrelated industry	+++++	+++++	+++++	+++++
Extreme Outsider				

The greater the number of plusses, the stronger the tendency: + equals very little tendency, while +++++ equals a very strong tendency.

probably knows many of the company's senior executives and is knowledgeable about (and has perhaps even ratified) current strategic directions. A recent example is Stanley Gault, a board member of Goodyear Corporation who was made CEO.

The final group are new hires from outside the company. But even here there are gradations. Some new hires come from the same industry (such as Lee Iacocca, who moved from Ford to Chrysler) and are knowledgeable about that industry but perhaps cognitively wedded to industry conventions or "recipes" (Spender 1989; Hambrick, Geletkanycz, and Fredrickson 1993). More "outside" are new hires who come from different but related industries, such as Raymond Gilmartin, who moved from Becton Dickinson (medical products) to Merck (pharmaceuticals). Finally, the most extreme outsider is the executive who comes from an unrelated industry, such as Lewis Gerstner who went from RJR Nabisco (tobacco and food) to IBM (data-processing equipment and services).

Figure 6–3 also presents, tentatively, the degree to which the four possible objectives of "going outside" (as noted above) might reasonably be expected from each type of appointment. The closer the new CEO is to the extreme outsider, the more the four expected accompaniments can be expected. However, not all the gradations are equal. For instance, a new CEO with medium tenure (five to fifteen years) in the firm can be expected to have somewhat more social/interpersonal openness to change, as a result of fewer long-standing relationships, than one who has long tenure. However, it is unlikely that the appointment of the medium-tenure executive would send any greater external signal of change.

The ratings represented by the plusses, and even the specific ordering of the continuum, in Figure 6–3 are admittedly speculative. However, the concept of the continuum should clearly signify that researchers will achieve stronger predictions—of who will be selected, as well as of the consequences of different types of appointments—if they develop more fine-grained conceptions of inside versus outside. As important, such subtlety in thinking about "outsiderness" could allow much more practical insights for boards, executive search firms, and others involved in executive selection than have been afforded by the dichotomous approaches taken so far.

The Broader Case of Continuity versus Change

The matter of inside versus outside in CEO selection is a variation of the broader issue of continuity versus change. In general, inertia exerts a great force on executive succession. This can occur because of entrenched power configurations, administrative routines, or organizational culture. For example, some companies appoint CEOs, decade after decade after decade, all from the same functional area (Pfeffer 1981a). Sameness in successive CEOs is also due to the human tendency for leaders to believe that their successors should be just like them (Kanter 1977; Hambrick, Geletkanycz, and Fredrickson 1993). In general, there is a striking tendency for new CEOs to resemble their predecessors (Smith and White 1987; Vancil 1987).

Thus, unless there is a countervailing force, not only will successors tend to be insiders, but they will also be the insiders who are most similar to the predecessors. The countervailing, inertia-breaking forces could be environmental shifts, strong boards, or poor performance.

The following propositions can be set forth:

PROPOSITION 6-9

The more stable the environment, the more a successor CEO resembles the predecessor in terms of company tenure, industry tenure, functional track, line-of-business experience, and education.

PROPOSITION 6-10

The more powerful the predecessor CEO, the more the successor resembles the predecessor.

PROPOSITION 6-11

The less powerful or less vigilant the board, the more a successor resembles the predecessor.

PROPOSITION 6-12

The higher the recent performance of the organization, the more a successor resembles the predecessor. Conversely, poor performance leads to a CEO who differs from the predecessor.

Not only will poor performance favor the selection of a new CEO who differs from the incumbent, but also the specific form of the performance shortfall will lead the board toward a new CEO whose credentials and expertise suit the particular challenge confronting the firm. Thus:

PROPOSITION 6-13

Specific types of performance shortfalls are associated with specific successor characteristics. For instance:
1. Poor growth favors candidates with marketing or sales experience or track records for growing businesses.

2. Poor profits, but with satisfactory growth or market share, favor candidates with operations and control experience or track records for consolidating or rationalizing businesses.
3. Problems of litigation or apparent ethical misdeeds favor candidates with legal experience.

In a recent study of 232 CEO successions, Zajac and Westphal (in press) found support for the general argument just set forth and even for some of the specific propositions. Conceiving of CEO selection as a contest between the incumbent CEO and the board, the authors found that the lower the presuccession performance (measured both by stock returns and profitability) and the weaker the predecessor's power (as gauged by the predecessor's tenure, whether he or she held both the chairman and CEO posts, and the proportion of outside directors appointed during his or her tenure), the more dissimilar the new CEO was from the predecessor (in terms of functional background, age, type of educational degree, and type of educational institution). Even more intriguing, Zajac and Westphal found that the same factors that caused a new CEO to be dissimilar from the predecessor were strongly associated with the degree of similarity the new person bore to the average profile of the board. One might conclude, then, that the CEO and the board engage in a contest to clone themselves. As is true of so much in organizations, the result depends on who has the most power. Also apparent is that succession outcomes can be anticipated on the basis of the precipitating conditions and the selection process.

WHAT ARE THE CONSEQUENCES OF SUCCESSION?

Perhaps understandably, researchers have devoted more effort to understanding the consequences of succession, or the "So what?" question, than to the other facets of top executive transitions. Unfortunately, this preoccupation with succession effects has often led researchers to ignore some critically important contextual factors, resulting in many weak and contradictory conclusions.

The care that must be brought to any study of the consequences of executive succession is illustrated by the findings of two studies that played a pivotal role in launching contemporary scholarship on executive succession: Gouldner's (1954) study of management succession in a gypsum plant and Guest's study (1962) in an automobile factory. The new manager of the gypsum plant in Gouldner's study, Peele, succeeded a very popular leader who was socially comfortable with the work force, to the point of being loose and indulgent. The productivity of the plant had slipped, which was why Peele, an outsider, was brought in. However, other inside managers felt that one of them should have been appointed the new leader; moreover, Peele adopted a stern, disciplinarian management style, meting out punishments liberally. Worker morale and productivity plummeted.

The new head of the automobile plant in Guest's study, Cooley, similarly was brought in from the outside to deal with a low-performance situation. His predecessor, however, had many of Peele's qualities—authoritarian, punitive, abrasive. Members of the organization were happy to be rid of him, and Cooley further rallied their support through a participative management style, laxity in enforcing unpopular company rules, and an approachable demeanor. Worker morale and productivity increased greatly.

These two studies, each of which could be a data point in a statistical study of the effects of managerial succession, illustrate by their contrasting outcomes how difficult it is to arrive at general conclusions. Or, put another way, if a researcher wants to develop general conclusions about the effects of executive succession, the predictive model inevitably must encompass an array of factors. Gordon and Rosen (1981) made the same point in a thoughtful article in which they proposed a succession model with numerous "pre-arrival" and "post-arrival" factors. Figure 6–1, a somewhat more formalized variation of Gordon and Rosen's ideas, indicates our thinking: One cannot make cogent predictions about the effects of succession without considering the factors precipitating the succession, the succession process, and the characteristics of the successor. Moreover, events and actions following the succession affect each other; these include the new leader's behaviors, organization changes, organizational performance, and stakeholder reactions.

The New Executive's Behaviors and Organizational Change

The new executive faces a difficult dilemma that complicates the scholar's ability to predict leader behaviors and organizational activities early in a tenure. On the one hand, the new executive often lacks the information to make prudent decisions. On the other, he or she is under great pressure to demonstrate worthiness for the job and managerial efficacy, generally requiring that *some* early actions be taken.

A new executive, even one internally appointed, enters the position at a disadvantage in terms of knowledge of the task at hand; pertinent facts, contacts, trends, and issues are not yet well understood. This is illustrated by a quote from a new general manager studied by Gabarro:

> You go through an early period of first trying like hell to learn about the organization. You're faced with a set of problems that are foreign to you. You have to learn about the people and their capabilities awfully fast and that's the trickiest thing to do. At first you're afraid to do anything for fear of upsetting the apple cart. The problem is you have to keep the business running while you learn about it. (1987, p. 1)

Accordingly, the new executive devotes a great deal of effort to scanning (Aguilar 1967), immersion (Gabarro 1987), and general learning. Mintzberg (1973) proposed that new managers spend relatively more time on developing contacts and collecting information ("liaison" and "monitor" roles) than in substantive strategic decision making. Other researchers have further emphasized the need for the new executive to develop reliable and constructive relationships with members of the top management team (Gabarro 1987; Greiner and Bhambri 1989).

At the same time, the new executive will feel pressure to show promptly that he or she was the right choice for the job. One tendency is for the new leader to spend an extraordinary amount of time with higher-ups (say, the board chair or other board members) to seek information and clarification on what needs to be done (Stewart 1967). A related tendency is for the new executive to try to persuade the board to set "realistic" expectations, as did an executive interviewed by Vancil:

> I felt that it was very important in that first meeting with them [the board] to calibrate their expectations. I didn't want them to think that I was arriving with some magical elixir that would solve our problems immediately. (1987, 59)

Constructive and supportive relationships with members of the management team and the board may well be the most important factors for surviving the first two to three years in a new executive position (Gabarro 1987; Vancil 1987; Greiner and Bhambri 1989). But, in general, the casualty or failure rate among new executives is relatively great. A disproportionate number of dismissals occur in the first several years of executives' tenures (Fredrickson, Hambrick, and Baumrin 1988; Ocasio 1994). New executives generally do not have as much power as more established ones (Hambrick and Fukutomi 1991; Miller 1993). If new executives are vulnerable and must demonstrate their efficacy, they cannot only engage in learning and establishing relationships. They must engage in some substantive actions.

The Going-In Mandate.   We now turn to the types of strategic actions taken by new executives. While no universal pattern occurs, we can improve our predictions and understanding of actions taken by a new executive if we extend a key point made by Gordon and Rosen: "Newly appointed leaders do not function totally independently of their sponsors and of how those around them expect them to function" (1981, 239). Most new executives have a mandate, even if implicit, stemming from the organization's current performance and prospects (Vancil 1987). New executives often are selected because their experiences and credentials align with the mandate, and thus their initial actions also tend to—or should—align with the mandate (Gabarro 1987). Hambrick and Fukutomi illustrated the confluence of organizational situation, mandate, choice of successor, successor credentials, and successor action through a now well-known CEO appointment:

> . . . in 1981 General Electric was extremely profitable, but had a very low growth rate and was weighted down with primarily mature businesses. Among several contenders to replace Reginald Jones as CEO, Jack Welch, the person picked by the board, was known for his impatience and track record of innovation and growing businesses. Even his demographic profile lined up with what seemed to be needed: youth, advanced education in technology, and experience in R&D. There seems little question that Welch had a mandate to inject youth and dynamism into GE; he was picked precisely because it was thought that his paradigm . . . would make the growth and dynamism occur; he was under pressure to behave in line with such expectations. It was not surprising that Welch immediately sold off numerous low-growth businesses, put major resources into high-growth businesses, and sought technological advantage in industries that had not recently been considered in "technological" terms, such as appliances and lighting. (1991, 722)

As a broader indication of the same phenomenon, researchers have consistently found that new executives brought in from the outside make more changes in strategy and staffing than do those from the inside (Grusky 1960; Carlson 1962; Helmich and Brown 1972; Kesner and Dalton 1994). Based on our discussion earlier in the chapter, we may reasonably expect that an outside successor is a mere single indicator of a gestalt: poor performance or environmental shift, the board's desire to break with the past, appointment of an outside successor, and a mandate for major change. However, none of these is binary; all can be considered in scalar, continuous terms. In keeping with our earlier discussion, we propose the following:

PROPOSITION 6–14

The worse the performance of the organization prior to the succession, the greater the strategic, structural, and staffing changes made by the successor.

PROPOSITION 6–15

The more dissimilar the successor is from the predecessor, the greater the changes made by the successor.

PROPOSITION 6–16

The more the successor is an extreme outsider (as portrayed in Figure 6–3), the greater the changes made by the successor.

Further, we anticipate that the combination of 1) a "going-in mandate," 2) the selection of an executive whose credentials align with the mandate, and 3) the new executive's need to demonstrate early efficacy will serve to bring about early strategic actions that strongly reflect the new executive's background. Therefore:

PROPOSITION 6–17

The correspondence between an executive's background characteristics (e.g., insider versus outsider, functional experience, international experience) and the amount and type of strategic actions taken is stronger in the first years of tenure than at any other time in the position.

The Executive's Early Survival Prospects. Executives are well advised to understand and adhere to their early mandates. This is illustrated by a seeming anomaly in Gabarro's (1987) study. At odds with almost all other studies on the topic, Gabarro found that the few new executives from outside the industry that were in his sample made fewer organizational changes in their first three years than did the insiders. His explanation was that insiders possessed more relevant knowledge and could take informed actions faster than the outsiders who had more of a knowledge deficit. However, as noted, the finding itself departed from other available evidence.

But this odd result is put in perspective when coupled with another of Gabarro's findings: a disproportionate number of the few outsiders he studied failed within the first three years. As we have emphasized, outsiders tend to be brought into difficult situations in which the general probability of failure is relatively great, but they are brought in because the board or senior management wants a significant change. If the outsider makes fewer changes than the higher-ups hoped they would get (as seems to be the case in Gabarro's small sample), then he or she has behaved at odds with the mandate.

To deviate from one's early mandate is to increase the likelihood of failure or dismissal for two reasons. First, the executive is probably acting outside the range of his or her primary repertoire, with a relative absence of experience and insight, and misjudgments and missteps may occur. Second, the actions are not consistent with what the board wanted; if an executive embarks in a direction other than the one the board had envisioned, the slightest misstep will evoke much more scorn and retribution than a similar falter in the agreed-upon direction. Thus, someone with a strong background in product innovation who is brought in to instill innovation is well advised not to turn instead to cost rationalization—at least not at the outset.

Consider a further example. After a long reign as CEO of ITT Corporation, Harold Geneen retired and was replaced by a long-time inside lieutenant, Lyman Hamilton, who promptly started divesting many of Geneen's acquisitions. This was not what the board expected or wanted from this particular successor, and he was soon fired (The fact that Geneen remained on the board did not help Hamilton.) (Fredrickson, Hambrick, and Baumrin 1988). Thus, a new CEO's mandate, even if only implicit, restricts his or her discretion (Hambrick and Finkelstein 1987).

We propose:

PROPOSITION 6-18

The greater the correspondence among 1) the new executive's mandate, 2) his or her experiences, and 3) the amount and direction of change initiatives, the greater the likelihood of the executive's survival beyond three years.

In sum, executives' behaviors entering into their positions vary widely and cannot be universally predicted. However, by incorporating the precipitating context, succession process, and successor characteristics into a predictive model, a greatly improved understanding of early executive actions can be achieved. Now we turn more generally to the issue of the performance implications of executive succession.

Implications for Organizational Performance

Does executive succession help or hurt an organization's performance? There can be no general answer to this question. If succession clearly were salutary, it would become quickly known, and organizations would start replacing their executives weekly. If succession were unequivocally harmful, that too would become readily apparent, and organizations would start putting healthy twenty-five-year-olds in top offices and doing everything possible to prolong their lives and connection to the organization, including eliminating mandatory retirement policies for them.

As unpromising as the above research question may seem, it was the initial focus of post-World War II research on managerial succession (Grusky 1963). Fortunately, scholars moved on to more fruitful questions, such as: When do successions hurt or help the most? and What kinds of successors help or hurt the most under different situations? We trace the evolution of this line of research and extract its chief conclusions and implications.

The Sports Team Studies.   Large-sample research on the performance implications of succession began with a series of studies on sports teams. This type of organization, while perhaps only marginally like other organizations, provides researchers the important advantages of a well-controlled sampling procedure and, most appealing, undisputable performance measures.

Grusky (1963) launched this stream with evidence from sixteen baseball teams over a twenty-year period. He found that "rates of administrative succession [of field managers] and degree of organizational effectiveness are negatively correlated" (1963, 21). Rather than impute a one-way causal direction, Grusky concluded that a "vicious circle" operates: poor performing teams tend to replace their managers; and new managers are disruptive to team morale and social structure, hence further hurting performance. Grusky further asserted that the "vicious circle" theory (harmful effects of succession) had won out over the "common-sense" theory (that succession brings improved performance).

However, Gamson and Scotch (1964) reanalyzed Grusky's data and concluded that it was not the "vicious circle" theory, but rather the "ritual scapegoating—no effects" theory that was supported. They contended that managers often are replaced during temporary "slumps"; performance then improves but not because of the manager; and the improvement is not sustained. By examining a subsample of midseason successions, they indeed found that team performance improved immediately following the succession but was rarely sustained. Gamson and Scotch went on to use an analogy that every student of executive succession should bear in mind:

> If we compared average rainfall in the month preceding and the month following the performance of the Hopi rain dance, we would find more rain in the period after. The dance is not performed unless there is a drought, so such a comparison would be misleading. Nevertheless, this "slump-ending" effect may help to account for the tenacity of belief in the effectiveness of the ritual. (1964, 71)

In this anecdote, Gamson and Scotch remind us of two things. First, successions occur disproportionately, albeit not exclusively, in low-performance situations. Even some voluntary departures are acts of escape, fatigue, or anticipation of dismissal in the face of poor performance. Second, a very poorly performing organization in one period is likely to be relatively poorly performing in the next period, but, on average, it will improve somewhat because it would be difficult to go any lower; it can only go up. This is the statistical phenomenon of "regression to the mean"—an essential concept for anyone interested in executive succession.

In a rejoinder, Grusky (1964) introduced the distinction between inside and outside succession. He found that teams experiencing inside succession improved in performance, whereas outside succession was associated with slight deterioration of performance. Grusky asserted that "inside successors tend to be less disruptive than outside successors" (1964, 74).

The next two sports team studies we will review represented considerable advances in this stream of research, with possibly important implications for successions in other types of settings. First was a study by Allen, Panian, and Lotz (1979), again on baseball teams. Their important contribution was in introducing careful controls for regression to the mean. In keeping with the overall thrust of this research stream, they also examined inside and outside successions separately.[4] Figure 6–4 shows how team performance compared between the prior season and the current one for different types of succession changes (the successions occurred between seasons or during the current season). These results, in our assessment, represent the type of results that would occur, on average, for these four succession situations in most organizational settings:

1. *Organizations with no executive succession:* These were high performing to start with, and in the following year, they were still high performing.
2. *Organizations with inside successions:* These were slightly inferior (below average) to start with, and in the following year, they were still slightly inferior.
3. *Organizations with outside successions:* These were very inferior to start with, and in the following year, they improved somewhat, but probably due primarily to regression to the mean.
4. *Organizations with multiple successions:* These were very inferior to start with. Regression to the mean somehow eluded them, and their performance deteriorated even more (no doubt accounting for the multiple successions, or "rain dances").

Thus, *succession events tend to occur under certain conditions.* This may create the erroneous impression that the successions caused the conditions. But the mere act of succession—particularly when the qualities required of the leader have not changed and there is no reason to believe the new

FIGURE 6–4 **Winning Percentages for Baseball Teams Studied by Allen, Panian, and Lotz (1979): Prior Season versus Current Season**

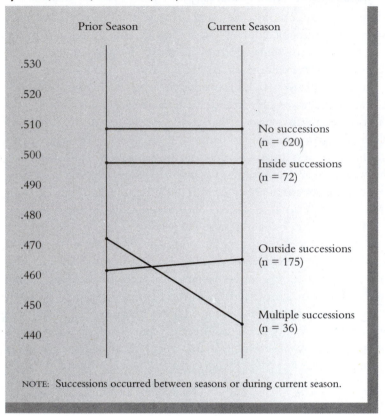

NOTE: Successions occurred between seasons or during current season.

leader is necessarily any better than the old one—allows no convincing predictions about new leader effects.

However, executives do vary in their ability, and that was the chief idea explored by the final sports team study we will review. In their analysis of data for twenty-two professional basketball teams over a five-year period, Pfeffer and Davis-Blake (1986) found, as we would expect, that mere coach succession had no effect on subsequent performance (when prior performance was controlled for). However, when the competence of new coaches was included in the analysis, succession did affect subsequent performance. New coaches who had good prior records, had prior experience coaching in professional basketball, and had led performance improvements in other teams brought more performance improvement to their new assignments than did new coaches without these qualifications. This study introduces the commonsense, but long-overlooked, idea that the effects of succession depend, among other things, on the capability of the new executive.

Research on managerial succession in sports teams has had a bumpy but still worthwhile ride. We know more about several aspects of succession, aided by the relatively reliable, uncontroversial measures of performance available for sports teams.

However, another aspect of sports teams has gone undiscussed in all this research, and it poses considerable limitations on observing any succession effects in such organizations. Specifically, sports teams (particularly in long-established sports) do not face major changes in their environments. Their rules, playing surfaces, ball size, and so on, all remain roughly the same over time. (We are sure baseball aficionados would love to set us straight on this, but even something like the introduction of artificial turf was nothing like deregulation in the airline industry or globalization of the automobile industry). The repertoires of sports coaches are rarely, if ever, fundamentally obsolesced. Succession as an adaptive device (Pfeffer and Salancik 1978) has little relevance in the sports setting.

When the rules change, when environments shift, when major new strategies have to be developed and implemented—these are conditions in which succession effects may be profound.

It Depends on the Succession Context.   Only by moving beyond sports teams can we consider how the context affects the performance implications of CEO succession. Here, we will examine projects that have focused on three particular contexts: young companies, turnaround situations, and environmental turbulence.

It is reasonable to expect that executive succession has differing effects, depending on the organization's stage of life. Carroll (1984) pursued this line of thought, arguing that the departure of the company's first chief executive would be extremely disruptive; because of the fragility of relatively young organizations, the likelihood of company failure after the departure would increase. Testing these ideas with a sample of newspapers founded over a 150-year period in seven randomly selected cities, Carroll's results supported his premise, revealing three interesting findings: 1) newspapers had disproportionately high failure rates following the departure of their first publisher (essentially, the CEO); 2) the failure rate was highest when the publisher was also the editor, presumably because the executive's personality and values had become even more embodied in the newspaper; and 3) the effect of executive departure on organization mortality was greater in the first two years of the newspaper's existence than in the later years studied (years three, six, and eleven). Apparently, as the organization becomes more substantial and institutionalized, departure of the first CEO is not as disruptive. Indeed, with the passing of years and accumulation of resources and legitimacy, CEO succession *per se* should come to have no general effect on failure rates.

In a similar study of local telephone companies in the early twentieth century, Haveman (1993) found results like Carroll's: presidential exit increased organization mortality. These effects were pronounced in younger organizations and diminished as time passed. Thus, there appear to be organizational conditions under which executive continuity is particularly important to organizational performance and survival.

However, there may be other organizational situations in which executive transition is generally beneficial. Writers on corporate turnarounds have consistently emphasized that new leadership is needed for a turnaround to be successful. Based on extensive case data, Hofer (1980) asserted that a change in leadership is needed if a turnaround is to be successful because incumbent management has a difficult time making the required changes and has lost too much credibility with key stakeholders. Bibeault (1982) made essentially the same point but also provided some quantitative data on CEO changes in troubled turnaround situations. Of eighty-two turnaround situations he studied, about three-fourths involved new CEOs. Of those new CEOs, about two-thirds were from the outside, supporting the general portrayal of the need for new perspective, energy, and credibility at the top of troubled firms.

These changes of CEOs could amount to little more than ritual scapegoating, or "rain dances." In fact, neither Bibeault nor other researchers, as far as we know, have provided telling evidence of the *results* that come from different CEO succession patterns in turnaround situations. We believe, in general, that a change of management, and particularly bringing in an outsider, provides the best chance for performance improvement in a turnaround.

Beyond considering the organizational context for executive succession, we must also incorporate the environmental context. If the environment is turbulent, and particularly if there is a major discontinuity, incumbent executive competencies may be obsolete. Under such conditions, executive succession may generally be salutary. Virany, Tushman, and Romanelli (1992) pursued this idea with a sample of companies in the minicomputer industry (1968 to 1980), an environment of great turbulence and, according to the authors, one in which fresh perspective (or "second-order learning") was a continuing imperative. The authors found that CEO succession, in general, was associated with profit improvements in the minicomputer industry. The authors also found that performance improved the most through a combination of CEO change, top management team change, and strategic change. But the essential conclusion here is that a turbulent environment tends to favor change at the top.

We earlier derided the idea that a change in CEO *per se* could have any generalizable effect on performance. Thus, we need to offer a line of defense for the conclusion that succession may be beneficial in certain environments. Here, we develop the idea of "fit—drift/shift—refit." We posit that a board, when selecting a chief executive, strives to appoint a person whose competencies or repertoire align, or *fit*, with the conditions facing the enterprise at that time and for the foreseeable future. The new executive may not fit perfectly (in fact, we have discussed the inertial and political factors that may make selections depart from the normative ideal), but, in general, the new executive will tend to be more appropriate than a randomly selected executive and, in many cases, highly appropriate.

The executive embarks on actions, drawing on his or her competencies and perhaps learning new ones. However, with the passage of time, the environment gradually *drifts*, or perhaps radically *shifts*, in a direction that requires competencies and perspectives different from those of the incumbent. The executive who can evolve cognitively at the same rate and in the same direction as the environment is exceedingly rare. Thus, the CEO who initially fit the specific contextual requirements will, over time, fit less well.

Whether the executive serves until mandatory retirement or departs in some other way, eventually the board has another opportunity to *refit* executive competencies with the new requirements of the environment and organization. So, on average, new executives will fit current and emerging requirements more than departing executives.

For example, when Reginald Jones was made CEO of General Electric in the early 1970s, the company was experiencing what observers called "profitless growth"—numerous entries into new industries and explosive expansion, but poor returns. Jones brought discipline and order to GE, and by the year of his mandatory retirement 1981, the company faced essentially the opposite situation: exceedingly high profits but little growth. International opportunities were untapped, new technologies had yet to be exploited, and the service economy was passing by GE. With Jones's departure, the board had an opportunity to refit executive capabilities with the new and emerging conditions. It chose to hire Jack Welch, known for his innovation, impatience, and expertise in technology (Aguilar, Hamermesh, and Brainard 1991; Tichy and Sherman 1993).

The "fit—drift/shift—refit" model is not a deterministic view; we are describing tendencies. Not all selection decisions are adaptive; naive scapegoating, cloning, and careless selection can occur. However, we believe this framework allows a coherent line of thought for explaining the important finding that succession in changing environments tends to bring performance improvements.

Reactions of Shareholders.   On the assumption that executive succession events may contain important signaling information, researchers have explored the reactions of shareholders. This has resulted in a quite sizable literature that can be best characterized as inconsistent: widely so in research designs (measures and model specifications) and correspondingly so in results. (See Warner, Watts, and Wruck 1988 and Furtado and Karan 1990 for extensive reviews; also see these recent works: Beatty and Zajac 1987; Friedman and Singh 1989; Lubatkin et al. 1989; Worrell, Davidson, and Glascock 1993).

One of the major obstacles to interpreting these studies is that they often include succession events that are routine and fully anticipated by investors; thus, they elicit no particular market reaction when the succession is announced or implemented. Perhaps only unexpected deaths of CEOs meet the requirements of an event-study test. Such a study found, on average, no stock market reaction (Johnson et al. 1985).

Doubt has even been expressed about whether most CEO dismissals are sufficiently "surprising" to meet the requirements of a satisfactory event-study test. However, at least two studies have found that firings or "board-initiated" departures of CEOs meet with positive stock market reactions (Friedman and Singh 1989; Worrell, Davidson, and Glascock 1993). Probably occurring disproportionately in troubled firms, these dismissals may give owners some hope that policies will be changed.

An important refinement in this stream of research has been to distinguish analytically between the departure announcement and the successor announcement. While this distinction has added to the complex variety of operationalizations, it has produced one interesting finding in at least three studies: the appointment of an outsider CEO elicits a favorable stock market reaction. But even here, the qualifications of each result diminish the clarity of the pattern: Reinganum (1985) found that CEO departure coupled with announcement of an external successor brought positive market response but only for the smaller firms in his sample;[5] Worrell, Davidson, and Glascock (1993) found that firings coupled with outsider appointments brought favorable market response (supporting the "change is on the way" theory); but Lubatkin and associates (1989) found that the appointment of outsiders into high-performing firms brought a favorable market response, casting doubt on the simple scapegoating theory. These disparate results are a microcosm of the varying results in this whole research stream.

We offer four suggestions to scholars who are considering their own studies of stock market reactions to executive succession. First, strive to incorporate some of the logics laid out in this chapter and elsewhere in the book: be alert to the concept of executive discretion and include in your model appropriate contextual factors (precipitating context, succession process, predecessor and successor characteristics). Second, only include in your sample those succession events that are near or total surprises to the investment community; otherwise, their reactions cannot be captured. For instance, a CEO's departure due to mandatory retirement or the appointment of a long-designated heir apparent is subtly and gradually factored into stock prices well before the actual event occurs. Third, consider doing very direct replications of some of the better-done prior studies. You might focus on different populations of firms or different time periods, but the aim should be to find out whether a given pattern has any stability or robustness. This stream of research has used an ever-shifting set of variables and models, yielding understandably inconsistent results. A direct replication could allow you to be the first researcher to find the same result that others have found! Fourth, consider comparing the market reaction to the succession announcement to the actual performance of the firm over the first two to three years of the executive's tenure. To what extent are positive (or negative) initial reactions borne out? Such a study might allow important insights about executive reputations, the "romance of leadership" (Meindl, Erlich, and Dukerich 1985), and investors' faith in "rain dances."

EXECUTIVE TURNOVER: A TOP MANAGEMENT TEAM PERSPECTIVE

Turnover in executive ranks, beyond the CEO, may also be reflective or predictive of important organizational phenomena. Although not studied as much as CEO turnover, the departures of other executives on top management teams have been examined in some research.

The most consistent predictor of top executive turnover, as with CEOs, is organizational performance. Wagner, Pfeffer, and O'Reilly (1984) found, in a sample of thirty-one large firms, that the correlation between the proportion of the top management group departing (over a five-year period) and the firm's profitability relative to its industry was -.44. Boeker (1992), in his study of semiconductor firms, found a similarly strong association between low performance and executive departures (specifically dismissals).

However, as with CEOs, performance does not fully explain executive turnover rates. Rather, other factors—including sociopolitical factors—are important as well. First, departure reflects power. In a very intriguing analysis, Boeker (1992) found that in poorly performing firms, highly powerful CEOs (those with large shareholdings and surrounded by a large proportion of inside board members) were not dismissed. However, the dismissal rate of their lieutenants was very high. The powerful CEOs were able to deflect scapegoating and pass it on to their fellow executives. Boeker did not examine which specific executives were dismissed, but we could reasonably expect that their individual power (their own stockholdings, their elite connections, the degree of fit between their competencies and the firm's critical contingencies, and so on [Finkelstein 1992]) would be highly predictive of their own retention versus departure. Thus:

PROPOSITION 6-19

The greater an executive's power within a top management group, the less likely he or she is to be dismissed when the firm is performing poorly.

Executive departure may be due to internal social forces as well. As Wagner, Pfeffer, and O'Reilly (1984) found, relational demography of the top management group affected executive turnover. Specifically, the more heterogeneous the group, in terms of tenure in the firm, the higher the departure rate of the executives. And at the individual level, the more distant a given executive is from other members of the group (in terms of age), the greater the likelihood of his or her specific departure. The authors argue, in line with a well-established line of thought in social psychology, that demographic similarity enhances social integration, which in turn aids communication and cohesion. When group members are dissimilar, social bonds are weak, and both voluntary and involuntary departures are greater. Those members most dissimilar from the majority of the group will be most likely to leave. Jackson and associates (1991) found the same result, using additional demographic dimensions. Thus:

PROPOSITION 6-20

The greater the demographic dissimilarity of top management group members, the greater the rate of turnover within the group.

PROPOSITION 6-21

The more dissimilar a specific executive from the demographic central tendencies of the top management group, the greater the likelihood of his or her departure.

However, an executive's likelihood of departure may be even greater to the extent that he or she is dissimilar from the characteristics of the *most powerful* group members, not simply from the *average* characteristics of all group members. Top management groups often have clear power strata—if only by hierarchical level—and an executive who is very unlike those in the highest strata experiences the combination of social distance described by Wagner, Pfeffer, and O'Reilly (1984) and the vulnerability of being distant from the political center. For example, if the three top-most executives, including the CEO, all have marketing backgrounds, a vice-president with a manufacturing background is relatively likely to depart. Due to a combination of social and political forces, we anticipate:

PROPOSITION 6–22

The more dissimilar a specific executive from the demographic characteristics of the most powerful executives in the group, the greater the likelihood of his or her departure. This will be a stronger association than the one described in Proposition 6–21.

Although dissimilarity may be a precursor to executive departure, there may be special circumstances when demographic similarity heightens the likelihood of turnover. Here, we speak specifically of the situation in which several executives share many characteristics—and particularly are about the same age—and all aspire to be the next CEO. Too much similarity can create direct rivalries that would not exist if executive characteristics were more dispersed (Vancil 1987). Not only may the rivals act antagonistically toward each other during the succession tournament (heightening chances of friction and departures); but after the succession decision has been made, the winner may engage in retaliatory actions (even unwittingly), and the tournament losers may leave voluntarily.

We consider the implications of CEO succession for the turnover of other executives to be very interesting and potentially important. Beyond the tendency for substantial turnover immediately following a CEO succession (Helmich and Brown 1972; Gabarro 1986), this general domain has not been studied. It may be that demographic similarity of contenders could affect departure rates, as we suggested above. And, the nature of the succession process—whether it is a horse race or a relay, how visible the horse race is, how many contenders there are, how close to the incumbent's departure the race is held—may have very strong effects on executive turnover.

The implications of top team turnover (beyond only CEO turnover) for organizational performance have received little attention by scholars. One study in the minicomputer industry, by Virany, Tushman, and Romanelli (1992), found two distinct patterns associated with high performance. The most typical mode was a combination of CEO succession, sweeping team changes, and strategic reorientation. The authors argued that this is the dramatic combination of events needed to adapt in a turbulent industry such as minicomputers. However, the second and rarer mode involved strategic reorientation and major team changes but continuity in the CEO. These firms, the authors argued, were able to simultaneously inject fresh perspective and learning (through major turnover within the team), while maintaining links to established organizational resources and competencies (through retention of the CEO). Across both modes, however, it becomes apparent that team turnover has implications for performance beyond those from CEO turnover. In this particular industry—turbulent, with frequent discontinuities—top team turnover appears to be beneficial.

However, as with CEO turnover, a different context may cause team turnover to have different effects. Here, a study of failing firms conducted by Hambrick and D'Aveni (1992) is instructive. This study of fifty-seven large bankruptcies and fifty-seven matched survivors examined the top management team characteristics associated with corporate failure. The failing firms showed divergence from survivors on several indicators of TMT composition, for each of the five years before bankruptcy (smaller management teams; shorter tenures; smaller proportions of executives with core function experience, i.e., in marketing or sales, operations, and R&D; and lower executive compensation). Moreover, those differences became more pronounced, at an accelerating rate, over the five-year period. Through cross-lagged analysis of team-changes and performance-changes, the authors concluded that a two-way causal process, or a "vicious circle," was at work (Figure 6–5): 1) team deficiencies bring about or aggravate corporate deterioration, either through strategic errors or stakeholder uneasiness with the visibly inadequate team; and 2) corporate deterioration brings about team deterioration, through a combination of voluntary departures (often of the most mobile and able executives), scapegoating, and limited resources for attracting new executive talent. Hambrick and D'Aveni posited that even though there may be ways to arrest this downward spiral, it has a compelling momentum that seriously complicates corporate turnarounds in a way that turnaround scholars and consultants had not previously considered.

Another context in which to consider top team turnover—both its causes and its effects—is in corporate acquisitions. Acquisitions are socially disruptive events that provide a crucible for studying turnover phenomena. Often, acquirers have strong preferences—one way or the other—about retaining acquired executives. On one matter, research data are highly consistent: executives in acquired firms depart at an extraordinarily high rate,

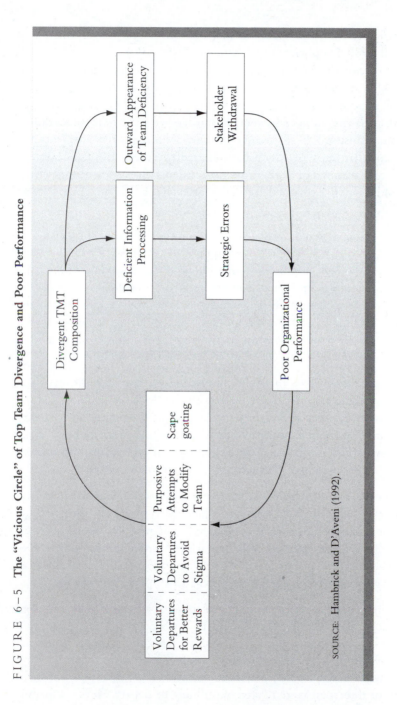

FIGURE 6-5   The "Vicious Circle" of Top Team Divergence and Poor Performance

SOURCE: Hambrick and D'Aveni (1992).

roughly twice the rate as under normal circumstances (Hayes and Hoag 1974; Walsh 1989; Hambrick and Cannella 1993).

But what are the factors that affect the rate of acquired executive departure? Under an agency perspective, the prior performance of the acquired firm should have a significant effect because the acquirers will want to dismiss the acquired executives if they deem them inadequate. Indeed, preacquisition performance of the acquired firm accounts for some variance in rates of executive departure (Walsh 1989). However, Hambrick and Cannella (1992) argued that departures of acquired executives could be best explained by the relatively robust concept of "relative standing":

> Acquisitions are often surrounded by an aura of conquest (Haspeslagh & Jemison, 1991; Hirsch, 1986). If the acquirers feel dominant or superior, and they reveal those feelings in their interactions with, and policies toward, the acquired executives (including, but not limited to, outright dismissal), the departure rate of the acquired executives will be affected. Similarly, if the acquired executives feel inferior, stripped of status, or locked in a struggle with the acquirers, they will tend to depart. Obviously, the attitudes and actions of the acquirers and the acquired influence each other. . . . (p. 735)

They tested these ideas on a sample of ninety-seven acquisitions, with several highly significant results in line with the "relative standing" argument. Not only did preacquisition performance of the acquired firm vary inversely with departure rates (as agency theory would predict), but the *gap* between the acquiring firm's and the acquired firm's preacquisition performance was an even stronger predictor. As the authors asserted:

> . . . perceptions and behaviors of superiority and inferiority are calibrated on the basis of both firms' performances. Where the gap between them is large, acquired executives are particularly likely to depart, possibly because of a variety of intervening factors: self-doubt about their capabilities and prospects in the combined firm, denigration and status degradation at the hands of the acquiring executives, and outright dismissal. (p. 756)

Other indicators of relative standing were also associated with acquired executive departure: friendly mergers led to low departure rates; contested tender offers were followed by high departure rates; the removal of autonomy (imposition of acquirer's policies) brought about more departure; and executives who were personally granted status in the postacquisition firm (as officers or directors) were relatively unlikely to depart. Hence, on multiple dimensions, the argument that "relative standing" is a major basis for acquired executive retention versus departure was supported.

In another paper, drawing from the same sample, Cannella and Hambrick (1993) sought to test the implications of executive departure for the postacquisition performance of the acquired entity. Using ratings of pre- and postacquisition performance from company executives and security analysts (who showed strong consistency in their ratings), the authors explored several hypotheses about the contingency conditions (prior performance, relatedness, and so on) that might moderate any effects between executive departure and performance. However, only a simple and straightforward relationship was found: the higher the rate of executive departure in the first two years after an acquisition, the worse the performance of the acquired entity four years after being acquired. Even among those acquisitions that had the worst preacquisition performance, the greatest improvement in performance came to those with the lowest departure rates. The authors concluded that acquisitions are so disruptive—to internal decision and social processes, as well as to relationships with stakeholders—that, in general, the departure of senior executives aggravates an already very strained and fragile situation.

As this research on acquired executive departure illustrates, there is ample and important need to focus on executive turnover beyond the CEO. Examining the determinants of executive turnover will allow useful insights into social and political phenomena in organizations. And studying the consequences of team-level turnover, particularly on performance, will allow eventually greater understanding than would be obtained by focusing only on CEO turnover.

In summary, turnover at the top is both a reflection of, as well as a cause of, important organizational phenomena. However, an understanding of these patterns and underlying processes can be achieved only if the various elements of executive and top team turnover—the precipitating context, succession events and processes, successor characteristics, and succession outcomes—are treated as an interdependent whole.

NOTES

1. See Furtado and Karan (1990) and Kesner and Sebora (1994) for alternative frameworks of executive succession.
2. In a survey of fifteen hundred senior executives of large companies in twenty countries, 80 percent of the respondents rated experience in the firm's primary industry as an important or very important (4 or 5 on a 5-point scale) credential for the company's future CEO (Korn/Ferry International and Columbia University 1989).
3. Some typical definitions of "outsider" include: anyone with fewer than two years' employment at the company (Cannella and Lubatkin [1993]); anyone who

has never worked for the company (Boeker and Goodstein [1993]); and anyone who did not report directly to the preceding CEO (Dalton and Kesner [1985]).

4. They also split out between-season and midseason successions. However, their use of overall season performance, no matter when in the current season the succession occurred, makes these comparisons tenuous in our opinion.

5. Our interpretation is that smaller firms allow more managerial discretion, that is, opportunity for executive impact, and hence, the stock market responds favorably to outside succession in such firms.

SEVEN

BOARDS OF DIRECTORS AND CORPORATE GOVERNANCE

All public companies have boards of directors, ostensibly to hire and fire senior executives, to set compensation, to review, approve, and evaluate firm strategy, and to generally act as overseers of company business (American Law Institute 1984). In spite of how seemingly straightforward these directives are, scholars studying boards of directors have raised numerous concerns about this normative model, challenging both its assumptions and implications. These efforts have produced a set of theoretical perspectives that examine what boards actually do and how they operate.

Resource dependence theorists have argued that boards can be used as a mechanism to reduce environmental uncertainty by co-opting external actors representing critical contingencies for the organization (Pfeffer 1972; Burt 1983). Social class theorists have focused more on managerial elites and board interlocks (Useem 1979; Mizruchi and Stearns

1988). Some earlier work of a more descriptive nature by management theorists examined what boards really do, often concluding that boards are more inert than active (Mace 1971; Herman 1981; Vance 1983; Wolfson 1984). More recently, agency theorists have placed boards at the center of corporate governance by emphasizing their role in monitoring[1] and disciplining top management (Fama and Jensen 1983). In this chapter, we discuss these various perspectives with the purpose of developing a model of boards of directors as we review appropriate research to suggest some new directions and guide future work on corporate governance. A primary goal is to spur further work on this topic that informs the study of both strategic leadership and the role of boards in strategic leadership.

Conceptually, boards of directors fulfill two roles in organizations. First, they act as buffers and boundary spanners, linking organizations to critical resources in the environment and to valuable information residing in a network of director interlocks (Price 1963; Zald 1969; Pfeffer 1972). Second, they play a role in administration and internal control, putatively responsible for setting policy and monitoring management (Zald 1969; Fama and Jensen 1983). These two roles, the first externally directed and the second internally focused, are implicit in virtually every theoretical formulation involving boards of directors. Nevertheless, alternative theoretical perspectives differ in the importance they place on each role and on the assessment of a board's effectiveness in fulfilling each role.

We consider both externally and internally focused board activities to the extent that they relate to strategic leadership. Our main interest in boards is focused on an understanding of 1) their structure and composition and 2) their direct and indirect effects on executive leadership and strategic choice. Such a treatment is consistent with the theme of this book and facilitates a focused discussion of boards; in addition, the huge volume of work in this area necessitates limiting our scope. Boards influence an organization's strategic choice to the extent they are involved in strategic decision making or, more commonly, in monitoring top management as they make strategic decisions.

Figure 7-1 presents a model of boards of directors that highlights how boards fit into executive leadership and strategic choice. The model depicts the major contextual conditions that influence board characteristics, such as composition and structure. These contextual conditions include critical contingencies faced by the firm, institutional forces (social class influences and managerial elites), and agency conditions. Board characteristics, in turn, affect board vigilance and behavior—both in terms of monitoring and disciplining top management and of involvement in setting strategy. These board actions have numerous and important consequences according to our

FIGURE 7-1 A Model of Boards of Directors

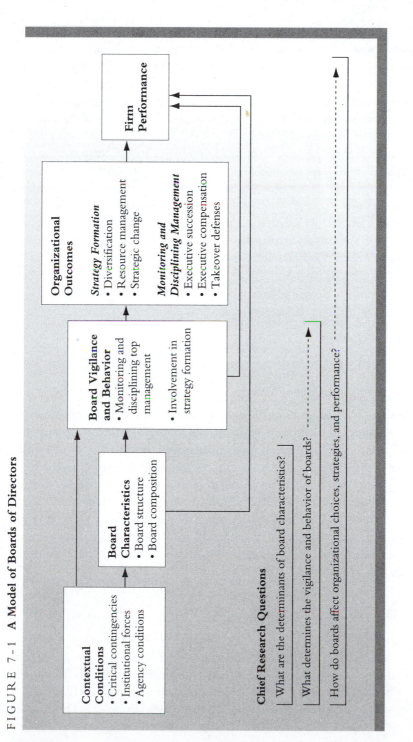

Contextual Conditions
• Critical contingencies
• Institutional forces
• Agency conditions

Board Characteristics
• Board structure
• Board composition

Board Vigilance and Behavior
• Monitoring and disciplining top management

• Involvement in strategy formation

Organizational Outcomes

Strategy Formation
• Diversification
• Resource management
• Strategic change

Monitoring and Disciplining Management
• Executive succession
• Executive compensation
• Takeover defenses

Firm Performance

Chief Research Questions

What are the determinants of board characteristics?

What determines the vigilance and behavior of boards?

How do boards affect organizational choices, strategies, and performance?

model. The organizational outcomes affected by board vigilance and strategic involvement reflect boards' dual external and internal roles in organizations and include various strategic outcomes, such as diversification, resource management, and change, as well as internal management activities related to executive succession, compensation, and entrenchment. In addition, our model also illustrates how board vigilance and strategic involvement can affect firm performance. This model is valuable for both its potential to develop a predictive framework of board phenomena and its parsimonious treatment of a wide-ranging literature. It also highlights a key set of research questions on boards of directors of special interest to those who desire to better understand strategic leadership: 1) What are the determinants of board characteristics? 2) What are the determinants of board vigilance and behavior? and 3) How do boards affect organizational choices, strategies, and performance? The remainder of this chapter is organized along the lines suggested by these questions.

DETERMINANTS OF BOARD STRUCTURE AND COMPOSITION

A useful starting point is consideration of the characteristics of boards of directors. While it is possible to identify numerous dimensions of boards, our focus is limited to structure and composition for several reasons.[2] First, board structure and composition are arguably the most fundamental of board dimensions, accounting for the vast majority of research on boards (Zahra and Pearce 1989). Second, the determinants and consequences of board structure and composition are strongly rooted in strategic leadership, since structure and composition address social, psychological, and economic aspects of strategic choice. In contrast, other board dimensions, such as processes and committees, have been studied less often and with less of a strategic orientation.

What Do We Mean by Board Structure and Composition?

Board structure refers to the formal organization of the board of directors; its major dimensions are size and the division of labor between the board chair and the CEO. The size of a board is straightforward, defined by the number of directors. Board size has been studied for a long time (Zald 1969) and has often been viewed as a key attribute (Pfeffer 1972). The second important component of board structure is the formal structure of the chair and CEO positions. CEO duality refers to the situation in which both titles are held by one person; the separation of chair and CEO positions can simply be called nonduality. CEO duality is one of the most contentious issues in public debates about the role of boards of directors, with most commentators recommending a separation of the top two positions in a firm (e.g., Lorsch 1989). However, the duality structure may be advantageous in situations requiring strong leadership (Finkelstein and D'Aveni 1994). Hence, CEO duality is an interesting structural characteristic of boards.

In contrast to structure, the composition of a board of directors defines the affiliations of each director. A corporate board is composed of the following: 1) top managers of the firm (inside directors); 2) representatives of other organizations that do not offer their services to the firm (outside directors); 3) representatives of other organizations that conduct business with the firm or with key persons within the firm (e.g., lawyers for family owners) or are otherwise affiliated with the firm (affiliated directors); and (4) members of the founding family of the firm or relatives of the incumbent top management, who are themselves not officers of the firm (family directors). Although each of these groups may have different motives and hence may behave differently (Van Nuys 1993), most earlier research on board composition employed the simpler categorization of insider and outsider. Board composition has been recognized as one of the most significant board dimensions, as witnessed by the overwhelming number of articles in which it is incorporated (Zahra and Pearce 1989).

Board composition can also be studied from a demographic perspective. Hence, composition is also defined by such characteristics as the age, tenure, managerial experience, industry experience, and heterogeneity of the members. Interestingly, this implies that it may be possible to extend upper-echelons theory to the board of directors and study the relationship between various board member characteristics and organizational outcomes. Later, we review the few studies that have been conducted along these lines (e.g., Goodstein, Gautum, and Boeker 1994).

One final aspect of composition is the shareholdings of each director; it may hold great potential to explain much about boards, such as their relative power. After outside director representation (typically measured as the percentage of directors on a board who are outsiders), director equity is the next most studied board characteristic. In many studies, however, the definition of director shareholdings depends on the definition of inside, outside, affiliated, and family directors. Thus, measures of composition and shareholdings are often correlated.

It is also important to study how the characteristics of boards change over time. This is especially relevant because changes in board characteristics are caused by exit of existing board members, and entry of new directors. Directors leave their positions for numerous reasons: mandatory retirement, illness or death, moving to a more prestigious directorship, insufficient time to perform effectively, dismissal by a new CEO, disagreement with other board members or the CEO, or avoidance of the stigma of associating with a poorly performing firm. Nevertheless, in contrast to the large body of work on CEO turnover (discussed in Chapter 6), studies on director turnover and selection are limited.[3]

We now turn to examining the first part of Figure 7-1, outlining the major contextual conditions that determine board characteristics—the impact of critical contingencies, institutional forces, and agency conditions.

Critical Contingencies

Critical contingencies emanate from multiple sources but find common ground in the challenge they represent for organizations to address the imperatives they impose. Although critical contingencies are sometimes considered solely in terms of environmental exigencies, we also consider imperatives that arise from firm strategy and performance.

A central tenet of resource dependence theory is that firms attempt to reduce the uncertainty associated with their environments (Thompson 1967). This uncertainty derives from the need to acquire critical resources from environmental actors (Pfeffer and Salancik 1978; Miles 1982). Boards of directors can be used to help reduce interorganizational dependencies by establishing interlocking directorates (Dooley 1969; Burt 1980; Pennings 1980; Mintz and Schwartz 1981;) or co-optation strategies (Thompson and McEwen 1958; Pfeffer 1972; Burt 1979). Co-optation is "the process of absorbing new elements into the leadership or policy-determining struc-ture of an organization as a means of averting threats to its stability or exis-tence" (Selznick 1949, 13). The implication is that directors are selected for their ability to reduce environmental uncertainty by providing access to resources critical to a firm.

Strong empirical support exists for this perspective. Pfeffer (1972), studying eighty manufacturing companies, found that firms with relatively greater financial needs had more bankers on their boards, more directors, and a greater proportion of outsiders and lawyers. In a follow-up study of fifty-seven hospitals, Pfeffer found that "hospitals operating with relatively more government money . . . tended to place more importance on select-ing board members for their political connections"(1973, 358). More gen-erally, organizational responsiveness to environmental requirements tends to increase both the size and diversity of boards (Pfeffer 1972; Pfeffer 1973).

These studies built on earlier work by sociologists such as Zald (1967), who found that directors of nonprofit organizations were selected on the basis of their ability to raise funds and to deal with environmental threats. The basic logic of the resource dependence approach has been supported in more recent studies as well (Provan 1980; Birnbaum 1984; Mizruchi and Stearns 1988; Boeker and Goodstein 1991; Pearce and Zahra 1992; Stearns and Mizruchi 1993).

Although co-optation strategies are generally described as mechanisms to reduce uncertainty (Pfeffer 1972), co-optation may work both ways. For example, a director who represents a bank may encourage a heavier debt load because this provides business for the director's firm. Thus, while directors may be appointed to enhance access to needed resources, they may also be fulfilling their own instrumental needs (Aldrich 1979; Mizruchi 1982; Mizruchi and Stearns 1988).

A second type of critical contingency may derive from the firm's strategy. Arguing that successful diversification requires 1) skills in portfolio management (Leontiades and Tezel 1981) and acquisition integration (Dundas and Richardson 1982), 2) access to external capital markets (Oster 1990), and 3) knowledge of different technologies (Roberts and Berry 1985), Pearce and Zahra (1992) found that diversification was positively associated with board size and outside director representation. These results are consistent with Baysinger and Zeithaml (1986), who also found differences in demographic characteristics of board members in diversified and nondiversified firms.

Firm performance may also affect board structure and composition. Considerable evidence exists that poorly performing firms have a higher rate of managerial turnover (e.g., Wagner, Pfeffer, and O'Reilly 1983). To the extent that some of this turnover affects insiders and these insiders are replaced by outsiders on the board (to offer fresh perspectives or to enhance monitoring), poor firm performance should lead to greater outside director representation. In a study of 142 large firms between 1971 and 1983, Hermalin and Weisbach (1988) found that decreasing profits were associated with more outsiders, consistent with the logic above. However, Pearce and Zahra (1992) reported an opposite result for their sample of 119 Fortune 500 firms in 1986, as did Hambrick and D'Aveni (1992) in their study of 114 bankrupt and surviving firms. Interestingly, in contrast to Hermalin and Weisbach (1988), Hambrick and D'Aveni showed how outside director turnover was part of a "downward spiral" of top team deterioration, with the departure rate of outsiders increasing as the firm neared bankruptcy (1992, 1464). In another study, however, Gilson (1990) examined 111 distressed firms between 1979 and 1985 and found no relationship between firm performance and outside director representation.

These inconsistent findings may be due to differences in performance measures (Hermalin and Weisbach used market-based measures, Pearce and Zahra used accounting-based measures, and Hambrick and D'Aveni, along with Gilson, identified samples of firms in or near bankruptcy), in the time periods studied, and in model specification (Hermalin and Weisbach measured both firm performance and outside director representation as changes from the previous year, Pearce and Zahra lagged firm performance and used an absolute measure of outside director representation, Hambrick and D'Aveni used several of these approaches, and Gilson reported simple means over time). Performance as an explanation for director turnover also may derive more from an institutional perspective than from a critical contingencies logic. The following section develops this line of argument.

Institutional Forces

Research on social class theory and managerial elites suggests a different explanation for the composition of boards. According to this stream of work, a capitalist class culture develops from interactions among directors (Useem 1979; Ratcliff 1980; Useem 1984). An individual's power in this so-called "business elite" depends on his or her position in the social network, which is determined in part by the directorships he or she holds (Warner and Abegglen 1955; Porter 1957; Clement 1975). The directorship is a means of establishing and maintaining contact with other important people in the business elite (Mariolis and Jones 1982). As Koenig, Gogel, and Sonquist (1979, 177) have argued, interlocking directorships allow "business leaders to occupy several influential positions simultaneously so that they can more effectively promote their own and allied interests in both the economic and social spheres." Often this upper echelon of business people enjoys memberships in the same elite social clubs, business groups, and government policy forums. For them, directorships provide intangible rewards and prestige that are valued in the business elite (Allen 1974; Useem 1979; Mizruchi 1982; Palmer 1983; Davis 1993).

The implication from this work is that directors may be selected to boards because of their personal connections throughout a community of individuals (Mintzberg 1983).[4] Although some have argued that boards really are not "old boys' clubs" anymore (Lorsch 1989, 4), persuasive evidence on board interlocks and the business elite continues to accumulate. For example, in a study of directors in the largest U.S. companies, Davis (1993) reported that the number of new boards to which directors were appointed in the 1980s depended on 1) the number of other boards of which they were already members and 2) the network interlock centrality of boards on which they already held directorships. Contrary to agency theory predictions (Fama and Jensen 1983),[5] directors of better performing firms were not more likely to join new boards than directors of poorer performers, and directors of hostile takeover targets were not less likely than other directors to join new boards. In sum, this study provided evidence in support of institutional factors, including director prestige and position in the managerial elite, as predictors of director selection but did not support predictions from an agency theory perspective.

Research on director interlocks and social class theory highlights the prestigious nature of a directorship and how it may enhance an individual's standing in the managerial elite (Allen 1974; Useem 1979). While membership in the managerial elite connotes success, however, it also implies an obligation to uphold a collective image of winning. Directors who sit on the board of a poorly performing firm may threaten their own position in the elite.[6] This idea is not much different from Fama and Jensen's (1983) contention that a primary motivation of outside directors is to protect and build their reputation. To the extent that directors are not successful in their fiduciary duties, there may even be an *ex post facto* "settling up" that exacts a price in terms of director reputation and the consequential rewards that accrue (Fama 1980; Gilson 1990; Kaplan and Rishus 1990; Hambrick and D'Aveni 1992). The logic of this argument suggests several propositions, only one of which has been tested.

PROPOSITION 7-1

The lower a firm's performance, the greater the likelihood of director turnover.[7] (Hermalin and Weisbach [1988] found no support for this proposition in their study, while Hambrick and D'Aveni's [1992] and Gilson's [1990] studies of distressed firms and Walsh and Kosnik's [1993] study of hostile takeovers were supportive.)

PROPOSITION 7-2

The greater the number and prestige of a director's other directorships, the greater the likelihood of that director's turnover in poorly performing firms.

PROPOSITION 7-3

Turnover by a director who is a CEO of his or her own firm will be more likely than by other directors when firm performance is low.[8]

Agency Conditions

We use the term "agency conditions" to refer to the distribution of power between a board and its CEO. As might be expected, agency conditions derive from a set of trade-offs between boards and CEOs, and often center around the ability of boards to effectively monitor top management. Although we discuss the issue of monitoring in more detail when we examine board vigilance and involvement in setting strategy later in this chapter, it is important to examine how agency conditions determine board characteristics, which we state in two propositions:

PROPOSITION 7-4

The greater the need for monitoring effectiveness, the greater the incidence of board characteristics that strengthen the independence of the board.

PROPOSITION 7-5

The greater the relative power of the board, the stronger the relationship between the need for monitoring effectiveness and board characteristics that strengthen the independence of the board.[9]

The first of these propositions has a significant normative element because it implies that boards have the power to strengthen their position when they need to. Although this may seem at odds with a strict distribution of power perspective, some support for this prediction exists. Harrison, Torres, and Kukalis (1988) found that return on assets was negatively associated with the consolidation of the chair and CEO positions, suggesting that boards in poorly performing firms (presumably in need of monitoring effectiveness) were able to enhance their independence by ensuring a separation of the CEO and chair positions.

Of relevance to Proposition 7-5, Finkelstein and D'Aveni (1994) recently reexamined the CEO duality issue and found that powerful boards were less likely to favor CEO duality when firm performance was poor. Interestingly, both this study and Harrison, Torres, and Kukalis (1988) reported a positive and significant association between outside director representation and CEO duality, ostensibly because CEO duality "contributes to a unity of command at the top that helps ensure the existence or illusion of strong leadership in a firm" (Finkelstein and D'Aveni 1994, 1099-1100).

Finally, in a recent study of board structure and composition in initial public offerings (a context that provides considerable power to principals),

Beatty and Zajac (1994) found that both the equity stakes held by top management and the noncash incentive portion of top managers' compensation (independent variables in this study) were negatively associated with the percentage of outside directors, the percentage of outside director-owners (although the coefficient for noncash incentive pay was not significant), and CEO duality. Hence, this study supports the logic of Propositions 7-4 and 7-5. It indicates that when the need for board monitoring is alleviated by alternative incentive alignment mechanisms (compensation plans and equity holdings) (see Chapter 8), boards need not maintain the same degree of independence as they might otherwise. As pointed out by Beatty and Zajac, these results highlight the trade-off between board monitoring and managerial incentives, suggesting that further studies of board trade-offs may help improve understanding of board structure and composition.

Although trade-offs between boards and CEOs surely exist, it also seems likely that CEOs have great influence in the selection of directors (Patton and Baker 1987). Because there are usually no legal requirements stipulating who may be selected to a board, membership may depend on influence and negotiation (Mintzberg 1983). Some have argued that CEOs will choose allies to sit on their boards (Lorsch 1989), and survey and anecdotal evidence supports this. For example, in a survey by Korn Ferry on how candidates for directorships are identified, "recommendation by the chairman" was the most commonly cited method (Jacobs 1991). Similarly, Anderson and Anthony note, "Although legally the board is elected by shareowners, as a practical matter boards are pretty much self-perpetuating bodies . . . . The chairman often dominates the decisions with respect to new board members (1986, 93)."

For anecdotal evidence, consider the actions of the board of directors at Paramount Communications Inc. in 1993, when the company was in the midst of being acquired by either Viacom or QVC. Martin Davis, the CEO of Paramount, strongly preferred the Viacom offer. The board had a fiduciary responsibility to assess all offers and make the best possible deal for shareholders. In a oft-quoted remark, Felix Rohatyn, general partner of Lazard Freres, Paramount's investment advisor throughout the Viacom-QVC bidding war, said in response to a question about why the Paramount board did not formally consider the QVC offer: "We haven't been asked." After QVC filed suit to force Paramount to consider its bid, Judge Jack Jacobs of the Delaware Chancery Court held: "The board did not even ask QVC to produce evidence of its financing. Meeting with QVC was the last thing management wanted to do, and by skillful advocacy, management persuaded the board that no exploration was required" (Roberts and Smith 1993).

What would explain the board's apparent resistance to formally considering the QVC offer? One answer may lie in the makeup of the Paramount board (Table 7-1). Of the fifteen board members, four were insiders, and another five had long-standing ties to Davis. The board included the following: Lester Pollack, a general partner of Lazard Freres (the Paramount advisor); Grace Flippinger, a former treasurer of Nynex (the telephone company ally of Viacom in the acquisition contest); Irving Fischer, an associate who worked with Davis on charitable activities; J. Hugh Liedtke, chairman of Pennzoil (a likely opponent of hostile bidders[10]); and, George Weissman, former chairman of Philip Morris (who knew Davis since Davis was a mail boy at Samuel Goldwyn) (Roberts and Smith 1993). Davis's ability to select directors with personal or business relationships to himself or his company is a good example of managerial power in action (Bowen 1994).

In one of the most complete studies on boards to date, Lorsch noted that "in most companies, selecting directors has been the responsibility of the CEO, who chose the candidates, then recommended them to the board for approval" (1989, 20). Lorsch quotes a director, "I think CEOs feel, justifiably, that they are entitled to select people of judgment, but who will also feel sympathetic to them" (1989, 22). Although such testimonials are impressive, empirical research on the association between managerial hegemony and director selection is relatively rare.[11]

TABLE 7-1 **Board of Directors of Paramount Communications, Inc. in 1993**

Director	Affiliation
Martin S. Davis	Chairman and CEO, Paramount
Grace J. Flippinger	Former treasurer, Nynex
Irving R. Fischer	Chairman and CEO, HRH Construction Corp.
Benjamin L. Hooks	Senior vice-president, Chapman Co.
	Former executive director, NAACP
Stanley R. Jaffe	President and COO, Paramount
J. Hugh Liedtke	Chairman, Pennzoil
Franz J. Lutolf	Former general manager, Swiss Bank Corp.
Ronald L. Nelson	CFO, Paramount
Donald Oresman	General Counsel and CAO, Paramount
James A. Pattison	Chairman and CEO, Jim Pattison Group
Lester Pollack	General partner of Lazard Freres
Irwin Schloss	President of Marcus Schloss & Co.
Samuel J. Silberman	Former chairman, Consolidated Cigar
Lawrence M. Small	President and COO, Fannie Mae
George Weissman	Former chairman, Philip Morris

One recent study is of particular note. Westphal and Zajac found that "(1) in firms where CEOs are relatively powerful, new directors are likely to be demographically similar to the firm's incumbent CEO; [and] (2) where boards of directors are more powerful relative to CEOs, new directors resemble the existing board, rather than the CEO" (1995, 29). These results provide the strongest evidence to date for the importance of the distribution of power between boards and CEOs in explaining board characteristics.

We build on this research with first a general proposition and then one that extends the Westphal and Zajac (1995) logic:

PROPOSITION 7-6
The greater the CEO's power, the greater the CEO's involvement in selecting new directors.

PROPOSITION 7-7
The greater the CEO's power, the greater the proportion of directors personally or professionally connected to the CEO.

In summary, boards are often strongly influenced by the contextual conditions under which they operate. We demonstrated how critical contingencies, institutional forces, and agency conditions can each affect the structure and composition of board of directors, as well as changes in structure and composition. Better predictive models of board characteristics will depend on the inclusion of these important contextual conditions. These contextual conditions, as well as characteristics of the board, affect board vigilance and behavior—a subject to which we now turn.

THE DETERMINANTS OF BOARD VIGILANCE AND BEHAVIOR

Our model of boards of directors places board vigilance and behavior at the center of a wide set of determinants and consequences. As Figure 7-1 illustrates, board vigilance and involvement in strategy formation may have potentially significant effects on such organizational outcomes as firm strategy and performance. As a result, gaining a clear understanding of the nature of board vigilance and strategic involvement and when they are more likely to occur is critical.

We first consider board vigilance. This construct is at the center of agency theory and is defined as the extent to which boards effectively monitor and discipline top managers. As we will argue, board vigilance is essentially a power construct; hence, it will have some application to board strategic involvement as well.

Board Vigilance in Monitoring and Disciplining Top Management

The descriptive literature on boards (e.g., Mace 1971) depicts directors as generally ineffective monitors of managerial activity. Agency theorists, however, place boards right in the center of corporate governance. For example, Gilson and Kraakman assert that "in the corporate governance debate, all arguments ultimately converge on the role of the board of directors" (1991, 873). For agency theorists, the role of the board is to ratify and monitor the decisions of top management (Fama and Jensen 1983). While there are alternatives to board monitoring, such as the market for corporate control (Jensen and Ruback 1983), competitive forces in capital and product markets (Williamson 1964), corporate law (Baysinger and Butler 1985), and managerial labor markets (Fama 1980), the board is considered central to ensuring that management act in the best interests of shareholders (Fama and Jensen 1983). Boards may accomplish this through various means, including implementing performance-contingent compensation plans, actively appraising and providing feedback to top managers on their performance, and even dismissing CEOs (Fama and Jensen 1983).

The difference between theory and practice in board vigilance has led many scholars to explore the reasons some boards are more vigilant than others. To understand why boards are not always vigilant monitors of top management, it is necessary to consider agency theory in some depth.[12] According to agency theory, shareholders and managers have different goals, driven to a large extent by the separation of ownership and control in modern organizations and by the different risks shareholders and managers face in an organization (Jensen and Meckling 1976; Shavell 1979; Holmstrom 1987). So, while shareholders can diversify their risk by investing in multiple firms, management is tied to a single organization by virtue of their position (Fama 1980; Baysinger and Hoskisson 1990). A clear implication of this difference in risk profiles is that top managers operate under a different set of incentives than do shareholders, potentially leading to such inefficient managerial behaviors as making short-term, risk-averse strategic investments (Lambert and Larcker 1985; Hill, Hitt, and Hoskisson 1988), shirking (Jensen and Meckling 1976), empire-building (Amihud and Lev 1981; Myers 1983; Benston 1985), and exploiting managerial perks (Williamson 1985).

Faced with this principal–agent problem, the primary responsibility of the board of directors is to ensure that top management actions are consistent with shareholder interests (Alchian and Demsetz 1972; Fama and Jensen 1983). According to this view, boards act to separate decision management from decision control, keeping for itself the roles of ratification and monitoring (Fama and Jensen 1983). We have already noted, however, that boards are not always effective monitors of top management. The underlying reason, as increasingly noted in empirical work (e.g., Kosnik 1987; Main, O'Reilly, and Wade 1994), relates to the distribution of power between boards and top management (especially CEOs).

Stated somewhat simplistically, when the balance of power favors boards, they will be more vigilant in monitoring and disciplining top management; when CEOs are more powerful, boards will be ineffective monitors. As Lorsch has argued:

> To govern effectively, directors must have enough power to influence the course of corporate direction, a power that is, at the least, slightly greater than the power of those the directors are to govern—the company's top managers and the employees who report to them. (1989, 13)

Hence, it is fundamental that the distribution of power between boards and top managers is carefully considered in studies of board vigilance:

PROPOSITION 7-8

The greater the relative power of the board over the top management team, the greater its vigilance.

The relationship between power and vigilance is strong because of the myriad ways a powerful CEO can affect the functioning of the board. As already discussed, powerful CEOs may be heavily involved in director selection. Choosing their own slate, or as much of it as possible, further strengthens a CEO's power base (Pfeffer 1981) and is often seen as a sign of entrenchment (Fama and Jensen 1983). A powerful CEO may also be able to take the chair position on the board, facilitating control of both the agenda and the debate in board meetings (Finkelstein and D'Aveni 1994). Such CEO duality can lead to further entrenchment because board chairs "give outsiders most of the information about the organization" (Mallette and Fowler 1992, 1028). Walsh and Seward (1990) point out a broad set of actions CEOs may take to entrench themselves, from seeking to attribute poor performance to external influences (Bettman and Weitz 1983; Staw, McKechnie, and Puffer 1983) to redefining relevant performance metrics (Jensen 1984)—entrenchment activities that are likely to be exacerbated by CEO power.

This logic is implicit in agency theory, at least as this theory has developed from its earliest formulations. While Fama and Jensen (1983) saw the board as the guardian of shareholder interests, scholars conducting empirical work focused on such board characteristics as outside representation (Weisbach 1988) and ownership equity (Morck, Shleifer, and Vishny 1988) as arbiters of board vigilance. Work in strategic management followed a similar path, with studies highlighting the role of such indicators of power as CEO tenure (Singh and Harianto 1989a), CEO ownership equity (Kosnik 1990), and whether the CEO appointed incumbent board members (Main, O'Reilly, and Wade 1994). These studies all recognized that board vigilance was a function of the distribution of power between boards (as representatives of shareholders) and CEOs (as the dominant top manager). Indeed, as Fama and Jensen noted, "the board is not an effective device for decision control unless it limits the decision discretion of individual top managers" (1983, 314).

Fundamentally, then, agency theory is a theory about power. The different goal orientations and risk horizons of boards and CEOs give rise to different incentive structures, creating a clear conflict of interest that is typically resolved through the use of power. Hence, the ability of boards to effectively monitor CEOs depends on board power, while the ability of CEOs to engage in activities that are not profit-maximizing depends on CEO power. To argue that boards are always effective or ineffective monitors of top management or that CEOs always prefer behaviors that are not profit-maximizing is theoretically unsatisfying because it ignores the fundamental role of power.

It is interesting to compare agency theory to earlier work on power in organizations. For example, Allen noted that "power theory holds that larger firm size and greater profits merely provide larger surpluses within these organizations which managers can allocate, at least in part, to their own compensation" (1981: 1114–15). This is not much different from agency theory arguments that CEOs may "take actions that deviate from the interests of residual claimants" (Fama and Jensen 1983, 304) and that CEO entrenchment can lead to opportunistic and inefficient behavior that reduces shareholder wealth (Jensen and Meckling 1976). The idea that power is central to the functioning of boards (Zald 1969) or that such consequences of board–CEO interactions as executive compensation (Lenski 1966) or CEO succession (Alexander, Fennell, and Halpern 1993) depend on the relative power of top managers is not new to organization theory (Mizruchi 1983). This hardly means that agency theory does not add value to our understanding of executive leadership, but rather it is important to identify the distribution of power between boards and CEOs as central to the theory.

This argument leads naturally to a call for a more explicit recognition of power in research on boards and top management. As part of this focus, more careful consideration of a broad set of power bases affecting board–CEO relations seems warranted. Research has concentrated on a few measures of board vigilance, as described above. But new studies may use different measures, making it difficult to directly compare findings across studies. A broader conceptualization of board–CEO power seems important.

Given the significance of board vigilance to understanding executive leadership, it is important to review how this construct has been measured in empirical work. As Figure 7-1 might suggest, with few exceptions (Pearce and Zahra 1991; Judge and Zeithaml, 1992; Johnson, Hoskisson, and Hitt 1993), board vigilance has been measured by its determinants, predominantly the proportion of outside directors on the board and the ownership equity of outside directors.

Numerous studies have imputed vigilance from outside director representation (Kosnik 1987; Weisbach 1988; Baysinger and Butler 1989; Singh and Harianto 1989a; Wade, O'Reilly, and Chandratat 1990; Davis 1991; Mallette and Fowler 1992; Johnson, Hoskisson, and Hitt 1993; Lambert, Larcker, and Weigelt 1993; Sundaramurthy and Wang 1993; Brickley, Coles, and Terry 1994; Buchholtz and Ribbens 1994; Finkelstein and D'Aveni 1994; Main, O'Reilly, and Wade 1994). Nevertheless, these studies have not explicitly differentiated between affiliated directors and outsiders with no affiliation to the firm, an oversight that may lead to misleading findings. Outsiders, as defined earlier, are expected to be more vigilant because 1) their focus on financial performance is a central component of monitoring (Fama and Jensen 1983; Johnson, Hoskisson, and Hitt 1993), 2) they are more likely to dismiss CEOs following poor performance (Coughlan and Schmidt 1985; Warner, Watts, and Wruck 1988; Weisbach 1988), 3) they have an incentive to monitor to protect their personal reputations as directors (Fama and Jensen 1983), and 4) they are likely to exercise greater objectivity by not being so clearly beholden to CEOs as are inside directors (Patton and Baker 1987; Schwenk 1989; Walsh and Seward 1990).

Although outside director representation is a commonly used measure of board vigilance, some have argued that the most effective directors are insiders because they are more informed than outsiders and thus can contribute more effectively to boardroom discussions (Hill and Snell 1988; Baysinger and Hoskisson 1990; Baysinger, Kosnik, and Turk 1991; Boyd 1994). One of the problems in trying to resolve this debate is that outside representation is an imprecise measure of board vigilance or involvement, leading to inconsistent findings across studies. Our view is that outsiders can enhance board vigilance more than insiders, while insiders have the potential to be more involved in board deliberations than outsiders. Nevertheless, board composition is only one factor influencing board vigilance and involvement. Thus, counts of insiders and outsiders are indirect measures of vigilance and involvement, only one of many determining factors. For this reason, Jensen conceded that "the idea that outside directors with little or no equity stake in the company could effectively monitor and discipline the managers who selected them has proven hollow at best" (1989, 64).

This discussion indicates that although board composition is often used as a measure of board vigilance, it is an indirect measure based on an assumption about the relationship between vigilance and composition that has not been tested. Hence, we propose the following direct test:

PROPOSITION 7-9
The greater the proportion of outside directors on the board, the greater the board vigilance.

As noted, board vigilance has also been measured quite often in terms of outside director ownership equity (Salancik and Pfeffer 1980; Gomez-Mejia, Tosi, and Hinkin 1987; Kosnik 1987; Holderness and Sheehan 1988; Finkelstein and Hambrick 1989; Mallette and Fowler 1992; Johnson, Hoskisson, and Hitt 1993; Lambert, Larcker, and Weigelt 1993; Beatty and Zajac 1994; Finkelstein and D'Aveni 1994; Hoskisson, Johnson, and Moesel, 1994). The notion here is that ownership stakes provide outside directors with an incentive to monitor CEO behavior to protect their personal wealth (Zald 1969; Alchian and Demsetz 1972; Shleifer and Vishny 1986). Once again, however, board vigilance is being measured by its determinants; direct tests have not been made of whether outsider equity is actually associated with board vigilance.

PROPOSITION 7-10
The greater the percentage of stock owned by outside directors on the board, the greater the board vigilance.

Several other measures of board vigilance appear often in the literature, including CEO nonduality (Mallette and Fowler 1992; Sundaramurthy and Wang 1993; Boyd 1994; Main, O'Reilly, and Wade 1994), (low) director compensation (Vance 1983; Main, O'Reilly, and Wade 1994), number of directors representing blockholders (Zald 1969), relative board tenure (Singh and Harianto 1989a; Wade, O'Reilly, and Chandratat 1990; D'Aveni and Kesner, 1993; Sundaramurthy and Wang 1993), and whether the CEO was appointed to the board before outside directors or directors serving on the compensation committee (Wade, O'Reilly, and Chandratat 1990; Lambert, Larcker, and Weigelt 1993; Main, O'Reilly, and Wade 1994; Westphal and Zajac 1994). Although there are critics of some of these measures (Baysinger and Hoskisson 1990; Walsh and Seward 1990; Gilson and Kraakman 1991), all have some merit and have often yielded interesting findings in empirical research. Nevertheless, they are also all removed from the actual actions or behaviors of boards. Without primary data, it is difficult to determine the actual level of board vigilance. Indeed, as we have argued, each of these measures of board vigilance are really determinants.

Another approach to improving the predictive power of models of board vigilance would be to study various contingency hypotheses predicting the conditions under which boards of directors "predisposed toward vigilance" (those with a majority of outsiders, high ownership equity, or some other director characteristic thought to affect vigilance) will be more effective monitors of top management. Such a study would implicitly recognize that most of the time the balance of power between boards and CEOs favors the CEO. Aside from the taboo against directly challenging the CEO except in critical circumstances (Mace, 1971), boards are constrained by a lack of time to prepare for meetings and to interact with the CEO, limited information and expertise, and the dominance of the CEO (Lorsch 1989). However, as we will argue in our discussion of board involvement in strategy formation, circumstances exist that may promote board vigilance.

One such circumstance may occur when the firm is facing a crisis. For example, several writers have asserted that the likelihood boards will discipline top managers increases during crises (Mace 1971; Lorsch 1989). It may not be clear what constitutes crises,[13] but when they occur, they tend to empower boards (Zald, 1969). There are a number of recent examples. James D. Robinson III resigned as CEO of American Express on January 29, 1993, only four days after three directors resigned in protest and following a long series of strategic setbacks (Myerson 1993). The CEO of Eastman Kodak, Kay Whitmore, was dismissed in a boardroom coup in August of 1993, as directors showed their displeasure after years of below-par performance (Mathews 1993). At General Motors, multibillion dollar losses in 1991 and 1992 precipitated the removal from office of Robert Stempel as CEO and former CEO Roger Smith as a director (Solomon, Washington, and Stokes 1992).

In some ways, these examples are not new: Studies of CEO succession consistently find turnover associated with poor firm performance (e.g., Brown 1982; Coughlan and Schmidt 1985; Warner 1988). Nevertheless, important questions remain unresolved: Why do some boards act more quickly than others in responding to poor performance (after all, General Motors had been losing market share for years)? Does it matter whether boards are dominated by outsiders or have members with large shareholdings in the firm, both traditional measures of board vigilance? Do the experiences of a CEO affect how much time the board allows to elapse before taking action? Are some CEOs, by virtue of their tenure, age, or position in the business elite, given more time to fix whatever is wrong with the firm? Is it coincidental that in all three companies—American Express, Kodak, and General Motors—the board was led by a CEO of another firm: Richard Furlaud, CEO of Bristol-Myers Squibb, at American Express; Roberto Goizueta, CEO of Coca-Cola, at Kodak; and John Smale, retired CEO of Procter & Gamble, at General Motors?

The increased vigilance of boards in poorly performing firms is also evident in the Finkelstein and D'Aveni (1994) finding that vigilant boards were associated with CEO duality when firm performance was high but not when it was low. It may be that boards give CEOs the benefit of the doubt, but when they are eventually driven to act, they do so with some conviction. Or perhaps the balance of power between boards and CEOs is fluid, with such factors as firm performance tipping the balance. These questions and issues are important and clearly require further work to resolve.

Board Involvement in Strategy Formation

Several descriptive studies have been conducted on what boards of directors actually do, and this work is instructive for the clear message it sends about board actions (Mace 1971; Mueller 1979; Herman 1981; Vance 1983; Whistler 1984; Wolfson 1984; Patton and Baker 1987). The virtually uniform conclusion that comes out of this research stream is that boards of directors are not involved in strategy formation. As Clark has argued,

> It is unrealistic to view directors as making any significant number of basic business policy decisions. Even with respect to the broadest business policies, it is the officers who generally initiate and shape the decisions. The directors simply approve them, and occasionally offer advice and raise questions. (1986, 108)

As an example, consider the only partly tongue-in-cheek analysis by Whistler (1984) (based on interviews with about sixty directors) and the following norms of director conduct he noted:

Rule I (A) No fighting

Rule I (B) Support your CEO

Rule I (C) Serve your apprenticeship

Rule I (D) No crusades

Rule II (C) We don't manage the company

Rule II (D) We don't set strategy

Rule III (A) Keep your distance from subordinate company executives

A common theme in these norms is that directors should avoid confrontation, stay in the background, and not rock the boat. This profile of director behavior has held in the management literature for some time and is in contrast to work in agency theory that generally posits a central role for boards of directors (Fama and Jensen 1983). Agency theorists, however, focus almost exclusively on the governance role of boards (the board's "most important role is to scrutinize the highest decision makers in the firm" [Fama 1980, 294]) and not on the role of boards in strategy formation.[14]

In recent years, demand has increased for boards of directors to become more active in strategic decision making (Weidenbaum 1985; Power 1987; Galen 1989). Indeed, as Figure 7-2 indicates, boards may have the legal authority to make major business decisions and establish corporate strategy (Clark 1986). Concerns about director liability (Galen 1989), the influence

FIGURE 7-2 **Responsibilities of Boards of Directors According to the American Law Institute**

1. Elect, evaluate and, where appropriate, dismiss the principal senior executives.

2. Oversee the conduct of the corporation's business, with a view to evaluation on an ongoing basis, whether the corporation's resources are being managed in a manner consistent with [enhancing shareholder gain, within the law, within ethical considerations, and while directing a reasonable amount of resources to public welfare and humanitarian purposes].

3. Review and approve corporate plans and actions that the board and principal senior executives consider major and changes in accounting principles that the board or principal senior executives consider material.

4. Perform such other functions as are prescribed by law, or assigned to the board under a standard of the corporation.

SOURCE: American Law Institute (1984, 66-67).

of pension funds (Dobrzynski 1988), and the market for corporate control (Brickley and James 1987) have all added to the pressure on boards. Moreover, as Lorsch (1989) reports, directors want to become more involved in the strategy-making process. Most directors he surveyed stressed the importance of board involvement in strategy formation, and writers such as Kenneth Andrews (1981) are strong advocates for such an arrangement. Nevertheless, the directors in Lorsch's (1989) study also recognized that the board's primary role in the strategy formation process was in advising and evaluating, rather than initiating, a division of labor driven to some extent by a lack of time and information. Board members may also become co-opted over time to not challenge management, in part because such activity may be demoralizing to managers and in part because there are often strict norms against doing so.

So, in some ways, we may be at a crossroads in developing norms for director involvement in strategic decision making. The generally older descriptive studies indicate that boards are largely ineffectual, while newer work suggests that boards need to become more active in spite of the constraints they face. To some extent, these opposing views may simply be a reflection of changing norms about board involvement. On the other hand, we only have limited empirical evidence on the extent to which boards are active in strategy formation. Nevertheless, these studies are informative because they may point the direction for new research on the conditions that give rise to board of director involvement in strategic decision making.

In one such study, Johnson, Hoskisson, and Hitt (1993) argued that boards become involved in corporate restructuring when firm performance decreases. This hypothesis was supported in a sample of ninety-two firms between 1985 and 1990, with board involvement measured with a survey instrument where "high scores represent significant board pressure or involvement in the decision to restructure or acquire business units" (1993, 40). They also found that characteristics of the board itself, such as outside director representation and outside director equity (both indicators of board vigilance), were predictors of involvement. Thus, according to this study, board characteristics do affect board involvement.

In a study of forty-two firms in four different industries (biotechnology, hospitals, textiles, and "diversified firms"), Judge and Zeithaml (1992) reported several interesting findings. First, in line with the notion that diversified firms face diluted environmental pressures to conform to emerging norms on board involvement, they found a negative association between diversification and board involvement in strategic decision making.[15] Second, contrary to the expectations of the authors and others who see insiders as contributing valuable insights and information to boardroom discussions (Tashakori and Boulton 1983; Ford 1988; Baysinger and Hoskisson 1990), outside director representation increased board involvement. This result, however, is consistent with a power perspective on board-CEO relations (e.g., Lorsch 1989), as discussed earlier. Finally, board size was negatively associated with board involvement.

These studies stand out for two reasons. First, they are among the only studies to date that have examined direct associations between board characteristics and involvement in strategy formation. Second, they carefully assessed board involvement through interviews with multiple informants in each organization (Judge and Zeithaml 1992) and through the development of multi-item scales of board involvement (Judge and Zeithaml 1992; Johnson, Hoskisson, and Hitt 1993). Building on these studies, we suggest two propositions—one for board size and one for board diversity.

The huge body of literature on group size generally concludes that larger groups can be unwieldy (Gladstein 1984), are too diverse to reach consensus (Shaw 1981), and increase conflict (O'Reilly, Caldwell, and Barnett 1989), while smaller groups may be too homogeneous (Jackson, et al., 1991) and have limited information-processing capability (Haleblian and Finkelstein 1993). This is corroborated by Clendenin, whose CEO informants told him that: "large boards . . . are unmanageable" (1972, 62), and by Alexander, Fennell, and Halpern (1993), who reported a positive association between board size and heterogeneity. These studies suggest that the "excess baggage" carried by larger boards reduces their ability to become involved in strategy formation.

PROPOSITION 7-11

The larger the board, the less involved it is in strategic decision making.

In a similar vein, the demographic diversity of the board may also hinder strategic involvement. For example, in a study of over fifteen hundred hospitals between 1980 and 1988, Alexander, Fennell, and Halpern (1993) found that leadership instability (defined as a systematic pattern of frequent succession among top managers) was greater when boards were smaller and more homogeneous. In addition, Goodstein, Gautam, and Boeker (1994) reported that occupationally diverse boards were less likely to make strategic changes than more homogeneous boards. When boards are constructed to reflect the diverse views of various constituencies organizations may be dependent on, they lose some cohesiveness (Clendenin 1972) and, by implication, power (Lorsch 1989). Diversity diffuses board power by promoting differences, when a strong consensus about shared purposes may enhance board power (Hackman 1986). If this logic is valid, then we might expect the following:

PROPOSITION 7-12

The greater the homogeneity of board member backgrounds, the more involved are boards in strategic decision making.

Although Judge and Zeithaml (1992) and Johnson, Hoskisson, and Hitt (1993) are valuable, they provide only partial evidence on the conditions that give rise to greater board involvement in strategic decision making—partly because the construct of board involvement is considerably more complex than typically assumed. Consider Figure 7-3. This schematic outlines five stages of strategic decision making, each of which may be subject to greater or lesser board involvement. There is much we do not know about board involvement. Some questions that remain unanswered include: Are boards equally involved at each stage? What determines the degree of involvement at each stage? How is involvement at one stage related to involvement at others? Although questions such as these clearly call for empirical investigation, we offer the following working proposition for study:

PROPOSITION 7-13

Board involvement in strategic decision making varies across the various stages of the process. Boards will be involved in the following strategic decision-making stages, in descending order: evaluating strategic alternatives, evaluating strategic results, selecting strategies, generating strategic alternatives, and implementing strategies.

This proposition, while provocative, must be also be considered speculative because of the dearth of work on board involvement in strategic decision making. While other patterns may be possible, the conditions that give rise to alternative patterns remain to be investigated. In the following section, we develop some ideas on potential precipitating conditions. Although we refer to "board involvement" in a general sense, we also suggest, where warranted, how these conditions might differentially affect each stage of board involvement in strategic decision making.

Contextual Conditions Predicting Board Strategic Involvement

Most observers agree that strategy formation is not the primary job of the board of directors (Fama and Jensen 1983). Hence, board involvement is likely to be an exception rather than a rule unless norms change in a much more radical fashion than they have. Even as an exception, however, it is interesting to consider the conditions that might give rise to greater

FIGURE 7-3   **Board Involvement in the Strategic Decision-Making Process**

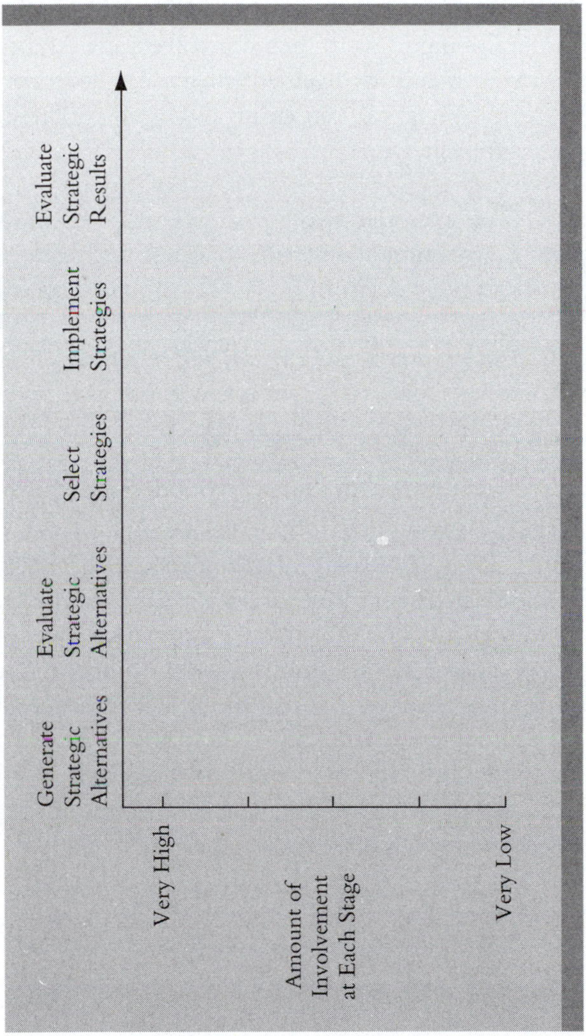

involvement. Because work on this question has been infrequent, we have only limited guidance in developing ideas on board involvement. As a first step toward stronger theory on board involvement in strategy formation, we broadly consider the same contextual conditions discussed earlier, and then we provide suggestive propositions.

Critical Contingencies.   We consider two types of critical contingencies, one emanating from the environment and the other deriving from earlier work by Zald (1969) on strategic decision points. In our analysis of the resource dependence perspective, we noted that board members may be selected for their ability to manage interorganizational dependencies. To the extent this is true, boards of firms facing the greatest environmental uncertainty should be more involved in strategic decision making. These boards might have the appropriate expertise to substantively aid top management. Indeed, several scholars have argued that the strategic role of the board of directors is particularly critical during periods of environmental uncertainty (Boulton 1978; Mintzberg 1983; Goodstein, Gautam, and Boeker 1994). However, we also noted earlier how board members may be co-opted, an interpretation that implies lesser influence for them. Complicating matters is the notion that because environmental uncertainty promotes greater ambiguity about means-ends relationships (Thompson 1967), board deliberations on strategy may become politicized, thereby reducing board members' effectiveness and ability to have an impact (Olson 1982). Hence, how environmental uncertainty affects board involvement is not entirely clear, and two alternative propositions are suggested:

PROPOSITION 7-14A
The more uncertain the environment, the more involved are boards in strategic decision making.

PROPOSITION 7-14B
The more uncertain the environment, the less involved are boards in strategic decision making.

Beyond critical contingencies that derive from the environment, we develop a different set of critical contingencies based on a promising theoretical logic first described by Zald (1969) and offer propositions that build on this work. Referring to the extent to which top management found it "necessary to be bound by (the board's) perspectives and ideas" (p. 99), Zald (1969) noted that it is at "strategic decision points that board power is most likely to be asserted" (p. 107). Strategic decision points, according to Zald, were related to life cycle problems and choosing a successor.

Several propositions based on these notions can be considered. For example, boards may be more involved in newer organizations because such firms have a greater need for policy formulation and the development of "guidelines for action" (Zald 1969, 107). In the only empirical test of this idea thus far, Judge and Zeithaml (1992) found that board involvement in strategic decision making and organization age were positively related. This unexpected result was attributed to the tendency of a board to develop a broader repertoire of skills over time, making it possible for it to contribute to substantive discussions on strategy formation. Nevertheless, since Judge and Zeithaml (1992) studied hospital boards (which are considerably different than the boards of most businesses) (e.g., Alexander, Fennell, and Halpern 1993), the applicability of this finding to other settings is unclear. In addition, although they used multiple measures of board involvement in the decision-making process ("formation" covering roughly the first three stages in Figure 7-3, and "evaluation" representing the final stage), they did not suggest more targeted hypotheses. One such hypothesis might distinguish between board involvement in generating and evaluating strategic alternatives, and selecting strategies (all of which may be more salient for newer firms) from board involvement in evaluating strategic results (which may be a more generalized board activity). Thus, we propose:

PROPOSITION 7-15

The older the organization, the less involved is the board in strategic decision making. Board involvement in generating and evaluating strategic alternatives and selecting strategies is more negatively associated with organization age than board involvement in implementing strategies and evaluating strategic results.

In a similar vein, boards in smaller firms may be more active in strategic decision making. Smaller firms are unlikely to have the same breadth of managerial talent available to larger firms, possibly requiring a larger board role. Indeed, some have argued that board members are often chosen for their strategic expertise (Vance 1983); it seems even more likely that such a criterion for director selection would be used in smaller firms. Certainly, Zald's (1969) argument that boards can provide more valued counsel on policy formulation to younger firms should apply to smaller firms as well.

PROPOSITION 7-16

The larger the organization, the less involved is the board in strategic decision making. Board involvement in generating and evaluating strategic alternatives, and selecting strategies is more negatively associated with organization size than board involvement in implementing strategies and evaluating strategic results.

Other organizational transitions may also call for greater board involvement. Acquisitions, divestitures, and joint ventures represent important strategic decision points where a board may be more prominent, and indeed boards are legally required to hold a vote on these decisions. In addition, the acquisition process in particular is time-consuming, absorbing managerial (Hoskisson and Hitt 1994), and likely board, energy along the way. As a result, boards may be more involved throughout the strategy formation process under these conditions.

PROPOSITION 7-17

The greater the acquisition, divestiture, and joint venture activity of a firm, the more involved is the board in all stages of the strategic decision-making process.

As noted above, selecting a new chief executive is a critical strategic decision point for a firm, and numerous studies have documented the board's role in succession (Brown 1982; Coughlan and Schmidt 1985; Johnson, Hoskisson, and Hitt 1993). Virtually all of these studies, however, tested the relationship between attributes of board structure and composition, and CEO turnover. Missing has been a more direct test of the implications of turnover for board strategic involvement. Once again, this involvement may occur throughout the strategy formation process.

PROPOSITION 7-18

Appointment of a new CEO increases board involvement in all stages of the strategic decision-making process.

PROPOSITION 7-19

CEO tenure decreases board involvement in all stages of the strategic decision-making process.

Institutional Forces. Earlier we described institutional forces as those emanating from the role played by prestigious managerial elites in corporate governance. Membership in the managerial elite provides an independent means through which directors gain power, and as a result, director prestige is a key antecedent to both the selection and turnover of board members. Hence, it is only a slight extension of this same logic to suggest that director prestige may offer board members greater opportunity to participate throughout the strategy formation process. These prestigious directors are unlikely to serve solely as "rubber stamps" because 1) they may very well have been in a position to select among multiple directorship offers and they likely would not have decided to sit on a board where they would have no impact, and 2) prestige may be accepted as a signal of managerial competence by a firm's top managers (D'Aveni and Kesner 1993), opening the door to a wider director role in strategy formation.

PROPOSITION 7-20

The more prestigious a board's directors, the greater its involvement in all stages of the strategic decision-making process.

Agency Conditions.   Earlier we suggested that board vigilance depends on the distribution of power between the board and top management. Powerful boards are more vigilant than weak boards. As such, powerful boards should be more involved than weak boards in strategy formation.

PROPOSITION 7-21

The more powerful a board, the greater its involvement in all stages of the strategic decision-making process.

The distribution of power between boards and top managers should also act as a moderator of all previously proposed relationships because they are subject to the constraining influence of limited power. Thus, board power should act as both a direct effect on strategy involvement and an indirect effect that accentuates any predisposition boards may have (due to various critical contingencies) to be involved in strategy formation. For example, the first part of Proposition 7-15 asserted that board involvement in strategic decision making will be greater in newer organizations. Considering agency conditions, an additional proposition might predict that the greater the power of the board, the stronger the (negative) association between organizational age and board involvement in strategic decision making. In this way, critical contingencies serve as "precipitating conditions" for board involvement, but the actual extent of such involvement will depend on the distribution of power between boards and top managers. The following proposition is offered as an overarching statement of this relationship:

PROPOSITION 7-22

The greater the power of a board, the stronger the relationship between critical contingencies and board involvement in strategic decision making.

This section suggested possible explanations for board strategic involvement. Other predictors may also be worthy of study. Nevertheless, we may conclude that even though there are generally severe constraints on board behavior, boards may, indeed, have an impact on strategy formation—and this impact will depend on various contextual conditions, as well as the power of the board. A fundamental implication of this argument is that board structure and composition, as well as board vigilance and strategic involvement, may be related to organizational choices, strategies, and performance, a subject to which we now turn.

Consequences of Board Vigilance and Board Involvement in Strategy Formation

Although boards do not always use their implicit power to directly affect organizational outcomes, such as strategy, they are influential in a wide range of outcomes related to executive leadership. Consider how boards can affect top management: they are involved in the selection and succession of CEOs, the determination of compensation systems and levels, and the setting of various takeover defenses and postures, and their vigilance affects how much discretion CEOs have in leading their organizations. So, despite the relatively limited role often ascribed to boards of directors, they may be involved in a broad range of activities that affect how top managers and CEOs do their jobs. These effects are borne out in a review of empirical research on the consequences of board monitoring and strategic involvement. We begin at the far right of Figure 7-1, with an examination of the performance consequences of board vigilance and involvement.

Boards and Firm Performance

Given the various interpretations of the role of boards of directors in the literature, the existence of considerable research raising doubts about the scope of board influence in strategy formation, and the rather large gap between board behavior and actual performance outcomes, one might expect to find relatively few studies investigating the direct association between boards and firm performance. However, this relationship appears to be quite enticing for scholars, for dozens of empirical studies have been published over the course of several decades. Researchers have investigated the performance effects of board size (Pfeffer 1973; Provan 1980; Chaganti, Mahajan, and Sharma 1985; Zahra and Stanton 1988; Pearce and Zahra 1992), outside director representation (Vance 1955; Vance 1964; Pfeffer 1972; Schmidt 1977; MacAvoy, et al. 1983; Baysinger and Butler 1985; Chaganti, Mahajan, and Sharma 1985; Kesner 1987; Hill and Snell 1988; Morck, Shleifer, and Vishny 1988; Zahra and Stanton 1988; Rosenstein and Wyatt 1990; Hermalin and Weisbach 1991; Hambrick and D'Aveni 1992; Pearce and Zahra 1992), director equity (Kesner 1987; Morck, Shleifer, and Vishny 1988; Schellenger, Wood, and Tashakori 1989), inside director equity (Vance 1955; Vance 1964; Pfeffer 1972), director and officer equity (Lloyd, Jahera, and Goldstein 1986; Kim, Lee, and Francis 1988; Oswald and Jahera 1991), director background and experiences (Norburn 1986), CEO duality (Berg and Smith 1978; Chaganti, Mahajan, and Sharma 1985; Rechner and Dalton 1991; Daily and Dalton 1992), board involvement in strategy making (Judge and Zeithaml 1992), board power (Pearce and Zahra 1991), and board attributes (Molz 1988). Inevitably, much of this work has produced mixed results, as an exhaustive review by Zahra and Pearce (1989) indicates.

Zahra and Pearce (1989) point out several reasons we should not be surprised by inconsistent findings: 1) contextual factors affecting boards, such as industry, organizational life cycle, and corporate strategy, have generally been ignored; 2) this research does not effectively consider how board members interact to make decisions; 3) emphasizing univariate analytical approaches, by considering one or two board attributes in isolation, makes comparability and integration across studies difficult; 4) researchers often do not measure board attributes, such as outside director representation, the same way; and 5) many studies use contemporaneous, as opposed to lagged, measures of firm performance, potentially confounding causal direction.[16] Perhaps most important, board structure and composition likely do not have universal effects on firm performance. Aside from doubts about board efficacy, there are too many intervening individuals and processes between boards and firm performance, too many potential contingency factors that might affect how boards are related to performance outcomes, and too many other influences on firm performance to expect a strong direct association.

Nevertheless, boards may have an indirect effect on firm performance through the quality of their managerial monitoring or their involvement in strategy formation. Indeed, investigations of how board monitoring and strategy involvement affect nonperformance outcomes may be quite promising. As Figure 7-1 indicates, rather than inducing a second-order effect, such as firm performance, boards may have a stronger impact on such outcomes as executive succession, executive compensation, and takeover defenses, and even on such strategic outcomes as diversification, resource management, and strategic change. We now turn to a consideration of these outcomes.

Board Effects on Strategy

Top managers are generally the most influential organizational actors determining a firm's strategic direction (Hambrick and Mason 1984). However, boards may also play a direct or indirect role in the strategic decision-making process, as Table 7-2 documents. Boards can directly affect strategy through involvement of their members on committees, recommendations to top management, and oversight of executive decisions. Boards can indirectly affect strategy by reducing interorganizational dependencies and by conveying information about other firms' strategies. Direct board effects have generally been empirically modeled using agency theory and strategic choice perspectives, while indirect board effects rely on resource dependence and institutional theories. This section reviews this research.

A small but important set of published studies examines how strategic outcomes are a direct consequence of board structure and composition. Goodstein, Gautam, and Boeker (1994), studying hospitals, examined whether board size and diversity were associated with strategic change. Arguing that larger boards and more diverse boards have inherently more internal conflict and dissensus, these authors hypothesized a negative association with strategic change. Results indicated that while both coefficients were negative, only board diversity was significantly related to multiple indicators of strategic change. That is, firms with diverse boards were less likely to initiate strategic changes than those with homogeneous boards.[17]

A different type of argument on how boards affect strategy has been advanced by Baysinger and Hoskisson (1990). Arguing that because outsiders tend to emphasize financial controls over strategic controls (i.e., more objective, performance-contingent control mechanisms), thus increasing managerial employment risk, outsider-dominated boards would be associated with greater diversification. Participation in multiple businesses allows top managers to diversify their employment risk by stabilizing the firm's income stream (Amihud and Lev 1981). What is interesting about this idea is that, according to the authors, increased diversification is an indirect consequence of outside director representation and is not due to (indeed, may be contrary to) the presumed vigilance of outsiders. While intriguing, only limited evidence speaks directly to this idea.

In a study of ninety-four R&D-intensive Fortune 500 firms in 1980, Hill and Snell (1988) found that the ratio of inside to outside directors was negatively associated with diversified scope and positively associated with both the specialization and relatedness ratios, contrary to their agency theory-based expectations but consistent with the Baysinger and Hoskisson (1990) logic. And a recent study of 203 restructuring firms between 1985 and 1990 by Hoskisson, Johnson, and Moesel (1994) found that outside director equity decreased the time spent restructuring and the number of divestitures. However, this study did not find support for the effects of other measures of outsider influence on diversification and restructuring.

Extending their ideas on financial versus strategic controls to R&D activity, Baysinger and Hoskisson (1990) also hypothesized that outside director representation would be associated with lower expenditures on R&D because outsiders' use of financial controls engenders risk aversion among managers. Both of the studies conducted to date on this question have been supportive (Hill and Snell 1988; Baysinger, Kosnik, and Turk 1991). Again, it is worth pointing out that a standard agency theory interpretation would predict that the enhanced vigilance of outsider-dominated boards ensures that firms limit unrelated diversification and promote R&D activity because such actions are consistent with shareholder interests.[18] Hence, such a commonly used measure of board vigilance as outside director representation may not be reliable.

Researchers drawing on organization theories have also examined how boards affect such strategic outcomes as corporate borrowing, diversification posture, and acquisition activity. Drawing on resource dependence theory, Mizruchi and Stearns documented how financial representation on boards is associated with corporate borrowing (Stearns and Mizruchi 1993; Mizruchi and Stearns 1994). Studying a group of 22 Fortune 500 firms over a twenty-eight year period, they found a consistent pattern of resource acquisition. For example, the presence of a life insurance executive on a board was positively associated with long-term private borrowing but negatively associated with long-term public borrowing. Investment bankers on the board, on the other hand, were more likely to be associated with borrowing from public sources than private sources. In all, these authors provide persuasive evidence that the presence of different types of financial representatives on a board is associated with the use of different types of financing.

Three recent studies have also examined how boards affect diversification. Using an institutional theory framework in a study of the adoption of the multidivisional organizational form by firms between 1963 and 1968, Palmer, Jennings, and Zhou (1993) tested the notions that 1) director interlocks provide information on strategic innovations in use in other firms and 2) the greater the number of interlocks with other firms that had already adopted the multidivisional form, the higher the likelihood of adoption by

TABLE 7-2 **Research on Board Effects on Strategy Formation**

Study	Theory	Dependent Variables	Independent Variables	Results	Sample
Hill and Snell 1988	Agency theory–power	R & D expenditures Number of industries firm is active in Specialization ratio Related diversification	Number of inside directors compared to number of outside directors	+ – + +	94 R & D intensive Fortune 500 firms in 1980
Baysinger, Kosnik, and Turk 1991	Agency theory–power	R & D expenditures	% inside directors	+	176 Fortune 500 firms in 1981 to 1983
Haunschild 1993	Institutional theory	Number of acquisitions in a particular year	Number of acquisitions by firms in which inside directors sit on the board Number of firms in which inside directors sit on the board	+, and inverted-U inverted-U	327 medium and large firms between 1981 and 1990
Palmer, Jennings, and Zhou 1993	Political theory Institutional theory	Adoption of multi-divisional form (MDF)	Family directors with 5% equity Banking representation on board with 5% equity Director interlocks with non-MDF firms Director interlocks with MDF firms	n.s. n.s. n.s. mixed	105 Fortune 500 firms between 1963 and 1968 with a unitary organization form in 1962

TABLE 7-2 **Research on Board Effects on Strategy Formation,** *continued*

Study	Theory	Dependent Variables	Independent Variables	Results	Sample
Stearns and Mizruchi 1993	Resource dependence	Corporate long-term, short-term, and private borrowing	Presence of different types of financial representatives on board	+	22 Fortune 500 firms between 1956 and 1983
Goodstein, Gautam, and Boeker 1994	Strategic choice	Strategic change	Board size	mixed	334 hospitals between 1980 and 1985
			Director occupational diversity	−	
			% outside directors	n.s.	
Haunschild 1994	Institutional theory	Size of acquisition premium	(1) Average premium paid by firms in which inside directors sit on the board	+	240 acquisitions between 1986 and 1993
			Target firm uncertainty x (1)	+	
Mizruchi and Stearns 1994	Agency theory Resource dependence	Corporate borrowing	Financial representation on board	+	22 Fortune 500 firms between 1956 and 1983

NOTES: Only findings related to boards of directors were included in this table. Significant results (denoted by + or −) were based on p<.05 or better. Identification of theoretical perspectives was based on our evaluation and not necessarily noted by the authors in their studies.

the focal firm. Surprisingly, results were mixed, with directional interlocks unexpectedly decreasing and nondirectional interlocks[19] increasing the likelihood of adoption; the results were attributed to different patterns of information dissemination associated with these interlocks. Nevertheless, the findings of this study were still generally supportive of an institutional theory story on how boards affect strategy.

These authors also tested board hypotheses based on political theory but found no significant results. Nevertheless, Palmer, Jennings, and Zhou (1993) is noteworthy for the multiple interpretations applied to board characteristics. This study highlights a general condition about research on boards: a reliance on objective characteristics of boards must start with strong theory because these characteristics are subject to multiple interpretations.

In a pair of studies that also examined boards from a social network perspective, Haunschild (1993; 1994) reported results that were strongly supportive. In the first study, she examined whether board interlocks were associated with acquisition activity in a sample of 327 medium and large firms between 1981 and 1990. Arguing that "director interlocks are an important source of personal contacts among those managers with the power to affect organizational merger and acquisition activity" (1993, 568), Haunschild found that focal firm acquisition activity was positively associated with the number of acquisitions made by firms that were tied to the focal firm through directorships. An inverted-U relationship was also found. These results held for different types of mergers and, after controlling for several alternative explanations, for acquisition activity as well.

The second study focused on the size of acquisition premiums, arguing that the size of prior premiums paid by firms tied to an acquiring firm through director ties should be a significant predictor (Haunschild 1994). This expectation was borne out in a sample of 240 acquisitions completed between 1986 and 1993. Taken together, the two Haunschild studies provide strong support for an institutional theory perspective on the relationship between boards of directors and strategy formation.

When considered in its entirety, research on how boards affect strategy is quite limited. Overall, there have been few empirical studies to date. In addition, the contrast between institutional theory and a theory of strategic controls advanced by Baysinger and Hoskisson (1990) is a stark one. Institutional theory pays less attention to whether directors are insiders or outsiders than it does to the position of these directors in an interlocking network of business elite. Nevertheless, the promising results that have come out of the few studies on the institutional perspective are encouraging and suggest that researchers adopting agency theory or strategic controls approaches consider alternative explanations for their findings.

Another conclusion that emerges is that board structure and composition are both causes and consequences of various organizational outcomes. Consider the following two examples that come out of our evaluation of the relevant literature:

1. What is the relationship between boards and diversification? On the one hand, limited evidence exists that diversified firms tend to bring more outsiders to the board for information and expertise (Pearce and Zahra 1992). On the other, theory and some evidence has accumulated that indicates that outside directors, by focusing on financial controls, tend to be associated with greater firm diversification as CEOs seek to diversify their employment risk (Hill and Snell 1988; Baysinger and Hoskisson 1990).

2. What is the relationship between boards and corporate borrowing? Directors from the banking community may be appointed to the board because firms wish to ensure adequate capital resources (Pfeffer 1972), while corporate borrowing may be higher in firms with more banking representatives on the board (Mizruchi and Stearns 1994). Hence, it is difficult to disentangle what is really happening in such relationships. As we noted earlier, co-optation works both ways, with banking directors and firms both having something to gain from mutual interaction.

Implications of this for research on boards and strategy include: 1) investigators must consider alternative explanations for their results that derive from the multiple theoretical perspectives bearing on boards; and 2) conceptually and analytically, researchers must explicitly take into consideration the possibility of a reverse causal direction to that posited.

Boards as Supra-Top Management Teams

Future research should extend upper-echelons theory to boards of directors. Few studies have explicitly tested upper-echelons hypotheses to a large extent because of the limited decision-making ability of most boards and the relatively greater role of top managers in effecting such organizational outcomes as strategy and firm performance. Nevertheless, there may be instances when board discretion is quite high, and in those cases, it is sensible to test upper-echelons hypotheses. For example, in a study of hospital boards referred to earlier, Goodstein, Gautam, and Boeker (1994) found that larger boards were associated with less reorganization of hospital services. Although these authors did not formally posit an upper-echelons framework for their hypotheses, the logic they used to support hypotheses and their subsequent findings are clearly consistent (Hambrick and Mason 1984).

If boards are seen as decision-making units operating analogously to top management teams, perhaps the upper-echelons perspective should be extended in this way. If so, then two important refinements to upper-echelons theory are especially relevant to boards—the moderating roles of *discretion* and *power* (Finkelstein 1988). As argued throughout this chapter, boards of directors are not always able to directly affect organizational outcomes; they have limited discretion. They are constrained by their own power relative to the CEO and other top managers, and their choices, as well as their ability to make choices, are constrained by many of the same environmental, organizational, and individual factors that limit executives. Hence, because many of the same forces may be at work, upper-echelons propositions must take account of these constraints.[20]

The second important consideration is the power of individual board members with respect to other board members. Although numerous studies have examined the distribution of power between boards and top managers, with a lesser number on the distribution of power within top management teams, we know of no study that has empirically investigated the distribution of power among board members. To the extent that boards affect organizational outcomes, such an analysis may help improve explained variance and is a potentially exciting line of inquiry. In addition, it would be interesting to develop a typology of director power and compare this with related work on top management teams (Finkelstein 1992). If boards are supra-TMTs, many of the same phenomena that drive power relations among top managers may also be relevant for board members.

Consider the four major power types identified by Finkelstein (1992): structural, ownership, expertise, and prestige. Each of these power types appears to be operative among board members. Structural power arises from formal hierarchical relations within the board, such as whether the CEO position is structurally separate from the board chair position. Ownership power emanates from shareholdings in the firm and family relations, both of which are important drivers of board power. Expertise power is defined by the ability of board members to reduce uncertainty arising from critical contingencies, something that has long been considered a central task of boards (Pfeffer 1972). Prestige power is a major component of the influence structure of top managers and has been used as an indicator of board power (D'Aveni and Kesner 1993). Nevertheless, boards of directors have several unique characteristics that may require a more complex model of the power distribution, chief among them being that both insiders and outsiders are members. It is not clear which director type will necessarily be more powerful, so development of these ideas requires special consideration of such differences.

If boards are supra-TMTs, it is possible to suggest numerous propositions that build on the original upper-echelons ideas. We offer two as examples.

Boards and Functional Tracks.   Several studies have investigated the idea that a manager's functional background will be related to the strategies the firm employs (e.g., Hitt and Tyler 1991). As Hambrick and Mason argued, "this functional-track orientation may not dominate the strategic choices an executive makes, but it can be expected to exert some influence" (1984, 199). Extending this line of thought to the board level suggests the following proposition:

PROPOSITION 7-23

The firm's resource allocation among different functions is positively associated with the extent to which these functions are reflected in the backgrounds of board members.

Boards and Tenures.   Perhaps the most studied of all demographic characteristics is the duration of service, or tenure. As we discussed in Chapter 4, long tenures are associated with strategic persistence to a course of action (Finkelstein and Hambrick 1990). Hence, at the board level, we propose:

PROPOSITION 7-24

The longer the tenures of board members, the less the strategic change that will ensue in the organization.

Moderators of the Board—Organizational Outcome Association. Keeping with our discussion earlier on how discretion and power represent key refinements to the upper-echelons logic, it is important to underscore how propositions such as those presented above are subject to moderating influences. We offer two generic propositions to address this issue:

PROPOSITION 7-25

The greater the discretion of the board, the stronger the association between board demographic characteristics and organizational outcomes.

PROPOSITION 7-26

The association between board demographic characteristics and organizational outcomes is moderated by the relative distribution of power among board members.

Our purpose here is simply to suggest some testable propositions on the relationship between boards of directors and strategy formation, and not to formally develop theory that extends the upper-echelons perspective to boards. Nevertheless, abundant research opportunities are apparent.

Board Monitoring and Disciplinary Behavior

The idea that boards fulfill a monitoring role in organizations is more widely held than the notion that boards are actively involved in strategic decision making. Research has investigated several different outcomes attributed to boards, including executive succession, the setting of managerial pay, and the adoption of takeover defenses. In Chapter 6, we examined CEO selection and succession, and thus do not review this literature here. Nevertheless, it is important to reiterate a point made in Chapter 6: CEOs do not get hired and fired without boards of directors playing a central role in these actions. Indeed, of all activities boards of directors engage in, the hiring and firing of CEOs are the most representative of their ultimate responsibility to discipline top management (Zald 1969).

Before reviewing research on the actual consequences of board monitoring and disciplining, it is important to consider the operative mechanisms through which boards may have this effect. Empirical studies seldom specify these mechanisms. Rather, hypotheses often argue that outside directors (or other measures of board vigilance) are associated with various organizational outcomes. An implicit assumption is that outsiders pressure top managers to behave in a manner consistent with shareholder interests. What is unclear is how vigilant boards do so.[21] In particular, do top managers work harder, or better, when boards are vigilant? How do vigilant boards actually influence top management to "do the right thing"? Although scholars have raised such questions in the past (e.g., Perrow 1986; Finkelstein and Hambrick 1988; Barkema 1993; Davis and Thompson 1994), empirical work has yet to directly specify, measure, and test how board monitoring actually affects organizational outcomes. We believe such a research program is in order. Nevertheless, in spite of this omission, considerable research has been conducted on the consequences of board monitoring, which we now review.

Boards and Executive Compensation.   Boards have long been considered to play an important role in the establishment of executive pay (Fama and Jensen 1983), and Table 7-3 highlights much of this work. While agency theorists tend to portray the board's role in aligning managerial and shareholder interests as primary, researchers working from an organizational perspective are beginning to accumulate evidence suggesting a different role for boards in the compensation-setting process.

In one of the earliest and most persuasive studies from an organization theory perspective, O'Reilly, Main, and Crystal (1988) found that CEO compensation was positively associated with the pay levels of compensation

TABLE 7-3 **Research on Board Effects on Executive Compensation**

Study	Theory	Dependent Variables	Independent Variables	Results	Sample
Allen 1981	Managerial power	CEO compensation	Classification of firms into control configurations based on director equity	mixed	218 large industrial firms in 1975
O'Reilly, Main, and Crystal 1988	Social comparison theory	CEO compensation	Compensation committee salary Outside directors' salary	+ +	105 firms from *Business Week's* executive compensation survey in 1984
Finkelstein and Hambrick 1989	Managerial power	CEO compensation	Outside directors' equity	n.s.	110 leisure-industry firms in 1971, 1976, 1982, and 1983.
Kerr and Kren 1992	Agency theory-power	CEO compensation	% inside directors	n.s.	63 R & D intensive firms in 1986 and 1987
Lambert, Larcker, and Weigelt 1993	Agency theory-power	Executive compensation	% outside directors appointed by the CEO Outside directors' equity % outside directors Non-CEO inside directors own ≥5% of company shares	+ mixed + mixed	303 large firms between 1982 and 1984
Main, O'Reilly, and Wade 1994	Agency theory-power	CEO compensation	*Study 1* Compensation committee pay Absence of compensation committee	+ +	89 firms from *Business Week's* executive compensation survey in 1984

TABLE 7-3 Research on Board Effects on Executive Compensation, *continued*

Study	Theory	Dependent Variables	Independent Variables	Results	Sample
			% outside directors	+	
			CEO appointed before compensation committee chair	+	
			CEO on nominating committee	+	
			CEO duality	+	
			% non-CEOs on compensation committee	+	
			CEO age similarity with compensation committee	+	274 firms partially owned by CALPERS in 1988
			Study 2		
			CEO compensation committee pay	+	
			% outside directors	mixed	
			CEO appointed before outsiders	mixed	
			CEO duality	n.s.	
Westphal and Zajac 1994	Managerial power	(1) Adoption of long-term incentive plans (LTIP) (2) Likelihood of LTIP use (3) Magnitude of LTIP		(1) (2) (3)	
			Number of inside directors compared to number of outside directors	n.s. n.s. n.s.	570 large firms between 1972 and 1990
			Number of outside directors appointed after the CEO	+ – n.s.	
			CEO duality	+ – –	

NOTES: Only findings related to boards of directors were included in this table. Significant results (denoted by + or −) were based on p<.05 or better. Identification of theoretical perspectives was based on our evaluation and not necessarily noted by the authors in their studies.

committee members and outside directors. Drawing on social comparison theory, this article suggests that the composition of board committees contains potentially valuable information on how boards and CEOs interact and that boards may not necessarily act as true principals in a principal-agent relationship. These notions were further supported in a more elaborate follow-up study (Main, O'Reilly, and Wade 1994).

One way to reconcile this organizational perspective of compensation with an agency theory approach is by explicitly modeling agency theory in terms of power. Indeed, this approach has been adopted in several studies. For example, in a study of 218 large industrial firms in 1975, Allen (1981) tested whether various measures of director equity (an indicator of board power or vigilance) were associated with CEO compensation. Results were not clearly supportive, as was the case in other studies testing similar relationships (Finkelstein and Hambrick 1989; Lambert, Larcker, and Weigelt 1993). On the other hand, outside director representation was positively associated with compensation in two recent studies (Lambert, Larcker, and Weigelt 1993; Main, O'Reilly, and Wade 1994), although no significant effects were found for total pay (Kerr and Kren 1992) or the adoption of long-term incentive plans (Westphal and Zajac 1994). A new measure that is beginning to be used in empirical work is the percentage of outsiders appointed to the board by the CEO. Generally, this measure of CEO power has been found to be positively related to CEO compensation (Lambert, Larcker, and Weigelt 1993; Main, O'Reilly, and Wade 1994; Westphal and Zajac 1994). Finally, CEO duality, another indicator of CEO power over a board, was a significant predictor of executive compensation in two studies (Main, O'Reilly, and Wade 1994; Westphal and Zajac 1994). Hence, although findings have not been consistent, these studies provide support for the idea that the distribution of power between boards and CEOs is an important determinant of executive compensation. This suggests that some boards' ability to effectively monitor top management through the use of compensation contracts is severely restricted by their limited power. As such, this research represents relatively strong support for our earlier conceptualization of agency theory as a theory of power.

Boards and Response to Takeover Threats.   Beyond compensation arrangements, boards play a potentially large role in spearheading a firm's response to takeover. This response need not await an actual takeover attempt, as boards can institute numerous antitakeover amendments or actions to reduce the chances of a successful takeover. Doing so is generally not considered to be an enhancement of shareholder value because actions that reduce the probability of takeover have the effect of insulating

TABLE 7-4 **Research on Board Effects on Takeover Defenses**

Study	Theory	Dependent Variables	Independent Variables	Results		Sample
Cochran, Wood, and Jones 1985	Agency theory-power	Incidence of golden parachutes	% inside directors	−		406 Fortune 500 firms in 1982
			Director equity	n.s.		
Kosnik 1987	Agency theory-power	Resistance to greenmail	% family directors	mixed		110 large firms that were greenmail targets between 1979 and 1983
			% outside directors with company's executives on their own board	mixed		
			% affiliated directors	+		
			% outside directors	+		
			% outside directors who are executives	+		
			Outside directors' equity	−		
Brickley, Lease, and Smith, 1988	Agency theory	% Votes cast on anti-takeover amendments	Directors' and officers' equity	n.s.		288 management-sponsored antitakeover amendments in 1984
		% Affirmative votes cast		+		
		% Negative votes cast		−		
Singh, and Harianto 1989a	Agency theory-power	Adoption of golden parachutes	Managerial tenure compared to outside directors' tenure	n.s.		213 large firms (79 had adopted golden parachutes by December 1985; 134 had not)
			% outside directors	+		
			Board size	n.s.		
Singh and Harianto, 1989b	Agency theory-power	(1) Number of executives covered by golden parachutes	Managerial tenure compared to outside directors' tenure	(1) n.s.	(2) +	89 Fortune 500 firms that adopted golden parachutes as of December 1985
		(2) Size of golden parachutes	% outside directors	mixed	n.s.	
			% insiders on compensation committee	−	n.s.	
			Board size	n.s.	−	

TABLE 7-4 **Research on Board Effects on Takeover Defenses,** *continued*

Study	Theory	Dependent Variables	Independent Variables	Results	Sample
Kosnik 1990	Demography Agency theory-power	Resistance to greenmail	(1) Outside directors' equity compared to outside directors' compensation	n.s.	110 large firms that were greenmail targets between 1979 and 1983
			(2) Outside directors' tenure	+	
			(3) Outside directors' tenure variation	n.s.	
			(4) Outside directors' occupational variation	−	
			Managers' equity compared to managers' compensation		
			x (1)	+	
			x (2)	n.s.	
			x (3)	−	
			x (4)	n.s.	
Wade, O'Reilly, and Chandratat 1990	Agency theory-power	Incidence of golden parachutes	CEO board tenure compared to directors' tenure	n.s.	89 firms from *Business Week's* executive compensation survey in 1984
			Number of outside directors appointed after CEO	mixed	
			Board size	n.s.	
			CEO board tenure	−	
Davis 1991	Agency theory-power Social class theory and inter-organizational cohesion	Adoption of poison pills	% inside directors	n.s.	440 Fortune 500 firms between 1984 and 1989
			Inside directors' equity	−	
			Network centrality	+	
			Ties to adopters	+	

TABLE 7-4 **Research on Board Effects on Takeover Defenses,** *continued*

Study	Theory	Dependent Variables	Independent Variables	Results	Sample
Mallette and Fowler 1992	Agency theory-power	Adoption of poison pills	% outside directors	n.s.	673 manufacturing firms between 1985 and 1988
			CEO duality	+	
			Outside directors' tenure	n.s.	
			Inside directors' equity	−	
			Outside directors' equity	n.s.	
D'Aveni and Kesner 1993	Social class theory Resource dependence Agency theory-power	Resistance to tender offers	Number of inside directors compared to number of outside directors	−	106 tender offers between 1984 and 1986
			% CEO family directors	−	
			Inside directors' tenure compared to outside directors' tenure	n.s.	
			% directors with vice-chair or chair titles	+	
			% lawyers on board	+	
Sundaramurthy and Wang 1993	Agency theory-power	Adoption of classified board provisions	% outside directors	n.s.	181 S & P 500 firms that had not adopted classified board provisions before 1984
			CEO duality	n.s.	
			Outside directors' tenure compared to CEO tenure	n.s.	
			Board size	−	
Buchholtz and Ribbens 1994	Agency theory-power	Resistance to tender offers	% outside directors	n.s.	406 firms subject to tender offer between 1986 and 1989
			Directors' equity	−	

NOTES: Only findings related to boards of directors were included in this table. Significant results (denoted by + or −) were based on p<.05 or better. Identification of theoretical perspectives was based on our evaluation and not necessarily noted by the authors in their studies.

top managers from the market for corporate control and reduce the opportunity for shareholders to capitalize on the returns that often accrue to target-firm owners (Jensen and Ruback 1983; Kosnik 1987; Mallette and Fowler 1992). As Table 7-4 indicates, researchers have examined how boards influence the adoption of golden parachutes,[22] poison pills,[23] classified board provisions,[24] and antitakeover amendments in general, as well as the paying of greenmail,[25] and takeover resistance.

This work constitutes a significant research stream on corporate governance. Driven largely by an agency theory logic, these studies have grown in importance because takeover defenses exemplify the boards' exercise of fiduciary responsibility. To the extent that boards adopt various mechanisms that protect top managers at the expense of shareholder interests, there is clear evidence of a breakdown of the principal-agent relationship. And in almost every case where such breakdown is observed, it is driven by a distribution of power that favors top managers over boards. Hence, the major contribution of this work is the identification of the distribution of power between boards and top managers as the key driving force in the agency relationship.

Several studies have examined the association between boards of directors and the granting of golden parachutes. In the first study of this type, Cochran, Wood, and Jones (1985) hypothesized that because insiders were more likely beholden to the CEO than outsiders, the incidence of golden parachutes would be greater in firms with more insiders on the board. They tested this idea on a sample of 406 Fortune 500 firms in 1982 and found that the percentage of insiders on the board was actually negatively associated with the incidence of golden parachutes. Singh and Harianto (1989a) reported similar results in a different sample of firms over a longer period. These authors also noted that managerial shareholdings were negatively associated with golden parachutes, suggesting that stock ownership may substitute for takeover-contingent compensation. Other board attributes were not significantly associated with golden parachutes, including director equity (Cochran, Wood, and Jones 1985), and board size and relative board tenure (Singh and Harianto 1989a; Wade, O'Reilly, and Chandratat 1990), although CEO tenure on the board was a negative predictor (Wade, O'Reilly, and Chandratat 1990). In addition, Singh and Harianto (1989b) reported that the percentage of insiders on the compensation committee was negatively associated with the number of executives covered by golden parachutes in a firm, and relative managerial tenure (positive) and board size (negative) were significant predictors of the magnitude of golden parachute contracts.

Two studies examined board effects on the adoption of poison pills. A comparison of these two studies is instructive, because the firms and time periods sampled overlapped significantly. Although the models tested and the analytical techniques employed differed, reported results had important similarities. Both Davis (1991) and Mallette and Fowler (1992) found inside director equity to be negatively associated, but inside or outside director representation not associated, with the adoption of poison pills.[26] In addition, Mallette and Fowler (1992) reported that such characteristics of outside directors as their equity and tenure were unrelated to poison pill adoption. However, these authors also found CEO duality to be positively related to poison pill adoption.

These results are generally consistent with an agency theory-CEO power perspective. Davis (1991) also tested the notion that intercorporate interactions drive the adoption of poison pills and found that network centrality—especially director ties with firms that have already adopted poison pills—were significant predictors of adoption by the focal firm. Thus, this study stands out as one of the few to explicitly test alternative theoretical perspectives on how boards affect organizational outcomes.

In another study related to antitakeover amendments, Sundaramurthy and Wang (1993) found that board size was negatively associated with the adoption of classified board provisions. Yet, outside director representation, CEO duality, and the ratio of outside director tenure to CEO tenure were not significant predictors. In addition, earlier work by Brickley, Lease, and Smith (1988) found that director and officer equity was positively associated with the percentage of affirmative votes cast for management-sponsored antitakeover amendments.

Some of the earliest work in this research stream was conducted by Kosnik (1987). In a study designed to test the effect of board characteristics on resistance to paying greenmail, Kosnik (1987) found that outside director representation, but not outside director equity, was positively related to resistance. In a follow-up study, Kosnik (1990) reported that a refined measure designed to assess the incentives outside board members face (the ratio of an outside director's equity to his or her compensation) was also unrelated to greenmail resistance. The interaction of this measure with a similar one constructed for top managers was positive and significant, although the main effect for "management's equity ratio" lost significance when the interaction term was added to the regression. As summarized in Table 7-4, both of these studies developed interesting measures relating to the distribution of power between boards and managers, and the more recent article also tested the effects of various measures of board demography.

Finally, two recent studies have examined the role of boards during takeover attempts. Adopting multiple theoretical perspectives, D'Aveni and Kesner (1993) argued that firms were more likely to resist tender offers when their top managers were more powerful than board members. Using a variety of measures of relative managerial power, these authors did not find support for this hypothesis. Instead, results indicated support for the notion that relatively powerful managers were more likely to cooperate with bidders. In contrast, a study by Buchholtz and Ribbens (1994) with a larger sample of firms subject to tender offer found that director equity was negatively associated with takeover resistance. However, outside director representation was not at all related to takeover resistance. Both of these studies are interesting in that they were carefully done yet yielded mostly counterintuitive findings.

Our review of the literature on how boards are associated with organizational outcomes shows a strong reliance on an agency theory-power perspective. While some refer to managerial hegemony theory (e.g., Mallette and Fowler 1992) or more loosely connected ideas on managerial power, (e.g., Allen 1981) rather than agency theory, virtually all consistently highlight the distribution of power between boards and CEOs as a central theoretical idea that drives this research stream. As such, empirical research is reflective of our earlier conceptualization of agency theory as a theory of power.

A second conclusion that emerges from this review is that, in spite of the generally consistent theoretical rationale across articles, results are far from uniform. One source of this confusion, the measurement of board vigilance, deserves greater emphasis in this research. Using such proxies for board vigilance as outside director representation or outside director equity may be part of the problem. Outside directors may not have sufficient information or independence to enforce shareholder interests on a potentially entrenched top management. However, virtually all studies testing the efficacy of board governance rely on such data.[27] More direct measures of board vigilance—ideally derived from field and survey data—are needed that can more accurately assess the true extent of board power. It would then be possible to examine whether commonly used board vigilance proxies are related to more direct measures of board vigilance and whether these more direct measures are related to organizational outcomes. Developing valid and reliable field- and survey-based measures of board vigilance clearly is no easy task; the potential benefit of such an undertaking, however, would appear to be large.

Researchers should expand the relatively narrow set of objective measures of board characteristics typically studied. For example, Eisenhardt notes such operational measures of board monitoring as "frequency of board meetings, number of board subcommittees, number of board members with long tenure, number of board members with managerial and industry experience, and number of board members representing specific ownership groups" (1989a, 65). These characteristics are consistent with our earlier conceptualization of board structure and composition; yet few of these attributes have been used in empirical research.

Another reason may account for the inconsistent results reported in previous work. In each study, authors selected a dependent variable and a set of independent variables, but no consideration was given to the interaction among different dependent variables and among different independent variables. For example, firms adopting poison pills may feel no need to also adopt classified board provisions. This suggests that different dependent variables may be substitutes for one another and that different measures of board vigilance may also be substitutes for one another. That researchers usually do not examine interrelationships among multiple outcomes of board monitoring or the substitutability of alternative measures of board vigilance[28] may explain why many studies report inconsistent results. This line of argument suggests the following illustrative proposition:

PROPOSITION 7-27

Boards that have adopted antitakeover provisions in the past are less likely to adopt subsequent antitakeover provisions.[29]

Relatedly, shareholders can rely on alternative monitoring and disciplining mechanisms, not all of which need be operative at any one time. For example, boards have several different internal monitoring and disciplinary mechanisms at their disposal, including compensation contracts, direct board monitoring, and dismissal (Walsh and Seward 1990). In addition, there are several external monitoring mechanisms on which shareholders may rely. However, with few exceptions (e.g., Morck, Shleifer, and Vishny 1989; Beatty and Zajac 1994; Rediker and Seth 1995), research has proceeded without consideration of alternative methods to keep top managers in line (Williamson 1983).

To the extent that agency costs can be minimized in a variety of ways, studies that model multiple monitoring mechanisms simultaneously are more likely to accurately assess how managerial behavior is constrained by such monitoring. Consider this simple example. Suppose a firm made extensive use of performance-contingent compensation, but the board of directors was dominated by insiders. Research that relies on a standard measure of board vigilance such as outside director representation may be misleading, because the tight link between pay and performance in this firm suggests that managers may actually be focused on shareholder interests.

Thus, it seems important that research on corporate governance adopt a more sophisticated approach that explicitly models the possibility that alternative monitoring mechanisms are substitutes. For example, we propose:

PROPOSITION 7-28

Alternative monitoring mechanisms (e.g., direct board monitoring, CEO compensation, the market for corporate control, market competition) act as substitutes for one another.

Finally, it is important to note that while the majority of research on board consequences is based on agency theory, several studies have adopted alternative theoretical approaches. One of the most promising of these approaches views boards as part of a social network (e.g., Galaskiewicz and Wasserman 1981) and is embodied most recently in work by Davis (1991) and Haunschild (1994). As Davis and Thompson argue,

> The corporate elite forms an identifiable category of actors connected by extensive formal and informal social ties. Of most interest for corporate governance is the interlock network formed by overlapping membership on boards of directors. Most large corporations are linked into a single network by sharing directors with other firms. This network . . . can serve as a basis for cohesion and collective action among professional managers (Useem, 1984) as well as a latent structure for spreading techniques for expanding corporate control. Because the board has ultimate authority within the firm in matters of governance, sharing directors provides a mechanism for innovations in governance to spread from board to board. (1994, 163)

Thus, research that relies solely on an agency theory perspective to explain board behavior may be neglecting an important alternative theory, one consequence of which may be the inconsistent results reported in the literature.

Our goal in this chapter was to develop an integrative model of boards of directors that depicted the board as a central player in strategic leadership—on the one hand, a monitor of top management and on the other, a supra-top management team. Consideration of the contextual conditions that give rise to board structure and composition, as well as the organizational outcomes that result from board vigilance and strategic involvement, allowed for an integrated treatment of the role of boards at the apex of organizations. This chapter also suggested numerous testable propositions to focus research on boards of directors as important strategic leaders and advocated a broader theoretical understanding of how boards affect, and are affected by, internal and external forces.

NOTES

1. Monitoring is defined as the direct and indirect observation of managerial behavior over time (Jensen and Meckling 1976). It "can be achieved through budgets, responsibility accounting, rules, and policies" (Tosi and Gomez-Mejia 1989, 171).
2. Beyond structure and composition, boards may be examined by focusing on process (how they interact as a group) (Vance 1983), style (their "personality" or modes of operation) (Mueller 1981), and internal organization (committee membership and the flow of information among committees) (Brown 1981).
3. Inside directors, as members of top management, have been studied somewhat more extensively (e.g., Wagner, Pfeffer, and O'Reilly 1984). As a result, we will focus on the turnover and selection of outside directors. The appointment of an executive of the firm to the board, however, is also interesting and worthy of study (the removal of an executive from the board is likely to coincide with his or her departure from the firm, so this aspect of director turnover is of somewhat less theoretical interest). For example, it may be that managers are selected to boards 1) when they are anointed as successors, or potential successors, of the CEO (Vancil 1987; Hermalin and Weisbach 1988), 2) as a reward for good performance (Vance 1983), or 3) as a consequence of their power (Finkelstein 1992). The selection of inside directors remains an interesting empirical question.
4. Although our discussion focuses on director selection from the perspective of the firm, social class theory also suggests that individuals seek directorships because it enhances their social standing in the business elite (Useem 1979).
5. Fama and Jensen (1983) argued that the reputation of outside board members in particular was an important consideration in their appointments. Hence, to the extent that firm performance is a positive indicator of reputation, agency theory predicts that directors of better performing firms would be more likely to be appointed to new board directorship positions.
6. The Gilson study (1990) noted earlier reported that the number of directorships held by individual directors of distressed firms who had resigned declined by 35 percent in the three years following resignation.
7. The idea that director turnover is associated with poor performance is consistent with theories of managerial turnover as well (Harrison, Torres, and Kukalis 1988). As a result, a negative association between director turnover and firm performance may reflect attributions about director responsibility. Nevertheless, although such an alternative explanation cannot be easily ruled out, it is not clear who would be making such attributions in a firm.
8. This proposition assumes that sitting CEOs will be more threatened by potential reputational losses than other outside directors.
9. This proposition implies that effective board monitoring requires certain board characteristics that promote board independence, even when boards themselves are relatively powerful. This may appear paradoxical until one considers that the primary mechanism through which boards may exert their power is dismissal of the CEO (Lorsch 1989); while an independent board has the potential to be involved throughout the strategy-making process.
10. In 1984, Pennzoil sued Texaco for damages when Texaco bought Getty Oil two days after Pennzoil had agreed to purchase 43 percent of Getty.

11. Hermalin and Weisbach (1988) report, however, that new CEOs were more likely to add outsiders than insiders to the board.

12. Although we emphasize the role of agency theory and managerial power in explaining why boards are not always vigilant, other reasons have been suggested. Building on work by Lorsch (1989), Main, O'Reilly, and Wade (1994) argued that because many shareholders have short-term interests that may be in conflict with the long-run goals of a firm, it may not make sense for directors to slavishly promote shareholder interests. Another explanation, suggested by Walsh and Seward (1990), is that because boards may have great difficulty accurately attributing organizational outcomes to top managers, ambiguity may creep into incentive systems. Also, as noted earlier, many boards have an implicit norm to support the CEO and his or her leadership of the firm (Patton and Baker 1987). Finally, outside directors may simply not have sufficient time and information to effectively evaluate managerial proposals and actions (Estes 1980; Baysinger and Hoskisson 1990), while inside directors tend to be more beholden to the CEO (Patton and Baker 1987).

13. Board attributions about firm performance and the responsibility of top management for that performance are not always straightforward (Fredrickson, Hambrick, and Baumrin 1988; Walsh and Seward 1990).

14. Although we discuss the board's governance and strategy formation roles separately for analytical purposes, these roles likely overlap somewhat. In the governance role, the board must approve the strategy that is developed. To do so effectively, board members must understand the strategy and believe that it will work in the context in which the firm operates. One of the best ways to understand the strategy is to be involved in developing it.

15. Board involvement was defined along two dimensions, "formation of new strategic directions" and "evaluation of prior strategic decisions," with respondents asked to rate the "board's general level of involvement in strategic decision making" (Judge and Zeithaml 1992, 793).

16. As noted earlier, Hermalin and Weisbach (1988) found that poor performance led to changes in board composition, so cross-sectional regression of performance on board composition may be biased because of changes in board composition resulting from past performance (Hermalin and Weisbach 1991).

17. Some of the problems in relating TMT heterogeneity directly to organizational outcomes discussed in Chapter 5 are likely relevant here as well.

18. For example, Amihud and Lev (1981) argued and found that unrelated diversification was greater in manager-controlled firms than in owner-controlled firms.

19. Directional interlocks are "created by people who are principally affiliated with (i.e., owners or officers of) one of the two firms they connect," while nondirectional interlocks are "created by people who are principally affiliated with a third institution" (Palmer, Jennings, and Zhou 1993, 107).

20. In Hambrick and Finkelstein's (1987) original statement of managerial discretion, they argued that powerful outside forces were an important constraint on executive choice. For boards of directors, perhaps the most important "powerful outside force" is the top management team. Hence, when we discuss board discretion, it makes sense conceptually to consider what we have defined as "vigilance" as an integral part of the construct. Nevertheless, vigilance and discretion

are not synonymous; while vigilance refers to a specific aspect of discretion, discretion is a broader construct encompassing a wide range of environmental and individual attributes that go beyond what is typically seen as vigilance.

21. The same criticism cannot as readily be made of research on top managers because 1) studies have explicitly documented how top managers affect organizational outcomes (e.g., Pettigrew 1973; Mintzberg 1985; Bower 1986), and 2) the relationship between top management and strategy and performance, while certainly not universally held (Hannan and Freeman 1977), has a stronger theoretical tradition (e.g., Child 1972; Hambrick and Finkelstein 1987).

22. Golden parachutes are contracts between employers and top managers that provide for additional compensation should a change in control or ownership occur (Krueger 1985).

23. Poison pills enable shareholders to purchase their shares in a firm at a discount or tender their shares at a premium. These rights impose unwanted financial obligations on a bidder, making takeovers more expensive.

24. A classified board amendment generally divides a board into three classes with only one class standing for election each year. As such, its provisions make a transfer of control more difficult (Sundaramurthy and Wang 1993).

25. Greenmail involves the purchase of a firm's stock from a corporate raider at a premium to prevent a takeover.

26. However, Brickley, Coles, and Terry (1994) reported that the average stock market reaction to announcements of poison pill adoption was positive when the board had a majority of outside directors and negative when it did not.

27. Tosi and Gomez-Mejia (1989) is an important exception.

28. There are some exceptions. For example, Davis (1991) controlled for other antitakeover mechanisms in his study of the adoption of poison pills. In addition, while some measures of board vigilance may be substitutes, others may be complements because of their construction. For example, outside director representation and outside director equity are definitionally related, so we might expect them to be correlated as well. An examination of the interrelationships among measures of board vigilance is needed.

29. Alternatively, it may be that once a board adopts one antitakeover amendment, it will be more likely to adopt others. In either case, this remains an important empirical question to sort out.

EXECUTIVE COMPENSATION

Few topics on strategic leadership generate the same degree of controversy as executive compensation. This debate spans academic, managerial, board of director, and governmental audiences, and tends to focus on a single question: What is the logic behind CEO pay? Academics generally try to answer this query with economic explanations that focus on incentives and principal-agent relations. CEOs and boards of directors, however, often have a broader set of forces that govern their behavior and frequently lead to conflicting goals in the compensation-setting process. CEOs and boards also are driven by concerns for comparability as they seek to legitimize pay structures. Meanwhile, governmental agencies, taking a different tack, advocate greater disclosure of executive compensation practices in response to pressure from various stakeholders.

Our goal in this chapter is to first develop a framework that captures the complexity of executive compensation and then suggest a research agenda to guide further work on this topic. While such a framework cannot encompass every stream of work on executive compensation (because of the broad range of disciplines represented), we attempt to offer a parsimonious yet integrative structure. This framework is based on three dimensions that characterize the assumptions often implicit in empirical research on executive compensation: 1) the direction of causality, 2) the theoretical perspective adopted, and 3) the unit of analysis. The following section describes these dimensions.

ORGANIZING DIMENSIONS FOR A FRAMEWORK OF EXECUTIVE COMPENSATION

Direction of Causality

Executive compensation can be considered as a dependent variable (i.e., something to be explained) or an independent variable (i.e., for explaining something else). Scholarly and popular interest in understanding why some CEOs are paid more than others has focused on compensation as a dependent variable. Thus, the prevailing research has been on the determinants of pay. Perhaps of greater interest for strategic choice and firm performance, however, are the consequences of executive compensation—an area of much less empirical work. Modeling executive compensation as an independent variable directs attention not only to firm performance, but also to a potentially wide set of strategic choices, organizational characteristics, and stakeholder reactions that may be responsive to executive compensation plans.

Theoretical Perspectives

Research on executive compensation has historically been driven by economic theory: for example, Berle and Means (1932), in one of the earliest and still most influential published works on corporate ownership structure, documented the increasing separation of ownership and control in modern organizations. This work led other economists to focus on the consequences of the separation of ownership and control, including the observation that "executive salaries appear to be more closely associated with the scale of operations than with its, the firm's, profitability" (Baumol 1967, 46). Consequently, early empirical research on executive compensation was dominated by economists' concerns about the relative importance of firm size and profitability as determinants of pay. Recent work based on agency theory represents a more sophisticated version of the same argument. Hence, economics-based theory has been the dominant influence on executive compensation research.

In spite of the prevalence of economic approaches to executive compensation, alternative perspectives based on social-psychological and political theories of organizations are becoming more common. The social-psychology perspective argues that the setting of executive compensation is a social phenomena (Barnard 1938; Hicks 1963) and, hence, is influenced by the actions of other individuals both within and outside of the organization. The political perspective suggests that executive compensation and executive power are closely related (Finkelstein and Hambrick 1988). Taken together, then, scholars interested in studying executive compensation can select from economic, social-psychological, and political theoretical perspectives. Predictably, most research has focused on only one of these theories, but each can offer valuable insights to the compensation puzzle. In addition, research that seeks to combine theoretical perspectives may be particularly valuable because such an approach can lead to critical tests that help distinguish the conditions where various theories are applicable (Platt 1964) and where they are not.

Unit of Analysis

The question of unit of analysis is seldom explicitly considered in research on executive compensation. Most work focuses on either the pay of the CEO or on the aggregate pay of a larger set of top managers. Relatively rare, but potentially very informative, is research on pay patterns within top management groups—such as pay dispersion and differentials—to understand both its determinants and consequences. Although research on pay at the group level is common for nonmanagers (Hirsch 1982), considerably less work has been done at the top managerial level.

When direction of causality, theoretical perspective, and unit of analysis are all considered together, a complex but analytically useful framework for the study of executive compensation emerges. The value of such a framework is twofold: 1) it provides a broad view of research on executive compensation that helps match pieces of a complex puzzle, and 2) it enables identification of research opportunities along multiple combinations of underlying dimensions. When all three possible dimensions are brought together in a two-by-two-by-three framework, as in Figure 8–1, twelve possible conditions emerge. However, because compensation research on the group level of analysis is sparse, it may be more effective to examine determinants and consequences together. Doing so allows an integrated discussion of pay distributions within top management teams that avoids repetition. Hence, we consider all three dimensions of executive compensation in a parsimonious yet integrated fashion.

FIGURE 8-1 **A Framework to Study Executive Compensation**

Perspective	Individual Unit of Analysis Direction of Causality		Group Unit of Analysis Direction of Causality	
	Determinants	**Consequences**	**Determinants**	**Consequences**
Economic	Managerialism versus neoclassical economics Human capital Marginal product Managerial labor markets	Managerial risk acceptance and acceptance of longer time horizons Firm performance	Tournament model and pay differentials	Tournament model and turnover Tournament model and firm performance
Social-Psychological	Mimetic and normative isomorphism Social comparison	Equity and turnover	Social comparison and pay dispersion	Pay inequality and turnover Pay inequality and firm performance
Political	Managerial power versus board power	Managerial manipulation of incentive systems Unintended consequences of pay	Distribution of power within top management teams	Politics as a contingency between pay inequality and firm performance Pay inequality and top management team politics Relative managerial pay and internal labor markets

Beyond compensation at the top executive level, some work also has been done on compensation for business unit general managers. Although some of this research has applied only theories and frameworks used in previous studies of corporate level compensation, specific issues arise in considering general manager compensation. Hence, we include a brief section that examines the determinants and consequences of general manager pay.

The remainder of this chapter is divided into four major sections, examining 1) the determinants of individual executive compensation, 2) the consequences of individual compensation, 3) the determinants and consequences of the distribution of pay within top management teams, and 4) the determinants and consequences of compensation for business unit general managers. Our goal in each section is to outline the key issues and research questions, major research findings, and unresolved or unanswered questions, and to recommend future research.

DETERMINANTS OF EXECUTIVE COMPENSATION

Economic Explanations for Executive Compensation

The economic determinants of executive compensation have been a major focus of research for some time. As we noted above, for many years economists have been interested in the relative importance of sales and profits in explaining compensation. The underlying theories, though not always explicit in some studies, can be described from both the managerial and neoclassical perspectives.

Managerialist.   According to this perspective, CEOs seek to maximize firm size because 1) size is more controllable than profits, 2) bigger firms have greater ability to pay more than smaller firms (Agarwal 1981), and 3) bigger firms offer larger nonpecuniary benefits, such as prestige, to managers (Marris 1964; Baumol 1967; Williamson 1985). The managerialist perspective leads naturally to a "corporate growth hypothesis"; namely, that firm size (sales or assets) will be positively associated with executive compensation (Ciscel and Carroll 1980). It is also possible to argue that maximizing firm size is a worthy goal for which CEOs should be rewarded because larger firms may have greater market power and access to more resources and, hence, involve more complex and demanding responsibilities (Ungson and Steers 1984; Henderson and Fredrickson 1993). Nevertheless, if a CEO is rewarded for increasing firm size and if bigger firms tend to pay more than smaller firms, an association between size and pay is mutually reinforcing: CEOs are paid more to manage a large firm, so they increase the size of the firm to be paid more (Lenski 1966). Perhaps for this reason, significant empirical support for the managerialist perspective exists, spanning several decades (Roberts 1959; Marris 1964; Ciscel 1974; Cosh 1975; Meeks and Whittington 1975; McGuire, Chiu, and Elbing 1975; Bentson 1985; Kerr and Bettis 1987; Rajagopalan and Prescott 1990). A very strong association exists between organization size and CEO pay.

Neoclassical. Neoclassical economists support the "profit maximization hypothesis," which translates in the compensation arena to an expectation that executive pay will be significantly related to firm profitability (Ciscel and Carroll 1980). According to this perspective, because corporations, through the decisions of management, seek to maximize profitability, profits should "have a strong and persistent influence on executive rewards" (Lewellen and Huntsman 1970, 718). Over the last twenty years, the idea that pay and firm performance are related has been promulgated by agency theorists (Jensen and Meckling 1976; Holmstrom 1979). Rather than only assuming that managerial interests are aligned with shareholder interests, however, agency theorists emphasize the importance of incentives in promoting this alignment (Smith and Watts 1982). Hence, most empirical work from the agency theory perspective hypothesizes a significant association between managerial pay and firm performance—generally under the assumption that effective incentives are included in compensation contracts (Raviv 1985). Although conceptual support in agency theory is strong, Jensen and Murphy (1990), in probably the most complete empirical examination of the effectiveness of incentives in compensation contracts, found these incentives to be particularly small. For example, these authors demonstrated that a $1,000 change in corporate value corresponded to a 6.7 cents change in CEO salary and bonus, hardly an incentive at all. Thus, agency theory research does not always find a strong association between pay and performance. In part as a response to these disappointing findings, agency theorists have begun to suggest that social–psychological and political factors may play a role in determining executive compensation (Baker, Jensen, and Murphy 1988).

In spite of the dominance of economic perspectives, a simple model of size and profitability is of limited value in moving the study of executive compensation forward. Rather than asking whether size or profits determine compensation, it is more logical to examine the conditions under which size and profits determine compensation. Indeed, there has been some progress in recent work on developing explanations for the varying relationship between firm profits and executive compensation, with studies examining the role of managerial discretion (Kerr and Kren 1992; Rajagopalan and Finkelstein 1992), corporate control (McEachern 1975; Gomez-Mejia, Tosi, and Hinkin 1987; Finkelstein and Hambrick 1989; Hambrick and Finkelstein 1995), and board information about CEO ability (Murphy 1986). Other factors probably affect the pay–performance relationship as well, and their identification and examination should be of value. Yet, research on firm size has not progressed much beyond that described above (see Lambert, Larcker, and Weigelt 1991, for an exception). In all, while work on the economic determinants of executive pay has a long history, more remains to be learned. To do so will require moving away from traditional models and toward developing more complex contingency relationships.

Both the managerialist and neoclassical schools are implicit in virtually all studies of the determinants of executive compensation. Although agency theory has modernized the neoclassical perspective, it remains at the heart of most work on compensation. In fact, the agency perspective has become almost paradigmatic in research on the determinants of executive compensation. In a similar vein, the managerialist perspective recently has become more sophisticated as scholars have clarified and expanded the role of power that is at the heart of this perspective (Hill and Phan 1991; Hambrick and Finkelstein 1995). Nevertheless, this work has also helped make clear that the managerialist view is really a political perspective that provides a clear counterpoint to an economic perspective.

Research on corporate control has probably come closest to developing these opposing theoretical perspectives on executive compensation. This work differentiates externally controlled firms (where some single nonmanager owns a significant portion of the stock) from managerially controlled firms (where no single party is a significant shareholder) (McEachern 1975; Gomez-Mejia, Tosi, and Hinkin 1987; Hambrick and Finkelstein 1995). When externally controlled and managerially controlled firms are compared directly, the underlying logic behind the neoclassical and managerialist schools becomes clear. Table 8–1 presents such a comparison. The underlying theory in explaining executive compensation in externally controlled firms is agency theory (neoclassical). The locus of corporate control in agency theory rests with the board of directors, who try to ensure that shareholder and CEO objectives are aligned (Fama and Jensen 1983). Hence, externally controlled firms seek to reward performance while simultaneously minimizing CEO pay (i.e., to limit the upper bound of compensation within the firm and to reduce overall compensation). The key driving forces

TABLE 8-1   **Externally Controlled versus Managerially Controlled Firms**

	External Control	**Managerial Control**
Underlying theories	Neoclassical Agency theory	Managerialist Managerial hegemony theory
Locus of corporate control	Board of directors	CEO
Compensation depends on	Alignment of shareholders' and CEO's objectives	Dominance of CEO preferences
Guidelines in setting compensation	Reward performance Minimize CEO pay	Legitimize process Maximize CEO pay
Key driving forces	Profit maximization Supply and demand Marginal product	Sociopolitical forces Institutional norms Bureaucracy

in the setting of executive compensation are supply and demand, concerns for marginal product, and maximizing firm profits.

In the managerially controlled firm, on the other hand, the underlying theory to explain compensation is managerial hegemony (managerialist) theory. According to this perspective, the locus of corporate control is the CEO because the board lacks the motivating influence of a large shareholder (Shleifer and Vishny 1986). Without this countervailing pressure, compensation is based on CEO preferences, leading to higher CEO pay subject only to a need to ensure that the process appears legitimate to stakeholders. The managerialist view thus is driven by sociopolitical factors increasing pay and bureaucratic and institutional pressures legitimizing pay.

These alternative perspectives were recently examined in a study by Hambrick and Finkelstein (1995). Sampling 188 firms in seven industries between 1978 and 1982, they found dramatic differences in CEO compensation patterns in externally controlled and managerially controlled firms. As Figure 8–2 illustrates, consistent with our depiction of differences in pay patterns across ownership categories, annual changes in sales had a big impact on CEO pay raises in managerially-controlled firms but a nonsignificant effect in externally controlled firms.

Some of the most interesting findings came from an examination of the effects of changes in firm performance (return on equity [ROE]):

> Our results suggest that CEOs of [managerially controlled firms install] asymmetric incentive plans which yield substantial pay increases when profits go up, but no change in pay when profits go down. As Crystal (1988,76) cynically surmised, ". . . pay for performance, see?" This is a graphic indication of

FIGURE 8-2 **Some Key Drivers of Δ CEO Pay (Cash and Stock Options)**

Predictor	Externally controlled	Managerially controlled
Δ Sales	• No effect	• Big effect
Δ ROE	• Minor upward effect for ROE increases	• Big upward effect for ROE increases
	• Big downward effect for ROE declines	• No downward effect for ROE declines
Δ CEO pay in industry	• Moderate effect	• Big effect

how CEOs in management-controlled firms strive to maximize their pay while appearing to abide by the basic conventions of contemporary business practice. (Hambrick and Finkelstein 1995, 31)

In externally controlled firms, CEO pay increased marginally (and non-significantly) when ROE improved but decreased by 0.51 percent for every 1 percent decline in ROE. These results indicate that externally controlled firms also create asymmetric pay plans but in a direction very much different from the pattern apparent in managerially controlled firms. This finding is not consistent with the idea that externally controlled firms seek to align shareholder and CEO interests. Hambrick and Finkelstein (1995) suggest these results may reflect the attributions of major owners: "When the firm performs well, the owner's interpretation is that the managers have done nothing exceptional; they have done their jobs. They have fulfilled their responsibilities as stewards of the inherently valuable assets of the firm. However, when performance is poor, at odds with expectations about the worth of the firm, management is seen as the problem."[1]

Hambrick and Finkelstein (1995) also uncovered interesting differences in the effects of changes in CEO pay in the industry on changes in CEO pay. To the extent that industry pay conditions reflect normative expectations about what is an appropriate level of pay, managerially controlled firms should attend closely to prevailing norms, while externally controlled firms should focus more on shareholder value criteria. Results were supportive of this logic: while coefficients for both ownership categories were positive and significant, managerially controlled firms were significantly more responsive to industry pay conditions than externally controlled firms. In fact, for every 1 percent increase in CEO pay in the industry, CEOs in managerially controlled firms received a 1.37 percent raise.

This comparison makes clear that differences between neoclassical and managerialist perspectives on executive compensation are fundamental and can be understood much more clearly when critical contingency factors (such as corporate control) are taken into consideration. More broadly, it is apparent that research asking whether pay and performance are associated is too simplistic: the more compelling question is, under what conditions are pay and performance related? Although a comparison of neoclassical and managerialist perspectives leads to a focus on corporate control, other potentially important contingency relationships exist as well. For example, in line with arguments by Myron Scholes on the trade-off between incentives and risk-sharing (Journal of Applied Corporate Finance, 1992) recent work by Beatty and Zajac (1994) found a negative association between the risk that top managers bear in firms going through initial public offerings and 1) the use of stock options and 2) the level of noncash incentives in compensation plans. Because top managers in riskier firms already face considerable uncertainty, pay packages tend to de-emphasize risky components, such as stock options and noncash incentives.

Another promising approach for understanding agency relationships comes from a managerial discretion perspective. Stated simply, the greater the level of managerial discretion, the greater the potential impact of managers on organizational outcomes and the more important it is to ensure that their pay is related to performance (Hambrick and Finkelstein 1987). As we noted in Chapter 2, there has already been some empirical work supporting this notion (Rajagopalan and Finkelstein 1992). Hence, although the traditional neoclassical-versus-managerialist debate in executive compensation may seem old, a new focus on contingency variables and managerial discretion may give rise to fresh ideas on the pay-for-performance question. We summarize this discussion with the following propositions:

PROPOSITION 8-1

The association between CEO compensation and firm performance is not a direct one. Rather, the nature of the pay-performance relationship depends on such contingency factors as managerial discretion, corporate control, and firm risk.

PROPOSITION 8-1A

The greater the level of managerial discretion, the stronger the relationship between CEO compensation and firm performance.

PROPOSITION 8-1B

The greater the level of external control, the stronger the relationship between CEO compensation and firm performance.[2]

PROPOSITION 8–1C

The greater the level of firm risk, the weaker the relationship between CEO compensation and firm performance.

Other economics-based theories have been used to explain executive compensation. These perspectives focus on human capital (Becker 1975), marginal product (Frank 1984), and the managerial labor market (Fama 1980; Fama and Jensen 1983). Although these theories are often invoked to explain compensation, they have seldom been formally operationalized in empirical research on executive pay. Hence, we will only briefly consider them here.

Human capital derives from the experiences and background of a manager, and is an important source of compensation to the extent that it is recognized and valued in a firm. Examples of relevant human capital factors are managerial experience, education, and tenure (Hogan and McPheters 1980). For top managers, research has yet to establish human capital as a key determinant of compensation. While it may be that certain human capital is advantageous in reaching the top echelons of a firm (Leonard 1990) or in being selected as an outsider to run a company, it is not clear how this will translate more directly into higher pay. Once in a senior management position, compensation is likely to be based less on one's abilities and experiences and more on what one does with them. In addition, researchers may need to more precisely measure human capital skills, some of which may be industry-specific and some generic (such as leadership talent) (Harris and Helfat 1995). Nevertheless, to the extent that some executive experiences are associated with risk acceptance (Gupta and Govindarajan 1984), human capital factors may be related to the use of contingent and long-term compensation. These experiences may affect managerial preferences for different types of compensation (contingent versus fixed, short-term versus long-term), since some managers are more comfortable with risk than others. Hence, if a top manager has some control over the setting of his or her pay (as most CEOs do), executive compensation can be tailored to managerial risk preferences, thus representing one way in which human capital (i.e., experiences with risk) may be related to executive compensation.

As noted, few studies have attempted to test a human capital theory of executive compensation. Finkelstein and Hambrick (1989) found that CEO general management experience was related to CEO bonuses (but not total cash compensation or salaries), and Agarwal (1981) reported a significant association between job-related experience and executive compensation. Fisher and Govindarajan (1992) also reported that the compensation of business unit heads was positively associated with years of education. Several studies have investigated the effects of CEO tenure from a human capital perspective, typically yielding insignificant results (Deckop 1988; O'Reilly, Main, and Crystal 1988; Rajagopalan and Prescott 1990; Hambrick and Finkelstein 1995).[3] In all, the work on human capital indicates that 1) it is unlikely to account for much variance in executive compensation and 2) unresolved questions remain, particularly with respect to compensation type.

Finally, while it seems likely that an executive's compensation depends in part on his or her marginal product (Frank 1984; Finkelstein and Hambrick 1988) and the workings of the managerial labor market (Fama 1980; Jensen and Murphy 1990), no empirical work has attempted to directly measure an executive's marginal product or model the managerial labor market. On the other hand, several factors that have been found to determine executive compensation—managerial complexity, degree of regulation, firm size, and firm performance—may be indirect proxies for a manager's marginal product. For example, complex managerial jobs tend to offer managers more choices, which increase their discretion and, hence, their potential contribution to a firm. In this vein, evidence that 1) CEOs in regulated firms earn substantially less than CEOs in unregulated firms and 2) the association between pay and performance is weaker in regulated than in unregulated firms (Joskow, Rose, and Shepard 1993) is consistent with the notion that managerial discretion is lower in regulated firms (Hambrick and Finkelstein 1987; Rajagopalan and Finkelstein 1992). To the extent that these findings are a reflection of the marginal products of CEOs, we offer the following proposition:

PROPOSITION 8-2

The greater the marginal product of a CEO, the greater his or her compensation.

Unfortunately, the effects of the managerial labor market are somewhat more intractable to gauge because the market's boundaries are so diffuse. At any point in time, it is unclear how many "eligible" candidates exist for available positions. Perhaps for this reason, consideration of managerial labor markets has been limited to conceptual discussion and has not been extended to empirical investigation (Fama 1980).[4] Clearly, both a manager's marginal product and the operation of the managerial labor market are important influences on compensation. An important challenge for researchers is to consider how to model these effects in empirical work.

Social Explanations for Executive Compensation

While much work has been done on the economic determinants of executive compensation, the effects of social factors have hardly been studied at all. Nevertheless, the potential contribution of such an approach is sizable. In this section, we develop ideas that may provide fruitful directions for research on the role of social factors in the setting of managerial pay, along two related themes: social comparison processes and isomorphic pressures toward conformity.

Given the dominance of economic explanations for executive compensation, it is important to make clear why social factors might be expected to affect compensation. Perhaps most fundamental, the setting of executive compensation has several unique attributes that support a "social" explanation. First among these is the often pervasive influence of compensation consultants (Baker, Jensen, and Murphy 1988). Consultants act as disseminators of information about compensation, reporting on what they see and making recommendations. Consultants tend to focus on comparability, leading to more homogenization of CEO pay than would exist if CEOs were compensated according to their own marginal products (Finkelstein and Hambrick 1988). Because the notion of comparability leads naturally to an emphasis on social processes and the setting of pay in accordance with "social norms," we should consider ways in which executive compensation is influenced by institutionally driven isomorphic pressures and social comparison processes.

Beyond the actions of consultants, several additional factors promote a social explanation. First, the publication annually in corporate proxy statements of information on executive compensation in publicly held firms removes secrecy and facilitates comparisons; indeed, research on pay secrecy suggests that open information about pay typically promotes social comparison pressures (Leventhal, Michaels, and Sanford 1972; Pfeffer and Davis-Blake 1990). Second, extensive reporting on compensation by the national business media further facilitates pay comparisons both across and within firms (Lawler and Jenkins 1992). Third, the wide availability of data on executive pay enhances its value as a scorecard of professional status and attainment, and thus may motivate top managers to keep track of their relative standing (Patton 1961; Lawler 1966; Crystal 1991).

Isomorphism of Executive Compensation.   Isomorphic pressures to conform to "pay norms" are evident in many studies of executive compensation. If we consider an industry as a working definition of an organizational field (Fligstein 1990), the results of several studies documenting strong industry effects on pay gain additional meaning (Eaton and Rosen 1983; Deckop 1988; O'Reilly, Main, and Crystal 1988; Rajagopalan and Prescott 1990; Ely 1991). For example, Rajagopalan and Prescott (1990) highlighted how the determinants of compensation varied systematically across industries, and Hambrick and Finkelstein (1995) found that changes in industry pay patterns were significantly associated with changes in CEO pay. However, most of these studies did not rely on isomorphism as an explanation for industry differences in compensation; indeed, while most research models industry as a control variable and uses dummy variables or single industry samples (Finkelstein and Hambrick 1989), other studies consider industry as a reflection of structural economic characteristics (O'Reilly, Main, and Crystal 1988; Rajagopalan and Prescott 1990). Thus, the idea that executive compensation differs by industry because of isomorphic pressures for conformity has yet to be fully tested. Unfortunately, such a hypothesis may not be amenable to empirical investigation because this explanation only predicts that differences across industries will exist and does not offer guidance on why CEO pay in one industry may be greater than CEO pay in another. In addition, there are explanations other than social ones for why compensation would vary across industries (for example, in addition to structural economic characteristics, managerial discretion—which varies by industry—also affects compensation).

Rather, the effect of "industry norms" may be observed most directly in terms of the variability of CEO compensation within an industry. Industries with particularly strong isomorphic pressures toward conformity will have more homogeneous pay patterns than those that are less constrained in this way. In addition, managerial discretion increases the potential marginal product of a CEO and creates greater outcome uncertainty in an industry (Rajagopalan and Finkelstein 1992), accentuating differences in CEO compensation across firms. These ideas give rise to the following propositions:

PROPOSITION 8–3

The greater the level of managerial discretion in an industry, the greater the variation in CEO compensation within that industry.

PROPOSITION 8–4

The greater the isomorphic pressures in an industry, the lesser the variation in CEO compensation within that industry.

Although work on isomorphic pressures on executive pay is not highly advanced, it is a promising area of inquiry given the information generally available on compensation in firms. For example, a current study examines the role of mimetic and normative isomorphism on the adoption of contingent executive compensation plans (Finkelstein and Rajagopalan 1996). The main hypothesis in this study suggests that the adoption of performance-contingent compensation plans is a function of the proportion of firms in an industry that have previously adopted that plan (mimetic isomorphism). To understand the driving forces for imitative behavior, the effects on adoption rates of CEO pay patterns in other firms with which board members were affiliated were also examined. Preliminary results indicated that firms were more likely to adopt particular pay plans when board members already had knowledge and experience with them, suggesting that normative isomorphic pressures arising from judgments about "appropriate" compensation plans may govern executive pay. Hence, it seems reasonable to expect that isomorphic pressures toward imitation operate in executive compensation similar to how they operate for other administrative innovations (Teece 1980; Burns and Wholey 1993) and that further exploration of such effects may be fruitful. The following propositions summarize this line of argument:

PROPOSITION 8-5

The greater the proportion of other firms within an industry that have already adopted performance-contingent compensation plans, the greater the likelihood of subsequent adoption by a focal firm.

PROPOSITION 8-6

The greater the affiliation of board members with other firms that have already adopted performance-contingent compensation plans, the greater the likelihood of subsequent adoption by a focal firm.

Social Comparison Processes in the Setting of Executive Pay. Our discussion of isomorphism is closely related to ideas on how social comparison processes can affect executive compensation. According to Festinger (1954), individuals have a need to evaluate their own opinions, attributes, and abilities, and select comparison others who are seen as similar in some way (Goodman 1974). O'Reilly, Main, and Crystal (1988) argue that this social comparison process leads compensation committee members to rely on their own experience and that of similar others (CEOs). In a study of 105 large firms in 1984, these authors found that compensation committee members' pay in their own firms was highly related to compensation levels for sample CEOs. Nevertheless, while this result is supportive of a social comparison explanation, it may also reflect that "the largest corporations are headed by the most able, and . . . offer the most prestigious and highest-paying directorships" (Lazear 1991, 94).

The idea that social comparison processes are made and acted upon in the setting of executive compensation is different from the traditional perspective in economics.[5] While it is a particularly compelling perspective because, according to this theory, social comparisons are prevalent, several questions arise in testing these notions. First, because social comparisons can and are made by all top managers, as well as the board, disentangling the relevant comparisons can be confusing. The CEO evaluates his or her own pay, as does the board, and this theory provides little guidance on which actor to emphasize. (As we discuss later, a political model does just this, suggesting the value of a multidisciplinary approach.)

Second, executives may consider the trade-off between, say, level of pay and prestige of position in evaluating their compensation. This point suggests that compensation may be only one type of reward a manager receives, and evaluation of its worth may vary dramatically across individuals. Along these lines, Finkelstein and Hambrick argued that financial compensation is only one of a variety of incentives available to CEOs and that "prestige, challenge, and power might rival or even greatly surpass pay in their importance to executives" (1988, 543). The value executives attach to alternative rewards is likely to depend on a wide set of factors, including personal wealth and career experiences, firm size and profitability, and even industry conditions. For example, we might hypothesize that some executives may be willing to take a pay cut for the opportunity to become CEO or that the challenge of leading a cutting-edge, high-profile company may be more important than immediate financial rewards. Financial and nonfinancial incentives may be substitutes for each other. As long as the entire package of inducements is sufficient to ensure appropriate contributions, executives will remain on the job (March and Simon 1958). It could even be argued that the tournament model (discussed in detail later in this chapter), which postulates that top managers will accept lower pay in exchange for the opportunity to be promoted to the next hierarchical level, is a manifestation of this phenomenon. Hence, we offer the following:

PROPOSITION 8–7
Financial incentives are negatively associated with nonfinancial incentives.

Third, it is not clear what reference groups are used when individuals make comparisons. For example, do CEOs compare their compensation to other CEOs, CEOs in firms of similar size, CEOs in the same industry, or some other reference group? The potential comparisons board members make may be even more complex, because they also include comparisons to their own firms, to other firms on whose boards they sit, and perhaps even to the experiences of other directors at other firms with whom they interact. Nevertheless, when these complex interactions are examined together, the process of social comparison begins to resemble the engine that may drive isomorphic pressures toward compensation conformity. In spite of some of these conceptual difficulties, further work is needed to understand how social comparison processes affect compensation patterns in organizations.

Political Explanations for Executive Compensation

Power, an important factor in explaining behavior in top management teams, plays a central role in the strategic decision-making process (Eisenhardt and Bourgeois 1988; Finkelstein 1992). Hence, it would not be surprising to find that managerial power is a critical determinant of pay. Indeed, some have argued that executive compensation is an indicator of power (Finkelstein 1992; Hambrick and D'Aveni 1992; Haleblian and Finkelstein 1993). While several studies have used power-based explanations for compensation, virtually none has attempted to develop and test a complete model of the effects of power on compensation.[6]

At the heart of a political model of executive compensation is the realization that the board of directors—acting as monitors of managerial behavior—and top managers, are fundamentally in conflict (Jensen and Meckling 1976). Boards have a fiduciary responsibility to maximize shareholder value, while top managers are more concerned with maximizing their own utility.[7] As a result, the setting of executive compensation brings together boards and managers with different interests that are often resolved through political means.[8] For example, a study by Westphal and Zajac (1994) highlights the symbolic aspects of compensation: they found that CEO power was significantly associated with the adoption of long-term incentive plans and negatively associated with their actual use. That is, firms with powerful CEOs were more likely to put in place long-term incentive plans, ostensibly to mollify shareholder pressures for performance-based pay, but were less likely to actually use these plans because they raised CEOs' employment risk. These authors argued that while compensation plans may be set up for symbolic reasons, the real test of how closely compensation is tied to performance is whether these plans are operative. Hence, these findings suggest that the compensation-setting process is highly political.

The consequence of conceptualizing the compensation-setting process in such a political manner is that the key predictor of executive pay becomes the relative power of a manager (typically the CEO in empirical work) over the board. An implicit assumption here is that managerial power will be associated with greater levels of compensation. However, consistent with our earlier description of compensation-setting in managerially controlled firms, power allows individual managerial preferences for type and mix, as well as amount, of compensation to affect pay determination. While some research has incorporated managerial preferences (Mahoney 1964; Finkelstein and Hambrick 1988; Hambrick and Snow 1989; Zajac 1992; Westphal and Zajac 1994), it has not attempted to directly model how preferences affect compensation. Thus, a model that considers the interaction of power and preferences in the determination of pay is needed.

PROPOSITION 8–8
CEO preferences for pay determine the amount, mix, and type of CEO compensation.

PROPOSITION 8–9
The more powerful the CEO, the stronger the relationship between CEO preferences for pay and the amount, mix, and type of CEO compensation.

Methodologically, relative power has been operationalized in a variety of ways in research on executive compensation, including CEO tenure (Finkelstein and Hambrick 1989; Hill and Phan 1991, Wade, O'Reilly, and Chandratat 1990; Westphal and Zajac 1994), relative CEO tenure (Singh and Harianto 1989a; Wade, O'Reilly, and Chandratat 1990), CEO duality (i.e., where one individual holds both the chair and CEO positions) (Boyd 1993; Main, O'Reilly, and Wade 1994; Westphal and Zajac 1994), CEO board directorships (Wade, O'Reilly, and Chandratat 1990), outsider director representation (Lambert, Larcker, and Weigelt 1993; Main, O'Reilly, and Wade 1994), CEO influence in appointing outside directors or compensation committee chairs (Wade, O'Reilly, and Chandratat 1990; Lambert, Larcker, and Weigelt 1993; Main, O'Reilly, and Wade 1994), CEO shareholdings (Allen 1981; Finkelstein and Hambrick 1989; Lambert, Larcker, and Weigelt 1993), CEO family shareholdings (Allen 1981; Finkelstein and Hambrick 1989), outsider shareholdings (McEachern 1975; Gomez-Mejia, Tosi, and Hinkin 1987; Finkelstein and Hambrick 1989; Lambert, Larcker, and Weigelt 1993; Hambrick and Finkelstein 1994), and with survey measures (Tosi and Gomez-Mejia 1989).

A review of this work reveals that while different measures of power have been used, the link between measurement and construct has yet to be fully developed. While a plausible case can be made for all of the measures used, there are really no theoretically based reasons one measure should be preferred to another. In some cases, one can even raise questions as to whether the measures employed are really appropriate. For example, tenure can be taken as a measure of power or, as we discussed earlier, of human capital. While CEO shareholdings may signify power, some researchers have taken shareholdings to indicate alignment with owners' interests (Jensen and Murphy 1990).

A broader conceptualization of power is needed in the context of executive compensation. Power is a multidimensional, complex construct (March 1966; Pfeffer 1981a; Finkelstein 1992), a consequence of which is the potential instability of results across studies that use different measures of power without grounding in a clear theory of board-CEO power. Such a model would need to 1) develop a conceptualization of board-CEO power grounded in theory, 2) use this grounding to identify appropriate dimensions of the construct, and 3) create a measurement methodology that adequately captures the multiple dimensions of board-CEO power. Although Finkelstein's (1992) model may be used as part of this process, it was based on the relative power of top management team members—which is not the same as the relative power of the CEO versus the board. This problem is analogous to our discussion of board vigilance in Chapter 7. As we argued in that chapter, the distribution of power between CEOs and boards is at the heart of agency theory and, hence, of central importance in understanding the compensation-setting process.

Consequences of Executive Compensation

Why is executive compensation of such compelling interest to so many people? We become fascinated with the huge sums of money CEOs and other top managers earn. Furthermore, the pay an executive receives for performing his or her job may have many consequences for that manager, the top management team, the organization, and stakeholders in the organization. Because the consequences of executive compensation are broad, the subject warrants careful consideration. The following sections review existing research and suggest new avenues to explore.

Economic Explanations for the Consequences of Executive Compensation

Agency theorists have for some time taken the lead in investigating the consequences of different compensation arrangements. This is not surprising, given that a primary focus of normative agency theory is to specify optimal incentive contracts that yield desired outcomes (no managerial shirking, strong effort and performance, no entrenchment) (Ross 1973; Harris and Raviv 1979; Holmstrom 1982; Holmstrom and Milgrom 1990). Indeed, a basic assumption of agency theory is that compensation contracts can be written to provide incentives to top managers to maximize firm performance, hence aligning managerial interests with shareholder interests (Alchian and Demsetz 1972; Fama and Jensen 1983; Raviv 1985).

Along these lines, empirical work has been directed toward demonstrating that long-term incentive compensation contracts[9] promote greater risk acceptance and longer time horizons for CEOs, outcomes presumed to be consistent with shareholder interests because they help direct risk-averse CEOs toward attractive but risky business opportunities (Lambert 1986). In a study testing the impact of bonus schemes on discretionary expenditures in banks, Larcker (1984) found that managers of banks adopting bonuses tended to make fewer nonpecuniary expenditures (such as expenditures for offices, furniture, and employee salaries) than managers of banks without bonuses. Similarly, Lambert and Larcker (1984) found that adoption of stock option plans tended to increase the variability of equity returns (taken as evidence of managers' greater propensity to undertake risky investments that may have longer time horizons but also the potential to increase shareholder wealth). Larcker (1983), in a well-known study, found that the adoption of long-term performance plans was associated with increases in capital expenditures (but only for an average of one year following adoption[10]), outcomes that are consistent with shareholder interests. Increases in capital expenditures tend to entail some risk, take longer to pay off than some other investments, and are seen as consistent with shareholder interests, according to agency theorists (Hoskisson and Hitt 1988). In three studies examining R&D expenditures (which are presumed to have a positive long-term effect on shareholder wealth [Baysinger and Hoskisson 1990]), Rappaport (1978) reported a positive correlation with long-term contingent pay, and Waegelein (1983) and Hoskisson, Hitt, and Hill (1993) reported negative associations with short-term bonus plan adoption and division financial incentives, respectively. Finally, Schotter and Weigelt (1992), in a laboratory experiment using college students, found that bonus schemes induced longer decision-making horizons among subjects. With the exception of laboratory studies (which have obvious problems of external validity), however, alternative explanations for managerial behavior in these studies cannot be ruled out (Lambert and Larcker 1987).

A stronger test of the effects of incentives would examine the proposition that "an incentive system that ameliorates the principal–agent problem creates greater incentives for executives to maximize profits, and so increases profits" (Leonard 1990, 24-S). Such a test has numerous problems, however, including ambiguity about casual direction between profits and compensation, as well as the possibility of manipulation by executives through aligning the payment of contingent compensation awards with expected periods of high performance. So, in one of the few studies to empirically examine the relationship of executive compensation to ROE, Leonard (1990) reported an ambiguous U-shaped association, with executive pay highest for the most successful and unsuccessful firms in his sample. Leonard acknowledged that this result was inconsistent with assumptions that pay is an incentive device and speculated that compensation was high in firms with very poor performance because "failing firms may need to pay a compensating differential to attract and retain skilled managers" (1990, 23-S).

Some have argued that the problem of causal direction may be resolved by using event studies (Lambert and Larcker 1984), but the evidence here is also mixed. While Tehranian and Waegelein (1985) in studying bonuses and Larcker (1983) and Brickley, Bhagat, and Lease (1985) in studying long-term compensation all reported positive abnormal returns following adoption of these compensation schemes, Gaver, Gaver, and Battistel (1992) found no such evidence in a sample of firms adopting performance plans. In trying to reconcile these findings, Gaver, Gaver, and Battistel (1992) note three differences: 1) some of the earlier studies relied on small sample sizes (Larcker studied twenty-one firms and Tehranian and Waegelein examined forty-two); 2) there is considerable uncertainty pinpointing the precise event date because information about compensation plans is available at various times (the Securities and Exchange Commission [SEC] stamp date, the board meeting date, and the proxy statement date); and 3) there appears to be a generalized "annual meeting effect" associated with positive abnormal returns independent of the content of the meeting (Brickley 1986).

Several points are worth making in assessing this research stream. First, the association between incentive compensation plans and abnormal market returns are subject to two alternative explanations in addition to the caveats put forth by Gaver, Gaver, and Battistel (1992): 1) compensation plans may be adopted to minimize the joint tax liability of a firm and its managers (Hite and Long 1982), and 2) compensation plans may be adopted when top managers expect profitability to be favorable in the future (Jensen and Zimmerman 1985). This latter point may help explain why firms adopt performance plans even after a stock option plan is in place, because it is unclear how an additional, and similar, long-term compensation plan will be motivational at the margin (Gaver, Gaver, and Battistel 1992).

Second, long-term compensation systems are used by virtually all large firms today (Leonard 1990; Sloan 1991), but few observers are prepared to argue that the principal-agent problem has been ameliorated. Hence, while some evidence exists that incentive compensation is associated with "good" CEO behavior, it is not at all clear that compensation contracts can effectively align shareholder and managerial interests.

Third, it is questionable whether compensation is really a motivator for top managers. We have already noted the complexity of a top manager's motivations; it is simplistic to assume that executives will work harder or better if they are paid more (Finkelstein and Hambrick 1988; Barkema 1993). Thus, when agency theorists posit a direct association between incentive compensation and value-maximizing managerial behavior, they are basing it on a clear assumption about top managerial motivations (Holmstrom 1979; Fama and Jensen 1983). We believe that this assumption is generally false and argue that it leads to confusion regarding why incentives do not always yield anticipated results (or why firm performance explains little variance in pay levels) (Lawler 1971; Baker, Jensen, and Murphy 1988). In one of the few studies that attempted to probe executive motivation, Donaldson and Lorsch (1983) interviewed top managers at twelve large companies. One of their major conclusions was that "contrary to conventional wisdom and most economic theory . . . top managers are [not] motivated by financial incentives" (Donaldson and Lorsch 1983, 20). Rather, top managers are driven by a desire to excel, to do better than their peers in similar firms. The portrait these authors draw of executive motivation raises doubts about the implicit assumptions made in agency theory about the incentive effects of compensation contracts and suggests that an alternative perspective based on social and political factors may be useful. This notion is also in line with an argument made by Chester Barnard about sixty years ago: "The real value of differences of money reward lies in the recognition or distinction assumed to be conferred thereby" (Barnard 1938, 145).

Fourth, executive compensation arrangements can elicit both intended and unintended consequences (from the point of view of the principal). These unintended consequences may include perception-shaping behaviors that March (1984) called the "management of accounts and reputations." Rather than respond to incentives by adjusting strategic behavior (as agency

theorists intended), CEOs may choose to manipulate measures of their performance. For example, Healey (1985) found that managers manipulated
accounting choices to increase the value of their bonuses. Similarly, CEOs
may attempt to shape board perceptions of their behavior through such
image-management techniques as courting the media to receive flattering
treatment or working long hours to demonstrate their commitment to their
jobs (Finkelstein and Hambrick 1988; Walsh and Seward 1990). The net
effects of such activities in response to incentives may be far afield from, even
opposite to, those envisioned by agency theorists.

Finally, most studies of compensation adopt inferential methods that do
not directly examine the extent to which boards actually monitor the compensation-setting process. However, in one recent study that asked the most
senior compensation officer in a firm to assess the level of board monitoring of CEO compensation, the "higher monitoring of CEO pay processes
[was] positively related to firm performance, but the effects of monitoring
on firm performance [were] weaker at higher levels of monitoring" (Tosi
and Gomez-Mejia 1994). This finding of diminishing returns to monitoring was consistent with notions that CEO abilities to affect performance
are necessarily limited when performance is already high (Holmstrom
1979) and that high levels of monitoring may induce CEOs to be overly
cautious in making strategic decisions (Baysinger and Hoskisson 1990).
Although there are questions concerning the reliability of subjective assessments of monitoring, this work holds promise for its ability to enter the
"black box" of monitoring processes.

In sum, a significant gap seems to exist between economic predictions
of the consequences of executive compensation and actual empirical results.
In addition, considerable problems arise in interpreting the results of this
work. To a sizable extent, these problems are due to the overly simplistic
assumptions about managerial motivations. The following sections focus on
social and political explanations for the consequences of executive compensation and offer alternative perspectives that warrant further consideration.

Social Explanations for the Consequences
of Executive Compensation

One of the most studied areas in organizational behavior is the relationship
between rewards and outcomes (Baron and Cook 1992). The outcomes
most commonly investigated include performance, satisfaction, absenteeism,
and turnover. While this literature is clearly too massive to review here and
is based almost entirely on lower-level individuals in organizations, we focus
on the two outcomes that have the most relevance to strategic leadership,

namely performance and turnover, and only consider them as they pertain to top managers.

The previous section on economic explanations for the consequences of compensation addressed the issue of top managerial motivation, concluding that there is much more to learn about it. Research on equity theory in the organizational behavior literature may offer one promising avenue in this regard. According to equity theory (Adams 1963; Adams 1965), "the presence of an inequitable state of affairs motivates behavior aimed at returning exchange participants to their formerly equitable conditions" (Greenberg 1982, 391). With respect to compensation, equity theory suggests that individuals compare their pay and productivity to referent others and adjust their behavior in response to this comparison. The adjustment of behaviors that equity theory suggests will come from over- or underpayment, however, such as working harder or working less hard (Greenberg 1982), and seem not to be very applicable to top managers.[11] As we noted earlier, managers have strong incentives to perform well in their jobs, and these incentives may not necessarily be monetarily based. For example, Donaldson and Lorsch note that the "desire to win or excel takes the form of an almost personal comparison with peers and friends who are the CEOs of other companies" (1983, 23). Hence, it is important to recognize that compensation may have its greatest motivational impact as a symbolic reward (Lawler 1966). Pay is a primary scorecard for managerial success; hence, top managers may not work harder in response to higher pay, but they probably will be highly dissatisfied with lower pay.

If equity theory allows only weak predictions about firm performance, perhaps it has more relevance to executive turnover. The association between compensation and turnover is predicated on the idea that underpaid executives will experience inequity and leave the organization. Of course, if the "underpaid" executive is an ineffective manager, he or she may not find the managerial labor market particularly welcoming. But in general, we would expect that executives who are paid less than their performance level would seem to warrant, as compared to their peers, would seek jobs elsewhere. Unsurprisingly, this proposition has not been subjected to empirical examination (although there are many supporting studies focused on lower-level employees and managers). Investigating this question raises thorny methodological issues, such as identifying the appropriate referent group, assessing labor market conditions, and considering countervailing nonpecuniary inducements (e.g., access to a company jet or a huge office with a large staff) that may keep top managers on the job even though they are "underpaid."[12]

The greater the compensation of executives relative to peer groups, the lower their turnover.

It is also important to recognize the implications of expectancy theory for executive compensation. Expectancy theory suggests that motivation is a function of employee perceptions of 1) the clarity of the association between effort and performance, 2) the clarity of the association between performance and reward, and 3) the value of that reward (Lawler 1971). Because one of the implications of installing contingent compensation plans is the increased likelihood that a reward will follow performance, employee efforts should increase. The idea that pay and performance should be related is also central to agency theory. From an expectancy theory point of view, however, it becomes clear why incentives may not yield the anticipated outcomes for top managers that they might with lower-level employees. First, the ambiguity of the top management task (Mintzberg 1973; March 1984) weakens managerial expectations that effort will result in performance. Executives have little control over numerous factors that might influence a company's performance, such as industry conditions, the economy, regulatory actions, and even luck. Hence, expectancy theory leads one to conclude that all top managerial incentives have a necessarily limited motivational impact because of the inherent uncertainty of executive leadership. Second, the marginal value of additional compensation for highly paid top managers may not be that great (Finkelstein and Hambrick 1988).[13] For top managers already earning millions of dollars, the motivational value of an increment in pay is not likely to be large. This points to the importance of distinguishing between the motivational impact of incremental pay and the natural desire to be paid as much as possible. Because executive compensation has great symbolic value as a scorecard of managerial status and success, we would not expect an executive to refuse a raise—yet the additional compensation may not necessarily be motivational.

Political Explanations for the Consequences of Executive Compensation

Political explanations for the consequences of executive compensation focus on how compensation plans may provoke unintended behaviors from stakeholders (as well as managers) seeking to maximize their own self-interest. Fundamental to a political explanation for the consequences of executive compensation is the idea that CEO power and CEO compensation are closely related. We consider these ideas in this section.

As noted earlier, compensation, especially contingent compensation, is subject to manipulation by CEOs (March 1984). Rather than responding to a long-term bonus by, say, evaluating investment decisions over long time horizons, CEOs may attempt to make accounting choices that are most favorable to them. Indeed, it could be argued that the use of incentive schemes triggers political activity in a firm. Other than a small number of studies from an accounting perspective (e.g., Healey 1985), however, no research has been conducted on managerial manipulation of incentive systems.

The amount of compensation top managers earn may also trigger political activity. In fact, it could even be argued that the more a top manager is paid, the more he or she will become risk-averse because there is more to lose if the firm does poorly. (This idea is contrary to agency theory expectations that large guaranteed compensation is required to ensure that CEOs will be willing to make risky but appropriate long-term investments [Eisenhardt 1989a]). Top managers would be expected to engage in much "management of accounts and reputations" under these circumstances—a further example of how incentive compensation systems may have unintended consequences. Thus, we propose:

PROPOSITION 8–11

The greater the level of executive compensation, the greater the degree of political behavior by executives (self-interested attempts to manipulate accounting systems or personal reputations).

PROPOSITION 8–12

The adoption of performance-contingent compensation plans increases the degree of political behavior by executives (self-interested attempts to manipulate accounting systems or personal reputations).

Executive compensation may also provoke behaviors from a wide range of stakeholders. Beyond the stock market reactions and incentive effects for top managers already discussed, compensation may also affect boards of directors, employees, suppliers, customers, competitors, and regulatory agencies (Finkelstein and Hambrick 1988). For example, Beatty and Zajac (1994) report that firm monitoring activities are more intense when top managers receive less incentive compensation. In addition, because compensation awards or plans may convey information about an organization's health and intentions, stakeholders may monitor company proxies and announcements for information content. Unfortunately, little research has been directed toward the signaling effect of compensation systems. There is considerable anecdotal evidence, however, that the compensation sections of corporate proxies often obfuscate factual data (Crystal 1991)—lending credence to the idea that various stakeholders attempt to interpret information on compensation in various ways.

The recent changes in SEC proxy reporting requirements that direct firms to identify a "peer group" for purposes of performance comparisons open an interesting window to corporate impression management.[14] While it is possible to imagine various decision rules used in the selection of a peer group (same industry, same firm size), Murphy (1994) reports that firms select peer groups that enhance their perceived relative performance. Thus, not only are stakeholders receptive to such information, firms may also want to actively manage compensation reporting to send "appropriate" signals to stakeholders.

Sometimes the signals that are broadcast by compensation plans have negative consequences for the firm. For example, large pay increases for CEOs may elicit objections from unions and lower-level employees whose compensation is considerably less generous (Finkelstein and Hambrick 1988). For example, when top executives at General Dynamics received large gain-sharing bonuses triggered by increased stock prices, employees and institutional investors expressed outrage:

> "Huge compensation packages that make employees independently wealthy make their personal financial future less tied to that of the company, not more. And huge salaries demoralize other employees and therefore ultimately harm performance." (Sarah Teslik, executive director of the Council of Institutional Investors, quoted in Dial and Murphy 1995)

In addition, "high pay may signify potential organizational slack, which a supplier may interpret as an exploitable opportunity to raise prices without fear of significant opposition. Similarly, competitors may learn about the financial health of business units by studying year-end bonuses. Regulatory officials may also read into pay levels something of an industry's financial health" (Finkelstein and Hambrick 1988, 553). Hence, executive compensation is open to multiple interpretations by a variety of stakeholders, each of whom may potentially find political advantage in this knowledge.

Finally, could CEO power and compensation be self-reinforcing, such that powerful CEOs are paid more, which allows them to gain additional power through equity ownership in the firm? In this way, compensation systems may help promote the institutionalization of CEO power in a firm, the consequences of which may be far-reaching with respect to corporate governance. If this is the case, it suggests a dual causal structure between power and compensation that has not yet been investigated. Doing so will require time series data with structural equation models to help disentangle causal direction.

In sum, there is a wide set of potential consequences of executive compensation—functional and dysfunctional, intended and unintended. We have highlighted many of these consequences by adopting a multitheoretical perspective. There are inconsistencies and conflicts among perspectives, given the differences in underlying assumptions. However, from a research point of view, they present great opportunities for theory testing and comparative analysis. Most research on executive compensation continues to focus on its determinants; this section has attempted to synthesize work on the consequences of executive pay, with an eye toward illustrating its research potential.

DISTRIBUTION OF COMPENSATION WITHIN TOP MANAGEMENT TEAMS

Up to this point, we have limited our discussion to the compensation of CEOs. Considering pay at a "group" level of analysis, however, may be quite important. Implicit in this treatment is the recognition that individual managerial compensation is not assigned in a vacuum and that senior management reward systems affect the pay of individual executives within a firm. The notion that the compensation of a group of top managers is of interest is implicit in such questions as, Why do some managers make so much more than others within the same firm? While alternative classifications may be possible, a review of research on compensation within top management teams highlights two central, and related, issues that will be reviewed in this section: 1) What accounts for, and what are the consequences of, the magnitude of pay differentials between CEOs and other top executives in a company? and 2) What are the determinants and consequences of pay dispersion among all the executives within a top team?

Pay Differentials between CEOs and Other Executives in the Firm

Perhaps the most developed theoretical perspective on pay differentials within top teams is the tournament model (Lazear and Rosen 1981; Rosen 1986). Based on work in economics, this perspective suggests that when monitoring is unreliable or costly, compensation systems based on rank rather than absolute individual performance are more efficient (Becker and

Huselid 1992). For top managers, this translates into an expectation that marked differences in levels of pay characterize different hierarchical levels (i.e., executive vice-president, president, CEO). An underlying assumption of this theory is that top managers are motivated to work hard and perform well because they wish to win each successive tournament (for promotion to the next hierarchical position) and the greater level of compensation that is the prize. Because the tournament for the position of CEO is the final one in which a top manager will be involved in any one organization, a particularly large pay increment is provided as incentive for that job (Rosen 1986). The resulting compensation structure within top management teams is thus defined by higher pay for successive positions and a particularly large gap in pay from the CEO to the second-highest position.

Three questions arise in considering the tournament model. First, has it been supported in empirical work at the top management team level? Second, what are the implications of a tournament model for such organizational outcomes as firm performance and managerial turnover? And third, does tournament theory really make sense?

Few empirical studies have focused on the tournament model regarding top management, and their results are not consistent. On the one hand, some evidence exists that compensation differentials between hierarchical levels increase as one moves up the organization (Leonard 1990; Lambert, Larcker, and Weigelt 1993; Main, O'Reilly, and Wade 1993). For example, Lambert, Larcker, and Weigelt found that "the difference in compensation level for the CEO relative to the next lower position in the organizational hierarchy [was] 'extraordinarily' large" (1993, 453). And Main, O'Reilly, and Wade found the number of vice-presidents (a measure of the number of contestants in the tournament and, hence, an indicator of the scale of the tournament) to be positively associated with CEO compensation (although they concluded that "promotion brings a raise, but not immediately on the order that would be expected if a . . . tournament were operating") (1993, 625). On the other hand, O'Reilly, Main, and Crystal (1988) reported that the number of vice-presidents was negatively associated with CEO compensation, a result that is opposite to the tournament expectation and implies that conditions designed to support a tournament actually reduce the gap between CEO pay and the average pay of vice-presidents. Thus, while a few studies support a tournament model, the results obtained are not robust, and alternative interpretations for these findings are possible.

The second issue addresses the likely consequences arising from the institution of tournaments for top managerial pay. If top managers recognize that a tournament model is in operation, there almost certainly will be 1) some self-selection either into or out of organizations with such structures, and 2) among those remaining, turnover is likely to occur in a step function, triggered by promotion decisions that define winners and losers at each stage. In other words, executives who are bypassed for promotion may be more likely to leave at each stage of the promotion ladder. This implies that, except when promotion decisions are made, top managerial turnover will be lower in firms that structure compensation on the basis of a tournament because executives may be less interested in leaving an organization while they are still in the running for promotion. Although these ideas are amenable to empirical work, such tests have not yet been conducted.

PROPOSITION 8–13

In firms whose compensation systems are structured as a tournament, executive turnover is lower.

PROPOSITION 8–14

In firms whose compensation systems are structured as a tournament, the promotion of other executives to higher hierarchical positions increases executive turnover.

Beyond top managerial turnover, because tournaments are designed to provide incentives, companies with such systems should perform better than firms that do not have tournament structures. While there is some evidence in nonorganizational settings (auto racing and golf) that individual performance may be affected by tournaments and that the magnitude of the spread between winners and losers is especially informative (Ehrenberg and Bognanno 1990; Becker and Huselid 1992), these ideas have not been directly studied for top managers or even in organizational settings. Nevertheless, a recent study reported a direct positive association between pay inequality in top management teams and firm performance (Main, O'Reilly, and Wade 1993), suggesting that further investigation is required.

One final point concerns the concept of pay as a scorecard (Lawler 1966). To the extent that executive compensation carries symbolic meaning, pay differentials among senior managers may signal the distribution of power within the top team. This may be especially true when these differentials are not based on hierarchical position, which as an "objective" sign of structure can be discounted as an indicator of real power. It may be possible to learn much about internal labor markets—promotions, fast tracks, deadwood—by studying pay patterns at the top. For example, relative compensation can be used as a predictor of subsequent promotion under the assumption that relatively higher-paid managers are being singled out as promising and induced to stay with the company. While such work may have its greatest predictive value for middle- to upper-level management, such signaling undoubtedly takes place at the top management team level.

PROPOSITION 8–15
The relative power of top managers determines the magnitude of pay differentials among them.

PROPOSITION 8–16
The greater the compensation of an executive relative to other top managers within the same firm, the greater the probability of his or her promotion to a higher position.

Finally, we need to understand whether the tournament model is logical in the context of executive compensation. There are four points to make here. First, differences in compensation levels across hierarchical levels may be due to the need to demarcate a firm's organizational structure (Simon 1957). The increasing magnitude of compensation differentials the higher up the organization one goes may be a reflection of different levels of structural power. The "extraordinary" gap between CEO pay and the next lower position may also be due to the relatively unconstrained power a CEO holds relative to other top managers. In addition, one of the prime ways for a CEO, having reached the top, to continue to earn recognition is to boost his or her pay as a symbol of status and success (Patton 1961). Relatedly, the magnitude of the differential between a CEO's pay and the compensation of the next highest executive may be an indicator of CEO autocracy, reflecting "the gap between the CEO's assessment of his own worth to the firm and his assessment of others' worth" (Hambrick and D'Aveni 1992, 1452).

Second, there are at least two conflicting sociopolitical explanations for CEO pay differentials in organizations. Wide pay gaps may be characteristic of firms that need not cooperate much across levels (e.g., unrelated diversified firms with business unit general managers one level below the most senior top management [Michel and Hambrick 1992]) because the incentive effects of tournament structures may promote excessive political activity, which disrupts the ability of top managers to work together. Hence, pay differentials may depend on the extent to which cooperation and interdependence characterize top managerial work. Alternatively, pay differentials based on rank are exactly what one would expect because of the relative status of formal positions in an organization (Berger, Cohen, and Zelditch 1972; Berger, et al. 1983). According to status-value theory, the need for status consistency drives compensation differences across hierarchical levels

(Cook and Hegtvedt 1983). Although the second of these alternative explanations does not appear to be directly testable, the first explanation clearly is:

PROPOSITION 8–17

The greater the degree of strategic interdependence among top managers, the less the magnitude of pay differentials among them.

Third, the tournament model, like other economically based models of executive compensation, tends to overemphasize the need for externally driven incentive structures and underestimate the degree to which most top managers are self-driven (Donaldson and Lorsch 1983; Finkelstein and Hambrick 1988). CEOs, in particular, are highly motivated because of the challenging nature of the job (Patton 1971; Roche 1975), the intrinsic value of the job (Barnard 1938; Patton 1961), a need for security (Patton 1961), a need to achieve (McClelland 1972; Kraus 1976), a need for power (Zalesnik and Kets de Vries 1975; Ungson and Steers 1984), and a desire to build a successful reputation in the managerial labor market (Patton 1961; Fama 1980).

Fourth, often it is the CEO, and not the board, who hires the people who report directly to him or her (Lorsch 1989). What incentive does the CEO have to set up a tournament where the prize is his or her job? According to this logic, a wide pay gap between a CEO and a firm's vice-presidents is less likely to represent the existence of a tournament than to reflect CEO power. Thus, much more work is needed to understand the implications of a tournament model for top managers. This work should focus not only on examining the original ideas of Rosen and colleagues (Lazear and Rosen 1981; Rosen 1986), but also on disentangling potentially confounding explanations for pay differentials based on political and social theories of organizations. While some evidence exists that promotion tournaments occur in organizations (Vancil 1987), when they occur and their implications for compensation structures among top managers remain important, and unresolved, research questions.

Pay Dispersion within Top Management Teams

While the tournament model focuses on pay differentials, considering social comparison processes at the top management team level gives rise to a focus on pay dispersion. Pay dispersion, defined as the variance in pay within top management teams, is a critical, though seldom studied, element of executive compensation for three reasons. First, the distribution of compensation within a top team may have important substantive consequences for how the team functions as a group. Second, studying pay dispersion may be one of the best ways to assess the importance of social factors in the setting of executive compensation because social comparisons occur at a group level; hence, they can be easily overlooked by researchers who focus on the compensation of an individual, such as the CEO. Third, there have been no published studies of the determinants of pay dispersion at the top management team level.

Two basic research questions must be considered: why is there great variance in pay among top management team members in some firms but not in others? and what are the organizational consequences of pay dispersion within top management teams? A social-psychological perspective might suggest that in organizations where cooperation, coordination, and social integration among top management team members are critical to the success of the firm, pay dispersion will be reduced (Finkelstein 1995). This may be expected because some of the consequences of pay dispersion, such as political infighting (Lazear 1989), conflict (Leventhal 1976; Frank 1984), and low trust and information sharing (Whyte 1955), tend to be disruptive in organizations where coordination and integration are important. As Deutsch (1975) has argued, pay dispersion signifies that some group members are not as valuable to the group as others. These findings are robust in the social psychology literature (Cook and Hegtvedt 1983), but they have not yet been tested in the context of top management teams.

One of the challenges in attempting to test these ideas at the top team level is to specify the conditions under which the potentially negative consequences of pay dispersion will be most detrimental to the functioning of management. While research is generally limited on the nature of interaction within top management teams, more is known about diversification. The literature on differences in managerial work among firms with different diversification postures indicates that the degree of interdependence and social integration is greater in less diversified firms (Vancil 1979; Galbraith and Kazanjian 1986). In contrast, in highly diversified firms, "corporate managers exist as discrete technical resources rather than as a coordinative entity" (Michel and Hambrick 1992, 17). Hence, our expectation would be that pay dispersion is more likely in highly diversified firms than in less diversified ones; accordingly, some evidence suggests that firms consider these issues in setting compensation. Top executives in broadly diversified firms tend to be compensated on the basis of their own unit's performance, rather than the performance of the overall organization (Pitts 1974; Kerr and Slocum 1987). To the extent that the performance of a firm's divisions varies, as seems likely, such policies will tend to increase pay dispersion in broadly diversified firms and decrease pay dispersion in more focused ones. In less diversified firms, pay is based more on overall firm performance to promote cooperation among the separate businesses to achieve synergy (Hoskisson and Hitt 1994).

PROPOSITION 8–18
The more diversified the firm, the greater the pay dispersion within the top management team.

The group level of analysis not only lends itself to a consideration of social determinants of compensation, it also leads quite naturally to a focus on power. Power is essentially a relative concept, meaningful only to the extent that the object or application of one's power is specified (Emerson 1962; Blau 1964). Hence, a basic proposition to consider is:

PROPOSITION 8–19
The greater the dispersion of power among top management team members, the greater the pay dispersion within the team.

As straightforward as this proposition appears, little research has directly offered an empirical test. The importance of behavioral factors (social and political) in explaining executive pay is being increasingly recognized, quite often by scholars who have traditionally adopted an economic orientation in their work (Baker, Jensen, and Murphy 1988; Lazear 1989; Jensen and Murphy 1990). What remains for researchers interested in executive compensation to develop is an integrated and balanced perspective on how economic, social, and political factors affect top managerial pay. To some extent, this has occurred at the individual level of analysis (e.g., Zajac 1990), but more work is needed. At the group level of analysis, scholars have a great opportunity to develop new directions in research on executive compensation that hold the potential for deeper understanding.

In contrast to research that attempts to account for pay dispersion, a relatively large body of literature on the social consequences of reward allocations in organizations focuses primarily on groups not at top managerial levels (Homans 1961; Martin 1981; Greenberg 1982). This work argues that the social consequences of various reward allocations depends on the distribution rule adopted (Cook and Hegtvedt 1983). Although several different distribution rules are possible (Eckoff 1974), most work has focused on the consequences of pay distributions based on equity. Typically, research indicates that inequity leads to such negative consequences as higher turnover and lower performance (Cook and Hegtvedt 1983; Greenberg 1987). An alternative distribution rule, that of equality, has not been studied as often, even though it appears particularly relevant for top managers. Hence, the remainder of this section focuses on the consequences of equal and unequal pay allocations in top management teams.

There is often significant pressure to reduce pay differentials within groups (Leventhal 1976): individuals from unionized workers (Hirsch 1982) to automobile salespersons (Frank 1984) to university faculty (Pfeffer and Langton 1993) all tend to prefer relatively equal pay within their work groups. These preferences for equality are generally assumed to derive from a process of social comparison (Festinger 1954), with pay compression valued because of the group social integration and stability it promotes (Deutsch 1975; Sampson 1975; Leventhal 1976). In contrast, unequal pay can engender conflict, reduce commitment, and discourage group cooperation (Leventhal, Michaels, and Sanford 1972; Rhodes and Steers 1981; Lawler and Jenkins 1992). Considerable research indicates that rewards based on group performance tend to elicit more collaborative behavior than rewards based on individual performance (Miller and Hamblin 1963; Mitchell and Silver 1990; Harder 1992). To the extent that compensation based on group performance leads to a more equal distribution of rewards than compensation based on individual performance, this research provides additional support for the notion that individuals prefer more equal pay within their work groups. The net effect of this research is to suggest that pay inequality is positively associated with turnover and negatively related to performance (Adams 1965; Pfeffer and Davis-Blake 1992).

We believe that pay inequality within top management teams may lead to such negative outcomes as higher turnover and lower performance. Indeed, a top management group may well be highly susceptible to the negative consequences of pay inequality. For example, research indicates that pay differences within groups become more compressed when successful completion of a group's task requires interaction and cooperation (Greenberg 1982; Cook and Hegtvedt 1983). High levels of contact among group members increase the likelihood that social comparisons will occur (Deutsch 1975) and that such comparisons will create pressure toward pay compression (Deutsch 1985; Pfeffer and Langton 1988). In addition, preferences for equal pay tend to be enhanced when a group is involved in a stable, long-term relationship because individuals are more likely to perceive themselves as a team that shares a "common fate" (Leventhal, Michaels, and Sanford 1972; Cook and Hegtvedt 1983; Deutsch 1985). Further, the negative consequences of unequal pay tend to be more severe the more intense the degree of group interaction (Frank 1984). Hence, to the extent top management teams are characterized by interaction, cooperation, and stability, pay inequality may promote higher turnover and lower firm performance. Relatedly, because political activity reflects and promotes conflict (Pfeffer 1981a), top management teams that are less politicized may perform best when pay is relatively compressed.

PROPOSITION 8-20

The greater the pay dispersion among top management team members, the greater the turnover within the team.

PROPOSITION 8-21

The greater the pay dispersion among top management team members, the lower the firm performance.

Three additional points regarding pay inequality are important. First, these arguments are based on research on lower-level employees and on laboratory studies; thus, it is not clear that top management teams behave in a similar manner. In addition, although many top management teams are characterized by high degrees of cooperation and stability, this is not always the case. Thus, the consequences of pay inequality on turnover and firm performance may vary across organizations—depending on the extent of interaction, cooperation, and stability of top teams. Nevertheless, Main, O'Reilly, and Wade (1993) found no relationship between the interaction of pay inequality and a measure of top management team interdependence, and return on assets.

Second, the distribution rules of equity and equality are not the same (Eckoff 1974) and suggest alternative interpretations of top managerial preferences for compensation. Although we indicated how pay distributions based on equality may be preferred by top managers, counterarguments could be marshaled in favor of equity. Hence, future research may examine if different distribution rules are preferred under different circumstances.

Third, the implications of our arguments on equality are different from those predicted by a tournament model. Rather than pay differentials providing incentives, as tournament theory holds (Rosen 1986), pay differentials within the top group may be disruptive and dysfunctional. In acknowledging this possibility, Lazear (1989), an original proponent of tournament theory (Lazear and Rosen 1981), suggests that pay compression may be preferred to pay inequality across ranks because unequal pay promotes disruptive political activity in organizations. As Main, O'Reilly, and Wade (1993) suggest, tournament theory and social comparison theory offer opposite predictions for how pay inequality is associated with firm performance.[15] In spite of these difficulties, the notion that pay inequality is associated with higher levels of executive turnover and lower firm performance is unresolved and requires further research.

The social composition of top management teams may affect the distribution of rewards at the top in other ways. Research on senior executives is increasingly focused on social dimensions driven to a large extent by the recognition that top management teams are really groups and that much can be learned from a group perspective (Hambrick 1994).

COMPENSATION FOR BUSINESS UNIT GENERAL MANAGERS

To this point, we have focused on the compensation of corporate top managers. As we noted at the beginning of this chapter, however, there is a related stream of compensation research on business unit general managers (GMs), to which we now turn our attention. A review of this work suggests that this research stream has not been an abundant one. Much of it has focused on the implications of corporate strategy on divisional GM pay (Berg 1973; Lorsch and Allen 1973; Salter 1973; Merchant 1989; Hoskisson and Hitt 1994), with some conceptual and empirical support of the idea that reward systems for GMs in highly diversified firms, with few strategic interdependencies, tend to emphasize performance-based pay, objective criteria, and relatively higher incentive pay than reward systems for GMs in less diversified firms (Pitts 1974; Kerr 1985; Napier and Smith 1987). The underlying logic is that compensation systems must fit the strategic context to ensure appropriate managerial motivation and performance (Hambrick and Snow 1989).

Herein, we focus on the unanswered or unresolved issues relating to business unit GM pay. Multiple theoretical perspectives, for the most part, have not been employed to study business unit GM pay; most of the work has focused solely on the determinants of GM pay. Thus, we address three basic questions about business unit GM pay: 1) what is different about business unit GM pay? 2) what are the determinants of GM compensation? and 3) what are the consequences of GM compensation?

The administration of business unit GM compensation differs from CEO compensation in several ways. First, divisional GMs are generally subject to greater constraint than CEOs by virtue of being in middle management and thus have less direct influence in the setting of their pay. Nevertheless, it is incorrect to disregard the role of power in business unit GM pay because the level of compensation earned by general managers may be influenced by top managers' perceptions of GMs' upward mobility. A second difference between business unit GM pay and CEO pay is that the latter's pay is formally set by the board of directors, while general manager pay is based on internal evaluations. Future work may build on this observation by modeling agency relationships within firms, with the CEO acting as principal and the business unit general manager as agent. Third, pay may be less of a motivator for CEOs than for business unit GMs because CEOs generally have greater wealth and may be motivated by other factors, such as power and prestige (Fisher and Govindarajan 1992). Thus, business unit GMs may be more responsive to financial incentives than are CEOs. Finally, the measurement of managerial performance is even more difficult for business unit GMs than it is for CEOs. Although there is controversy over appropriate measurement (Antle and Smith 1986), CEO performance can be measured in several ways, including stockholder returns. In contrast, business unit performance is difficult to measure with either accounting or market-based measures (Fisher and Govindarajan 1992).

Although the work cited earlier on the determinants of divisional reward systems has been informative, little research has been done on the determinants of the actual level of GM pay. To some extent, this is because such information is difficult to obtain. In a study that relied on data collected by compensation consultants, however, Fisher and Govindarajan (1992) tested a model of business unit GM pay. Their model applied findings on CEO pay (Finkelstein and Hambrick 1988; O'Reilly, Main, and Crystal 1988; Finkelstein and Hambrick 1989) to the profit center manager and found that such variables as firm size, profit center size, firm performance, and the human capital of the GM were significant predictors. As these authors acknowledge, they were unable to test the association between business unit profitability and business unit GM pay because of measurement difficulties. Although this study is informative, it still begs the question: If the business unit GM job is different from the job of the CEO, should we not be able to develop a model of business unit GM compensation that does not depend on arguments originally ascribed to CEO pay? Indeed, Fisher and Govindarajan note that "the results from studies on CEO pay cannot be directly transferred" to the business unit level (1992, 205).

Many of the same questions that arose in our discussion of CEO compensation may also be relevant for business unit GMs. For example, do general managers compare their compensation with each other, and does this affect their motivation to stay in the organization? The answer is not obvious because business unit GM pay is seldom publicly available, and organizations often have a norm of pay secrecy. Beyond this, much of the work on business unit GM compensation adopts a contingency framework that implies certain outcomes in response to strategy-reward system alignment or misalignment (Kerr 1985; Galbraith and Kazanjian 1986; Napier and Smith 1987; Balkin and Gomez-Mejia 1990; Govindarajan and Fisher

1990; Fisher and Govindarajan 1993). Nevertheless, no direct empirical tests have been made of such a hypothesis. We might expect however, that, all things being equal, the closer the alignment between corporate diversification and performance-based pay for business unit general managers, the greater the firm performance.[16]

PROPOSITION 8-22

The more diversified the firm, the stronger the relationship between performance-contingent compensation and firm performance.

Hambrick and Snow (1989) also developed a set of prescriptions that differentiated between emerging and established general managers, arguing that each group has its own needs, desires, and values, and, hence, may respond to different reward systems. Emerging GMs are "in the 35–50 age range, often have less than ten years tenure with the firm, and, while part of the general management ranks, tend to preside over smaller, lower-level units than their more seasoned counterparts" (Hambrick and Snow 1989, 350). Established GMs are older, have longer company tenures, and "have largely achieved the positions of power and responsibility that their

FIGURE 8-3 **Incentive Systems for Different Managerial Contexts**

	Incentive Types and Amounts	Criteria for Receipt	Incentive Administration
Emerging General Managers	Promotion and advancement of paramount importance Pay emphasis on cash, reliable base salary, high incentive leverage and hurdles	Emphasis on unit performance Emphasis on quantitative, "objective" indicators	Explicit and unambiguous incentives
Established General Managers	Perquisites and recognition of primary importance Blend of cash and deferred stock compensation, competitively average base salary, moderate incentive leverage and low hurdles	Balanced emphasis on unit and corporate performance Balanced emphasis on quantitative and qualitative measures	Somewhat implicit, flexible, and ambiguous incentives

SOURCE: Hambrick and Snow (1989)

younger counterparts seek" (Hambrick and Snow 1989, 350). As Figure 8–3 illustrates, these differences extend to the type and amount of incentives, payment criteria, and incentive administration. For example, established GMs tend to prefer a combination of cash and deferred compensation, while emerging GMs favor cash compensation. The implication of this logic is that firm performance depends in part on the degree to which reward systems and GMs' characteristics are aligned. Each of the cells in Figure 8–3 represents hypotheses on business unit GM pay that require empirical tests. Hence, firm performance should be greater to the extent that emerging and established general managers are rewarded through the pattern of incentives, criteria for receipt, and administration described for each in Figure 8–3.

CONCLUSIONS

This chapter was devoted to an in-depth analysis of executive compensation research using a framework that facilitated examination of a broad range of work. Because numerous propositions were suggested throughout, we do not summarize them here. Rather, we end the chapter with summary comments on three critical issues for subsequent work on executive compensation.

Managerial Discretion

The role of managerial discretion in explaining executive compensation has been emphasized in this chapter, with the basic idea being that higher levels of discretion imply greater potential marginal product and, hence, higher pay (Hambrick and Finkelstein 1987). Because the discretion concept draws upon economic, social, and political perspectives, it represents an example of an integrative model of executive compensation. In addition, as Rajagopalan and Finkelstein (1992) argued (and as we noted in Chapter 2), managerial discretion implicitly underlies much of the work linking strategy to compensation. For example, the idea that corporate diversification is associated with higher pay and more incentive pay is common in the strategy literature (Murthy and Salter 1975; Napier and Smith 1987; Hambrick and Snow 1989; Hoskisson, et al. 1989; Henderson and Fredrickson 1993). To the extent that more diversified contexts increase managerial discretion by expanding potential strategic options (Finkelstein and Hambrick 1989), such arguments are logical.

Measuring Executive Compensation

The majority of research on executive compensation has used measures of salary and bonus, as reported directly in proxy statements or indirectly through compensation consultants and the business media. The question that arises is whether or not relying on salary and bonus, rather than on more inclusive measures of pay that include contingent and long-term compensation, is appropriate.[17] Recent years have seen the rise of stock options as key components of executive compensation, and some well-publicized and large option gains (e.g., Peers and Kansas 1994) have sensitized researchers to their potential importance. In addition, normative agency theorists have emphasized the value of formally structuring compensation "contracts" to provide managerial incentives (Holmstrom 1979), implying that empirical researchers should study how pay and performance are related (Jensen and Murphy 1990). Thus, it seems important, conceptually, to value stock options and other long-term contingent compensation in empirical work.

In practice, however, significant problems are associated with valuing contingent compensation. For example, although some version of the Black–Scholes model is typically used to value stock options, "the ultimate proceeds from a stock option grant . . . depend on the firm's stock price performance after the employee's risk preferences . . . and changes in the tax law" (Lambert, Larcker, and Weigelt 1993, 444), considerations that are not part of the Black–Scholes computation. In addition, the assumptions of Black–Scholes are not precisely met with executive stock options (Kerr and Kren 1992). There may be even greater uncertainty in valuing other types of long-term contingent compensation (Antle and Smith 1986). These problems have yet to be resolved in the literature (Lambert, Larcker, and Verrecchia 1991), leading to variety in how executive compensation is measured in empirical studies.

Beyond problems in valuation, several studies on different aspects of compensation indicate that results are appreciably the same whether or not long-term pay is included in the measure of executive compensation (Lewellen and Huntsman 1970; Benston 1985; Ely 1988; Lambert, Larcker, and Verrechia 1991; Lambert, Larcher, and Weigelt 1993; Hambrick and Finkelstein 1995). As a result, while the inclusion of long-term contingent compensation does provide additional information on executive pay, the marginal gain in information may be offset by potentially unreliable measurement.

Pay and Performance

Countless articles have attempted to test the relationship between pay and performance, with inconclusive results. Indeed, one of the most perplexing problems in agency theory is why the association between pay and performance is not more robust (Jensen and Murphy 1990). Our review of social and political factors strongly suggests that a prime reason for the often weak reported association between pay and performance is that the "agent" in the principal-agent framework is not necessarily a fully "rational," risk-averse, self-interested optimizer, but rather an individual whose complex motivations and interests cannot be scripted. Coupled with breakdowns in the vigilance of the "principal" (as Chapter 7 documents), it is not hard to see why the pay and performance relationship is not simple and straightforward.

The implications of these arguments are fundamental: 1) pay and performance are not always related; 2) pay and performance should not necessarily be structured to be closely related; and 3) the relationship between pay and performance is contingency-driven, depending on an assessment of such factors as principal (board of directors) effectiveness, agent (managerial) preferences for different types and amounts of compensation, existence of alternative monitoring devices, and the nature of top managerial work and discretion in different contexts. A focus on social and political, as well as economic, factors is needed to not only develop more complete understanding of compensation, but also to begin to resolve such fundamental dilemmas as the pay-performance relationship.

NOTES

1. The greater vigilance of boards in externally controlled firms may help account for why CEOs in Japanese firms earn less than their U.S. counterparts. In many Japanese companies, large institutional shareholders are common, and often hold extensive corporate debt as well, giving them considerable influence over management (Prowse 1990). Hence, it may not be that surprising that CEOs in Japan are paid much less than those in the United States (Snyder and Bird 1994).
2. However, the Hambrick and Finkelstein (1995) results suggest important subtleties in this relationship.
3. Whether CEOs are appointed from inside or outside the organization does seem to make a difference, however, with new insiders generally being paid less than their predecessors and new outsiders paid much more than the CEOs they replace (Gilson and Vetsuypens 1992; Joskow, Rose, and Shephard 1993; Hambrick and Finkelstein 1995).
4. Nevertheless, one study is noteworthy for its consideration of executive reputation in the managerial labor market. Harris (1986) found that reputation moderated the relationship between performance and compensation during an executive's external succession, suggesting that the relationship between pay and performance is stronger for new outsider CEOs with greater standing in the managerial labor market.
5. More recently, economists have begun to incorporate ideas from psychology and sociology in an attempt to refine traditional notions of efficient wages. For

example, several writers have discussed the possibility that social comparisons do take place among employees and that this process of comparison can affect productivity (e.g., Akerlof and Yellon 1988; Lazear 1989; Lazear 1991).

6. A recent paper by Main, O'Reilly, and Wade (1994) may be the only exception to date. These authors find support for a model of CEO compensation based on social influence that attempts to explain why boards of directors are not the effective monitors agency theorists typically assume (e.g., Fama and Jensen 1983).

7. Executive utility, as we discuss later in this chapter, is not limited to preferences for compensation. Top managers may also desire greater responsibility, achievement, and power.

8. It is difficult to imagine a power-based model of executive compensation that does not use these observations as a starting point. However, one exception may occur in regulated industries, where some have argued that regulatory agencies, in seeking to avoid public dissatisfaction with "excessive" compensation earnings, use their political power to both reduce overall levels of CEO pay and the magnitude of incentives offered to CEOs (to reduce the possibility of large nominal payouts) (Joskow, Rose, and Shepard 1993). Nevertheless, it could be argued that regulatory agencies are really acting as supernormal, and vigilant, boards of directors (Stigler 1971).

9. One recent study found evidence that firms may also use nonincentive cash compensation to promote desired strategic behaviors (Ramanan, Simon, and Harris 1993).

10. Finkelstein and Hambrick suggest that this short-term effect may be evidence of a "Hawthorne" effect and that "a steady stream of new incentive schemes is required to kindle managerial action" (1988, 552).

11. In this regard, traditional equity theory provides a motive for what agency theorists refer to as "shirking" by suggesting that inequity breeds resentment.

12. This expectation may not hold as strongly for CEOs since, as we argued earlier, they benefit most from the prestige and status of their positions.

13. It could also be argued that the motivational impact of incentive-based compensation should be evaluated against the actual wealth of the executive, rather than his or her guaranteed compensation. Zajac (1990), testing this hypothesis, found that firms whose CEOs perceived greater connection between their personal wealth and the wealth of their firm tended to be more profitable.

14. This initiative is itself a political response to executive compensation practices.

15. Strictly speaking, however, tournament theory refers to pay differentials across hierarchical levels, especially between the CEO and the next level, while pay inequality emphasizes the degree of pay dispersion among a group of top managers. While the ratio of CEO pay to the pay of executives at the next level is likely to be highly correlated with pay dispersion, these two constructs are not the same.

16. This hypothesis is analogous to Michel and Hambrick's (1992) study of the performance effects of the interaction of diversification and top management team characteristics.

17. One problem that arises occasionally is the use of figures representing "long-term compensation" or "stock options" directly from such sources as *Business Week* or *Forbes*. Unfortunately, because these surveys do not value such contingent pay but typically report data directly from proxies, they are potential-

ly very misleading. For example, simply counting the gain on exercise of options (which is reported in the proxy) disregards when these options were first granted and the changes in their value over time, both of which may have closer conceptual links to firm performance.

NINE

An Integrated Analysis of Contemporary Research on Strategic Leadership

The previous chapters focused on a specific topic within strategic leadership, offering both a synthesis and a set of research priorities for the future. We have examined the role and consequences of managerial action, the impact of executive experiences on strategic choice, individual and group bases of executive action, executive turnover and succession, board-management relations, and executive compensation. In this chapter, we consider research on strategic leadership in a more integrative yet analytical fashion by investigating the following questions: What are the content and foci of contemporary research on strategic leadership? What are the major research questions, theoretical perspectives, causal models, and methodological approaches employed? How have these design choices changed over time?

What can we learn from an analysis of this work? And what does this analysis tell us about the future direction of research on strategic leadership?

This chapter has several purposes. First, we identify the articles and books that have had the greatest constructive impact on current scholarly understanding of strategic leadership. Such a list is useful for the information it conveys about the various contributions to this research area, and it provides a foundation for the chapter's other purposes. The second goal of this chapter is to analyze strategic leadership research over time, to see how the topic has been studied and how it is evolving. Third, such an integrative analysis is valuable for the lessons it offers for future research on strategic leadership. In a sense, this chapter enables an analysis of the empirical record, an integrative examination of leading works on strategic leadership that brings us full circle back to the ideas contained in each preceding chapter. The ultimate goal of this process is to ensure that we understand both the contributions and the limits of what has been done, so that we can move forward to the next stage of research on strategic leadership with an appreciation for its past.

To accomplish these objectives, we undertook an empirical study of the most noted works on strategic leadership. This chapter reports on this analysis. We first describe how the study was conducted and then discuss our findings. Because our goals are to understand what has been done and to employ this understanding to build on earlier chapters and provide more specific recommendations for future research programs, findings are reported both in terms of description and analysis. Thus, the results of this study are closely tied to the recommendations we make.

DESCRIPTION OF THE STUDY

Research on strategic leadership has grown considerably in recent years. To make an analysis of this work manageable, we examined only those select works that have had the greatest impact on the field. We chose 1980 as the starting point of our analysis because there was little systematic scholarly research on strategic leadership before that date, and it coincided with two events that have helped accelerate strategic management research in general: publication of the Schendel and Hofer (1979) volume summarizing the views of many leading figures in the field and calling for the rechristening of "business policy" as "strategic management" and the founding of the *Strategic Management Journal*. We extended our analysis through early 1994. Thus, the time frame of the study encompasses what might be called the modern era of strategic management, defined by a dominant concern for scholarly research, and especially theory-based, empirical investigation, of strategic management problems.

We studied these works in two different sets because it is difficult to compare older studies with those published more recently. The first set covered research published between 1980 and 1990, while the second included post-1990 works.

Identification of the leading works on strategic leadership published between 1980 and 1990 went through several stages. In the first screen, our goal was to draw as broadly based a population as possible. We searched for *any* published work—whether a journal article, book, or book chapter—on strategic leadership. For journal articles, we went through the table of contents of each issue of seventeen different journals using the list of journals identified by MacMillan (1991) as offering "appropriate, significant, or outstanding quality" as a forum for publication of strategic management research.[1] We selected all articles that were judged to address at least some component of strategic leadership as we have broadly defined it. Meanwhile, books on strategic leadership were identified via various word searches in library databases; we also asked colleagues to recommend books that might be appropriate. Similarly, book chapters were identified by using word searches and by examining the tables of contents of two leading book series that regularly publish works on strategic leadership *(Research in Organizational Behavior* and *Advances in Strategic Management)*. This procedure produced a list of over two hundred works on strategic leadership.

To reduce these books, book chapters, and journal articles to a more manageable set and to identify those that have had the greatest impact on the study of strategic leadership, we used citation counts. Because works on the initial list were published at various times over a fifteen-year span, however, it was important to develop a method that did not favor articles published at the beginning of our study period (since they obviously would have had greater opportunity to be cited). We chose to count citations within the first four years of publication and included all works that were cited eight or more times during this time period. Beyond "leveling the playing field" for works published at different times, using four-year citation counts enables research published more recently, which may not have had adequate time to be disseminated in the literature, to be treated separately. In other words, and as noted earlier, we formally differentiated between works published during 1980 to 1990 and those after 1990 because the relative newness of the latter set of works renders comparisons with more established research potentially unfair. In addition, exploratory analyses of the relationship between the total number of citations since publication and the number of citations as of three, four, five, and six years after publication indicated that the four-year cutoff was most predictive of total citations.

Thus, this procedure yielded two lists. Using the rule of eight citations within four years of publication, the first list includes the eighty-three most-cited works on strategic leadership between 1980 and 1990, and is reported in Table 9-1.[2] The average number of citations per year and the average survey rating (discussed below) are provided as additional information.

The second list, which includes all works on strategic leadership published after 1990, was constructed as follows. First, we selected journal articles, books, and book chapters published during this time period without regard to number of citations. But rather than reviewing all journals and book series (which would have created a very large list), we limited our search to those journals and book series that appeared in the 1980 to 1990 list. Hence, we included the *Academy of Management Journal (AMJ), Academy of Management Review (AMR), Administrative Science Quarterly (ASQ), Harvard Business Review (HBR), Management Science (MS), Organization Science (OS)*, and the *Strategic Management Journal (SMJ)*, as well as *Research in Organizational Behavior (ROB)* and *Advances in Strategic Management (ASM)*. This led to a list of sixty-three works.

Then, to gain additional information on these sixty-three works, as well as the ones from 1980 to 1990, we surveyed the authors of the works identified in either of the two lists—to provide expert ratings (on a five-point scale) of the extent to which each work has had *or* will have a "constructive impact on scholarly understanding of strategic leadership."[3] We then averaged the scores to arrive at a survey rating for each work.[4] We did not list these works by average survey rating, however, because our metric, while informative, was not designed to be applied to a ranking exercise. Nevertheless, we do provide both the average survey rating and average number of citations per year as additional information in Table 9-2, which lists alphabetically all sixty-three works published after 1990.

The lists in Tables 9-1 and 9-2 are not meant to represent any sort of popularity index. By identifying the "most highly cited works on strategic leadership," we have only done just that. Some research is cited as often for its limitations as for its contributions. In addition, the survey ratings represent an assessment of an expert audience at one point in time; trends and fashions in academic research may lead to different results at another point in time. These lists have their greatest value as the raw material for this chapter: inventories of relatively well-known research on strategic leadership that enable examination of prevailing themes and patterns over time.

TABLE 9–1 **Works on Strategic Leadership Published between 1980 and 1990 with at Least Eight Citations within the First Four Years of Publication (Ranked by Number of Citations within First Four Years of Publication and Alphabetically in the Case of Ties)**

Citation	Four-year Citations	Citations per Year	Survey Rating
Eisenhardt, K. M. 1989. Agency theory: An assessment and review. *Academy of Management Review* 14 (1): 57–74.	54	14.8	3.33
Kotter, J. P. 1982 *The general managers*. New York: Free Press.	32	14.3	3.24
Hambrick, D. C., and Mason, P. A. 1984. Upper echelons: The organization as a reflection of its top managers. *Academy of Management Review* 9 (2): 193–206.	28	16.4	4.43
Lorsch, J. W. 1989. *Pawns or potentates: The reality of America's corporate boards*. Cambridge: Harvard Business School Press.	26	7.2	2.96
Dutton, J. E., and Jackson, S. E. 1987. Categorizing strategic issues: Links to organizational action. *Academy of Management Review* 12 (1): 76–90.	25	9.4	3.10
Hambrick, D. C. 1981. Environment, strategy, and power within top management teams. *Administrative Science Quarterly* 26: 253–76.	22	7.2	3.66
Boeker, W. 1989. Strategic change: The effects of founding and history. *Academy of Management Journal* 32(3): 489–515.	21	5.0	3.21
Dutton, J. E., and Duncan, R. B. 1987. The creation of momentum for change through the process of strategic issue diagnosis. *Strategic Management Journal* 8 (3): 279–95.	21	6.4	3.21
Eisenhardt, K. M. 1989. Making fast strategic decisions in high-velocity environments. *Academy of Management Journal* 32 (3): 543–76.	21	6.8	3.84
Nutt, P. C. 1984. Types of organizational decision-processes. *Administrative Science Quarterly,* 29 (3): 414–50.	21	8.5	2.85
Eisenhardt, K. M., and Schoonhoven, C. B. 1990. Organizational growth: Linking founding team, strategy, environment, and growth among U.S. semiconductor ventures, 1978–1988. *Administrative Science Quarterly* 35 (3): 504–29.	20	5.0	3.23

TABLE 9–1 *Continued*

Citation	Four-year Citations	Citations per Year	Survey Rating
Mintzberg, H. 1987. Crafting strategy. *Harvard Business Review* 65 (4):66–75.	20	5.7	3.08
Bourgeois, L. J. 1980. Strategy and environment: A conceptual integration. *Academy of Management Review* 5 (1): 25–39.	19	7.9	2.95
Thomas, J. B., and McDaniel, R. R. 1990. Interpreting strategic issues: Effects of strategy and the information-processing structure of top management teams. *Academy of Management Journal* 33 (2): 286–306.	19	4.8	2.88
Vancil, R. F. 1987. *Passing the baton: Managing the process of CEO succession.* Cambridge: Harvard Business School Press.	19	5.0	3.35
Brown, M. C. 1982. Administrative succession and organizational performance: The succession effect. *Administrative Science Quarterly* 27: 1–16.	18	4.8	2.86
Jensen, M. C., and Murphy, K. J. 1990. CEO incentives: It's not how much you pay, but how. *Harvard Business Review* 68 (3): 138–49.	18	4.5	2.69
Kerr, J., and Bettis, R. A. 1987. Boards of directors, top management compensation, and shareholder returns. *Academy of Management Journal* 30 (4): 645–64.	18	4.3	2.65
Kotter, J. P. 1988. *The leadership factor.* New York: Free Press.	18	4.3	2.52
Donaldson, G. and Lorsch, J. W. 1983. *Decision making at the top: Shaping of strategic direction.* New York: Basic Books.	17	6.5	3.18
Fredrickson, J. W., and Iaquinto, A. L. 1989. Inertia and creeping rationality in strategic decision-processes. *Academy of Management Journal* 32 (3): 516–42.	17	4.8	3.05
Fredrickson, J. W., 1986. The strategic decision process and organizational structure. *Academy of Management Reveiew* 11 (2): 280–97.	17	4.9	2.95
Reinganum, M. R. 1985. The effect of executive succession on stockholder wealth. *Administrative Science Quarterly* 30: 46–60.	17	4.7	2.90

TABLE 9-1 *Continued*

Citation	Four-year Citations	Citations per Year	Survey Rating
Baysinger, B., and Hoskisson, R. E. 1990. The composition of boards of directors and strategic control: Effects on corporate strategy. *Academy of Management Review* 15 (1): 72–87.	16	4.0	3.06
Gupta, A. K., and Govindarajan, V. 1984. Business unit strategy, managerial characteristics, and business unit effectiveness at strategy implementation. *Academy of Management Journal* 27 (1): 25–41.	16	7.8	3.73
Hambrick, D. C., and Finkelstein, S. 1987. Managerial discretion: A bridge between polar views of organizational outcomes. *Research in organizational behavior.* vol. 9, 369–406. Greenwich, Conn. JAI Press.	16	5.9	3.93
Meindl, J. R., Ehrlich, S. B., and Dukerich, J. M. 1985. The romance of leadership. *Administrative Science Quarterly* 30: 78–102.	16	5.4	3.55
Tosi, H. L., and Gomez-Mejia, L. R. 1989. The decoupling of CEO pay and performance: An agency theory perspective. *Administrative Science Quarterly* 34 (2): 169–89.	16	4.2	3.05
Finkelstein, S., and Hambrick, D. C. 1990. Top management team tenure and organizational outcomes: The moderating role of managerial discretion. *Administrative Science Quarterly* 35 (3): 484–503.	15	3.8	3.80
Fredrickson, J. W. 1984. The comprehensiveness of strategic decision processes: Extension, observations, future directions. *Academy of Management Journal* 27 (3): 445–66.	15	5.3	3.29
Salancik, G. R., and Meindl, J. R. 1984. Corporate attributions as strategic illusions of management control. *Administrative Science Quarterly* 29: 238–54.	15	6.2	3.29
Walsh, J. P., and Seward, J. K. 1990. On the efficiency of internal and external corporate control mechanisms. *Academy of Management Review* 15 (3): 421–58.	15	3.8	3.00
Carroll, G. R. 1984. Dynamics of publisher succession in newspaper organizations. *Administrative Science Quarterly* 29: 93–113.	14	4.8	3.02

TABLE 9-1 *Continued*

Citation	Four-year Citations	Citations per Year	Survey Rating
Fredrickson, J. W., and Mitchell, T. R. 1984. Strategic decision processes: Comprehensiveness and performance in an industry with an unstable environment. *Academy of Management Journal* 27 (2): 399–423.	14	5.6	3.07
Kotter, J. P. 1982. What effective general managers really do. *Harvard Business Review* 60 (6): 156–67.	14	3.1	2.88
Pfeffer, J., and Davis-Blake, A. 1986. Administrative succession and organizational performance: How administrator experience mediates the succession effect. *Academy of Management Journal* 29 (1): 72–83.	14	3.9	3.00
Schweiger, D. M., Sandberg, W. R., and Ragan, J. W. 1986. Group approaches for improving strategic decision making: A comparative analysis of dialectical inquiry, devil's advocacy, and consensus. *Academy of Management Journal* 29 (1): 51–71.	14	4.8	2.62
Singh, H., and Harianto, F. 1989. Management-board relationships, takeover risk, and the adoption of golden parachutes. *Academy of Management Journal* 32 (1): 7–24.	14	4.4	2.82
Walsh, J. P. 1988. Selectivity and selective perception: An investigation of managers' belief structures and information-processing. *Academy of Management Journal* 31 (4): 873–96.	14	3.3	3.14
Bourgeois, L. J., and Eisenhardt, K. M. 1988. Strategic decision processes in high velocity environments: Four cases in the microcomputer industry. *Management Science* 34 (7): 816–35.	13	4.8	3.57
Isenberg, D. J. 1984. How senior managers think. *Harvard Business Review* 62 (6): 80–90.	13	4.7	2.47
Kosnik, R. D. 1990. The effects of board demography and directors' incentives on corporate greenmail decisions. *Academy of Management Journal* 33 (1): 129–50.	13	3.3	2.65
Sonnenfeld, J. A. 1988. *The hero's farewell: What happens when CEOs retire?* New York: Oxford University Press.	13	2.8	2.87

TABLE 9–1 *Continued*

Citation	Four-year Citations	Citations per Year	Survey Rating
Bantel, K. A., and Jackson, S. E. 1989. Top management and innovations in banking: Does the composition of the top team make a difference? *Strategic Management Journal* 10 (Special Issue): 107–24.	12	4.0	2.97
Bourgeois, L. J. 1985. Strategic goals, perceived uncertainty, and economic performance in volatile environments. *Academy of Management Journal* 28 (3): 548–73.	12	5.8	3.13
Eisenhardt, K. M., and Bourgeois, L. J. 1988. Politics of strategic decision-making in high-velocity environments. *Academy of Management Journal* 31 (4): 737–70.	12	5.0	3.32
Jackson, S. E., and Dutton, J. E. 1988. Discerning threats and opportunities. *Administrative Science Quarterly* 33 (3): 370–87.	12	5.3	3.26
Mintzberg, H., and Waters, J. A. 1982. Tracking strategy in an entrepreneurial firm. *Academy of Management Journal,* 25 (3): 465–99.	12	4.9	3.10
Wagner, W. G., Pfeffer, J., and O'Reilly, C. A., III. 1984. Organizational demography and turnover in top-management groups. *Administrative Science Quarterly* 29 (1): 74–92.	12	6.8	3.65
D'Aveni, R. A. 1990. Top managerial prestige and organizational bankruptcy. *Organization Science* 1 (2): 121–42.	11	2.8	2.79
Dess, G. R. 1987. Consensus on strategy formulation and organizational performance: Competitors in a fragmented industry. *Strategic Management Journal* 8: 259–77.	11	4.7	2.97
Finkelstein, S., and Hambrick, D. C. 1989. Chief executive compensation: A study of the intersection of markets and political processes. *Strategic Management Journal* 10 (2): 121–34.	11	3.8	3.29
Miller, D., DeVries, M. F. R. K., and Toulouse, J. M. 1982. Top executive locus of control and its relationship to strategy-making, structure, and environment. *Academy of Management Journal* 25 (2): 237–53.	11	6.7	3.24
Miller, D., and Toulouse, J. M. 1986. Chief executive personality and corporate strategy and structure in small firms. *Management Science* 32 (11):1389–1409.	11	4.5	3.14

TABLE 9-1 *Continued*

Citation	Four-year Citations	Citations per Year	Survey Rating
Daft, R. L., Sormunen, J., and Parks, D. 1988. Chief executive scanning, environmental characteristics, and company performance: An empirical study. *Strategic Management Journal* 9: 123–39.	10	4.2	2.89
Friedman, S. D., and Singh, H. 1989. CEO succession and stockholder reaction: The influence of organizational context and event content. *Academy of Management Journal* 32 (4): 718–44.	10	3.2	2.59
Govindarajan, V., and Fisher, J. 1990. Strategy, control systems, and resource sharing: Effects on business unit performance. *Academy of Management Journal* 33 (2): 259–85.	10	2.5	2.94
Kesner, I. F. 1988. Directors' characteristics and committee membership: An investigation of type, occupation, tenure, and gender. *Academy of Management Journal* 31 (1): 66–84.	10	2.5	2.39
Kosnick, R. D. 1987. Greenmail: A study of board performance in corporate governance. *Administrative Science Quarterly* 32: 163–85.	10	5.0	3.11
Kotter, J. P. 1990. What leaders really do. *Harvard Business Review* 68 (3): 103–11.	10	2.5	2.56
Robey, D., and Taggart, W. 1981. Measuring managers' minds: The assessment of style in human information-processing. *Academy of Management Review* 6 (3): 375–83.	10	2.9	2.21
Schwenk, C. R. 1984. Cognitive simplification processes in strategic decision-making. *Strategic Management Journal* 5: 111–28.	10	5.4	2.78
Szilagyi, Jr., A. D., and Schweiger, D. M. 1984. Matching managers to strategies: A review and suggested framework. *Academy of Management Review* 9 (4): 626–37.	10	3.1	2.44
Hitt, M. A., Ireland, R. D., and Palia, K. A. 1982. Industrial firms' grand strategy and functional importance: Moderating effects of technology and uncertainty. *Academy of Management Journal* 25 (2): 265–98.	9	3.4	2.63

TABLE 9–1 *Continued*

Citation	Four-year Citations	Citations per Year	Survey Rating
Huber, G. P., and Power, D. J. 1985. Retrospective reports of strategic-level managers: Guidelines for increasing their accuracy. *Strategic Management Journal* 6: 171–80.	9	4.6	2.31
Miller, D., and Dröge, C. 1986. Psychological and traditional determinants of structure. *Administrative Science Quarterly* 31 (4): 539–60.	9	4.9	2.97
Sheridan, J. E., Vredenburgh, D. J., and Abelson, M. A. 1984. Contextual model of leadership influence in hospital units. *Academy of Management Journal* 27 (1): 57–78.	9	2.0	1.82
Smith, J. E., Carson, K. P., and Alexander, R. A. 1984. Leadership: It can make a difference. *Academy of Management Journal* 27 (4): 765–76.	9	2.8	2.39
Thomas, A. B. 1988. Does leadership make a difference to organizational performance? *Administrative Science Quarterly* 33 (3): 388–400.	9	2.7	2.87
Walsh, J. P. 1989. Doing a deal: Merger and acquisition negotiations and their impact upon target company top management turnover. *Strategic Management Journal* 10 (4):307–22.	9	2.4	2.88
Worrell, D. L., Davidson, W. N., Chandy, P. R., and Garrison, S. L. 1986. Management turnover through deaths of key executives: Effects on investor wealth. *Academy of Management Journal* 29 (4):674–94.	9	1.8	2.19
Zajac, E. J. 1990. CEO selection, succession, compensation and firm performance: A theoretical integration and empirical analysis. *Strategic Management Journal* 11 (3): 217–30.	9	2.3	3.15
Bourgeois, L. J. 1980. Performance and consensus. *Strategic Management Journal* 1 (3): 227–48.	8	5.1	3.21
D'Aveni, R. A., and MacMillan, I. 1990. Crisis and the content of managerial communications: A study of the focus of attention of top managers in surviving and failing firms. *Administrative Science Quarterly* 35 (4): 634–57.	8	2.0	3.13
Duhaime, I. M., and Schwenk, C. R. 1985. Conjectures on cognitive simplification in acquisition and divestment decision-making. *Academy of Management Review* 10 (2): 287–95.	8	3.2	2.65

TABLE 9–1 *Continued*

Citation	Four-year Citations	Citations per Year	Survey Rating
Finkelstein, S., and Hambrick, D. C. 1988. Chief executive compensation: A synthesis and reconciliation. *Strategic Management Journal* 9 (6):543–58.	8	2.7	3.49
Fredrickson, J. W., Hambrick, D. C., and Baumrin, S. 1988. A model of CEO dismissal. *Academy of Management Review* 13 (2):255–70.	8	3.2	3.05
Hitt, M. A., and Ireland, R. D. 1985. Corporate distinctive competence, strategy, industry and performance. *Strategic Management Journal* 6 (3):273–93.	8	4.2	2.87
Levinson, H. 1984. *CEO: Corporate leadership in action*. New York: Basic Books.	8	1.9	2.35
Miller, D. 1987. Strategy making and structure: Analysis and implications for performance. *Academy of Management Journal* 30 (1): 7–32.	8	3.3	3.07
Nutt, P. C. 1986. Tactics of implementation. *Academy of Management Journal* 29 (2): 230–61.	8	2.6	2.41
O'Reilly, C. A., Main, B. G., and Crystal, G. S. 1988. CEO compensation as tournament and social comparison: A tale of two theories. *Administrative Science Quarterly* 33 (2): 257–74.	8	3.3	3.41
Wade, J., O'Reilly, C. A., and Chandratat, I. 1990. Golden parachutes: CEOs and the exercise of social influence. *Administrative Science Quarterly* 35 (4): 587–603.	8	2.0	2.72

TABLE 9–2 **Works on Strategic Leadership Published After 1990 (up to date of survey—Spring, 1994) (in alphabetical order)**

Citation	Survey Rating	Citations Per Year
Boeker, W. 1992. Power and managerial dismissal: Scapegoating at the top. *Administrative Science Quarterly* 37 (3): 400–21.	3.23	4.0
Boeker, W., and Goodstein, J. 1991. Organizational performance and adaptation: Effects of environment and performance on changes in board compostition. *Academy of Management Journal* 34 (4): 805–26.	2.82	2.7
Boeker, W., and Goodstein, J. 1993. Performance and successor choice: The moderating effects of governance and ownership. *Academy of Management Journal* 36 (1): 172–86.	2.61	3.0
Boone, C., and Debrabander, B. 1993. Generalized versus specific locus of control expectancies of chief executive officers. *Strategic Management Journal* 14 (8):619–25.	2.11	1.0
Cannella, A. A., and Lubatkin, M. 1993. Succession as a sociopolitical process: Internal impediments to outsider selection. *Academy of Management Journal* 36 (4): 763–93.	2.94	N/A
Chen, C. C., and Meindl, J. R. 1991. The construction of leadership images in the popular press: The case of Donald Burr and People Express. *Administrative Science Quarterly* 36 (4): 521–51.	2.80	3.5
Clapham, S. E., and Schwenk, C. R. 1991. Self-serving attributions, managerial cognition, and company performance. *Strategic Management Journal* 12 (3): 219–29.	2.54	1.0
Cowherd, D. M., and Levine, D. I. 1992. Product quality and pay equity between lower-level employees and top management: An investigation of distributive justice theory. *Administrative Science Quarterly* 37 (2): 302–20.	2.70	1.5
D'Aveni, R. A., and Kesner, I. F. 1993. Top managerial prestige, power and tender offer response: A study of elite social networks and target firm cooperation during takeovers. *Organization Science* 4 (2): 123–51.	3.07	1.0
Davis, G. F. 1991. Agents without principles: The spread of the poison pill through the intercorporate network. *Administrative Science Quarterly* 36 (4): 583–613.	3.16	3.3
Dutton, J. E., and Ashford, S. J. 1993. Selling issues to top management. *Academy of Management Review* 18 (3): 397–428.	3.18	N/A
Finkelstein, S. 1992. Power in top management teams: Dimensions, measurement, and validation. *Academy of Management Journal* 35 (3): 505–38.	3.63	3.5

TABLE 9–2 *Continued*

Citation	Survey Rating	Citations Per Year
Fisher, J., and Govindarajan, V. 1992. Profit center manager compensation: An examination of market, political and human capital factors. *Strategic Management Journal* 13 (3): 205–17.	2.67	1.0
Gomez-Mejia, L. R. 1992. Structure and process of diversification, compensation strategy, and firm performance. *Strategic Management Journal* 13 (5): 381–97.	2.82	1.0
Goodstein, J., and Boeker, W. 1991. Turbulence at the top: A new perspective on governance structure changes and strategic change. *Academy of Management Journal* 34 (2):306–30.	3.03	4.0
Goodstein, J., Gautam, K., and Boeker, W. 1994. The effects of board size and diversity on strategic change. *Strategic Management Journal* 15 (3): 241–50.	2.50	N/A
Grimm, C. M., and Smith, K. G. 1991 Management and organizational change: A note on the railroad industry. *Strategic Management Journal* 12 (7): 557–62.	2.25	0.7
Haleblian, J., and Finkelstein, S. 1993. Top management team size, CEO dominance, and firm performance: The moderating roles of environmental turbulence and discretion. *Academy of Management Journal* 36 (4): 844–63.	3.30	N/A
Hambrick, D. C., and D'Aveni, R. A. 1992. Top team deterioration as part of the downward spiral of large corporate bankruptcies. *Management Science* 38 (10): 1445–66.	3.32	0.5
Hambrick, D. C., and Fukutomi, G. D. S. 1991. The seasons of a CEO's tenure. *Academy of Management Review* 16 (4): 719–42.	3.51	1.0
Hambrick, D. C., Geletkanycz, M. A., and Fredrickson, J. W. 1993. Top executive commitment to the status quo: Some tests of its determinants. *Strategic Management Journal* 14 (6): 401–18.	3.15	N/A
Hart, S. L. 1992. An integrative framework for strategy-making processes. *Academy of Management Review* 17 (2): 327–51.	2.56	2.0
Haveman, H. A. 1993. Ghosts of managers past: Managerial succession and organizational mortality. *Academy of Management Journal* 36 (4): 864–81.	2.91	2.0
Hill, C. W. L., and Phan, P. 1991. CEO tenure as a determinant of CEO pay. *Academy of Management Journal* 34 (3): 707–17.	2.36	1.0

TABLE 9–2 *Continued*

Citation	Survey Rating	Citations Per Year
Hitt, M. A., and Tyler, B. B. 1991. Strategic decision models: Integrating different perspectives. *Strategic Management Journal* 12 (5): 327–51.	2.63	4.0
House, R. J., Spangler, W. D., and Woycke, J. 1991. Personality and charisma in the United States presidency: A psychological theory of leader effectiveness. *Administrative Science Quarterly* 36 (3): 364–96.	2.51	2.0
Jackson, S. E. 1992. Consequences of group composition for the interpersonal dynamics of strategic issue processing. *Advances in strategic management.* vol. 8, 354–89. Greenwich, Conn.: JAI Press.	2.92	2.5
Judge, W. Q., and Zeithaml, C. P. 1992. Institutional and strategic choice perspectives on board involvement in the strategic decision process. *Academy of Management Journal* 35 (4): 766–94.	2.65	2.7
Keck, S. L., and Tushman, M. L. 1993. Environmental and organizational context and executive team structure. *Academy of Management Journal* 36 (6):1314–44.	3.06	N/A
Kerr, J. L., and Kren, L. 1992. Effect of relative decision monitoring on chief executive compensation. *Academy of Management Journal* 35 (2): 370–97.	2.52	1.0
Kim, W. C., and Mauborgne, R. A. 1993. Procedural justice, attitudes, and subsidiary top management compliance with multinationals' corporate strategic decisions. *Academy of Management Journal* 36 (3): 502–26.	2.48	1.0
Lambert, R. A., Larcker, D. F., and Weigelt, K. 1991. How sensitive is executive compensation to organizational size? *Strategic Management Journal* 12 (5):395–402.	2.23	0.7
Lambert, R. A., Larcker, D. F., and Weigelt, K. 1993. The structure of organizational incentives. *Administrative Science Quarterly* 38 (3): 438–61.	3.00	N/A
Lant, T. K., Milliken, F. J., and Batra, B. 1992. The role of managerial learning and interpretation in strategic persistence and reorientation: An empirical exploration. *Strategic Management Journal* 13 (8): 585–608.	3.18	N/A
Mallette, P., and Fowler, K. L. 1992. Effects of board composition and stock ownership on the adoption of poison pills. *Academy of Management Journal* 35 (5): 1010–35.	2.22	0.5
Michel, J. G., and Hambrick, D. C. 1992. Diversification posture and top management team characteristics. *Academy of Management Journal* 35 (1): 9–37.	2.92	5.5

TABLE 9–2 *Continued*

Citation	Survey Rating	Citations Per Year
Miller, D. 1991. Stale in the saddle: CEO tenure and the match between organization and environment. *Management Science* 37 (1): 34–52.	3.22	3.0
Miller, D. 1993. Some organizational consequences of CEO succession. *Academy of Management Journal* 36 (3): 644–59.	2.95	N/A
Milliken, J., and Lant, T. K. 1991. The effect of an organization's recent performance history on strategic persistence and change: The role of managerial interpretations. *Advances in strategic management.* vol. 7, 129–56. Greenwich, Conn.: JAI Press.	2.91	N/A
Nutt, P. C. 1993. The formulation processes and tactics used in organizational decision-making. *Organization Science* 4 (2): 226–51.	2.57	2.0
Nutt, P. C. 1993. The identification of solution ideas during organizational decision making. *Management Science* 39 (9): 1071–85.	2.35	0.7
Pagonis, W. G. 1992. The work of the leader. *Harvard Business Review* 70 (6): 118–26.	2.30	N/A
Pearce, J. A., and Zahra, S. A. 1991. The relative power of CEOs and boards of directors: Associations with corporate performance. *Strategic Management Journal* 12 (2): 135–53.	2.65	0.5
Powell, G. M., and Butterfield, D. A. 1994. Investigating the glass ceiling phenomenon: An empirical study of actual promotion to top management. *Academy of Management Journal* 37 (1): 68–86.	2.74	N/A
Priem, R. L. 1992. An application of metric conjoint analysis for the evaluation of top managers' individual strategic decision-making processes: A research note. *Strategic Management Journal* 13 (Special Issue, Summer): 143–151.	2.00	1.0
Puffer, S. M., and Weintrop, J. B. 1991. Corporate performance and CEO turnover: The role of performance expectations. *Administrative Science Quarterly* 36 (1): 1–19.	2.85	4.3
Rajagopalan, N., and Finkelstein, S. 1992. Effects of strategic orientation and environmental change on senior management reward systems. *Strategic Management Journal* 13 (Special Issue, Summer): 127–41.	3.12	N/A
Rechner, P. L., and Dalton, D. R. 1991. CEO duality and organizational performance: A longitudinal analysis. *Strategic Management Journal* 12 (2): 155–60.	2.55	1.3

TABLE 9-2 *Continued*

Citation	Survey Rating	Citations Per Year
Rotemberg, J. J., and Saloner, G. 1993. Leadership style and incentives. *Management Science* 39 (11): 1299–1314.	1.94	N/A
Schotter, A. 1992. Behavioral consequences of corporate incentives and long-term bonuses: An experimental study. *Management Science* 38 (9): 1280–98.	1.94	N/A
Shanley, M. T., and Correa, M. E. 1992. Agreement between top management teams and expectations for postacquisition performance. *Strategic Management Journal* 13 (4): 245–66.	2.14	0.5
Simons, R. 1991. Strategic orientation and top management attention to control systems. *Strategic Management Journal* 12 (1): 49–62.	2.35	N/A
Simons, R. 1994. How new top managers use control systems as levers of strategic renewal. *Strategic Management Journal* 15 (3): 169–90.	2.62	N/A
Thomas, A. S., Litschert, R. J., and Ramaswamy, K. 1991. The performance impact of strategy-manager coalignment: An empirical examination. *Strategic Management Journal* 12 (7): 509–22.	2.44	0.3
Virany, B., Tushman, M. L., and Romanelli, E. 1992. Executive succession and organization outcomes in turbulent environments: An organization learning approach. *Organization Science* 3 (1): 72–91.	3.33	4.5
Walsh, J. P., and Ellwood, J. W. 1991. Mergers, acquisitions, and the pruning of managerial deadwood. *Strategic Management Journal* 12 (3): 201–17.	2.77	2.0
Walsh, J. P., and Kosnik, R. D. 1993. Corporate raiders and their disciplinary role in the market for corporate control. *Academy of Management Journal* 36 (4): 671–700.	2.77	N/A
Wiersema, M. F., and Bantel, K. A. 1992. Top management team demography and corporate strategic change. *Academy of Management Journal* 35 (1): 91–121.	3.17	1.0
Wiersema, M. F., and Bantel, K. A. 1993. Top management team turnover as an adaptation mechanism: The role of the environment. *Strategic Management Journal* 14 (7): 485–504.	2.86	N/A
Wiersema, M. F., and Bird, A. 1993. Organizational demography in Japanese firms: Group heterogeneity, individual dissimilarity, and top management team turnover. *Academy of Management Journal* 36 (5): 996–1025.	2.62	N/A

TABLE 9-2 *Continued*

Citation	Survey Rating	Citations Per Year
Worrell, D. L., Davidson, W. N., and Glascock, J. L. 1993. Stockholder reactions to departures and appointments of key executives attributable to firings. *Academy of Management Journal* 36 (2): 387–401.	2.32	N/A
Zajac, E. J., and Bazerman, M. H. 1991. Blind spots in industry and competitor analysis: Implications of interfirm (mis)perceptions for strategic decisions. *Academy of Management Review* 16 (1): 37–56.	3.27	2.7
Zaleznik, A. 1992. Managers and leaders: Are they different? *Harvard Business Review* 70 (2): 126–35.	2.74	N/A

A Descriptive and Analytic Assessment of Research on Strategic Leadership

In this section, we describe research on strategic leadership in two parts. First, we focus on a substantive assessment of strategic leadership through the unit of analysis selected, the theoretical perspectives used, the causal logics employed, and the underlying assumptions about managerial work. Second, we discuss this research from a methodological perspective, concentrating on methodological and analytic patterns.

To extract appropriate data to address these issues, we analyzed the content of the 146 articles that comprise both the 1980 to 1990 and post-1990 lists. Although dimensions that could be examined in such an analysis are virtually unlimited, we focused on a limited number of major issues: primarily an assessment of the theoretical approaches that form the basis for this work, as well as some of the key methodological design choices researchers have made.

We begin by reporting on two basic choices researchers make about their work, the nature of the study (conceptual versus empirical) and the publication outlet. Of the 146 journal articles, books, and book chapters, 109 (75 percent) were empirical and 37 were conceptual—indicating that both theory development and theory testing were occurring simultaneously in our sample. By way of comparison,[5] an early study of research on "business policy" conducted in 1980 found that 42 percent of all research-oriented papers submitted to the Business Policy and Planning Division of the Academy of Management in 1979 were empirical; a study by Hambrick (1986) of strategic management works published between 1980 and 1985 found that 46 percent were empirical; and Schwenk and Dalton (1991) reported that in their survey of strategic management research published in five major journals in 1986 and 1987, the percentage of empirical articles had increased to 60 percent.

Our sample of well-known works on strategic leadership exhibited a similar pattern over time, as Figure 9-1 indicates. The increased incidence of empirical work over time probably reflects an enhanced familiarity with important data sources for strategic leadership research (e.g., *Dun & Bradstreet's Reference Book of Corporate Management,* corporate proxy statements, compensation surveys, etc.), as well as the legitimate need to test some early concepts and constructs in strategic leadership (e.g., upper echelons, organizational demography, agency relationships, managerial discretion, etc.). Nevertheless, a risk may be associated with these trends: Are we developing enough new theories and ideas, or are we excessively relying on idea-testing in our work?

Beyond the nature of the study itself, it is also useful to examine where strategic leadership research is published. Most of the research on our two lists appeared in a relatively small number of journals. Prominent among the most cited works, however, are several books and book chapters. The distribution of publication outlets is summarized in Figure 9-2. Four journals

FIGURE 9-1 **Incidence of Empirical Works over Time**

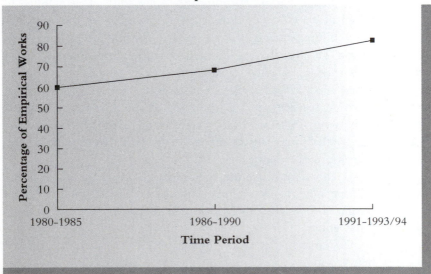

FIGURE 9-2 **Publication Outlet**

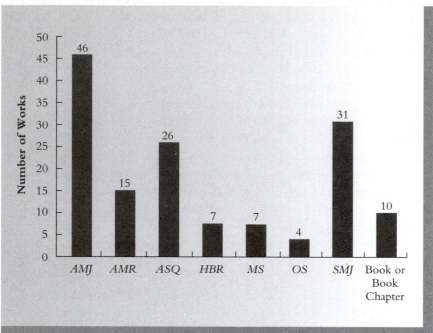

account for the vast majority of publications—AMJ, SMJ, ASQ, and AMR. The other three journals, HBR, MS, and OS (a new journal), are much less well-represented in our sample. Although the selection criteria applied to works published after 1990 favored these seven journals, research on strategic leadership published during 1980 to 1990 in any one of seventeen outlets was surveyed. The fact that such a small set of journals emerged as the dominant outlets for highly cited research on strategic leadership is not that surprising, given MacMillan's (1991) findings about journal impact, and it is consistent with an earlier survey of the most oft-cited works on strategic management between 1980 and 1985, which found that thirty-five of thirty-six journal articles listed among the top fifty works were published in the same seven journals (Hambrick 1986).

Figure 9-3 reports on how the representation of these journals has changed over time; note that several patterns are in evidence. First, although AMJ has continued to be the dominant outlet for work on strategic leadership, SMJ has emerged in recent years as an important journal for this research. From a journal that was originally seen as primarily oriented toward strategy content and economic paradigms, SMJ has more recently published dedicated issues on strategic leadership (Summer 1989) and strat-

FIGURE 9-3   **Publication Outlets over Time**

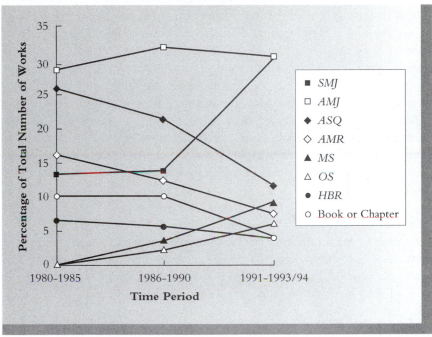

egy process (Summer and Winter 1992), which reflects the increasing importance of behavioral and top-management research in the field of strategic management. A second pattern is the gradually decreasing incidence of strategic leadership articles in AMR and especially ASQ. Among the possible reasons for these trends is the decline in theory-building and conceptual research noted earlier (AMR publishes only conceptual, not empirical, research) and ASQ's increasing attention to ecological and deterministic models of organizations.

We now turn to a description of the works on strategic leadership we have identified. Here, we consider both substantive and methodological attributes of these works along a series of key dimensions. For each, we first provide a descriptive assessment, and then we analyze the nature of the changes that have occurred over time.

Conceptual Issues in Research on Strategic Leadership

In this section, we examine four important conceptual attributes of research on strategic leadership: unit of analysis, underlying theory, causal logic, and assumption about managerial work.

Unit of Analysis.   For research on strategic leadership, the selection of a unit of analysis is a critical conceptual choice that may have implications for the theoretical development of an article. For example, as we argued in Chapter 5, focusing solely on the CEO in a study of how top managerial choices affect organizational outcomes implies that only the CEO can affect outcomes. One of the arguments made throughout this book, however, is that CEOs are often quite constrained in their ability to change an organization—and these constraints arise not only from general limits to managerial discretion throughout an organization, but also from practical bounds imposed by the actions of other top managers and the board of directors. Hence, in a conceptual sense, selecting a unit of analysis carries significant meaning.

We classified unit of analysis into six categories: CEO, top management team, board of directors, strategic business unit (SBU) manager, the firm or some process within the firm, and unspecified executives. Authors in some works examined multiple units of analysis, which we counted as well. As a result, the sum of the works assigned to each unit of analysis adds up to more than 146. This method of counting secondary and even tertiary attributes of the research pieces was employed throughout this chapter to help ensure we were capturing as much information as possible.

Figure 9-4 provides data on the distribution of units of analysis in our sample. As is evident from this figure, a majority of the works in our sample employed an individual unit of analysis—either the CEO, the SBU manager, or unspecified top executives (86 works, or 59 percent). That so much research has concentrated on the CEO is expected, given the prevailing traditional focus on the single leader. However, only eleven works examined the SBU manager, indicating that while a general manager focus is the purported hallmark of work on strategic management, in reality scholars have devoted considerably more effort to studying corporate-level general managers (i.e., CEOs) than business-level general managers. This gap is important because, although business-level data is difficult to collect, contemporary firms have many SBU positions, and it is precisely at this level that competitive strategy is formulated and executed.

There are two other important points. First, although only thirteen works focused on boards of directors, we would expect this number to grow as strategy researchers adopt the agency perspective and as scholars turn their attention to the very timely issues of board behavior and reform. Nevertheless, difficulty in obtaining primary data (as opposed to archival data) on boards will always be great. Second, consistent with the general impression of a strong emphasis on top management teams in the literature, these studies employed either TMT or firm units of analysis 54 of 146 times (37 percent).

FIGURE 9-4   **Unit of Analysis**

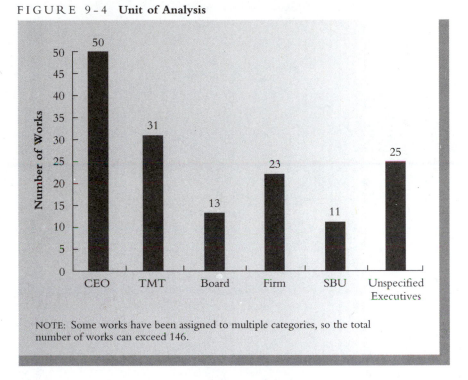

NOTE: Some works have been assigned to multiple categories, so the total number of works can exceed 146.

We also examined how the selection of unit of analysis has changed over the last fifteen years. Basing our analysis on three different time periods, 1980 to 1985, 1986 to 1990, and 1991 to 1993-94—with each period accounting for a significant portion of the works from our sample—we report the incidence of each characteristic as a percentage of the total number of works published during that period.[6]

Figure 9-5 depicts how the adoption of various units of analysis in the works has changed over time. Standing out is the continuing dominant focus on the CEO, followed by the recent emergence of the TMT as a secondary unit of analysis, reflecting upper-echelons arguments on the importance of TMTs.[7] Other changes worth noting are the reduction in work adopting the firm and unspecified executives units of analysis, perhaps reflecting increasing precision about specific types of executives. Also, there has been an increase in studies of boards of directors, driven by the timeliness and importance of this work and the availability of tools from agency theory.

Theoretical Perspective.   One of the recurring themes in our synthesis of strategic leadership is that a wide set of theoretical perspectives may be relevant to understanding the characteristics, behaviors, and

FIGURE 9-5   **Unit of Analysis over Time**

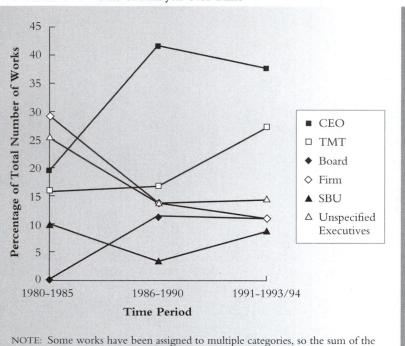

NOTE: Some works have been assigned to multiple categories, so the sum of the percentages in any one time period may exceed 100.

effects of executives. In this vein, it is interesting to examine the array of theoretical perspectives employed in the 146 scholarly works we are examining here.

We initially attempted our categorization with a relatively small set of major theories (e.g., agency, upper echelons, resource dependence, population ecology, and institutionalization), to which we planned to assign the various works. It became apparent, however, that a much broader set of theoretical perspectives was in evidence and that some of these perspectives were not really theories as much as they were collections of ideas. As a result, we changed our coding scheme to capture this range, in the process loosening our initially strict definition of what constitutes a theory. In the end, seventeen "theoretical perspectives" were identified in our studies, as depicted in Figure 9-6.

The most commonly used theoretical perspective was upper echelons theory, which has the advantage of allowing straightforward tests of executive effects and has been instrumental in persuading researchers to focus on top management teams, not just single executives. By recognizing the sep-

FIGURE 9-6 **Theoretical Perspectives**

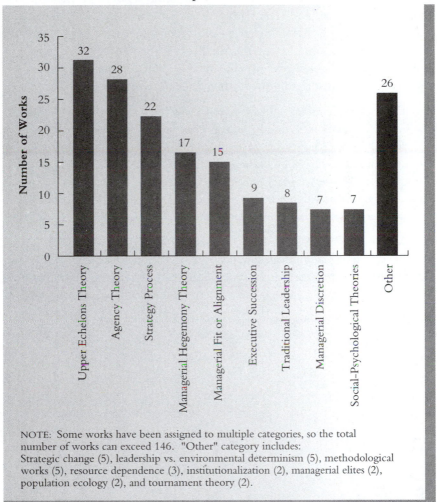

NOTE: Some works have been assigned to multiple categories, so the total
number of works can exceed 146. "Other" category includes:
Strategic change (5), leadership vs. environmental determinism (5), methodological
works (5), resource dependence (3), institutionalization (2), managerial elites (2),
population ecology (2), and tournament theory (2).

aration of ownership and control in contemporary firms, agency theory has
also proved to be a prominent theoretical perspective for scholars of strategic leadership. Work by Eisenhardt (1989a) and Walsh and Seward (1990),
in particular, have made this theory accessible for strategic leadership
researchers. Less often employed was the "traditional leadership" perspective, perhaps a reflection of skepticism about "great man" conceptions of
CEOs. Also little used was managerial discretion, a promising perspective,
but relatively new, somewhat abstract, and difficult to operationalize.

The wide array of different theoretical perspectives found was consistent
with our own review of the literature and indicates that strategic leadership

is a broad domain that can be studied in numerous ways. Nevertheless, it also indicates that we are a long way from developing any paradigmatic focus in this area, something that might bring more coherent knowledge generation (Pfeffer 1993). To some extent, this plethora of theoretical perspectives may mirror what one sees in the overall strategic management (Shrivastava and Lim 1989) and organization theory literatures (Pfeffer 1993):

> Theories of the middle range (Merton 1968; Pinder and Moore 1979) prolif-erate, along with measures, terms, concepts, and research paradigms. It is often difficult to discern in what direction knowledge of organizations is progress-ing—or if, indeed, it is progressing at all. Researchers, students of organization theory, and those who look to such theory for some guidance about issues of management and administration confront an almost bewildering array of vari-ables, perspectives, and inferred prescriptions." (Pfeffer 1982, 1)

Although scholars of strategic leadership continued to employ a vari-ety of different theoretical perspectives over time, significant changes occurred in the relative importance of these theories over the last fifteen

FIGURE 9-7 **Theoretical Perspectives over Time**

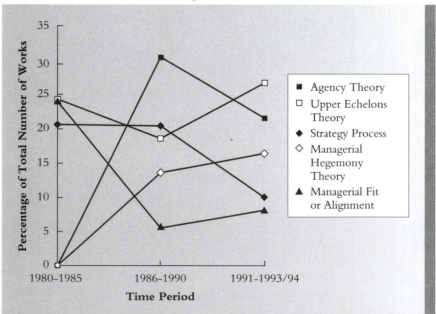

NOTE: Some works have been assigned to multiple categories. Only the theoretical perspectives that appeared most often in our sample are illustrated; however, percentages are of the total number of works in each time period and not just of those with the theoretical perspectives depicted.

years. An examination of Figure 9-7 documents the rise of agency theory and, to a lesser extent, managerial hegemony theory as major theoretical perspectives in the study of strategy leadership. That these two theories appear to be adopted in tandem is not surprising, given their underlying similarity. Other shifts are also evident in Figure 9-7, such as the relative decline of work on managerial fit and strategy process and the renewed emphasis on upper-echelons ideas in the early 1990s. Much more research on managerial fit or alignment in particular appears to be needed, given the importance of contingency approaches to strategy; it is well known that universal ideas do not often hold (Miller 1987).

Causal Logic.   The underlying causal logic employed in an empirical or conceptual work has to do with the types of conceptual relationships being considered. By causal logic we mean the underlying set of relationships among major constructs that form the basis for propositions tested, generated, or implied. These underlying causal logics exist in both conceptual and empirical research, since most works either present arguments on a particular relationship or a test a relationship. The existence of a causal logic in an empirical study, however, should not be taken to mean that formal statistical causal modeling methods are actually being employed. Indeed, we found that very few empirical works in our sample were able to establish strict causality.

There are many ways to conceptualize causal logics. In this analysis, we view strategic leadership as a distinct construct that extends the classic strategic management framework linking environment, organization form or conduct, and firm performance. Strategic leadership refers to any aspect of executives (whether characteristics or behavior) and any executives, (whether CEO, TMT, or board). Environment is defined to include any stimuli external to the organization (e.g., industry structure, environmental uncertainty). Organization form or conduct encompasses all aspects of the organization that are distinct from the strategic leadership construct, including strategies, structures, and organizational processes. Finally, firm performance refers to the organization's effectiveness, as indicated by such factors as return on equity, stock market returns, and survival of the entity. Figure 9-8 illustrates how these four constructs are interrelated.

Taking these four constructs together, it is possible to analytically distinguish the implicit or explicit causal logics used in most strategic leadership research. We classified causal logics on the basis of how strategic leadership was envisioned in each work: as an independent construct, dependent construct, moderator construct, or both an independent and dependent construct.[8] Table 9-3 provides a breakdown of the different types of relationships examined or proposed in the studies we examined, and Figure 9-9 further illustrates the relative volume of work in each category.[9]

FIGURE 9-8   **Causal Logics in Strategic Leadership Research**

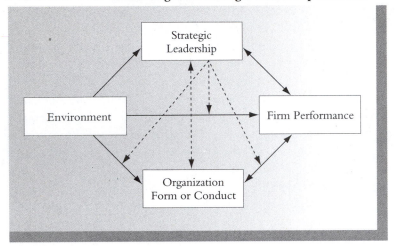

FIGURE 9-9   **Causal Logics**

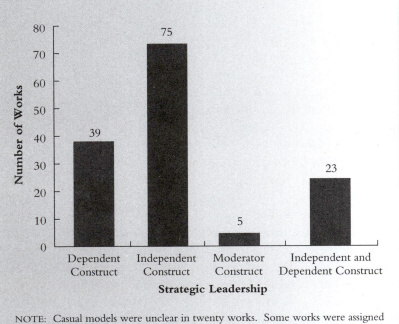

NOTE: Casual models were unclear in twenty works. Some works were assigned to more than one category.

TABLE 9–3   **Types of Causal Logics**

	Number of Works
Strategic Leadership As a Dependent Construct	43
Environment ————————————→ Strategic Leadership	7
Organization Form or Conduct ————————→ Strategic Leadership	15
Firm Performance ————————→ Strategic Leadership	21
Strategic Leadership As an Independent Construct	81
Strategic Leadership ————→ Organization Form or Conduct	31
Strategic Leadership ————————→ Firm Performance	50
Strategic Leadership As a Moderator Construct	5
Environment X Strategic Leadership ————→ Organization Form or Conduct	1
Environment X Strategic Leadership ————————→ Firm Performance	1
Organization Form or Conduct X Strategic Leadership ————————→ Firm Performance	3
Firm Performance X Strategic Leadership ————→ Organization Form or Conduct	0
Strategic Leadership As an Independent and Dependent Construct Simultaneously	
Strategic Leadership ————————→ Strategic Leadership	23

It is evident that strategic leadership has more often been modeled as an independent construct than a dependent one and especially as an antecedent to firm performance. This is not surprising, given strategists' focus on performance outcomes. Studies in this category include work on CEO alignment (with organizational form or conduct) and on the consequences of executive succession for firm performance. However, although management scholars tend to focus on the effects of managers and their behaviors, much more understanding of the determinants of executive characteristics and behaviors is needed; only with that can we get at the root forces for change or intervention. Not well-represented are studies with strategic leadership as a moderator construct, perhaps reflecting researchers' design choices as much as anything else, since research on managerial fit with organizational or environmental contexts is not uncommon. Thus, strategic leadership

FIGURE 9-10   **Causal Logics over Time**

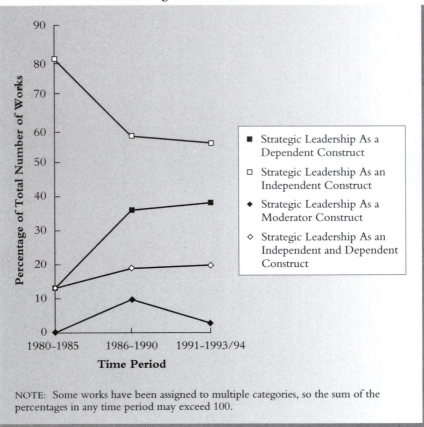

NOTE: Some works have been assigned to multiple categories, so the sum of the percentages in any time period may exceed 100.

may be modeled as an independent construct with environment, or organization form or conduct, as moderators, rather than the reverse.

Figure 9-10 shows how the prevalence of different causal logics has changed over the last fifteen years. Of primary interest is the consistency of relative rankings over time. Strategic leadership was most often modeled as an independent construct in all three time periods, followed as a dependent construct, both an independent and dependent construct, and finally, a moderator construct. That this pattern held so closely over time may indicate a tendency for researchers to accept established patterns of relationships among major constructs. If so, there may be research opportunities for those interested in breaking out of traditional mind-sets on how strategic leadership fits into our broader models of environments, organizations, and outcomes. In many places throughout this book, we have tried to offer suggestions regarding some of these newer conceptualizations and the types of research questions that could be pursued. For example, in Chapter 8, we presented a multidimensional framework on executive compensation that indicated how executive pay patterns are more than phenomena to be explained: they can be predictive of other organizational activities as well. Similarly, the framework we developed on boards of directors in Chapter 7 considers both the determinants and consequences of board characteristics. Conceptualizations such as these have the potential to help us broaden our understanding of how strategic leadership fits into the wider environmental and organizational configurations that some strategists and organization theorists have been studying for some time.

Underlying Assumptions about Managerial Work.   The final way in which we analyzed the conceptual attributes of the works was to identify their underlying assumptions about managerial work. Although many works do not explicitly state the assumptions that underlie their view of managerial work, virtually all researchers make such assumptions. It is important to uncover these underlying perspectives because they help us understand the point of view authors adopt in a project and, by implication, the complexity and even sophistication of our collective research. We have argued in many places in the book (and especially in Chapter 3) that managerial work is rarely characterized by a simple nexus of utility–maximizing decisions. Rather, top managers operate under considerable ambiguity, complexity, and information overload (Mintzberg 1973; Kotter 1982), with decision making often involving political and social factors as well as economic ones. The question we asked here, then, was whether the top works on strategic leadership reflected these diverse assumptions on the nature of managerial work.

We classified the underlying assumption of each work as follows:

Strategic Rationality: The general management task is to identify techno-economic opportunities and problems, systematically search for and weigh alternatives, and make choices that maximize firm performance.

Bounded Rationality: Organizations and individuals within them have bounded rationality. The management task is to accommodate these limitations or develop ways to minimize them (improved information flows, staffing, etc.).

Political: The general management task is to maintain the organizational coalition by acquiring, using, allocating, and channeling power (both externally and internally).

Symbolic: The general management task is to maintain the organizational coalition by creating and manipulating symbols (for both internal and external consumption).

Garbage Can: Because organizations are "garbage cans" into which problems, solutions, and people are thrown together, the general management task is either 1) futile, 2) a matter of dealing with chaos, or 3) not amenable to coherent description and analysis.

Hambrick (1986), in his earlier study of the top works on strategic management between 1980 and 1985, used a similar classification scheme and so offers a point of comparison.

Using these definitions, we coded each article according to which set of assumptions about managerial work appeared strongest. Because some authors relied on more than one assumption about managerial work, we counted each one separately to keep with our approach of "inclusivity." Nevertheless, we were unable to clearly categorize the underlying assumption in twenty-seven works.

Figure 9-11 provides a bar chart of the distribution of underlying assumptions in our two lists. A clear plurality of works adopted underlying

FIGURE 9-11   **Underlying Assumption about Managerial Work**

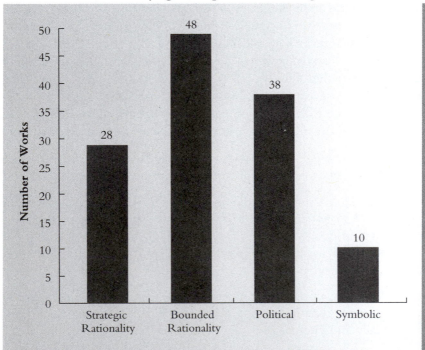

NOTE: Underlying assumptions were unclear in twenty-seven works. Some works were assigned to more than one category.

assumptions about managerial work that reflect the imperfections of organizational life. Forty percent of all works (in which we could identify underlying assumptions) employed the bounded rationality framework, and an additional 32 percent adopted a political model of organizations. This is in contrast to 21 percent and 12 percent, respectively, in the Hambrick (1986) study of strategic management research. We see this profile as encouraging and consistent with the realistic premise that managerial work is defined more by incomplete cognitions, cliques, biases, distorted sensors and information channels, and selfishness than by economic maximizing behavior.

There are, however, two caveats to this picture. First, only ten articles (8 percent) focused on the symbolic nature of managerial work—suggesting that there is still an instrumental bias in our collective perceptions of what managers do. Assumptions of strategic rationality, bounded rationality, and organizational politics are all based on the idea that top managerial work is purposeful and forward-directed; it is the underlying capabilities and motivation of managers that are different across these views. Yet, an alternative perspective that emphasizes the symbolic nature of managerial jobs—of how executives are symbols for their organizations and for their organizations' success or failure (Pfeffer and Salancik 1978)—does not appear to be adequately represented among the top works. Second, the more extreme set of assumptions that are embodied in the garbage can model have yet to be employed at all in research on strategic leadership. Thus, while our studies of strategic leadership have adopted more complex assumptions about managerial work than those observed by Hambrick (1986), there is still opportunity to push this work further.

Figure 9-12 reports on how the underlying assumptions about managerial work employed in a study changed over time. In line with the increasing attention scholars are paying to top management teams (and to a lesser extent boards of directors), the biggest change in our sample was the increased adoption of a political assumption about managerial work. From being the most rarely employed underlying assumption during 1980 to 1985 (except the garbage can model, which was not used at all throughout the fifteen years of our study), researchers have increasingly viewed managerial work in terms of power and politics to the extent that it now is the most common one. The relative importance of bounded rationality, strategic rationality, and symbolic management has not changed much at all over the three time periods, with scholars of strategic leadership consistently relying on bounded rationality more than strategic rationality of symbolic management to describe how managers perform their jobs. Nevertheless, we expect to see more work on the symbolic nature of managing as we improve our understanding of such phenomena as prestige, reputations, attributions, and stigma as applied to executives.

FIGURE 9-12   **Underlying Assumptions about Managerial Work over Time**

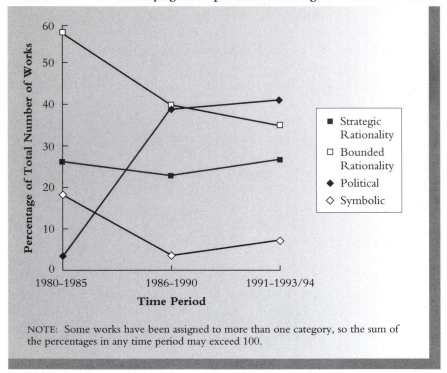

NOTE: Some works have been assigned to more than one category, so the sum of the percentages in any time period may exceed 100.

    In summary, our analysis indicates that the primary conceptual charac-teristics of research on strategic leadership have exhibited considerable sta-bility over the last fifteen years, with one significant exception. Greater consideration has been given to the political nature of managerial work and how the distribution of power among organizational members affects mul-tiple facets of organizational life. In some ways, the rise of a political per-spective on strategic management and strategic leadership complements the prevailing theme of bounded rationality and constraint on strategic choice as drivers of executive action. When these themes are brought together, the picture of strategic leadership that emerges is a complex one, far removed from rational–economic prescriptions, but characterized by constraints, lim-itations, flaws, biases, selfishness, and coalitions.

Methodological Issues in Research on Strategic Leadership

As might be expected, a variety of design and methodological choices have been made across studies. As with conceptual issues, we decided to focus on

FIGURE 9-13 **Data Source**

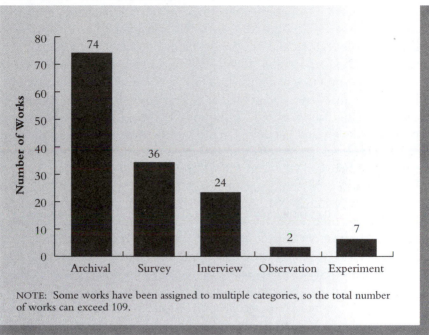

NOTE: Some works have been assigned to multiple categories, so the total number of works can exceed 109.

a small set of key characteristics that describe the methods employed in this work: data sources, sample size, the theoretical model and time frame of the study, and statistical techniques. Because we are interested in the methodological details of strategic leadership research, this section only examines empirical studies.

Data Sources. We classified data sources into five types—archival, survey, interview, observation, and experiment—with each empirical work assigned to at least one of these categories. Figure 9-13 provides information on the distribution of data sources across the 109 empirical articles in our sample. Data derived from archival sources were far and away the most commonly employed (in evidence for 68 percent of the empirical works), reflecting abundant, highly reliable data sources for research on top executives and the many ways those data can be used (e.g., Finkelstein 1992). In contrast, data from direct observation and experiments were rarely used. Observation techniques are difficult in the strategic leadership arena, because the phenomena studied are inherently sensitive and ego-involving; while it would be desirable if more such data were collected, we recognize how difficult it is to do so. Experiments should also be encouraged because they often allow rigorous controls; however, they raise inevitable problems of generalizability. One inference to make from this distribution of data sources is that strategic leadership research may suffer from a reliance on relatively sterile archival and survey data. Still, interviews were used to collect data in 22 percent of the studies, a not insignificant number.

Table 9-4 provides a comparison of the results from our sample to other studies that have coded similar information on research methods using studies by Saunders and Thompson (1980) on papers submitted to the Business Policy and Planning Division of the Academy of Management in 1979, Hambrick (1986) on twenty-three empirical projects on strategic management between 1980 and 1985, Shrivastava and Lim (1989) on doctoral dissertations in strategy completed between 1960 and 1982, and Schwenk and Dalton (1991) on research on strategic management published between 1986 and 1987 in selected journals. Although each of these studies does not offer the same level of detail or cover the same population of works, several interesting findings emerge. First, on the basis of this table, the use of archival data sources seems to be increasing somewhat over time. Only 28 percent of dissertations and 39 percent of Academy papers employed this method of data collection, considerably less than the more recent surveys and especially our own, at 68 percent. Second, usage of survey and experimental methods has been quite consistent across studies, with surveys commonly employed and experiments hardly at all. Finally, although the patterns for interview and observation are more difficult to

TABLE 9-4 **Comparison of Studies on Strategic Management Research**

	Saunders and Thompson (1980) (n=18)	Hambrick (1986) (n=23)	Shrivastava and Lim (1989) (n=98)	Schwenk and Dalton (1991) (n=91)	Finkelstein and Hambrick (1995) (n=109)
Years Reviewed in Study	1979	1980–1985	1960–1982	1986–1987	1980–1994
Data Sources					
Archival	39%	65%	28%	49%	68%
Survey	39%	39%	28%	32%	33%
Interview	50%	} 43%	} 33%	} 5%	22%
Observation	28%				2%
Experiment	11%	0	11%	3%	6%

gauge, their usage appears to have declined. While it is interesting to speculate on the origins of these patterns, what is both striking and encouraging to us is the multiple and relatively wide set of data collection methods that continue to be used by strategy scholars in general and strategic leadership scholars in particular.

A more detailed analysis of changes over time is possible with our own data, yielding an interesting pattern. In contrast to the observed stability of conceptual attributes over the last fifteen years, methodological changes have been more pronounced. Figure 9-14 indicates this with respect to data sources. In particular, it is apparent that archival data has become more important over time, to the point where it was used in 76 percent of all empirical articles published between 1991 and 1993-94. This is understandable, given the relatively low cost of obtaining archival data and its superior reliability. Nevertheless, it also raises the danger that our research is becoming more sterile over time, with much of the real top managerial activity buried within the "black box." It appears that researchers have

FIGURE 9-14 **Data Sources over Time**

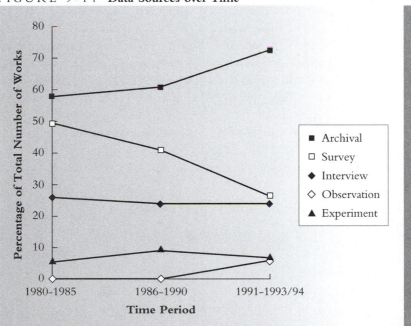

NOTE: Some works were assigned to multiple categories, so the sum of the percentages in any time period may exceed 100.

employed archival data to replace survey data, which has steadily diminished. The relative percentages for interview, experimental, and even observational data have remained stable across the three time periods. The consistently low use of observational and experimental data is worrisome because such data can draw out the richness and subtleties of strategic leadership is a way that other data sources cannot.

Sample Size.   Researchers make numerous choices in designing a sample for an empirical study, such as size, industry, type of firm, years, and so on. One problem that arises in trying to summarize these design choices, however, is the great variation across studies. For example, industries studied range from paint and coatings (Fredrickson 1984; Dess 1987) to professional basketball (Pfeffer and Davis-Blake 1986) to the Fortune 500 (many articles). As a result, we focus on sample size alone.

To facilitate an examination of sample sizes across a large set of articles and to aid comparability, it seems important to control for unit of analysis. For example, because data on SBUs are generally more difficult to obtain, we might expect sample sizes to be smaller. Reference to unit of analysis in a study provides an additional anchor with which to evaluate the appropriateness of sample size. It also seems to make sense to define sample size in terms of the number of observations on a particular unit of analysis. Hence, we report data on sample size in Table 9-5 by referring to units of analysis. In general, these data indicate that large sample sizes are the norm, with remarkable similarities across units of analysis. The only exception is research on TMTs—where the mean sample size is somewhat smaller, though still quite sizable. In all, these summary statistics attest to the prominence of relatively large-scale database research in strategic leadership.

Not only are large sample sizes evidenced in the empirical articles we studied, but this trend appears to have accelerated somewhat from the early

TABLE 9–5   **Sample Characteristics by Unit of Analysis**

	Unit of Analysis					
	CEO (n=41)	**TMT** (n=29)	**Board** (n=10)	**Firm** (n=18)	**SBU** (n=10)	**Executive** (n=5)
Sample Size						
Average	152.0	81.3	250.4	139.7	124.9	172
Standard deviation	167.4	65.0	193.3	111.9	130.4	122.1
Minimum	10	2	42	18	16	50
Maximum	690	243	673	438	322	303

1980s. For example, comparing medians across time periods, the number of observations in studies conducted between 1986 and 1990 increased to one hundred from forty-four during 1980 to 1985, while the median sample size for the 1991 to 1993-94 studies did not change over the middle time period. To some extent, this may be a reflection of the greater use of archival data over time—its accessibility facilitates larger samples.

Theoretical Model and Time Frame of the Study.   One of the most commonly heard refrains about research in strategic management is that the models and methods employed are too static. This is an especially serious weakness for a field that focuses on managerial problems for which timing, sequence, and change are key elements. Strategic leadership is no different. Thus, we examined the dynamism embedded in the research projects in our samples by focusing on two dimensions: 1) the extent to which the theoretical model is static or dynamic, a dynamic model being one that involves changes over time—growth, stages, sequence, decay, timing, and so on; and 2) whether the data used for the study were cross-sectional or longitudinal.

Figure 9-15 combines these two dimensions to offer an integrated portrayal of the dynamism of research on strategic leadership. It is readily apparent that the majority (61 percent) of works are both static and cross-sectional—a pattern that runs directly counter to what is often espoused in the literature and to what our own conceptualization of strategic leadership would recommend. By comparison, this static-cross-sectional pattern was observed in 52 percent of the articles Hambrick (1986) surveyed and 75 percent of the articles in the Schwenk and Dalton (1991) study. Encouraging,

FIGURE 9-15 **Number of Empirical Articles Arrayed by Theoretical Model and Time Frame of the Study**

| | **Theoretical Model** | |
	Static	Dynamic
Cross-sectional	66	0
Data		
Longitudinal	14	29

however, are the twenty-nine studies (27 percent) employing dynamic theoretical models with longitudinal data, an improvement over the 17 percent and 12 percent rates reported by Hambrick, and Schwenk and Dalton, respectively. Fourteen empirical projects (13 percent) in our study collected longitudinal data but only used static models, a large portion of which were pooled time series cross-sectional studies (Schwenk and Dalton also reported 13 percent, while Hambrick did not observe any). These works have an advantage over single time period cross-sectional analyses because they provide more stable parameter estimates but fall short of addressing causal issues that the fully dynamic–longitudinal studies incorporating change can. Finally, the remaining category of cross-sectional dynamic projects was not populated at all, as would be expected, given the impossibility of modeling dynamic relationships with data from a single time period.

Figure 9-16 illustrates how theoretical models and time frames used in empirical articles on strategic leadership have changed in the last fifteen years. Although most work is of a cross-sectional and static nature, the relative percentage of these studies has declined recently. Longitudinal dynamic studies (often held up as an "ideal" type) declined in the middle time

FIGURE 9-16 **Theoretical Model and Time Frame over Time**

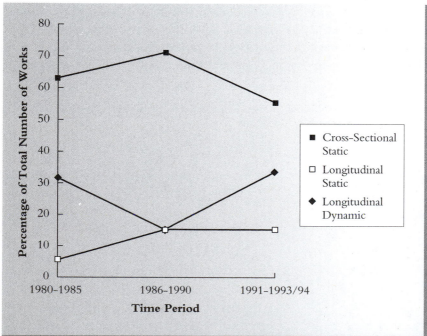

period but increased to about the same relative percentage in 1991 to 1993-94 as in 1980 to 1985. In absolute terms, however, there were more longitudinal dynamic studies in the more recent time period than earlier. The decline in traditional cross–sectional static studies from the 1986 to 1990 period to 1991 to 1993-94 means that the percentage of empirical research with a longitudinal data component increased to 48 percent in the early 1990s, an encouraging pattern.

Statistical Techniques.   We identified all statistical techniques used to test for significance in an article and then summed across all articles to arrive at a total number for each technique employed in our sample. Figure 9-17 portrays this information in the form of a bar graph. Three techniques appear to be in greatest use, with one clearly dominant: regression techniques (multiple, moderated, pooled, etc.) were employed in 54 percent of empirical projects, while ANOVA (including MANOVA, MANCOVA, and repeated measures ANOVA) and correlation (including partial, cross-lag, and canonical correlation) were used in 18 percent and 16 percent, respectively.[10] By comparison, other techniques were rarely used. The greater use of regression techniques may be interpreted as a favorable trend since it reflects the inclusion of important control variables in the analyses.

FIGURE 9-17   **Statistical Techniques**

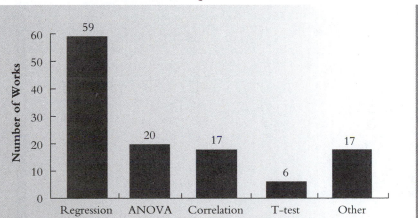

Some works have been assigned to multiple categories, so the total number of articles can exceed 109. "Other" category includes: path analysis (4), case study without analytical techniques (4), cluster analysis (3), event history (2), frequency counts (2), discriminant analysis (1), and metric conjoint analysis (1).

Changes in the use of various statistical techniques have exhibited two contradictory patterns over time. On one level, as Figure 9-18 makes clear, regression techniques have increased in importance to the extent that they dominate the next three most commonly employed approaches. Most striking has been the decline in the use of simple correlations to test hypotheses, from 42 percent in 1980 to 1985 to 7 percent in 1991 to 1993-94. However, on another level, the same four techniques continue to be used more than any other for fifteen years. No new statistical technique has gained prominence, at least in terms of general usage, in spite of the large variety of alternative methods occasionally used (i.e., cluster analysis, discriminant analysis, path analysis, and event history). This conservatism of approach is exacerbated when one considers the strong similarity among regression, ANOVA, and correlation (Cohen and Cohen 1983) and it counters occasional complaints that strategists use more complex statistical

FIGURE 9-18 **Statistical Techniques over Time**

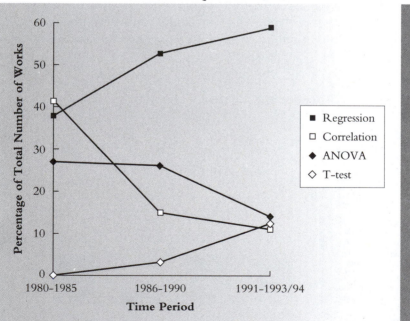

NOTE: Some works have been assigned to multiple categories, so the sum of the percentages in any one time period may exceed 100. Only the analytical techniques that appeared most often in our sample are illustrated; however, percentages are of the total number of works in each time period and not just of those with the analytical techniques depicted.

techniques than necessary (Daft 1986). It is unclear whether "newer" techniques will yield original insights; nevertheless, it would seem that a move toward a wider set of statistical methods would at least help ensure that we are not unnecessarily constrained to established approaches, and it might even help establish the robustness of our findings.

In summary, we have documented several key methodological attributes of the empirical works in our sample and how they have changed. Empirical research on strategic leadership is relying more on archival data sources than survey sources, employing larger sample sizes, and using regression techniques more than correlational ones. Taken together, these changes appear to represent a move toward greater methodological "objectivity" and "sophistication," a conclusion that is subject to multiple interpretations. For example, the use of more sophisticated methods may enhance reliability and reduce the possibility of alternative explanations, or it may be seen as further evidence that we are becoming more removed from the phenomena we seek to study. While there is truth in both interpretations, it seems important to encourage alternative approaches—such as case studies of a more inductive nature—to complement the now-dominant trends. Hence, a combination of methods, either within the same study or across studies, likely will be needed to help move our understanding of strategic leadership to the next level.

Our goal in this section was to document and discuss the key conceptual and methodological attributes of strategic leadership research and to analyze how these works have changed over the last fifteen years, using the studies in our sample as exemplars. We have sought to break down the study of strategic leadership into relatively fine analytical components to provide information on where we have been and guidance on what this means for where we are going. In addition to the insights gained, this analysis is important as the raw material for synthesis. In the following section, we turn to an exploration of the major themes that are suggested by this analysis and how they relate to each of the chapters of this book.

SYNTHESIS AND RECONCILIATION

The analysis presented thus far underlined differences in conceptual and methodological attributes that characterize the major recent works on strategic leadership. Hence, to a large extent, this analysis has crossed chapter boundaries and the research questions that distinguish each chapter. Each chapter, however, represents a differentiated body of work, characterized by a set of research questions and phenomena that provide some structure for conceptual and empirical exploration. This is not to say that research topics and issues do not overlap, for they clearly do. Nevertheless, the research embodied in each chapter of this book is different, suggesting that it is important to offer unified portrayals of the research issues represented by each chapter. Doing so will go a long way toward providing a needed synthesis to our discussion.

Research Questions in Each Book Chapter

We begin by considering the major research questions studied in each work to understand how much scholarly research has been conducted on the subject matter of each chapter in this book. Hence, we coded articles on executive succession as part of Chapter 6 on executive turnover and succession, works on organization cognitions were assigned to Chapter 3 on individual bases of executive action, and so on. A significant number of articles addressed research questions spanning multiple chapters; for example, studies of board vigilance of compensation arrangements were clearly relevant for both Chapters 7 and 8. To avoid arbitrarily assigning such articles to a single chapter, we coded the primary, secondary, and (for some works) tertiary research questions addressed to arrive at a more inclusive categorization of work into chapters. Thus, articles that examined expansive issues covering material in two chapters were coded as addressing research questions in both chapters. As a result, and as was the case for many of the other attributes investigated here, the sum of the number of articles assigned to each chapter adds up to more than 146. Figure 9-19 summarizes the allocation of articles to chapters.

Several observations can be made from Figure 9-19. First, research on top management teams accounted for the largest number of works in our two lists. As we discussed in Chapter 5, the prospect of studying a group of top managers, rather than a single individual, is intuitively appealing and has important consequences for how we think about the strategic decision-making process.

Perhaps the most unexpected result was the relatively small number of articles on executive experiences and strategic choice (Chapter 4). The original Hambrick and Mason (1984) piece is well-cited, but only fifteen other works on our lists focused on this topic. To some extent, this may reflect the power of the upper-echelons perspective: support for many of the Hambrick and Mason (1984) propositions has been found.[11] Further advances in research on the role of executive experiences may depend on newer conceptualizations that are now emerging, such as managerial dis-

FIGURE 9-19 **Research Questions (as Defined by Book Chapters)**

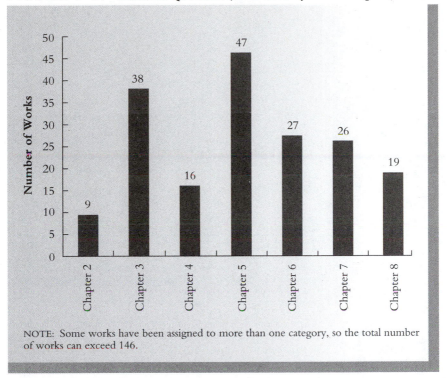

NOTE: Some works have been assigned to more than one category, so the total number
of works can exceed 146.

cretion (Finkelstein and Hambrick 1990), managerial power (Finkelstein
1992), distributional properties of TMTs (see Chapter 5), and a wide set of
contingency factors of the type discussed in Chapter 4.

Finally, and in contrast to research on executive experiences from a
demographic perspective, work on individual bases of executive action is a
major area of study within strategic leadership. Fully thirty-eight works (26
percent) addressed research questions on psychological properties of executives as a basis for executive action, considerably more than were published
on demographic characteristics. The search for values, cognitions, and other
elements of personality has intrigued scholars for a long time—a result that
stands in contrast to the sometime contention that research on strategic
leadership pays insufficient attention to the internal processes of key decision makers in organizations (Walsh 1994).

In addition to the distribution of works across book chapters, we were
also interested in how the incidence of each research question changed across
the three time periods under consideration. As illustrated in Figure 9-20, several noteworthy patterns were evidenced. First, between 1980 to 1985 and

FIGURE 9-20   **Research Questions (as Defined by Book Chapters)
over Time**

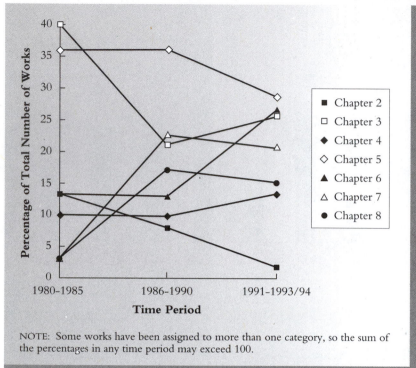

NOTE: Some works have been assigned to more than one category, so the sum of
the percentages in any time period may exceed 100.

1986 to 1990, research on boards of directors and executive compensation
increased dramatically (Chapters 7 and 8). In contrast, the percentage of works
on individual bases of executive action (Chapter 3) declined during this time
period. Second, there was considerable stability in the relative importance of
different research questions between 1986 to 1990 and 1991 to 1993-94, with
the exception of research on executive succession (which increased to
become the second-most studied topic in the latest time period).

Overall, perhaps the most interesting pattern is that all seven topic
areas—which form the core of strategic leadership—have continued to be
the subject of investigation for fifteen years. The relative importance of a
topic may shift somewhat over time, but in a broader sense, we continue to
study the same phenomena. Such persistence can have both positive and
negative implications: on the one hand, it implies that we have not made
sufficient progress to allow consideration of new research questions; on the
other, it suggests that these research questions may indeed be fundamental,
multifaceted, and worthy of such enduring attention.

Finally, we also report how the major conceptual and methodological attributes of the works we examined clustered across chapters. Table 9-6 provides these data and offers a more fine-grained picture of research in the strategic leadership arena. In the interests of space, however, we do not elaborate on the patterns evident in this chart. Rather, in the next section, we offer more integrated portrayals of research in each of the topic areas on strategic leadership examined in this book.

Research Record and Research Priorities

Throughout this book, we have made a series of recommendations, often propositional in nature, but thematic as well. As we try to set an agenda for future research on strategic leadership, the analysis conducted in this chapter thus far serves as a litmus test indicating just how far, or close, we are to achieving these ends. To help calibrate "where we are" to "where we need to go," this section explores the research priorities identified in each chapter and compares them to the research record. We conclude with several emerging integrative themes.

Chapter 2: Do Top Managers Matter?   There can be no question as fundamental as the one asked in Chapter 2. To some extent, the strategic leadership works analyzed in the present chapter, in combination with the various models, frameworks, and propositions developed throughout the rest of the book, go a long way toward answering this question. Nevertheless, when we consider the major research priorities that emerged from Chapter 2—the need for empirical investigation of managerial roles and the need to incorporate managerial discretion as a central construct in strategic leadership—it is clear that we have made only limited progress toward these goals.

We did not explicitly examine managerial roles in our analysis. Yet, the extent to which the determinants of such roles involve institutional forces, critical contingencies, and agency conditions, the works in our sample probably can offer only limited guidance because agency theory singly accounts for a large percentage of the theoretical perspectives employed (see Figure 9-6). Indeed, institutionalization theory (twice) and resource dependence theory (three times) were rarely used in the works we investigated.

The results reported in this chapter provide a more effective assessment of managerial discretion. Only seven works incorporated managerial discretion as a theoretical perspective, but because several of these articles spanned multiple chapters, discretion was used to address all but one topic (executive succession) within strategic leadership (see Table 9-6). The relevance of

TABLE 9-6 Frequency Counts of Attributes of Strategic Leadership Research by Research Question (Chapter)

Conceptual Issues	Book Chapter						
	2	3	4	5	6	7	8
(A) Unit of Analysis							
CEO	5	14	2	6	15	8	13
TMT	2	1	9	24	8	2	1
Board	0	0	3	0	2	12	0
Firm	3	4	0	11	3	3	1
SBU	0	4	1	1	1	1	4
Unspecified Executives	0	15	1	5	0	1	4
(B) Theoretical Perspective							
Upper Echelons Theory	0	18	10	12	3	1	1
Agency Theory	0	2	1	2	4	18	10
Strategy Process	0	2	0	22	0	0	0
Managerial Hegemony Theory	1	0	2	3	2	6	6
Managerial Fit or Alignment	0	7	4	5	1	1	1
Executive Succession	0	0	0	0	9	2	0
Traditional Leadership	0	5	0	1	2	2	0
Managerial Discretion	4	1	2	2	0	2	2
Social-Psychological Theories	1	1	0	1	2	1	2
Other	6	4	0	6	7	5	3
(C) Causal Logic							
Strategic Leadership As a Dependent Construct	2	8	1	10	12	9	10
Strategic Leadership As an Independent Construct	6	17	10	29	12	10	5
Strategic Leadership As a Moderator Construct	1	1	1	2	0	1	0
Strategic Leadership As an Independent and Dependent Construct	1	6	4	5	3	8	6

TABLE 9–6 Frequency Counts of Attributes of Strategic Leadership Research by Research Question (Chapter), *continued*

	Book Chapter						
Conceptual Issues	2	3	4	5	6	7	8
(D) Underlying Assumption							
Strategic Rationality	1	10	1	4	5	5	5
Bounded Rationality	2	19	10	26	3	2	2
Political	2	2	2	6	8	17	12
Symbolic	3	2	0	1	4	2	0
Methodological Issues							
(E) Data Source							
Archival	8	9	10	21	23	18	12
Survey	0	10	4	19	2	2	6
Interview	2	6	0	13	1	2	1
Observation	0	1	0	1	0	0	0
Experiment	1	1	1	3	1	0	1
(F) Theoretical Model and Time Frame							
Static and Cross-sectional	0	18	10	28	10	10	8
Static and Longitudinal	2	2	3	3	4	3	3
Dynamic and Cross-sectional	0	0	0	0	0	0	0
Dynamic and Longitudinal	6	2	1	6	10	6	6
(G) Statistical Technique							
Regression	5	9	10	16	17	12	15
ANOVA	3	2	2	10	4	3	1
Correlation	1	8	0	7	1	1	1
T-test	0	2	0	2	1	0	1
Other	0	6	2	6	1	4	0

managerial discretion for a variety of research questions on strategic leadership is even more apparent in the various chapters of this book, which have offered managerial discretion as a potentially useful construct to resolve different theoretical dilemmas. As a result, research conducted to date has only begun to consider the implications of managerial discretion to a broad range of strategic leadership issues. More work is clearly required.

Chapter 3: Individual Bases of Executive Action. Chapter 3 synthesized what we know about executive values, cognitive models, and other personality characteristics, and suggested several illustrative propositions to further develop our understanding of individual bases of executive action. Among the priorities identified were 1) research on the determinants of executive values and cognitive models in general, and examination from agency and especially institutional theory perspectives in particular, and 2) additional attention to the implications of values and cognitions to executive behavior and strategic choices.

First, as Panel C of Table 9-6 indicates, research on the determinants of executive values and cognitions has been limited. Of the eight studies of this type, only two adopted an agency theory perspective, and none used institutionalization theory. Hence, of the thirty-eight works addressing individual bases of executive action, only 5 percent focused on agency conditions, and none focused on institutional forces, as determining factors. Clearly, our calls for more attention to these problems seem well-placed.

Considerably more work has been published on the consequences of certain executive characteristics, but none of the work we analyzed here has been on executive values. Somewhat better represented are studies of executive personality characteristics, such as locus of control (e.g., Miller, Kets de Vries, and Toulouse 1982) and tolerance for ambiguity (Gupta and Govindarajan 1984), and some more recent studies have examined executive cognitions (e.g., Hitt and Tyler 1991). As we discussed in Chapter 3, however, numerous propositions can be tested on the effects of cognitive content, structure, and style. Hence, while we have made some progress toward fulfilling these research priorities, many unresolved issues still require study.

Chapter 4: Executive Experiences and Strategic Choice. Chapter 4 focused on how executive experiences affect organizational outcomes and extended a promising social-psychological framework to the study of top managers. The research priorities from this chapter center on the application of this "interactional" perspective to senior executives. Hence, we called for more research on the moderating effects of various forces on the association between executive experiences and outcomes.

Of the works we analyzed in Chapter 4, ten modeled strategic leadership as an independent construct (see Table 9-6, Panel C). Of these, seven considered the impact of moderating constructs as well. For example, Hambrick and Mason (1984) developed propositions on the moderating role of environment, Finkelstein and Hambrick (1990) and Haleblian and Finkelstein (1993) empirically examined managerial discretion as a moderator, and several studies (Gupta and Govindarajan 1984; Michel and Hambrick 1992) have modeled firm strategy to interact with executive experiences. Hence, some progress has been made in specifying how executive experiences interact with other constructs to affect organizational outcomes. Nevertheless, these studies have focused on situational moderators and have yet to identify which traits, behaviors, and people most improve our ability to predict executive choices from background characteristics.

Chapter 5: Top Management Teams: Group Bases of Executive Action.   This chapter focused on the distributional properties of TMTs and developed a model of the antecedents and consequences of TMT dynamics. The research priorities we identified centered on empirical concerns: the need for scholarly work on the determinants of TMTs, dynamics within TMTs, and relationships among TMTs, decision processes, and organizational outcomes. Of these three areas, we especially noted how little had been done to explain TMT characteristics.

Table 9-6 (Panel C) indicates that most work on TMTs focuses on its consequences and is largely based on theories of strategy process (Panel B). Much less common are studies of the determinants of TMTs. Even in studies of the consequences of TMTs, however, researchers rarely develop or test models of managerial fit. Such models would propose that a particular alignment of TMT characteristics with contextual conditions would enhance firm performance. As Panel B of Table 9-6 indicates, only five works on TMTs employed such a theoretical perspective. Thus, in spite of the large number of studies on TMTs, the research priorities we identified in Chapter 5 remain unfulfilled.

Chapter 6: Changes at the Top: Executive Turnover and Succession. Research on executive turnover and succession has a long history, as discussed in Chapter 6. To try to make sense of this work and offer some new research directions, we developed a conceptual framework that integrated the precipitating context, the process of succession and the event itself, successor characteristics, and the effects of succession. While we used this framework to make several suggestions for future work, many of these ideas relate to the importance of developing a stronger theoretical footing for our investigations and focus in particular on the role of managerial power in executive turnover and succession.

Our analysis of the 146 works identified 27 articles, books, or book chapters on succession. Of these, eight (30 percent) viewed managerial work as politically based (Table 9-6, Panel D), though only two (7 percent) focused specifically on managerial hegemony theory (Panel B). In contrast, we were unable to identify a strong, central theory in one-third of the works on succession, leading us to characterize the theoretical perspective employed simply as "executive succession." This research was not without theory—however, the theory developed was based on a disconnected or loosely connected set of ideas. For example, in studies of the performance consequences of succession, various works argued for alternative outcomes and relied on ideas about organizational adaptation, disruption, and scapegoating. However, while often reasonably developed, these perspectives lacked certain elements of good theory—development of a refutable and parsimonious set of causal constructs tied together in an internally consistent pattern, with a specified limited range of application, that can broaden our knowledge and understanding by predicting and explaining phenomena of interest (Hempel 1966).

We argued in Chapter 6 that closer integration of managerial power with formulations of executive succession is warranted. The research record indicates that we still have a long way to go in this regard. The development of stronger theory on executive succession and the elaboration of the role of managerial power in this theory remain important targets for future research.

Chapter 7: Boards of Directors and Corporate Governance. We developed an integrative model of boards of directors in Chapter 7 that we asserted could serve as a blueprint for future research in this area. Since the model was based in part on existing research, some of the works analyzed here have influenced its development. However, two important research priorities we identified appear to be particularly critical, given the results of the analysis reported in the first part of this chapter. First, we argued in Chapter 7 that boards of directors may be viewed as supra-TMTs, charged with nontrivial strategic responsibilities in many instances. As a result, research on boards of directors needs to employ 1) the TMT unit of analysis more often, 2) theoretical perspectives that can address the board's strategic role, such as upper echelons theory and strategy process, and 3) an assumption about managerial work that appreciates the cognitive and social constraints that directors operate under (bounded rationality). As Table 9-

6 indicates in each case, however, research on boards of directors has yet to incorporate these attributes.

Second, although agency theory is a major component of our model of boards of directors, it is too simplistic to be the only theoretical perspective of value in understanding boards. The dominance of agency theory ideas in research on boards is clear when one considers that of the twenty-six works on boards we sampled, eighteen (69 percent) relied on agency theory. Our model discusses how institutional forces and critical contingencies can also be key driving forces in how boards operate, but for the most part, these alternative perspectives are of secondary concern in the works analyzed. Given that the large increase in work on boards has been fueled by agency-based research (see Figures 9-7 and 9-20), a priority for future research must surely be to broaden our theoretical focus to encompass other perspectives as well.

Chapter 8: Executive Compensation. We developed a new integrative framework on executive compensation in Chapter 8 that was designed to help remove the blinkers on how we study this phenomenon and suggest a broad-based research agenda. The framework we developed was based on three dimensions: unit of analysis, theoretical perspective, and causal model. It is interesting to assess the extent to which the works we analyzed in this chapter address these dimensions.

Table 9-6 provides an appropriate backdrop for this assessment. We argued in Chapter 8 that executive compensation can be studied at both the individual executive (typically the CEO) and the TMT unit of analysis. In the latter case, important questions arise on pay dispersion within the TMT and pay differentials across individuals within the TMT. Thus far, however, these concerns have not been addressed. The TMT unit of analysis was employed in only one of the works in our sample, while CEO (thirteen times) and executive (four times) foci have dominated (Panel A).

The distribution of studies do a somewhat better job of reflecting the recommended research priorities for the other two dimensions of the framework. Looking first at theoretical perspective (Panel B), managerial hegemony theory and social-psychological theories were employed a total of eight times, while agency theory was used in ten works. Although agency theory and managerial hegemony theory are closely related, much of the work from the agency perspective was economically based. So, it appears that multiple theoretical perspectives were used in the study of executive compensation, although social-psychological approaches clearly lag behind.

Finally, Table 9-6 (Panel C) indicates that executive compensation is most typically (ten times) considered a dependent variable, which is traditional in this work. In contrast, only one-half as many works modeled executive compensation as an independent variable, indicating that our call for examination of the consequences of executive pay is, indeed, warranted. Overall, our analysis of research on strategic leadership points out that while some progress has been made, considerably more work is needed to address the research priorities identified in Chapter 8.

In summary, the research record on strategic leadership is impressive—in terms of breadth of research questions examined, variety of theoretical perspectives employed, quality of contributions made, and volume of work conducted. Nevertheless, clear research priorities warrant our renewed attention as the study of strategic leadership builds on and moves beyond its initial concerns. The further development of strategic leadership as a topic of study will require us to develop new questions and new theories that address the fundamental nature of top management and their role in organizations.

Conclusions

One of the goals of this book was to develop theory on strategic leadership from social-psychological and political perspectives, conceptualizations that we believe are particularly informative for the study of executives and their effects on organizational outcomes. Analysis of the top works of 1980 to 1990 and works more recently published allows us to make certain assertions in this regard.

First, considerable evidence exists that the study of strategic leadership relies heavily on theoretical perspectives based on social-psychological and political ideas. For example, many of the major theories used in our sample—such as upper echelons theory, strategy process, and managerial hegemony theory—can be fairly classified in this way. And, if our arguments on agency theory being a theory of power hold true, this pattern is further accentuated.

Second, we can go much further in developing a theory of strategic leadership from social-psychological and political perspectives. Many of the propositions offered in the previous chapters are an attempt to move toward this ultimate goal. Our reconciliation of this chapter's findings with the research priorities of earlier chapters highlighted the extent to which this remains an important area for future research.

A second theme, manifested in both conceptual and empirical research, relates to the nature of our theorizing on causal direction. Earlier, we presented data on the various causal models employed by scholars of strategic leadership, pointing out apparent patterns in these data. It is evident that, in spite of repeated calls for examining causal direction, significant progress has not been made in this regard. Fundamentally, and as Figure 9-8 illustrates, there are both determinants and consequences of strategic leadership, involving relationships that have been modeled throughout this book. Yet these determinants and consequences are seldom considered simultaneously, even though it is not difficult to construct arguments on the interactive nature of strategic leadership. For example, in Chapter 5, we argued that a firm's diversification posture affects the diversity of the TMT, but it may also be that team (functional) heterogeneity reduces the chances of information-sharing and other synergistic activities, thus promoting greater diversification. Nevertheless, we tend not to study such potentially circular patterns of relationships, even though they are plausible. Longitudinal time frames and dynamic theoretical models, which are gaining in use, as Figure 9-16 documented, need to be more fully employed. In addition, as the fourteen studies employing static theoretical models with longitudinal data attest, researchers need to take full advantage of the data they collect. Effectively addressing causality remains an essential challenge in our research.

A third theme that is central to our approach is the idea that strategic leadership does not reside solely in the chief executive officer. Throughout this book, we have been concerned with all executives who have overall responsibility for an organization—a conceptualization that includes top management teams and other senior executives, boards of directors, and business unit general managers. This theme is shared by other scholars of strategic leadership. Nevertheless, studies rarely examine more than one type of organizational actor. Hence, research that adopts multiple units of analysis and explores interrelationships among these key organizational actors seems particularly warranted.

To conclude, the study of strategic leadership is broad-based, encompassing numerous research questions. At one level, the breadth of phenomena under consideration makes it difficult to define strategic leadership as a unique sphere of knowledge. On another level, however, great similarities in the underlying perspectives help explain each of these phenomena. Hence, although research on strategic leadership is multifaceted, we believe the greatest contributions will emerge from the development of strong theory that spans different research questions and topics. Such fundamental driving forces as critical contingencies, institutional forces, and agency conditions are important in multiple arenas. The effects from different top executives, whether CEOs or boards, seem to be broad and important, with implications for organizational processes, structures, strategies, and performance. Thus, the integrative and overlapping nature of strategic leadership challenges us to develop theories and methods that simultaneously advance knowledge across multiple fronts. This book is one step in this direction.

NOTES

1. Actually, MacMillan (1991) listed sixteen journals; we added *Organization Science*, which began in 1990. The other journals were: *Academy of Management Journal, Academy of Management Review, Administrative Science Quarterly, Harvard Business Review, Management Science*, and *Strategic Management Journal ("outstanding quality"); California Management Review* and *Sloan Management Review ("significant quality");* and *Academy of Management Executive, Decision Sciences, Journal of International Business Studies, Journal of General Management, Journal of Management, Journal of Management Studies, Omega*, and *Rand Journal of Economics ("appropriate quality").*

2. An alternative method to rank the most-cited works while controlling for recency effects is to compute the average number of citations per year since publication. While we considered this option, we selected the four-year citation count rule because of the clear demarcation it creates between the most recent research published after 1990 and earlier work, which cannot be fairly compared. As it turns out, while the ordering of works is different, the composition of the two lists is quite similar. For example, using an alternative criterion of the average of three citations per year as a cutoff added only five articles that are not presently included.

3. The survey asked about research published between 1980 and 1990 in a separate section from the more recent works. The survey instrument is included as Appendix 1 of this chapter.

4. The survey was sent in Spring 1994 to every person who was listed as an author of one of 146 works (83 plus 63). Thus, only journal publications received as of March 1994 were included in the list of post-1990 works. Nine surveys were returned uncompleted, because respondents said they were unfamiliar with much of the research included on the two lists, correct mailing addresses for some respondents were unavailable, or respondents were deceased. Of the remaining 150 surveys mailed out, 51 were returned with usable responses, for an effective response rate of 34 percent.

5. Where possible, we tried to compare our results to those of others who have conducted similar analyses on strategic management research. Nevertheless, none of the various projects we refer to in this chapter specifically examined strategic leadership or employed exactly the same methods we did. Thus, the comparisons we draw are meant only to provide additional context within which to evaluate our results and should not be taken as definitive.

6. In some cases when we were unable to code an article along an attribute (e.g., causal logic), the percentages were computed after subtracting out that article. Hence, the reported percentages were based on nonmissing data in every case. In addition, because in many instances we were able to identify multiple attributes in a single article (e.g., when two or three different research ques-

tions were addressed in the same work), the sum of the percentages for each attribute does not usually add up to 100.

7. All such comparisons are really relative ones, since the graph depicts percentages and not absolute numbers, of published works. So, the percentage of articles with the TMT unit of analysis in our list of top works increased from 17 percent of all work published between 1986 and 1990 to 27 percent of published research during 1991 to 1993-94.

8. In coding the top works along these dimensions, however, we found we were unable to clearly determine causal logics in 20 cases (14 percent), so the analysis that follows refers to the remaining 126 works.

9. The total number of works that appear in Table 9-3 and Figure 9-9 for each causal logic are not the same because a work that modeled, say, strategic leadership as an independent construct may have included both organization form or conduct and firm performance as dependent variables, counted separately in Table 9-3 but not in Figure 9-9.

10. Schwenk and Dalton (1991) also found these three techniques to be the most commonly used, but with a different pattern: regression, 27 percent; ANOVA, 34 percent; and correlation, 26 percent.

11. Nevertheless, several studies on TMTs (Chapter 5) also adopted a demographic approach that is consistent with Hambrick and Mason (1984).

APPENDIX 1

Survey on Strategic Leadership

Definition: The study of strategic leadership focuses on the executives who have overall responsibility for an organization—their characteristics, what they do, and how they do it; and how they affect organizational outcomes. The executives who are subjects of strategic leadership research can be individuals (CEOs or division general managers), groups (or "top management teams"), or other governance bodies (e.g., boards of directors).

Part 1: The following works, published between 1980 and 1990, are listed alphabetically. For each, please rate its importance—the degree to which it has had, and/or you expect it will have, a constructive impact on scholarly understanding of strategic leadership, as defined above. Obviously, some of these works were published several years ago, so their constructive impact may already be clear; others are more recent work, so your assessment may need to weigh more heavily on their potential for constructive impact. If, for any reason, you do not wish to rate an item, use the column designating as such.

Use the following scale in rating the works:

1-Unimportant: adds very little
2-Somewhat important: marginally interesting ideas or research results
3-Moderately important: interesting ideas or research results
4-Very important: significant ideas or research results
5-Highly important: extremely significant ideas or research results
X-Unable to rate

1	**2**	**3**	**4**	**5**	**X**
Unimportant				**Highly Important**	**Unable to Rate**

_____ Bantel, K. A., and Jackson, S. E. 1989. Top management and innovations in banking: Does the composition of the top team make a difference? *Strategic Management Journal* 10 (Special Issue): 107-24.

_____ Baysinger, B., and Hoskisson, R. E. 1990. The composition of boards of directors and strategic control: Effects on corporate strategy. *Academy of Management Review,* 15 (1): 72-87.

_____ Boeker, W. 1989. Strategic change: The effects of founding and history. *Academy of Management Journal* 32 (5): 489-515.

_____ Bourgeois, L. J. 1980. Performance and consensus. *Strategic Management Journal* 1 (3): 227-48.

_____ Bourgeois, L. J. 1980. Strategy and environment: A conceptual integration. *Academy of Management Review* 5 (1): 25-39.

_____ Bourgeois, L. J. 1985. Strategic goals, perceived uncertainty, and economic performance in volatile environments. *Academy of Management Journal* 28 (3): 548-73.

_____ Bourgeois, L. J. and Eisenhardt, K. M. 1988. Strategic decision processes in high velocity environments: Four cases in the microcomputer industry. *Management Science* 34 (7): 816-35.

_____ Brown, M. C. 1982. Administrative succession and organizational performance: The succession effect. *Administrative Science Quarterly* 27: 1-16.

_____ Carroll, G. R. 1984. Dynamics of publisher succession in newspaper organizations. *Administrative Science Quarterly* 29: 93-113.

_____ Daft, R. L., Sormunen, J., and Parks, D. 1988. Chief executive scanning, environmental characteristics, and company performance: An empirical study. *Strategic Management Journal* 9: 123-39.

_____ D'Aveni, R. A. 1990. Top managerial prestige and organizational bankruptcy. *Organization Science* 1 (2): 121-42.

_____ D'Aveni, R. A., and MacMillan, I. 1990. Crisis and the content of managerial communications: A study of the focus of attention of top managers in surviving and failing firms. *Administrative Science Quarterly* 35 (4): 634-57.

_____ Dess, G. R. 1987. Consensus on strategy formulation and organizational performance: Competitors in a fragmented industry. *Strategic Management Journal* 8: 259-77.

_____ Donaldson, G., and Lorsch, J. W. 1983. *Decision making at the top: Shaping of strategic direction.* New York: Basic Books.

_____ Duhaime, I. M., and Schwenk, C. R. 1985. Conjectures on cognitive simplification in acquisition and divestment decision-making: *Academy of Management Review* 10 (2): 287-95.

_____ Dutton, J. E., and Duncan, R. B. 1987. The creation of momentum for change through the process of strategic issue diagnosis. *Strategic Management Journal* 8 (3): 279-95.

_____ Dutton, J. E., and Jackson, S. E. 1987. Categorizing strategic issues: Links to organizational action. *Academy of Management Review* 12 (1): 76-90.

_____ Eisenhardt, K. M. 1989. Making fast strategic decisions in high-velocity environments. *Academy of Management Journal* 32 (3): 543-76.

_____ Eisenhardt, K. M. 1989. Agency theory: An assessment and review. *Academy of Management Review* 14 (1): 57-74.

_____ Eisenhardt, K. M., and Bourgeois, L. J. 1988. Politics of strategic decision-making in high-velocity environments. *Academy of Management Journal* 31 (4): 737-70.

_____ Eisenhardt, K. M., and Schoonhoven, C. B. 1990. Organizational growth: Linking founding team, strategy, environment, and growth among U.S. semiconductor ventures, 1978-1988. *Administrative Science Quarterly* 35 (3): 504-29.

_____ Finkelstein, S., and Hambrick, D. C. 1988. Chief executive compensation: A synthesis and reconciliation. *Strategic Management Journal* 9 (6): 54-58.

_____ Finkelstein, S., and Hambrick, D. C. 1989. Chief executive compensation: A study of the intersection of markets and political processes. *Strategic Management Journal* 10 (2): 121-34.

_____ Finkelstein, S., and Hambrick, D. C. 1990. Top management team tenure and organizational outcomes: The moderating role of managerial discretion. *Administrative Science Quarterly* 35 (3): 484-503.

_____ Fredrickson, J. W. 1984. The comprehensiveness of strategic decision processes: Extension, observations, future directions. *Academy of Management Journal* 27 (3): 445-66.

_____ Fredrickson, J. W. 1986. The strategic decision process and organizational structure. *Academy of Management Review* 11 (2): 280-97.

_____ Fredrickson, J. W., Hambrick, D. C., and Baumrin, S. 1988. A model of CEO dismissal. *Academy of Management Review* 13 (2): 255-70.

_____ Fredrickson, J. W., and Iaquinto, A. L. 1989. Inertia and creeping rationality in strategic decision-processes. *Academy of Management Journal* 32 (3): 516-42.

_____ Fredrickson, J. W., and Mitchell, T. R. 1984. Strategic decision processes: Comprehensiveness and performance in an industry with an unstable environment. *Academy of Management Journal* 27 (2): 399-423.

_____ Friedman, S. D., and Singh, H. 1989. CEO succession and stockholder reaction: The influence of organizational context and event content. *Academy of Management Journal* 32 (4): 718-44.

_____ Govindarajan, V., and Fisher, J. 1990. Strategy, control systems, and resource sharing: Effects on business unit performance. *Academy of Management Journal* 33 (2): 259-85.

_____ Gupta, A. K., and Govindarajan, V. 1984. Business unit strategy, managerial characteristics, and business unit effectiveness at strategy implementation. *Academy of Management Journal* 27 (1): 25-41.

_____ Hambrick, D. C. 1981. Environment, strategy, and power within top management teams. *Administrative Science Quarterly* 26: 253-76.

_____ Hambrick, D. C., and Finkelstein, S. 1987. Managerial discretion: A bridge between polar views or organizational outcomes. *Research in organizational behavior.* vol. 9 369-406. Greenwich, Conn. JAI Press.

_____ Hambrick, D. C., and Mason, P. A. 1984. Upper echelons: The organization as a reflection of its top managers. *Academy of Management Review* 9 (2): 193-206.

_____ Hitt, M. A., and Ireland, R. D. 1985. Corporate distinctive competence, strategy, industry and performance. *Strategic Management Journal* 6 (3): 273-93.

_____ Hitt, M. A., Ireland, R. D., and Palia, K. A. 1982. Industrial firms' grand strategy and functional importance: Moderating effects of technology and uncertainty. *Academy of Management Journal* 25 (2): 265-98.

_____ Huber, G. P., and Power, D. J. 1985. Retrospective reports of strategic-level managers: Guidelines for increasing their accuracy. *Strategic Management Journal* 6: 171-80.

_____ Isenberg, D. J. 1984. How senior managers think. *Harvard Business Review* 62 (6): 80-90.

_____ Jackson, S. E., and Dutton, J. E. 1988. Discerning threats and opportunities. *Administrative Science Quarterly* 33 (3): 370-87.

_____ Jensen, M. C., and Murphy, K. J. 1990. CEO incentives: It's not how much you pay, but how. *Harvard Business Review* 68 (3): 138-49.

_____ Kerr, J., and Bettis, R. A. 1987. Boards of directors, top management compensation, and shareholder returns. *Academy of Management Journal* 30 (4): 645–64.

_____ Kesner, I. F. 1988. Directors' characteristics and committee membership: An investigation of type, occupation, tenure, and gender. *Academy of Management Journal* 31 (1): 66–84.

_____ Kosnik, R. D. 1987. Greenmail: A study of board performance in corporate governance. *Administrative Science Quarterly* 32: 163–85.

_____ Kosnik, R. D. 1990. The effects of board demography and directors' incentives on corporate greenmail decisions. *Academy of Management Journal* 33 (1): 129–50.

_____ Kotter, J. P. 1982. *The general managers.* New York: Free Press.

_____ Kotter, J. P. 1982. What effective general managers really do. *Harvard Business Review* 60 (6): 156–67.

_____ Kotter, J. P. 1988. *The leadership factor.* New York: Free Press.

_____ Kotter, J. P. 1990. What leaders really do. *Harvard Business Review* 68 (3): 103–11.

_____ Levinson, H. 1984. CEO: *Corporate leadership in action.* New York: Basic Books.

_____ Lorsch, J. W. 1989. *Pawns or potentates: The reality of America's corporate boards.* Cambridge: Harvard Business School Press.

_____ Meindl, J. R., Ehrlich, S. B., and Dukerich, J. M. 1985. The romance of leadership. *Administrative Science Quarterly* 30: 78–102.

_____ Miller, D. 1987. Strategy making and structure. Analysis and implications for performance. *Academy of Management Journal* 30 (1): 7–32.

_____ Miller, D., DeVries, M. F. R. K., and Toulouse, J-M. 1982. Top executive locus of control and its relationship to strategy–making, structure, and environment. *Academy of Management Journal* 25 (2): 237–53.

_____ Miller, D., and Dröge, C. 1986. Psychological and traditional determinants of structure. *Administrative Science Quarterly* 31 (4): 539–60.

_____ Miller, D., and Toulose, J-M. 1986. Chief executive personality and corporate strategy and structure in small firms. *Management Science* 32 (11): 1389–1409.

_____ Mintzberg, H. 1987. Crafting strategy. *Harvard Business Review* 65 (4): 66–75.

_____ Mintzberg, H., and Waters, J. A. 1982. Tracking strategy in an entrepreneurial firm. *Academy of Management Journal* 25 (3): 465–99.

_____ Nutt, P. C. 1984. Types of organizational decision-processes. *Administrative Science Quarterly* 29 (3): 414–50.

_____ Nutt, P. C. 1986. Tactics of implementation. *Academy of Management Journal* 29 (2): 230–61.

_____ O'Reilly, C. A., Main, B. G., and Crystal, G. S. 1988. CEO compensation as tournament and social comparison: A tale of two theories. *Administrative Science Quarterly* 33 (2): 257–74.

_____ Pfeffer, J., and Davis-Blake, A. 1986. Administrative succession and organizational performance: How administrator experience mediates the succession effect. *Academy of Management Journal* 29 (1): 72–83.

_____ Reinganum, M. R. 1985. The effect of executive succession on stockholder wealth. *Administrative Science Quarterly* 30: 46–60.

_____ Robey, D., and Taggart, W. 1981. Measuring managers' minds: The assessment of style in human information-processing. *Academy of Management Review* 6 (3): 375–83.

_____ Salancik, G. R., and Meindl, J. R. 1984. Corporate attributions as strategic illusions of management control. *Administrative Science Quarterly* 29: 238–54.

_____ Schweiger, D. M., Sandberg, W. R., and Ragan, J. W. 1986. Group approaches for improving strategic decision making: A comparative analysis of dialectical inquiry, devil's advocacy, and consensus. *Academy of Management Journal* 29 (1): 51–71.

_____ Schwenk, C. R. 1984. Cognitive simplification processes in strategic decision-making. *Strategic Management Journal* 5: 111–28.

_____ Sheridan, J. E., Vredenburgh, D. J., and Abelson, M. A. 1984. Contextual model of leadership influence in hospital units. *Academy of Management Journal* 27 (1): 57–78.

_____ Singh, H., and Harianto, F. 1989. Management-board relationships, takeover risk, and the adoption of golden parachutes. *Academy of Management Journal* 32 (1): 7–24.

_____ Smith, J. E., Carson, K. P., and Alexander, R. A. 1984. Leadership: It can make a difference. *Academy of Management Journal* 27 (4): 765–76.

_____ Sonnenfeld, J. A. 1988. *The hero's farewell: What happens when CEOs retire?* New York: Oxford University Press.

_____ Szilagyi, Jr., A. D., and Schweiger, D. M. 1984. Matching managers to strategies: A review and suggested framework. *Academy of Management Review* 9 (4): 626–37.

_____ Thomas, A. B. 1988. Does leadership make a difference to organizational performance? *Administrative Science Quarterly* 33 (3): 388–400.

_____ Thomas, J. B., and McDaniel, R. R. 1990. Interpreting strategic issues: Effects of strategy and the information-processing structure of top management teams. *Academy of Management Journal* 33 (2): 286–306.

_____ Tosi, H. L. and Gomez-Mejia, L. R. 1989. The decoupling of CEO pay and performance: An agency theory perspective. *Administrative Science Quarterly* 34 (2): 169–89.

_____ Vancil, R. F. 1987. *Passing the baton: Managing the process of CEO succession.* Cambridge: Harvard Business School Press.

_____ Wade, J., O'Reilly, C. A., and Chandratat, I. 1990. Golden parachutes: CEOs and the exercise of social influence. *Administrative Science Quarterly* 35 (4): 587–603.

_____ Wagner, W. G., Pfeffer, J., and O'Reilly, C. A., III. 1984. Organizational demography and turnover in top-management groups. *Administrative Science Quarterly* 29 (1): 74–92.

_____ Walsh, J. P. 1988. Selectivity and selective perception: an investigation of managers' belief structures and information-processing. *Academy of Management Journal* 31 (4): 873–96.

_____ Walsh, J. P. 1989. Doing a deal: Merger and acquisition negotiations and their impact upon target company top management turnover. *Strategic Management Journal* 10 (4): 307–22.

_____ Walsh, J. P., and Seward, J. K. 1990. On the efficiency of internal and external corporate control mechanisms. *Academy of Management Review* 15 (3): 421–58.

_____ Worrell, D. L., Davidson, W. N., Chandy, P. R., and Garrison, S. L. 1986. Management turnover through deaths of key executives: Effects on investor wealth. *Academy of Management Journal* 29 (4): 674–94.

_____ Zajac, E. J. 1990. CEO selection, succession, compensation and firm performance: A theoretical integration and empirical analysis. *Strategic Management Journal* 11 (3): 217–30.

In addition to the works listed above, are there any others that you believe have had an especially constructive impact on scholarly understanding of strategic leadership? If so, please note them below.

_____

_____

_____

_____

_____

_____

_____

_____

Part 2: The following works, published after 1990, are listed alphabetically. For each, please rate the degree to which you believe it will have a constructive impact on scholarly understanding of strategic leadership, as defined at the beginning of this survey.
Use the following scale in rating the works:

1   2   3   4   5   X
Unimportant   Highly Important   Unable to Rate

_____ Boeker, W. 1992. Power and managerial dismissal: Scapegoating at the top. *Administrative Science Quarterly* 37 (3): 400-21.

_____ Boeker, W., and Goodstein, J. 1991. Organizational performance and adaptation: Effects of environment and performance on changes in board composition. *Academy of Management Journal* 34 (4): 805-26.

_____ Boeker, W., and Goodstein, J. 1993. Performance and successor choice: The moderating effects of governance and ownership. *Academy of Management Journal* 36 (1): 172-86.

_____ Boone, C., and Debrabander, B. 1993. Generalized versus specific locus of control expectancies of chief executive officers. *Strategic Management Journal* 14 (8): 619-25.

_____ Cannella, A. A., and Lubatkin, M. 1993. Succession as a sociopolitical process: Internal impediments to outsider selection. *Academy of Management Journal* 36 (4): 763-93.

_____ Chen, C. C., and Meindl, J. R. 1991. The construction of leadership images in the popular press: The case of Donald Burr and People Express. *Administrative Science Quarterly* 36 (4): 521-51.

_____ Clapham, S. E., and Schwenk, C. R. 1991. Self-serving attributions, managerial cognition, and company performance. *Strategic Management Journal* 12 (3): 219-29.

_____ Cowherd, D. M., and Levine, D. I. 1992. Product quality and pay equity between lower-level employees and top management: An investigation of distributive justice theory. *Administrative Science Quarterly* 37 (2): 302-20.

_____ D'Aveni, R. A., and Kesner, I. F. 1993. Top managerial prestige, power and tender offer response: A study of elite social networks and target firm cooperation during takeovers. *Organization Science* 4 (2): 123-51.

_____ Davis, G. F. 1991. Agents without principles: The spread of the poison pill through the intercorporate network. *Administrative Science Quarterly* 36 (4): 583-613.

_____ Dutton, J. E., and Ashford, S. J. 1993. Selling issues to top management. *Academy of Management Review* 18 (3): 397-428.

_____ Finkelstein, S. 1992. Power in top management teams: Dimensions, measurement, and validation. *Academy of Management Journal* 35 (3): 505-38.

_____ Fisher, J., and Govindarajan, V. 1992. Profit center manager compensation: An examination of market, political and human capital factors. *Strategic Management Journal* 13 (3): 205-17.

_____ Gomez-Mejia, L. R. 1992. Structure and process of diversification, compensation strategy, and firm performance. *Strategic Management Journal* 13 (5): 381-97.

_____ Goodstein, J., and Boeker, W. 1991. Turbulence at the top: A new perspective on governance structure changes and strategic change. *Academy of Management Journal* 34 (2): 306-30.

_____ Goodstein, J., Gautam, K., and Boeker, W. 1994. The effects of board size and diversity on strategic change. *Strategic Management Journal* 15 (3): 241-50.

_____ Grimm, C. M., and Smith, K. G. 1991. Management and organizational change: A note on the railroad industry. *Strategic Management Journal* 12 (7): 557-62.

_____ Haleblian, J., and Finkelstein, S. 1993. Top management team size, CEO dominance, and firm performance: The moderating roles of environmental turbulence and discretion. *Academy of Management Journal* 36 (4): 844-63.

_____ Hambrick, D. C., and D'Aveni, R. A. 1992. Top team deterioration as part of the downward spiral of large corporate bankruptcies. *Management Science* 38 (10): 1445-66.

_____ Hambrick, D. C., and Fukutomi, G. D. S. 1991. The seasons of a CEO's tenure. *Academy of Management Review* 16 (4): 719-42.

_____ Hambrick, D. C., Geletkanycz, M. A., and Fredrickson, J. W. 1993. Top executive commitment to the status quo: Some tests of its determinants. *Strategic Management Journal* 14 (6): 401-18.

_____ Hart, S. L. 1992. An integrative framework for strategy-making processes. *Academy of Management Review* 17 (2): 327-51.

_____ Haveman, H. A. 1993. Ghosts of managers past: Managerial succession and organizational mortality. *Academy of Management Journal* 36 (4): 864-81.

_____ Hill, C. W. L., and Phan, P. 1991. CEO tenure as a determinant of CEO pay. *Academy of Management Journal* 34 (3): 707-17.

_____ Hitt, M. A., and Tyler, B. B. 1991. Strategic decision models: Integrating different perspectives: *Strategic Management Journal* 12 (5): 327-51.

_____ House, R. J., Spangler, W. D., and Woycke, J. 1991. Personality and charisma in the United States presidency: A psychological theory of leader effectiveness. *Administrative Science Quarterly* 36 (3): 364–96.

_____ Jackson, S. E. 1992. Consequences of group composition for the interpersonal dynamics of strategic issue processing. *Advances of strategic management.* vol. 8, 354–89. Greenwich, Conn. JAI Press.

_____ Judge, W. Q., and Zeithaml, C. P. 1992. Institutional and strategic choice perspectives on board involvement in the strategic decision process. *Academy of Management Journal* 35 (4): 766–94.

_____ Keck, S. L., and Tushman, M. L. 1993. Environmental and organizational context and executive team structure. *Academy of Management Journal* 36 (6): 1314–44.

_____ Kerr, J. L., and Kren, L. 1992. Effect of relative decision monitoring on chief executive compensation. *Academy of Management Journal* 35 (2): 370–97.

_____ Kim, W. C., and Mauborgne, R. A. 1993. Procedural justice, attitudes, and subsidiary top management compliance with multinationals' corporate strategic decisions. *Academy of Management Journal* 36 (3): 502–26.

_____ Lambert, R. A., Larcker, D. F., and Weigelt, K. 1991. How sensitive is executive compensation to organizational size? *Strategic Management Journal* 12 (5): 395–402.

_____ Lambert, R. A., Larcker, D. F., and Weigelt, K. 1993. The structure of organizational incentives. *Administrative Science Quarterly* 38 (3): 438–61.

_____ Lant, T. K., Milliken, F. J., and Batra. B. 1992. The role of managerial learning and interpretation in strategic persistence and reorientation: An empirical exploration. *Strategic Management Journal* 13 (8): 585–608.

_____ Mallette, P., and Fowler, K. L. 1992. Effects of board composition and stock ownership on the adoption of poison pills. *Academy of Management Journal* 35 (5): 1010–35.

_____ Michel, J. G., and Hambrick, D. C. 1992. Diversification posture and top management team characteristics. *Academy of Management Journal* 35 (1): 9–37.

_____ Miller, D. 1991. Stale in the saddle: CEO tenure and the match between organization and environment. *Management Science* 37 (1): 34–52.

_____ Miller D. 1993. Some organizational consequences of CEO succession. *Academy of Management Journal* 36 (3): 644–59.

_____ Milliken, J., and Lant, T. K. 1991. The effect of an organization's recent performance history on strategic persistence and change: The role of managerial interpretations. *Advances in strategic management.* vol. 7, 129–56. Greewich, Conn. JAI Press.

_____ Nutt, P. C. 1993. The identification of solution ideas during organizational decision making. *Management Science* 39 (9): 1071-85.

_____ Nutt, P. C. 1993. The formulation processes and tactics used in organizational decision-making. *Organization Science* 4 (2): 226-51.

_____ Pagonis, W. G. 1992. The work of the leader. *Harvard Business Review* 70 (6): 118-26.

_____ Pearce, J. A., and Zahra, S. A. 1991. The relative power of CEOs and boards of directors: Associations with corporate performance. *Strategic Management Journal* 12 (2): 135-53.

_____ Powell, G. M, and Butterfield, D. A. 1994. Investigating the "glass ceiling" phenomenon: An empirical study of actual promotion to top management. *Academy of Management Journal* 37 (1): 68-86.

_____ Priem, R. L. 1992. An application of metric conjoint analysis for the evaluation of top managers' individual strategic decision-making processes: A research note. *Strategic Management Journal* 13 (Special Issue, Summer): 143-51.

_____ Puffer, S. M., and Weintrop, J. B. 1991. Corporate performance and CEO turnover. The role of performance expectations. *Administrative Science Quarterly* 36 (1): 1-19.

_____ Rajagopalan, N., and Finkelstein, S. 1992. Effects of strategic orientation and environmental change on senior management reward systems. *Strategic Management Journal* 13 (Special Issue, Summer): 127-41.

_____ Rechner, P. L., and Dalton, D. R. 1991. CEO duality and organizational performance. A longitudinal analysis. *Strategic Management Journal* 12 (2): 155-60.

_____ Rotemberg, J. J., and Saloner, G. 1993. Leadership style and incentives. *Management Science* 39 (11): 1299-1314.

_____ Shanley, M. T., and Correa, M. E. 1992. Agreement between top management teams and expectations for post acquisition performance. *Strategic Management Journal* 13 (4): 245-66.

_____ Schotter, A. 1992. Behavioral consequences of corporate incentives and long-term bonuses: An experimental study. *Management Science* 38 (9): 1280-98.

_____ Simons, R. 1991. Strategic orientation and top management attention to control systems. *Strategic Management Journal* 12 (1): 49-62.

_____ Simons, R. 1994. How new top managers use control systems as levers of strategic renewal. *Strategic Management Journal* 15 (3): 169-90.

_____ Thomas, A. S., Litschert, R. J., and Ramaswamy, K. 1991. The performance impact of strategy-manager coalignment: An empirical examination. *Strategic Management Journal* 12 (7): 509-22.

_____ Virany, B., Tushman, M. L., and Romanelli, E. 1992. Executive succession and organization outcomes in turbulent environments: An organization learning approach. *Organization Science* 3 (1): 72-91.

_____ Walsh, J. P., and Ellwood, J. W. 1991. Mergers, acquisitions, and the pruning of managerial deadwood. *Strategic Management Journal* 12 (3): 201-17.

_____ Walsh, J. P., and Kosnik, R. D. 1993. Corporate raiders and their disciplinary role in the market for corporate control. *Academy of Management Journal* 36 (4): 671-700.

_____ Wiersema, M. F., and Bantel, K. A. 1992. Top management team demography and corporate strategic change. *Academy of Management Journal* 35 (1): 91-121.

_____ Wiersema, M. F., and Bantel, K. A. 1993. Top management team turnover as an adaptation mechanism: The role of the environment. *Strategic Management Journal* 14 (7): 485-504.

_____ Wiersema, M. F., and Bird, A. 1993. Organizational demography in Japanese firms: Group heterogeneity, individual dissimilarity, and top management team turnover. *Academy of Management Journal* 36 (5): 996-1025.

_____ Worrell, D. L., Davidson, W. N., and Glascock, J. L. 1993. Stockholder reactions to departures and appointments of key executives attributable to firings. *Academy of Management Journal* 36 (2): 387-401.

_____ Zajac, E. J., and Bazerman, M. H. 1991. Blind spots in industry and competitor analysis: Implications of interfirm (mis)perceptions for strategic decisions. *Academy of Management Review* 16 (1): 37-56.

_____ Zaleznik, A. 1992. Managers and leaders: Are they different? *Harvard Business Review* 70 (2): 126-35.

In addition to the works listed above, are there any others published after 1990 that you believe have had an especially constructive impact on scholarly understanding of strategic leadership? If so, please note them below.

_____

_____

_____

_____

_____

_____

_____

TEN

SYNTHESIS AND SUMMARY: STRATEGIC LEADERSHIP IN PRACTICE

This book is dedicated to an analysis and synthesis of research on strategic leadership, with an ultimate goal of suggesting a new research agenda for the future. Each chapter of the book has taken up this charge in a different arena of strategic leadership, resulting in a wide set of testable propositions intended to address unanswered, as well as previously unasked, questions. We hope each of these chapters encourages students of strategic leadership to continue to investigate this important topic and to undertake the challenge set forth herein to advance our understanding of senior executives and their effects on their organizations.

While we have maintained primarily a scholarly focus—and believe that such a focus is exceedingly important for this field of inquiry—we also recognize that many of the ideas we have discussed have profound practical significance to organizations and to the realities of strategic leadership. Executive values and cognitions, executive experiences, top management teams and strategic decision making, executive succession, corporate governance, and executive compensation have great consequences for organizations and top executives. Understanding how these facets of strategic leadership arise, interact, and affect strategy and performance is greatly aided by an in-depth comprehension of the phenomena we discuss in each chapter of the book.

In this final chapter, we offer an illustrative case study of strategic leadership that provides a vehicle to synthesize and summarize many of the ideas presented in the various chapters. The case study serves several purposes. First, it provides face validity and anecdotal evidence to support some of the ideas developed in previous chapters, enlivening the phenomena and demonstrating the practical significance of strategic leadership in organizations. Second, briefly summarizing the topics we have discussed in the book is difficult, given the number of propositions suggested in each chapter. Rather than repeat what has come before, a greater contribution of this final chapter is to illustrate some of these ideas in a broad but coherent practical example. Finally, a case analysis of strategic leadership allows for added context and richness that is not always apparent in more quantitative research and enables formation of an additional layer of understanding of issues fundamental to strategic leadership. We hope to encourage others to consider such ethnographic analyses of strategic leadership as an important complement to more quantitative approaches.

We have selected the story of William Agee for the case study. William Agee's career is fascinating, offering numerous examples of phenomena discussed in earlier chapters. We first briefly describe salient aspects of his career, then we analyze these events, drawing on many of the ideas contained in earlier chapters. Although both the case and the analysis are based on press reports, company documents, and secondary data sources, additional information not available to us may suggest interpretations that differ from those we present.

WILLIAM AGEE[1]

Over a ten-day period in February 1995, the events confronting William Agee, chairman and CEO of Morrison Knudsen, went from bad to worse and finally to professional ignomiy. Accompanying the news that the large engineering and construction company was going to report a large loss and possibly default on its loans, Agee issued a statement saying that he intended to retire as CEO in six months, but he left open the possibility that he would remain as chairman. After an emergency board meeting a few days later, however, Morrison Knudsen's directors summarily removed Agee from all posts immediately. Upon hearing this news, some employees at company headquarters in Boise, Idaho, reportedly brought out noisemakers and balloons to celebrate.

For Agee, there may have been feelings of deja vu in all this. A decade earlier, he had been the object of scathing headlines in the business press. As chief of Bendix Corporation, he attempted to take over Martin Marietta Corporation. But the bid backfired when Martin Marietta tried to buy Bendix, driving Agee's company into a shotgun marriage with Allied Corporation (now Allied Signal Inc.) and leaving Agee without a job.

Even before the episode with Martin Marietta, Agee's tenure at Bendix was marked by controversy. He quickly promoted his thirty-year-old executive assistant, Mary Cunningham, to vice-president, stirring widespread rumors about their romantic involvement. The two married after Cunningham left Bendix.

There are numerous similarities between Mr. Agee's two ill-fated chapters as corporate CEO, suggesting, at a minimum, that he was not particularly chastened by the first episode. In both cases, he built his early track record primarily through financial and accounting maneuvers, rather than through operational or strategic initiatives. For instance, he registered early profit improvements at Morrison Knudsen by selling off divisions and reporting large amounts of interest income. Also, in both cases, extreme risk-taking became his undoing: at Bendix, there was the grandiose pursuit of Martin Marietta; at Morrison Knudsen, the financial crisis hinged, in great part, on Agee's decision to sell rail cars to a large customer at a loss, in the hope that the customer would exercise an option to buy more cars later. In fact, according to critics, Agee consistently underbid on projects. Finally there were continuing signs of Agee's imperiousness and dubious judgment: he removed portraits of Morrison Knudsen's founders from the headquarters offices; he placed his wife in charge of the company's philanthropic foundation, with an office next to his; he moved his home to Pebble Beach, California, running the company by fax, phone, and weekly briefings from executives who shuttled between him and Boise. As one expert on corporate governance said, "This is not a company anyone would hold up as a model to be followed by Corporate America." (*NYT* 1995b)

To structure discussion of this case study, we consider how the events described relate to the specific chapters of the book. Since it is hardly feasible to address all of the issues discussed in every chapter, we focus on a select number that the case illustrates within each topic area of strategic leadership, drawing on additional company documents and press accounts for elaboration.

Individual Bases of Executive Action (Chapter 3)

Chapter 3 focused on the role of psychological factors, such as values and cognitions, in the strategic choice process. One possible interpretation of Agee's career is that his interest in prestige and status was a reflection of such values as materialism and power. Some indications of these values are apparent in the case narrative, such as removing the portraits of Morrison Knudsen's founders and operating the firm from his luxury home abutting the famed Pebble Beach golf course.[2] In addition, he converted the massive boardroom at Morrison Knudsen to his office upon becoming CEO, made extensive use of the company jet, and commissioned a life-size portrait of Mary Cunningham and himself at company expense. At least as telling are his actions as CEO at Bendix, when Michael Blumenthal, former CEO of Bendix and Agee's mentor, left the administration of President Jimmy Carter in 1979:

> Blumenthal returned to Detroit and joined Burroughs as heir apparent to Paul Mirabito, chief executive of the computer company. . . . No sooner did Agee hear that Blumenthal was in line for the Burroughs job than he went to Harry Cunningham [no relation to Mary Cunningham] and Paul Mirabito, who were directors of both Bendix and Burroughs, and made a pitch to get the Burroughs job for himself. . . . Agee said: "I know it will cost me a friend, but I can do a better job than Mike." (*Fortune* 1982a, 60)

To the extent these events reflect fundamental personal values of materialism and power, we would expect several effects on executive actions. For example, since extensive, multiple information sources help build and maintain power (Pettigrew 1973), it might be expected that Agee's field of vision would be broad. Press reports suggest this was the case. At both Bendix and Morrison Knudsen, Agee installed a "hot line" to facilitate direct communication with him, created "skunk works" that cut layers of management between the factory floor and the CEO's office, and managed by walking around, collecting information through various interactions with other managers. Evidence also exists that Agee selectively perceived and interpreted the information he collected. For example, critics charged that Morrison Knudsen consistently underbid on projects, despite the apparent losses caused by this practice.[3] And at Bendix, the selective perception and interpretation process was influenced by what is reported as his heavy reliance on Cunningham for counsel (*Fortune* 1982b). Overall, Agee's career as CEO provides considerable evidence of the process described in Chapter 3 as strategic choice under bounded rationality, in which the executive's psychological orientation serves as the filtering, screening, and priority-setting mechanism.

Executive Experiences and Strategic Choice (Chapter 4)

Executives' actions are shaped by their previous experiences. At Morrison Knudsen and at Bendix (and even earlier at Boise Cascade, where Agee was chief financial officer), Agee's background and experiences significantly affected the strategic choices made during his watch. As the case described, similarities in the pattern of strategic actions are evident in each situation. At Morrison Knudsen, Agee implemented a three-part strategy: 1) sell off businesses to generate investment capital to produce income, 2) concentrate on fewer but larger and higher-profile contracts by submitting low bids with the intention of recouping losses on follow-up purchases, and 3) create a major new business in repairing and building rail cars, under the assumption that governmental support for infrastructure and public works was set to accelerate. This emphasis on financially oriented and risky choices is also apparent at both Bendix (where he focused on asset sales and investments in financial securities, rather than operations, to generate cash flow) and Boise Cascade (where he helped build the company into one of the big conglomerates of the 1960s).

We proposed in Chapter 4 that executives often rely on familiar approaches, drawing on previous successful actions or at least on comfortable repertoires. Agee's reliance on financial strategies in three very different contexts[4] provides some support for this idea. Also noteworthy is the importance of past experiences, as reflected in such demographic characteristics as functional background, age, and tenure. For example, Agee reportedly told other top managers: "You construction guys have been trying to run the company for seventy-five years. Now I'm going to show you how the financial guys do it" (*WSJ* 1995b, B4). An analysis of the functional backgrounds of corporate officers at Morrison Knudsen provides further corroboration.[5] In 1987, the year before Agee became CEO, the dominant functional background of one-third of the firm's officers was operations. By 1993, none of the corporate officers then in power had operations backgrounds, according to company documents and the *Dun and Bradstreet Reference Book on Corporate Management*. Instead, 78 percent of the officers had primary functional affiliations in finance, law, and corporate communications.

Executive age and tenure are also suggestive of Agee's orientation. He became CFO at Boise Cascade when he was only thirty-one and CEO of

Bendix at thirty-eight. That these firms undertook somewhat risky strategies (such as innovating the conglomerate strategy at Boise Cascade and engaging in an aggressive, hostile takeover attempt at Bendix) is consistent with the research evidence on the effects of age (Hambrick and Mason 1984). That this orientation toward risk continued into Morrison Knudsen can be interpreted as a continuing reliance on an established repertoire. In addition, average company tenure among officers at Morrison Knudsen dropped from more than 20 years in 1987 to 10.9 in 1989—not only a reflection of massive turnover at the top immediately after Agee became CEO (see below), but also perhaps a further indication of a risk-taking orientation among senior managers.

The relatively consistent pattern of strategic choices engineered by Agee-managed firms may also indicate his lack of self-monitoring. Recall from Chapter 3 that self-monitoring refers to the tendency to comprehend and regulate one's behavior in the context of situational cues. Press reports of Agee's career suggest that he was, indeed, a low self-monitor. For example, the continuing role of Cunningham at Bendix (reportedly as a top advisor) and Morrison Knudsen (as head of the company's charitable foundation with an office next door to Agee's) in the face of much criticism suggests a lack of concern for others' perceptions of him. Thus, as proposed in Chapter 4, the importance of personal dispositions (especially as reflected in functional background) in affecting executive behavior may be greater when self-monitoring is low. Such executives unhesitatingly reveal their biases in their actions—time after time.

Top Management Teams: Group Bases of Executive Action (Chapter 5)

During Agee's tenure at Morrison Knudsen, the top management team (defined as all corporate officers of the firm) consisted of Agee and between five and eight other executives. Yet, it is reported that considerable decision-making power resided with Agee. For example, a Morrison Knudsen executive described Agee's decision-making style as follows: "When he makes a decision, he reminds me of the time Abraham Lincoln was outvoted eight to one at a Cabinet meeting. Lincoln said: 'The ayes have it, because I am the aye' " (*Business Month* 1990, 24). Another press report concluded: "Morrison Knudsen is a public company with 10,820 shareholders; Agee and his wife Mary own just 1.1 percent of the stock, but there is no doubt about who is running the company. It is Agee" (*Forbes* 1992, 91). Additional evidence exists of Agee's dominant position within the top management team: the number of insiders on the board gradually declined from four (44 percent) in the year before Agee was appointed CEO (1987) to one (9 percent) in 1994, leaving Agee as the sole inside director; Agee held both the chair and CEO positions throughout his tenure; and the ratio of CEO pay to that of the next highest-paid executive at Morrison Knudsen increased from 1.37 in 1987 to 2.02 in 1993.[6]

Chapter 5 suggests that CEO dominance affects the characteristics of the top management team and that these characteristics, in turn, have consequences for the effectiveness of the strategy formulation and implementation processes, as well as firm performance. We proposed that CEO dominance increases team homogeneity and size but decreases consensus. Earlier we noted how the backgrounds of Morrison Knudsen's corporate officers clustered around peripheral functions, such as finance, law, and corporate communications. Using the categories in Hambrick and Mason (1984),[7] the Blau index of functional heterogeneity was 78 percent higher in 1987 than in 1993.[8] Variation in company tenure among top management team members increased substantially right after Agee was selected CEO, largely because of the high executive turnover that accompanied his ascendancy to the top. Nevertheless, the coefficient of variation of company tenure declined by a third from 1988 to 1993. Hence, on several dimensions, top management team heterogeneity declined substantially since Agee became CEO, indicating an eventual senior group with relatively similar orientations and highly consistent with Agee's orientation. At the same time—and consistent with propositions in Chapter 5—the number of corporate officers increased from six in 1987 to nine in 1993.

While quantitatively gauging the degree of consensus among top management team members is more difficult, anecdotal evidence abounds that Agee's dominance created great friction and dissensus: Agee's comments about financial and engineering management styles and the high degree of turnover among senior executives suggest differences in point of view; in 1992, Morrison Knudsen "acknowledged that executive telephone calls had been secretly recorded by a security officer," suggesting a degree of distrust at the top (NYT 1995b, D4); and in 1994, senior managers at Morrison sent a letter to directors alleging financial improprieties and mismanagement by Agee, indicating that the CEO had "lost the confidence of his senior managers" (WSJ 1995b, B4). So, while Agee's quest for dominance led to a relatively homogeneous team, his behavior, ironically, created extraordinary tension and dissensus among top management team members.

The combination of top management team homogeneity and dissensus is expected to create problems in both strategy formulation and implementation and, hence, for firm performance. Effective strategy formulation depends on the generation of multiple feasible alternatives as well as the comprehensive evaluation of those alternatives, while effective implementation requires the integration of people and other resources, and the acceptance of and commitment to a strategic direction. There is evidence of problems on both counts. For example, press reports on Morrison Knudsen do not indicate that any alternatives to the strategy of financial engineering were considered; indeed, some have argued that Agee's financial ability was the reason he had been hired (*Fortune* 1989). Yet, such a strategy is inherently unsustainable because at some point, the company must create, produce, and sell products. As the letter to company directors pointed out, "the percentage of the company's pretax income from nonoperating sources such as asset sales and interest for the five years ending 1993 averaged 43 percent. In other words, Mr. Agee was sweetening profit reports by selling Morrison off piece by piece and investing Morrison's cash" (*WSJ* 1995b, B4).

Effective strategy implementation was hindered by Agee's management style and accompanying low morale of top managers, according to press reports. For example, commitment to corporate goals was impeded by Agee's alleged zeal for pushing for high profit projections, with little awareness of the realities of the company's businesses:

> Morrison executives say that Mr. Agee called up his business managers every quarter and asked them what profit they planned to deliver for the quarter; whatever the answer, he pushed for more. "If they hemmed and hawed, he nagged them until they said, 'Yeah, I could do that,'" says one former Morrison manager. By the time Mr. Agee finished the calls, the quarterly profit projections would be nearly double the original managers' targets, the executives say (*WSJ* 1995b, B4).

Dissatisfaction with this management style is evident in several other press accounts. For example, the *New York Times* reported that "employee morale slumped as experienced executives were replaced by people with insufficient experience and complex construction jobs were taken on without adequate engineering support" (1995b, D4). Consistent with the ideas we introduced in Chapter 5, significant performance difficulties ensued, culminating in a reported $310 million loss in 1994. Thus, the William Agee experience at Morrison Knudsen provides a particularly telling illustration of some of the dysfunctions associated with certain types of top management teams and the consequences for strategic decision making and firm performance.

Changes at the Top: Executive Turnover and Succession (Chapter 6)

The central event in the William Agee case was his dismissal from Morrison Knudsen. We now consider what this episode suggests for the framework developed in Chapter 6 to study executive turnover and selection. In addition, we also discuss initial selection factors and top management turnover.

It is not common for CEOs to be dismissed (Vancil 1987). Events surrounding Agee's dismissal provide insight to some of the reasons for this. In Chapter 6, we argued that understanding CEO turnover requires subtlety in assessing firm performance, and it appears from press accounts that firm performance was a particularly important factor at Morrison Knudsen. Although there were indications that the company's finances were not strong (lease obligations increased seven-fold from 1988 to 1993, to $266 million, reflecting sale and leaseback arrangements; maintaining consistent net income was dependent on continued asset sales and investments; a $40.5 million loss was reported in the second quarter of 1994), only when top executives sent their anonymous letter to directors did the board become alarmed. Revealingly, directors asserted "their chief beef was that Mr. Agee hadn't warned them about the perilous state of the balance sheet. 'People felt they should have gotten more of a head's up' from Mr. Agee, said one board member" (WSJ 1995b, B4). Thus, it appears that it was the unexpected, and from the board's point of view, sudden, performance downturn, more than other aspects of the company's performance, that precipitated the board's action.[9]

The performance of the firm, however, was not the critical event in Agee's dismissal. Rather, the actions of Morrison creditors apparently pushed the board to dismiss Agee immediately. The *Wall Street Journal* reported that while debt holders could extend the Morrison loan covenants, they said they were not "going to do it under current management"; in addition, "[t]he banks said they wouldn't provide cash in the future unless Mr. Agee was entirely removed from the board" (1995b, B4). Hence, the adoption of an agency theory perspective on executive turnover may have the effect of overemphasizing the importance of shareholders and underemphasizing the influence of other stakeholders, such as lenders. The important lesson for research on executive turnover is the need to extend consideration of external forces to a broader set of stakeholders than has typically been included in the past.

In light of the controversial nature of Agee's tenure at Bendix, the question arises as to why he was selected CEO of Morrison Knudsen. The answer lies in understanding the problems faced by Morrison Knudsen in 1988. At that time, the company reportedly was losing money, becoming excessively bureaucratic, and confronting the threat of takeover by a raider who had acquired 6.2 percent of the firm (*Fortune* 1989; *Business Month* 1990). These conditions suggest the company was facing a crisis, one that demanded a new CEO with financial expertise and experience in dealing with takeovers. William Agee, who sat on the Morrison board as an outsider, met these criteria. These events suggest a proposition worthy of more in-depth study: firms facing succession under crisis conditions will seek an individual who can deal with existing critical contingencies (see Proposition 6–13.)[10]

Finally, the pattern of entries and exits to Morrison's top management team after Agee was appointed CEO in 1988 can be interpreted as his attempt to consolidate power. First, within five weeks of taking office, Agee removed three senior managers (including the former CEO, who had remained as chairman), replacing them with two former Bendix executives. Overall, 83 percent of corporate officers at Morrison in the year before Agee became CEO were replaced within a year after his appointment. As a result, 89 percent of top team members were new by 1989. Second, as noted above, many of the new officers had primary experience in finance and law. Thus, the direction of top management team turnover was toward greater demographic similarity. Third, "[o]ver the years Mr. Agee had presented the board with several potential successors, including some they liked. But he habitually dropped the old ones for new ones, saying the old ones were no longer performing well" (*WSJ* 1995b, B4). Overall, these actions are consistent not only with prior research on management changes following CEO succession (Helmich and Brown 1972; Gabarro 1987; Virany, Tushman, and Romanelli 1992), but also with our earlier analysis of the distribution of power within the top management team at Morrison Knudsen.

Boards of Directors and Corporate Governance (Chapter 7)

The power distribution between CEOs and their boards is at the heart of agency theory. Boards are best able to fulfill their fiduciary responsibilities to shareholders when they have sufficient power to monitor and discipline top managers; as such, vigilant boards represent the front lines against CEO entrenchment (Fama and Jensen 1993). CEO entrenchment occurs when "managers gain so much power that they are able to use the firm to further their own interests rather than the interests of shareholders" (Weisbach 1988, 435). The press has reported, and we have already noted, several instances of such alleged behavior by Agee.[11] One of the accompaniments of entrenchment is slackened board vigilance. As one analyst remarked upon reflection of the weakening financial position of Morrison and the board's willingness to allow Agee almost unfettered control of the firm, "The question as to where was the board is not a bad one" (*WSJ* 1995b, B4).

Hence, of primary interest in understanding corporate governance at Morrison Knudsen is why the board was not more vigilant. There are several possible answers. First, after Agee was appointed CEO of Morrison, he steadily replaced incumbent directors with his own slate (*Fortune* 1995). The percentage of directors appointed by Agee reached 90 percent by 1992, with only one director a holdover from the previous administration. Interestingly, this board member, Robert McCabe, was reported to be more aggressive than others in seeking Agee's dismissal (*WSJ* 1995b). Hence, the percentage of board members appointed by an incumbent CEO is a telling indicator of board vigilance, or the lack thereof.

Second, the demographic profile of the Morrison board mirrors that of the top management team. Of the directors sitting on the board in the last year of Agee's tenure, only one had a title indicating operating responsibilities. The other directors (besides Agee) were active in finance (50 percent), government (20 percent), executive search (10 percent), and education (10 percent). The primary orientation of board members was not operations, thus they were relatively unlikely to challenge the finance–based strategy employed by Agee. In fact, one security analyst said of the board, "There was nobody who has ever run a large company" (*Fortune* 1995, 70).

Third, as indicated earlier, Agee held both the chair and CEO positions during his entire tenure. While such CEO duality may be advantageous in conveying a strong sense of leadership to stakeholders, it facilitates control of both the agenda and content of board meetings, making the board's monitoring role more difficult (Finkelstein and D'Aveni 1994). In fact, after dismissing Agee, the board amended the company's bylaws to forbid the same person from holding both the titles of chair and CEO.

Finally, several members of the Morrison board were reportedly part of the Agees' social network. For example, the *New York Times* reported that two of Agee's appointments to the board were "close friends" (1995b, D4). Another director, the chairman of an executive search firm, was characterized as a personal friend of Agee who placed Mary Cunningham in a new job when she left Bendix (*WSJ* 1995b, B4). More controversial is the association between Cunningham's philanthropic activities on behalf of Morrison Knudsen and the company's board:

> Further linking Mrs. Agee's charity work to Mr. Agee's corporation are the family connections between her board and his. Several of the corporate directors' wives have served as directors of [Mrs. Agee's foundation], according to the charity's corporate resolutions. Indeed, several corporate directors serve directly on the board, including Mr. Agee, and the company's board meetings were frequently held in tandem with the [foundation's] board meetings. (*NYT* 1995b, D4).

The close social and business ties in the Morrison Knudsen board create ambiguity about board independence and, as a prominent critic noted, "raises a question of prudent judgment" (*NYT* 1995b, D4).

Hence, there may be several reasons the Morrison board was not as vigilant as it could have been. In the end, the board did not act until three events occurred in close proximity: a letter was sent by mutinous senior executives to board members documenting alleged mismanagement, the company announced unexpected losses, and lenders refused to extend covenants. Along with the evidence of CEO dominance within the top management team, changes in board composition and culture under Agee can be interpreted as an attempt to institutionalize power, which is consistent with our earlier comments on the importance of power as one of Agee's core values.[12] When both board members and other top managers are constrained, the essential checks and balances of corporate governance are removed. And, as the Agee case indicates, significant risk is associated with such a governance failure.

Executive Compensation (Chapter 8)

We focus on two aspects of compensation at Morrison Knudsen: 1) how much William Agee was paid, and how this compared to the pay of other executives and to the firm's performance; and 2) what the consequences were of Agee's compensation.

Corporate proxy statements indicate that Agee's initial contract called for $425,000 in annual salary, as well as the right to participate in bonus and stock option plans. His total compensation increased to $2.43 million in 1993, representing an average annual pay increase of 45 percent, or 4.4 times that specified in the initial contract. A comparison of Agee's pay to the next-highest paid executive at Morrison indicates that Agee's compensation was several times that of the second-in-command, as follows:

Salary	1.8 times
Bonus	6.3 times
Long-term incentive plan	2.3 times
Value of unexercised options	4.2 times
Estimated pension benefits	3.3 times

While some may agree with Agee's contention that he was greatly responsible for the company's success and, hence, deserving of this remuneration, the gap in pay between Agee and other senior executives may also be taken as an indication of his dominant position within the top management team.[13] Some evidence exists that the wide pay differential between

Agee and others engendered conflict and dissatisfaction. For example, one account noted that Agee froze top executives' salaries at the same time as his own compensation increased significantly in 1991, concluding that such actions have "not endeared him to many of his executives" (*Forbes* 1992, 91). Agee's relatively high pay may also have contributed to the high turnover among senior executives and to the lack of consensus among senior managers at Morrison—culminating in the letter sent to directors. Hence, rather than indicating the presence of a tournament in senior management ranks, the pay differential between Agee and others may reflect Agee's power and his extraordinary quest for material gain.

Agee's compensation should also be compared to Morrison Knudsen's performance. There are two possible interpretations. First, relative to the condition of the company when Agee took over, profitability had improved significantly and was maintained until 1994. For example, Morrison lost $123 million in 1988 but reported net income of $35.7 million in 1989, Agee's first full year as CEO.[14] However, a more negative evaluation of Agee's performance results from an analysis of his strategy and its consequences. A reliance on asset sales, financial investments, and the risky rail car business for revenues; alleged underbidding on projects; sale and lease-back arrangements that damaged the balance sheet; and expenditures on such perks as corporate jets were all likely contributors to the large losses reported for 1994. Thus, the increases in Agee's pay over time are inconsistent with the lack of improved performance at Morrison on a year-to-year basis. In addition, it appears that the absolute level of Agee's compensation was substantial. The *Wall Street Journal* noted that "Mr. Agee's 1993 compensation of $2.4 million equaled 6.8 percent of Morrison Knudsen's net income, more than any other CEO of a company with earnings in that range, according to a *Forbes* magazine list" (1995a, B10).

We argued in Chapter 8 that there are important intended and unintended consequences of executive compensation arrangements. One of the most interesting, yet relatively unexplored, consequences is the "management of accounts and reputations" (March 1984), whereby executives respond to compensation plans by manipulating accounting choices and enhancing personal reputations to maximize their pay. Such behavior is attributed to William Agee in several press reports. For example, the *Wall Street Journal*, quoting from the letter sent to directors of Morrison Knudsen by disgruntled executives, noted that in the second quarter of 1994, "initial projections of loss reserves to be booked were at least $50 million greater than the approximately $90 million actually booked. The obvious question is—what happened to the balance?" (1995b, B4). Other reports indicate that the company avoided depressing net income by "capitalizing development costs instead of expensing them" (*Forbes* 1992, 90–91) and announced that "corporate employment had been trimmed 40 percent to 180 people to save costs when, in fact, half of the employees involved had simply been moved to subsidiaries " (*NYT* 1995a, D7). Hence, there is evidence that the company tried to "obscure its financial performance" (*NYT* 1995a, D7); critics even charged that Agee had engaged in "aggressive, if not illusory, balance-sheet accounting" (letter to directors, quoted in *WSJ* 1995a, B1).

One final point on the unintended consequences of executive compensation at Morrison Knudsen relates to agency theory. The *New York Times* observed that before spinning off a new division to shareholders and the public, "Mr. Agee asked the company's lawyers and accountants to give the board reports on how such transactions should be counted in his compensation formula" (1995b, D4), implying his preoccupation with how his strategic choices would affect his pay. According to agency theory, because compensation contracts should be designed to reward shareholder wealth maximization, CEOs should do everything they can to meet the criteria set in their contracts. Thus, what are sometimes referred to as unintended consequences may actually be predictable, at least for executives who pay careful attention to the incentives contained in their compensation plans.

In sum, executives may engage in the management of accounts and reputations to maximize their compensation and prestige (March 1984). The picture that emerges from press accounts of Morrison Knudsen is consistent with our earlier discussion of Agee's values. Indeed, to the extent a CEO is motivated by materialism and power, engaging in activities that contribute to their realization may be expected. Hence, different elements of strategic leadership are often closely intertwined in practice. Overall, our analysis of the William Agee case demonstrates that many of the ideas we discuss in each chapter have clear, practical relevance to strategic leadership and offer abundant opportunity for improved understanding of senior executives and their behavior.

CONCLUSION

S trategic leadership—the study of top executives, their characteristics, and the choices they make—is a fundamental component of strategic management. We cannot understand the strategies firms undertake without clearly understanding the strategists who make them. Although the arena of strategic leadership can be likened to the nerve center of strategic management, helping to explain the logics of related phenomena within this field, awareness of and appreciation for its importance have been insufficient. In an attempt to address such a challenge, this book has systematically integrated what we know about strategic leadership and offered a new, comprehensive research agenda for the future. Our review and analysis indicate that strategic leadership has great theoretical and practical importance for organizations, for the behavior of executives within organizations, and for the consequences of this behavior for organization performance. While we have offered a blueprint for further study of strategic leadership, it remains for the reader to accept the challenge. Doing so will enable important new insight into and understanding of top executives, the strategies they adopt, and the performance they deliver.

NOTES

1. This narrative is drawn primarily from *New York Times (NYT)*, 10 February 1995; *Wall Street Journal (WSJ)*, 2 February 1995; *Forbes* 1992; *Business Month* 1990.
2. While Agee was recovering from surgery in 1992, he received a "black rose, which he took as a death threat" (*Fortune* 1995, 65). It is reported that the Agees moved to Pebble Beach immediately after this incident.
3. For example, after Morrison won the contract to build transit cars for the Bay Area Rapid Transit District in Oakland, California, in 1992, one insider charged, "We were looking at a $14 million loss on the contract the day we won it" (*WSJ* 1995a, B10).
4. That a similar pattern of behavior may be observed across different contexts suggests a causal direction consistent with upper echelons theory.
5. Corporate officers are taken to define the boundaries of the top management team at Morrison Knudsen. The annual report consistently differentiated among executives, reserving for primary status (indicated by a demarcation in the listing of executives) a subset of all senior managers typically labeled as "corporate officers."
6. This indicator may be particularly revealing of CEO dominance (Finkelstein 1992; Hambrick and D'Aveni 1992).
7. They divided functional background into three categories: output, throughput, and peripheral.
8. The number two executive, Stephen Hanks was reported to be "Mr. Agee's biggest cheerleader" and an "Agee clone" (*WSJ* 1995b, B1).
9. Another issue is why the board waited as long as it did to take action. We take up this point in the next section.
10. As such, it is not surprising that Agee emphasized financial strategies as CEO. Such expertise may have been a reason he had been hired. It does suggest, however, that the qualifications desired in a new CEO may not necessarily translate into the appropriate expertise desired for the longer term. This may be why the "experimentation" phase of a CEO's tenure, occurring after entry mandates have been addressed but before an enduring organizational theme has been selected, is so critical (Hambrick and Fukutomi 1991).

11. In addition, it is reported that Morrison Knudsen made several expenditures on Agee's behalf, including the commissioning of a portrait of the Agees, purchases of Waterford crystal, legal expenses for Mary Cunningham, flower beds for the Pebble Beach home, and a guest house behind the Boise home (*NYT* 1995b; *WSJ* 1995b; *WSJ* 1995c).

12. Press accounts also indicate that while at Bendix, Agee engineered the resignations of four directors critical of his management of that company and appointed replacements who were loyal to him (*Fortune* 1982a).

13. Agee told an interviewer at *Forbes*, "Morrison Knudsen is a turnaround story that is not without precedent, but it ranks right up there in terms of turnaround stories in the country" (1992, 89).

14. Except for 1992 (when Morrison reported a net loss due to lower operating income and a charge for accounting changes), the company's net earnings remained essentially the same until 1994.

REFERENCES

Abrahamson, E., and Park, C. 1994. Concealment of negative organizational outcomes: An agency theory perspective. *Academy of Management Journal* 37: 1302–1334.

Ackerman, R. W. 1970. Influence of integration and diversity on the investment process. *Administrative Science Quarterly* 15: 341–51.

Adams, J. S. 1963. Toward an understanding of inequity. *Journal of Abnormal and Social Psychology* 67: 422–36.

Adams, J. S. 1965. Inequity in social exchange. In *Advances in experimental social psychology* ed. L. Berkowitz. vol. 2, 267–99. New York: Academic Press.

Agarwal, N. 1981. Determinants of executive compensation. *Industrial Relations* 20 (1): 36–46.

Agle, B. R., and Sonnenfeld, J. A. 1994. Charismatic chief executive officers: Are they more effective? An empirical test of charismatic leadership theory. In *Academy of Management Best Papers Proceedings*, ed. D. P. Moore, 2–6.

Aguilar, F. J. 1967. *Scanning the business environment.* New York: Macmillan.

Aguilar, F. J., Hamermesh, R., and Brainard, C. 1991. General Electric: Reg Jones and Jack Welch. Case, Harvard Business School.

Akerlof, G., and Yellon, J. L. 1988. Fairness and unemployment. *American Economic Review, Papers and Proceedings* 78: 44–49.

Alchian, A. A., and Demsetz, H. 1972. Production, information costs and economic organization. *American Economic Review* 62: 777–95.

Aldrich, H. E. 1979. *Organizations and environments.* Englewood Cliffs, N.J.: Prentice-Hall.

Alexander, J. A., Fennell, M. L., and Halpern, M. T. 1993. Leadership instability in hospitals: The influence of board-CEO relations and organization growth and decline. *Administrative Science Quarterly* 38: 74–99.

Allen, M. P. 1974. The structure of interorganizational elite cooptation: Interlocking corporate directorates. *American Sociological Review* 39: 393–406.

Allen, M. P. 1981. Power and privilege in the large corporation: Corporate control and managerial compensation. *American Journal of Sociology* 86: 1112–23.

Allen, M. P., and Panian, S. 1982. Power, performance and succession in the large corporation. *Administrative Science Quarterly*, 27: 538–47.

Allen, M. P., Panian, S., and Lotz, R. 1979. Managerial succession and organizational performance: A recalcitrant problem revisited. *Administrative Science Quarterly* 24: 167–80.

Allison, G. T. 1971. *Essence of decision: Explaining the Cuban missile crisis.* Boston: Little, Brown.

Allport, G. W., Vernon, P. E., and Lindzey, G. 1970. *Study of values.* New York: Houghton Mifflin.

Altemeyer, R. 1966. Education in the arts and sciences: Divergent paths. Unpublished Ph.D. dissertation, Carnegie Institute of Technology.

Amason, A. C., and Schweiger, D. M. 1992. Toward a general theory of top management teams: An integrative framework. Paper presented at the Academy of Management annual meeting, Las Vegas, Nevada.

American Law Institute. 1984. *Principles of corporate governance: Analysis and recommendation, draft 2*, 13 April, 66–67. Philadelphia.

Amihud, Y., and Lev, B. 1981. Risk reduction as a managerial motive for conglomerate mergers. *Bell Journal of Economics* 12: 605–17.

Ancona, D. G. 1990. Top management teams: Preparing for the revolution. In *Applied social psychology and organizational settings*, ed. J. Carroll, 99–128. Hillsdale, N.J.: Erlbaum.

Ancona, D. G. and Caldwell, D. F. 1992. Demography and design: Predictors of new product team performance. *Organization Science* 3: 321–41.

Anderson, C. A., and Anthony, R. N. 1986. *The new corporate directors: Insights for board members and executives.* New York: Wiley.

Anderson, C. R., Hellriegel, D., and Slocum, J. W., Jr. 1977. Managerial response to environmentally induced stress. *Academy of Management Journal* 20: 260–72.

Anderson, C. R., and Schneier, C. E. 1978. Locus of control, leader behavior, and leader performance among management students. *Academy of Management Journal* 21: 690–98.

Andrews, K. R. 1971. *The concept of corporate strategy.* Homewood, Ill.: Dow Jones–Irwin.

Andrews, K. R. 1981. Corporate strategy as a vital function of the board. *Harvard Business Review* 59(6):174–88.

Ansoff, H. I., 1965. *Corporate strategy: An analytic approach to business policy for growth and expansion.* New York: McGraw-Hill.

Antle, R., and Smith, A. 1986. An empirical investigation into the relative performance of corporate executives. *Journal of Finance* 18: 593–616.

Arrow, K. 1974. *The limits of organization.* New York: Norton.

Astley, W. G., Axelsson, R., Butler, R. J., Hickson, D. J., and Wilson, D. C. 1982. Complexity and cleavage: Dual explanations of strategic decision-making. *Journal of Management Studies* 19: 357–75.

Axelrod, R. M., (Ed.). 1976. Results. *Structure of decision: The cognitive maps of political elites*, 221–48. Princeton, N.J.: Princeton University Press.

Baker, G. P., Jensen, M. C., and Murphy, K. J. 1988. Compensation and incentives: Practice vs. theory. *Journal of Finance* 18: 593–616.

Balkin, D. B., and Gomez-Mejia, L. R. 1990. Matching compensation and organizational strategies. *Strategic Management Journal*, 11: 153–69.

Balkin, D. B., and Gomez-Mejia, L. R. 1987. Toward a contingency theory of compensation strategy. *Strategic Management Journal* 8: 169–82.

Bantel, K. A., and Finkelstein, S. 1995. The determinants of top management teams. In *Advances in group processes*, ed. B. Markovsky, J. O'Brian, and K. Heime. vol. 12. Greenwich, Conn.: JAI Press.

Bantel, K. A., and Jackson, S. E. 1989. Top management and innovations in banking: Does the composition of the top team make a difference? *Strategic Management Journal* 10 (Special Issue): 107–24.

Barbosa, R. R. 1985. Innovation in a mature industry. Unpublished Ph.D. dissertation, Columbia University, New York.

Bardach, E. 1977. *The implementation game*. Cambridge, MIT Press.

Barkema, H. G. 1993 Do top managers work harder when they are monitored?. Paper presented at the Strategic Management Society Meeting, Chicago.

Barnard, C. I. 1938. *The functions of the executive*. Cambridge: Harvard University Press.

Baron, J. N., and Cook, K. S. 1992. Process and outcome: Perspectives on the distribution of rewards in organizations. *Administrative Science Quarterly* 37: 191–97.

Bass, B. M. 1985. *Leadership and performance beyond expectations*. New York: Free Press.

Baumol, W. J. 1967. *Business behavior, value and growth*. New York: Harcourt, Brace and World.

Baumrin, S. W. 1990. New CEOs at the helm in large firms: The relationship of the succession context to subsequent organizational change and performance. Unpublished Ph.D. dissertation, Columbia University, New York.

Baysinger, B., and Butler, H. 1985. Corporate governance and the board of directors: Performance effects of changes in board composition. *Journal of Law, Economics, and Organization* 1: 101–24.

Baysinger, B. D., and Hoskisson, R. E. 1989. Diversification strategy and R&D intensity in multiproduct firms. *Academy of Management Journal* 32: 310–32.

Baysinger, B. D., and Hoskisson, R. E. 1990. The composition of the board of directors and strategic control: Effects of corporate strategy. *Academy of Management Review* 15: 72–87.

Baysinger, B. D., Kosnik, R. D., and Turk, T. A. 1991. Effects of board and ownership structure on corporate R&D strategy. *Academy of Management Journal* 34: 205–14.

Baysinger, B. D., and Zeithaml, C. P. 1986. *Corporate strategy and board of directors' composition: Theory and empirical evidence.* Paper presented at the Academy of Management annual meeting, Chicago.

Beatty, R. P., and Zajac, E. J. 1987. CEO change and firm performance in large corporations: Succession effects and manager shifts. *Strategic Management Journal* 8: 305–17.

Beatty, R. P. and Zajac, E. J. 1994. Managerial incentives, monitoring, and risk-bearing: A study of executive compensation, ownership, and board structure in initial public offerings. *Administrative Science Quarterly* 39: 313–35.

Becker, B. E., and Huselid, M. A. 1992. The incentive effects of tournament compensation systems. *Administrative Science Quarterly* 37: 336–50.

Becker, G. S. 1975. *Human capital.* 2d ed. Chicago: University of Chicago Press.

Becker, M. H. 1970a. Sociometric location and innovativeness: Reformulation and extension of the diffusion model. *American Sociological Review* 35: 267–304.

Becker, M. H. 1970b. Factors affecting diffusion of innovations among health professionals. *American Journal of Public Health*, 60: 294–304.

Begley, T. M., and Boyd, D. P. 1987. Psychological characteristics associated with performance in entrepreneurial firms and smaller businesses. *Journal of Business Venturing* 2: 79–93.

Bendix, R. 1956. *Work and authority in industry.* New York: Wiley.

Benston, G. J. 1985. The self-serving management hypothesis: Some evidence. *Journal of Accounting and Economics* 7: 67–84.

Berg, N. A. 1969. What's different about conglomerate management? *Harvard Business Review* 47(6): 112–20.

Berg, N. A. 1973. Corporate role in diversified companies. In *Business policy: Teaching and research*, ed. B. Taylor and K. MacMillan. New York: Halsted Press.

Berg, S. V., and Smith, S. K. 1978. CEO and board chairman. A quantitative study of dual versus unitary board leadership. *Directors and Boards* Spring: 34–39.

Berger, J., Cohen, B.P., and Zelditch, M. 1972. Structural aspects of distributive justice: A status value formulation. In *Sociological theories in progress*, ed. J. Berger, M. Zelditch, and B. Anderson. vol. 2, 119–46. Boston: Houghton Mifflin.

Berger, J., Fisek, H., Norman, R. Z., and Wagner, D. G. 1983. The formation of reward expectations in status situations. In *Equity theory: Psychological and sociological perspectives*, ed. D. M. Messick and K. S. Cook. 127–68. New York: Praeger.

Berle, A., and Means, G. C. 1932. *The modern corporation and public property.* New York: Macmillan.

Bettenhausen, K., and Murnighan, J. K. 1985. The emergence of norms in competitive decision-making groups. *Administrative Science Quarterly* 30: 350–72.

Bettman, J. R., and Weitz, B. A. 1983. Attributions in the boardroom: Causal reasoning in corporate annual reports. *Administrative Science Quarterly* 28: 165–83.

Bibeault, D. B. 1982. *Corporate turnaround.* New York: McGraw-Hill.

Birnbaum, P. H. 1984. The choice of strategic alternatives under increasing regulation in high technology companies. *Academy of Management Journal* 27: 489–510.

Blau, P. M. 1964. *Exchange and power in social life.* New York: Wiley.

Blau, P. M. 1970. A formal theory of differentiation in organizations. *American Sociological Review* 35: 201–18.

Blau, J. R., and McKinley, W. 1979. Ideas, complexity, and innovation. *Administrative Science Quarterly* 24: 200–19.

Boeker, W. 1992. Power and managerial dismissal: Scapegoating at the top. *Administrative Science Quarterly* 27: 538–47.

Boeker, W., and Goodstein, J. 1991. Organizational performance and adaptation: Effects of environment and performance on changes in board composition. *Academy of Management Journal* 34: 805–26.

Boeker, W., and Goodstein, J. 1993. Performance and successor choice: The moderating effects of governance and ownership. *Academy of Management Journal* 36: 172–86.

Boone, C., and Debrabander, B. 1993. Generalized versus specific locus of control expectancies of chief executive officers. *Strategic Management Journal* 14: 619–25.

Boulton, W. R. 1978. The evolving board: A new look at the board's changing roles and information needs. *Academy of Management Review* 3: 827–36.

Bourgeois, J. 1981. On the measurement of organizational slack. *Academy of Management Review* 6: 29–39.

Bourgeois, L. J. 1980. Performance and consensus. *Strategic Management Journal* 1: 227–48.

Bourgeois, L. J. 1985. Strategic goals, perceived uncertainty, and economic performance in volatile environments. *Academy of Management Journal* 28: 548–73.

Bowen, W. G. 1994. *Inside the boardroom.* New York: John Wiley and Sons.

Bower, J. L. 1970. *Managing the resource allocation process.* Boston: Division of Research, Harvard Business School.

Bower, J. L. 1986. *Managing the resource allocation process.* New York: McGraw Hill.

Bowman, E. H. 1976. Strategy and the weather. *Sloan Management Review* 17: 49–62.

Boyd, B. 1993. Board control and CEO compensation: An agency perspective. Paper presented at the annual meeting of the Academy of Management, Atlanta.

Boyd, B. 1994. Board control and CEO compensation. *Strategic Management Journal* 15: 335–44.

Brickley, J. A. 1986. Interpreting common stock returns around proxy statement disclosures and annual shareholder meetings. *Journal of Financial and Quantitative Analysis* 21: 343–49.

Brickley, J. A., Bhagat, S., and Lease, R. C. 1985. The impact of long-range managerial compensation plans on shareholder wealth. *Journal of Accounting and Economics* 7: 115–29.

Brickley, J. A., and James, C. M. 1987. The takeover market, corporate board composition, and ownership structure: The case of banking. *Journal of Law and Economics* 10: 161–80.

Brickley, James A., Coles, Jeffrey L., and Terry, Rory L. 1994. Outside directors and the adoption of poison pills. *Journal of Financial Economics* 35: 371–90.

Brickley, J. A., Lease, R. C., and Smith, C. W. 1988. Ownership structure and voting on antitakeover amendments. *Journal of Financial Economics* 20: 267–291.

Brockhaus, R. H. 1980. Psychological and environmental factors which distinguish the successful from the unsuccessful entrepreneur: A longitudinal study. *Academy of Management Proceedings,* 368–72.

Brown, J. K. 1981. *Corporate directorship practices: The planning committee.* New York: Conference Board.

Brown, M. C. 1982. Administrative succession and organizational performance: The succession effect. *Administrative Science Quarterly* 27: 1–16.

Buchholtz, A. K., and Ribbens, B. A. 1994. Role of chief executive officers in takeover resistance: Effects of CEO incentives and individual characteristics. *Academy of Management Journal* 37: 554–79.

Burgelman, R. A. 1983. A process model of internal corporate venturing in the diversified major firm. *Administrative Science Quarterly* 28: 223–44.

Burns, L. R., and Wholey, D. R. 1993. Adoption and abandonment of matrix management programs: Effects of organizational characteristics and interorganizational networks. *Academy of Management Journal* 36: 106–38.

Burns, T. and Stalker, G. M. 1961. *The management of innovation*. London: Tavistock.

Burrell, G., and Morgan, G. 1979. *Sociological paradigms and organizational analysis*. London: Heinemann.

Burt, R. S. 1979. A structural theory of interlocking corporate directorates. *Social Networks* 1: 415–35.

Burt, R. S. 1980. Cooptive corporate actor networks: A reconsideration of interlocking directorates involving American manufacturing. *Administrative Science Quarterly* 25: 557–82.

Burt, R. S. 1983. *Corporate profits and cooptation: Networks of market constraints and directorate ties in the American economy*. New York: Academic Press.

Burt, R. S. 1992. *Structural holes*. Cambridge: Harvard University Press.

Business Month. 1990. Born again. January, 22–34.

Business Week, 1993. Portrait of a CEO. 11 October: 64–65.

Byrne, B. M. 1984. The general/academic self-concept nomological network. *Review of Educational Research* 54: 427–56.

Byrne, D. 1961. Interpersonal attraction as a function of affiliation need and attitude similarity. *Human Relations* 14: 63–70.

Byrne, D. 1971. *The attraction paradigm*. New York: Academic Press.

Cafferata, G. L. 1979. An attribution theory of professional ideology. Working paper, University of Rochester, N.Y.

Cannella, A., and Hambrick, D. C. 1993. Effects of executive departures on the performance of acquired firms. *Strategic Management Journal* 14(Special Issue): 137–52.

Cannella, A., and Lubatkin, M. 1993. Succession as a sociopolitical process: Internal impediments to outsider selection. *Academy of Management Journal* 36: 763–93.

Carlson, R. 1962. *Executive succession and organizational change*. Danville, Ill.: Interstate Printers and Publishers.

Carroll, G. R. 1984. Dynamics of publisher succession in newspaper organizations. *Administrative Science Quarterly* 29: 93–113.

Carter, E. 1971. The behavioral theory of the firm and top-level corporate decisions. *Administrative Science Quarterly* 16: 413–28.

Chaganti, R. S., Mahajan, V., and Sharma, S. 1985. Corporate board size, composition and corporate failures in retailing industry. *Journal of Management Studies* 22(4): 400–17.

Chaganti, R., and Sambharya, R. 1987. Strategic orientation and characteristics of upper management. *Strategic Management Journal* 8: 393–401.

Chandler, A. D. 1962. *Strategy and structure: Chapters in the history of the American industrial enterprise.* Cambridge MIT Press.

Chatov, R. 1973. The role of ideology in the American corporation. In *The corporate dilemma*, ed. D. Votaw and S. P. Sethi 50–75. Englewood Cliffs, N.J.: Prentice-Hall.

Chattopadhyay, P., Glick, W. H., Miller, C. C., and Huber, G. P. In press. Determinants of executive beliefs: It's to whom you talk that counts. *Academy of Management Journal.*

Chen, C. C., and Meindl, J. R. 1991. The construction of leadership images in the popular press: The case of Donald Burr and People Express. *Administrative Science Quarterly* 36: 521–51.

Chen, M-J., and MacMillan, I. C. 1992. Nonresponse and delayed response to competitive moves: The roles of competitor dependence and action irreversibility. *Academy of Management Journal* 35: 539–70.

Cherrington, D. J., Condie, S. J., and England, J. L. 1979. Age and work values. *Academy of Management Journal* 22(3): 617–23.

Child, J. 1972. Organization structure, environment, and performance: The role of strategic choice. *Sociology* 6: 1–22.

Ciscel, D. H. 1974. Determinants of executive compensation. *Southern Economic Journal* 40: 613–17.

Ciscel, D. H., and Carroll, T. M. 1980. The determinants of executive salaries: An econometric survey. *Review of Economics and Statistics* 62: 7–13.

Clark, R. C. 1986. *Corporate law.* Boston: Little, Brown.

Clement, W. 1975. Inequality of access: Characteristics of the Canadian corporate elite. *Canadian Review of Sociology and Anthropology* 12: 33–52.

Clendenin, W. D. 1972. Company presidents look at the board of directors. *California Management Review* Spring: 60–66

Cochran, P. L., Wood, R. A. and Jones, T. B. 1985. The composition of board of directors and incidence of golden parachutes. *Academy of Management Journal* 28(3): 664–71.

Cohen, J. and Cohen, P. 1983. *Applied multiple regression/correlation analysis for the behavioral sciences.* Hillsdale, N.J.: Lawrence Erlbaum Associates.

Cohen, M. D., March, J. G., and Olson, J. P. 1972. A garbage-can model of organizational choice. *Administrative Science Quarterly* 17: 1–25.

Cook, K. S., and Hegtvedt, K. A. 1983. Distributive justice, equity, and equality. *Annual Review of Sociology* 9: 217–41.

Conger, J. A. 1990. The dark side of leadership. *Organizational Dynamics* 19(2): 44–55.

Conger, J. A., and Kanungo, R. 1988. *Charismatic leadership.* San Francisco: Jossey-Bass.

Corner, P. D., Kinicki, A. J., and Keats, B. W. 1994. Integrating organizational and individual information processing perspectives on choice. *Organization Science* 5(3): 294–308.

Cosh, D. H. 1975. The remuneration of chief executives in the United Kingdom. *Economic Journal* 85: 75–94.

Coughlan, A. T., and Schmidt, R. M. 1985. Executive compensation, managerial turnover, and firm performance: An empirical investigation. *Journal of Accounting and Economics* 7: 43–66.

Crystal, G. S. 1988. The wacky, wacky world of CEO pay. *Fortune*, 6 June: 68–78.

Crystal, G. S. 1991. *In search of excess: The overcompensation of American executives.* New York: Norton.

Cyert, R. M., and March, J. G. 1963. *A behavioral theory of the firm.* Englewood Cliffs, N.J.: Prentice-Hall.

Daft, R. L. 1986. The past and future of strategic management research: A fast track to nowhere? Paper presented at the annual meeting of the Academy of Management, Chicago.

Daft, R. L., Sormunen, J., and Parks, D. 1988. Chief executive scanning, environmental characteristics, and company performance: An empirical study. *Strategic Management Journal* 9: 123–39.

Daily, C. M., and Dalton, D. R. 1992. The relationship between governance structure and corporate performance in entrepreneurial firms. *Journal of Business Venturing* 7: 375–86.

Dalton, D. R., and Kesner, I. F. 1985. Organizational performance as an antecedent of inside/outside chief executive succession: An empirical assessment. *Academy of Management Journal* 28: 749–62.

D'Aveni, R. A. 1990. Top managerial prestige and organizational bankruptcy. *Organization Science* 1: 121–42.

D'Aveni, R. A., and Kesner, I. F. 1993. Top managerial prestige, power, and tender offer response: A study of elite social networks and target firm cooperation during takeovers. *Organization Science* 4: 123–51.

Davis, G. F. 1993. Who gets ahead in the market for corporate directors: The political economy of multiple board memberships. Paper presented at the Academy of Management meeting, Atlanta.

Davis, G. F. 1991. Agents without principles? The spread of the poison pill through the intercorporate network. *Administrative Science Quarterly* 36: 583–613.

Davis, G. F., and Thompson, Tracy A. 1994. A social movement perspective on corporate control. *Administrative Science Quarterly* 39: 141–73.

Day, D. V., and Lord, R. G. 1992. Expertise and problem categorization: The role of expert processing in organizational sense-making. *Journal of Management Studies* 29(1): 35–47.

Dearborn, D. C., and Simon, H. A. 1958. Selective perception: A note on the departmental affiliations of executives. *Sociometry* 21: 144–50.

Deckop, J. 1988. Determinants of chief ececutive officer compensation. *Industrial and Labor Relations Review* 41: 215–26.

Dess, G. G. 1987. Consensus on strategy formulation and organizational performance: Competitors in a fragmented industry. *Strategic Management Journal* 8: 259–77.

Dess, G. G., and Beard, D. 1984. Dimensions of organizational task environments. *Administrative Science Quarterly* 29: 52–73.

Dess, G. G., and Keats, B. W. 1987. Environmental assessment and organizational performance: An exploratory field study. *Academy of Management Proceeding*: 21–25.

Dess, G. G., and Origer, N. K. 1987. Environment, structure, and consensus in strategy formulation: A conceptual integration. *Strategic Management Journal* 12: 313–30.

Deutsch, M. 1975. Equity, equality, and need: What determines which value will be used as the basis of distributive justice? *Journal of Social Issues* 31: 137–49.

Deutsch, M. 1985. *Distributive justice: A social psychological perspective*. New Haven: Yale University Press.

Dial, J., and Murphy, K. J. 1995. Executive compensation and corporate strategy at General Dynamics. Working Paper, Harvard Business School, Division of Research, 18.

DiMaggio, P., and Powell, W. W. 1983. The iron cage revisited: Institutional isomorphism and collective rationality in organizational fields. *American Sociological Review* 48: 147–60.

DiMaggio, P. J., and Powell, W. W. 1985. The structure of corporate ownership: Causes and consequences. *Journal of Political Economy* 93: 1155–77.

Dobrzynski, J. 1988. Whose company is it, anyway? *Business Week*, 25 April, 60–61.

Donaldson, G., and Lorsch, J. W. 1983. *Decision making at the top*. New York: Basic Books.

Dooley, P. 1969. The interlocking directorate. *American Economic Review* 59: 314–23.

Drazin, R., and Kazanjian, R. 1993. Applying the del technique to the analysis of cross-classification data: A test of CEO succession and top management team development. *Academy of Management Journal* 36: 1374–99.

Duhaime, I. M. and Baird, I. S. 1987. Divestment decision making: The role of business unit size. *Journal of Management* 13: 483–98.

Duncan, R. 1972. Characteristics of organizational environments and perceived environmental uncertainty. *Administrative Science Quarterly* 17: 313–27.

Dundas, K. M., and Richardson, P. R. 1982. Implementing the unrelated product strategy. *Strategic Management Journal* 3: 287–301.

Dutton, J. E. and Duncan, R. B. 1987. The creation of momentum for change through the process of strategic issue diagnosis. *Strategic Management Journal* 8: 279–95.

Dutton, J. E., Fahey, L., and Narayanan, V. K. 1983. Toward understanding strategic issue diagnosis. *Strategic Management Journal* 4: 307–23.

Dutton, J. E., and Jackson, S. E. 1987. Categorizing strategic issues: Links to organizational action. *Academy of Management Review* 12: 76–90.

Eaton, J., and Rosen, H. S. 1983. Agency, delayed compensation, and the structure of executive remuneration. *Journal of Finance* 38: 1489–1505.

Ebadi, Y., and Utterback, J. 1984. The effects of communication on technological innovation. *Management Science* 30: 572–85.

Eckoff, T. 1974. *Justice: Its determinants in social interaction.* Rotterdam: Rotterdam Press.

Ehrenberg, R. G., and Bognanno, M. L. 1990. The incentive effects of tournaments revisited: Evidence from the European PGA tour. *Industrial and Labor Relations Review* 43: 74S–88S.

Eisenhardt, K. M. 1989a. Agency theory: An assessment and review. *Academy of Management Review* 14: 57–74.

Eisenhardt, K. M. 1989b. Making fast strategic decisions in high-velocity environments. *Academy of Management Journal* 32: 543–76.

Eisenhardt, K. M., and Bourgeois, L. J. 1988. Politics of strategic decision making in high–velocity environments: Toward a midrange theory. *Academy of Management Journal* 31: 737–70.

Eisenhardt, K. M., and Schoonhoven, C. B. 1990. Organizational growth: Linking founding team, strategy, environment, and growth among U. S. semiconductor ventures, 1978–1988. *Administrative Science Quarterly* 35: 504–29.

Eisenhardt, K. M., and Zbaracki, M. J. 1992. Strategic decision making. *Strategic Management Journal* 13(Winter, Special Issue): 17–38.

Ely, K. M. 1991. Interindustry differences in the relation between compensation and firm performance variables. *Journal of Accounting Research* 29 (1): 37–57.

Emerson, R. M. 1962. Power-dependence relationships. *American Sociological Review* 27: 31–41.

England, G. W. 1967. Personal value systems of American managers. *Academy of Management Journal* 10: 53–68.

England, G. W. 1973a. Personal value systems and expected behavior of managers—a comparative study in Japan, Korea, and the United States. In *Management research: A cross-cultural perspective*, ed. D. Graves. 270–92. San Francisco: Jossey-Bass.

England, G. W. 1973b. Personal value systems of managers and administrators. *Academy of Management Journal Proceedings* (August): 81–89.

England, G. W. 1975. *The manager and his values.* Cambridge, Mass.: Ballinger.

Estes, R. M. 1980. Corporate governance in the courts. *Harvard Business Review* 58(4): 50–54.

Etzioni, A. 1975. *A comparative analysis of complex organizations.* New York: Free Press.

Fama, E. F. 1980. Agency problems and the theory of the firm. *Journal of Political Economy* 88: 288–307.

Fama, E. F., and Jensen, M. C. 1983. Separation of ownership and control. *Journal of Law and Economics* 26: 301–25.

Farris, M. T. 1973. Purchasing reciprocity and antitrust. *Journal of Purchasing* 27 (February): 15–27.

Fayol, H. 1949. *General and industrial management.* London: Pitman.

Feldman, D. C. 1981. The multiple socialization of organization members. *Academy of Management Review* 6: 309–18.

Festinger, L. 1954. A theory of social comparison processes. *Human Relations* 7: 117–40.

Filley, A. C., House, R. J., and Kerr, S. 1976. *Managerial process and organizational behavior.* Glenview, Ill.: Scott Foresman.

Finkelstein, S. 1988. Managerial orientations and organizational outcomes: The moderating roles of managerial discretion and power. Unpublished Ph.D. dissertation, Columbia University, New York.

Finkelstein, S. 1992. Power in top management teams: Dimensions, measurement, and validation. *Academy of Management Journal* 35: 505–38.

Finkelstein, S. 1995. Understanding pay dispersion within top management teams: A social comparison approach. Working paper, Amos Tuck School of Business Administration, Dartmouth College, Hanover, N.H.

Finkelstein, S., and D'Aveni, R. A. 1994. CEO duality as a double-edged sword: How boards of directors balance entrenchment avoidance and unity of command. *Academy of Management Journal* 37: 1079–1108.

Finkelstein, S., and Hambrick, D. C. 1988. Chief executive compensation: A synthesis and reconciliation. *Strategic Management Journal* 9: 543–58.

Finkelstein, S., and Hambrick, D. C. 1989. Chief executive compensation: A study of the intersection of markets and political processes. *Strategic Management Journal* 10: 121–34.

Finkelstein, S., and Hambrick, D. C. 1990. Top management team tenure and organizational outcomes: The moderating role of managerial discretion. *Administrative Science Quarterly* 35: 484–503.

Finkelstein, S., and Rajagopalan, M. 1996. The adoption of performance-contingent compensation plans. Working paper, Amos Tuck School of Business Administration, Dartmouth College, Hanover, N.H.

Fiol, L. L. 1989. A semiotic analysis of corporate language: Organizational boundaries and joint venturing. *Administrative Science Quarterly,* 34(2): 277–303.

Fisher, J., and Govindarajan, V. 1992. Profit center manager compensation: An examination of market, political and human capital factors. *Strategic Management Journal* 13: 205–17.

Fisher, J., and Govindarajan, V. 1993. Incentive compensation design, strategic business unit mission, and competitive strategy. *Journal of Management Accounting Research* 5: 129–44.

Fizel, J. L., and Louie, K. K. T. 1990. CEO retention, firm performance and corporate governance. *Managerial and Decision Economics* July: 167–76.

Flatt, S. 1992. A longitudinal study in organizational innovativeness: How top management team demography influences organizational innovation. Unpublished Ph.D. dissertation, University of California, Berkeley.

Fligstein, N. 1987. The intraorganizational power struggle: Rise of finance personnel to top leadership in large corporations, 1919–1979. *American Sociological Review* 52 44–58.

Fligstein, N. 1990. *The transformation of corporate control.* Cambridge: Harvard University Press.

Forbes. 1992. The imperial Agees. 8 June: 88–92.

Ford, R. H. 1988. Outside directors and the privately owned firm: Are they necessary? *Entrepreneurship Theory and Practice* 13(1): 49–57.

Fortune. 1982a. The boardroom battle at Bendix. 11 January: 54–64.

Fortune. 1982b. "Our dream is to work together": An interview with Bill Agee and Mary Cunningham. 18 October: 163–66.

Fortune. 1989. Bill Agee gets a second chance. 27 March: 94–96.

Frank, R. 1984. Are workers paid their marginal products? *American Economic Review* 74: 549–71.

Fredrickson, J. W. 1984. The comprehensiveness of strategic decision processes: Extension, observations, future directions. *Academy of Management Journal* 27: 445–66.

Fredrickson, J. W., Hambrick, D. C., and Baumrin, S. 1988. A model of CEO dismissal. *Academy of Management Review* 13: 255–70.

Fredrickson, J. W., and Iaquinto, A. L. 1989. Inertia and creeping rationality in strategic decision-processes. *Academy of Management Journal* 32: 516–42.

Friedman, S. D., and Singh, H. 1989. CEO succession and stockholder reaction: The influence of organizational context and event content. *Academy of Management Journal* 32: 718–44.

Furtado, E., and Karan, V. 1990. Causes, consequences and shareholder wealth effects of management turnover: A review of the empirical evidence. *Financial Management* 19: 60–75.

Gabarro, J. J. 1986. When a new manager takes charge. *Harvard Business Review* 86: 110–23.

Gabarro, J. J. 1987. *The dynamics of taking charge*. Boston: Harvard Business School Press.

Galaskiewicz, J., and Burt, R. S. 1991. Interorganization contagion in corporate philanthropy. *Administrative Science Quarterly* 36(1): 88–105.

Galaskiewicz, J., and Wasserman, S. 1981. A dynamic study of change in a regional corporate network. *American Sociological Review* 46: 475–84.

Galbraith, J. 1973. *Designing complex organizations*. Reading, Mass.: Addison-Wesley.

Galbraith, J. R., and Kazanjian, R. K. 1986. *Strategy implementation: Structure, systems and processes*. St. Paul: West Publishing.

Galen, M. 1989. A seat on the board is getting hotter. *Business Week* 3 July: 72–73.

Gamson, W. A., and Scotch, N. A. 1964. Scapegoating in baseball. *American Journal of Sociology* 70: 69–72.

Gaver, J. J., Gaver, K. M., and Battistel, G. P. 1992. The stock market reaction to performance plan adoptions. *The Accounting Review* 67 (1): 172–82.

Geletkanycz, M. 1994. The external networks of senior executives: Implications for strategic innovation and imitation. Unpublished Ph.D. dissertation, Columbia University.

Gersick, C., and Hackman, R. 1990. Habitual routines in task-performing groups. *Organization Behavior and Human Decision Processes* 47: 65–97.

Gibbons, R., and Murphy, K. 1992. Optimal incentive contracts in the presence of career concerns: Theory and evidence. *Journal of Political Economy* 100: 468–505.

Gilson, S. 1990. Bankruptcy, boards, and blockholders: Evidence on changes in corporate ownership and control when firms default. *Journal of Financial Economics.* 27: 355–87.

Gilson S., and Kraakman L. 1991. Reinventing the outside director: An agenda for institutional investors. *Stanford Law Review* 43: 863–80.

Gilson, S. C., and Vetsuypens, M. R. 1992. CEO compensation in financially distressed firms. Working paper, Harvard Business School.

Gladstein, D. 1984. Groups in context: A model of task group effectiveness. *Administrative Science Quarterly* 29: 499–517.

Glick, W. H., Miller, C. C., and Huber, G. P. 1993. Upper-level diversity in organizations: Demographic, structural, and cognitive influences on organizational effectiveness. In *Organizational change and redesign: Ideas and insights for improving performance*, ed. G. P. Huber and W. H. Glick. New York: Oxford.

Gomez-Mejia, L., Tosi, H., and Hinkin, T. 1987. Managerial control, performance, and executive compensation. *Academy of Management Journal* 30: 51–70.

Goodman, P. S. 1974. An examination of referents used in the evaluation of pay. *Organizational Behavior and Human Performance* 12: 170–95.

Goodman, R. S. 1988. The determinants of banks' success and failure in a changing regulatory environment: Substantive, methodological, and statistical implications for corporate strategy. Unpublished Ph.D. dissertation, University of Minnesota.

Goodstein, J., Gautam, K., and Boeker, W., 1994. The effects of board size and diversity on strategic change. *Strategic Management Journal* 15: 241–50.

Gordon, G. W., and Rosen, N. A. 1981. Critical factors in leadership succession. *Organizational Behavior and Human Performance* 27: 227–54.

Gouldner, A. W. 1954. *Patterns of industrial bureaucracy.* Glencoe, Ill.: Free Press.

Govindarajan, V., and Fisher, J. 1990. Strategy, control systems, and resource sharing: Effects on business-unit performance, *Academy of Management Journal* 33: 259–85.

Granovetter, M. 1985. Economic action and social structure: The problem of embeddedness. *American Journal of Sociology* 91: 481–510.

Greenberg, J. 1982. Approaching equity and avoiding inequity in groups and organizations. In *Equity and justice in social behavior*, ed. J. Greenberg and R. L. Cohen. 389–435. New York: Academic Press.

Greenberg, J. 1987. A taxonomy of organizational justice theories. *Academy of Management Review* 12: 9–22.

Greiner, L. E., and Bhambri, A. 1989. New CEO intervention and dynamics of deliberate change. *Strategic Management Journal* 10(Summer): 67–86.

Grimm, C. M., and Smith, K. G. 1991. Management and organizational change: A note on the railroad industry. *Strategic Management Journal* 12: 557–62.

Grinyer, P. H., and Norburn, D. 1975. Planning for existing markets: Perceptions of executives and financial performance. *Journal of the Royal Statistical Society* 138: 70–97.

Gripsrud, G., and Gronhaug, K. 1985. Strategy and structure in grocery retailing: A sociometric approach. *Journal of Industrial Economics* 33: 339–47.

Grusky, O. 1960. Administrative succession in formal organizations. *Social Forces* 39: 105–15.

Grusky, O. 1961. Corporate size, bureaucratization, and managerial succession. *American Journal of Sociology* 67: 261–69.

Grusky, O. 1963. Managerial succession and organizational effectiveness. *American Journal of Sociology* 69: 21–31.

Grusky, O. 1964. Reply to scapegoating in baseball. *American Journal of Sociology* 70: 72–76.

Guest, R. 1962. Managerial succession in complex organizations. *American Journal of Sociology* 68:47–56.

Gupta, A. K. 1984. Contingency linkages between strategy and general manager characteristics: A conceptual examination. *Academy of Management Review* 9: 399–412.

Gupta, A. 1986. Matching managers to strategies: Point and counterpoint. *Human Resource Management* 25: 215–35.

Gupta, A. 1988. Contingency perspectives on strategic leadership: Current knowledge and future research directions. In *The executive effect: Concepts and methods for studying top managers*, ed. D. C. Hambrick. 141–78. Greenwich, Conn.: JAI Press.

Gupta, A. K., and Govindarajan, V. 1984. Business unit strategy, managerial characteristics, and business unit effectiveness at strategy implementation. *Academy of Management Journal* 27: 25–41.

Guth, W. D. and MacMillan, I. C. 1986. Strategy implementation versus middle management self-interest. *Strategic Management Journal* 7: 313–27.

Guth, W. D., and Taguiri, R. 1965. Personal values and corporate strategy. *Harvard Business Review* 43 (5): 123–32.

Hackman, J. R. 1976. Group influences on individuals. In *Handbook of industrial and organizational psychology*, ed. M. Dunnette. 1455–1525. Chicago: Rand McNally.

Hackman, J. R. 1986. The psychology of self-management in organizations. In *Psychology and Work: Productivity, change, and employment,* ed. M. S. Pallak and R. O. Perloff. Washington, D.C.: American Psychological Association.

Hage, J., and Aiken, M. 1969. Routine technology, social structure, and organizational goals. *Administrative Science Quarterly* 14: 366–76.

Hage, J., and Dewar, R. 1973. Elite values versus organizational struture in predicting innovations. *Administrative Science Quarterly* 18: 279–90.

Haleblian, J., and Finkelstein, S. 1993. Top management team size, CEO dominance, and firm performance: The moderating roles of environmental turbulence and discretion. *Academy of Management Journal* 36: 844–63

Hall, R. I. 1976. A system pathology of an organization: The rise and fall of the old *Saturday Evening Post. Administrative Science Quarterly* 21: 185–211.

Hambrick, D. C. 1981a. Specialization of environmental scanning activities among upper-level executives. *Journal of Management Studies* 18: 299–320.

Hambrick, D. C. 1981b. Environment, strategy, and power within top management teams. *Administrative Science Quarterly* 26: 253–76.

Hambrick, D. C. 1982. Environmental scanning and organizational strategy. *Strategic Management Journal* 3: 159–74.

Hambrick, D. C. 1984. Taxonomic approaches to studying strategy: Some conceptual and methodological issues. *Journal of Management* 10(1): 29–41.

Hambrick, D. C. 1986. Research in strategic management, 1980–1985: Critical perceptions and reality. Paper presented at the annual meeting of the Academy of Management, Chicago.

Hambrick, D. C. 1987. Top management teams: Key to strategic success. *California Management Review* 30: 88–108.

Hambrick, D. C. 1989. Guest editor's introduction: Putting top managers back in the strategy picture. *Strategic Management Journal* 10 (Special Issue): 5–15.

Hambrick, D. C. 1994. Top management groups: A conceptual integration and reconsideration of the "team" label. In *Research in organizational behavior*, ed. B. M. Staw and L. L. Cummings. Greenwich, Conn. JAI Press. 171–214.

Hambrick, D. C. 1995. Fragmentation and the other problems CEOs have with their top management teams. *California Management Review* 37: 110–27.

Hambrick, D. C., and Abrahamson, E. (1995). Assessing the amount of managerial discretion in different industries: A multimethod approach. *Academy of Management Journal* 38: 1427–1441.

Hambrick, D. C., Black, S., and Fredrickson, J. W. 1992. Executive leadership of the high-technology firm: What is special about it? In *Advances in global high-technology management*, ed. L. R. Gomez-Mejia and M. W. Lawless. Greenwich, Conn.: JAI Press. 3–18.

Hambrick, D. C., and Brandon, G. 1988. Executive values. In *The executive effect: Concepts and methods for studying top managers*, ed. D. C. Hambrick. 3–34. Greenwich, Conn.: JAI Press.

Hambrick, D. C., and Cannella, Jr., A. A. 1993. Relative standing: A framework for understanding departures of acquired executives. *Academy of Management Journal* 36: 733–62.

Hambrick, D. C., and D'Aveni, R. A. 1992. Top team deterioration as part of the downward spiral of large corporate bankruptcies. *Management Science* 38: 1445–66.

Hambrick, D. C., and Finkelstein, S. 1987. Managerial discretion: A bridge between polar views of organizations. In *Research in organizational behavior*, ed. L. L. Cummings and B. M. Staw. vol. 9, 369–406. Greenwich, Conn: JAI Press.

Hambrick, D. C., and Finkelstein, S. 1995. The effects of ownership structure on conditions at the top: The case of CEO pay raises. *Strategic Management Journal* 16: 175–194.

Hambrick, D. C., and Fukutomi, G. D. 1991. The seasons of a CEO's tenure. *Academy of Management Review* 16: 719–42.

Hambrick, D. C., Geletkanycz, M. A., and Fredrickson, J. W. 1993. Top executive commitment to the status quo: Some tests of its determinants. *Strategic Management Journal* 14: 401–18.

Hambrick, D. C., and Mason, P. 1984. Upper echelons: The organization as a reflection of its top managers. *Academy of Management Review* 9: 193–206.

Hambrick, D. C., and Snow, C. C. 1989. Strategic reward systems. In *Strategy, organization design and human resource management*, ed. C. C. Snow. 333–68. Greenwich, Conn. JAI Press.

Hannan, M., and Freeman, J. 1977. The population ecology of organizations. *American Journal of Sociology* 82: 929–64.

Harder, J. W. 1992. Play for pay: Effects of inequity in a pay-for-performance context. *Administrative Science Quarterly* 37: 321–35.

Harris, D. 1986. Executive succession, reputation, and wage revision. Unpublished Ph.D. dissertation, Kellogg Graduate School of Management, Northwestern University, Evanston, Ill.

Harris, D., and Helfat, C. 1995. How much do boards of directors pay for CEO skills? Working paper, Wharton School of Business, University of Pennsylvania.

Harris, M., and Raviv, A. 1979. Optimal incentive contracts with imperfect information. *Journal of Economic Theory* 63: 231–59.

Harris, R. G. 1979. *The potential effects of deregulation upon corporate structure, merger behavior, and organizational relations in the rail freight industry*. Washington, D.C.: Public Interest Economics Center.

Harrison, E. F. 1975. *The managerial decision-making process*. Boston: Houghton Mifflin.

Harrison, J. R., Torres, D. L., and Kukalis, S. 1988. The changing of the guard: Turnover and structural change in the top management positions. *Administrative Science Quarterly* 33: 211–32.

Haspeslagh, P. C., and Jemison, D. B. 1991. The challenge of renewal through acquisitions. *Planning Review* 19: 27–32.

Haunschild, P. 1993. Interorganizational imitation: The impact of interlocks on corporate acquisition activity. *Administrative Science Quarterly* 38: 564–92.

Haunschild, P. R. 1994. How much is that company worth? Interorganizational relationships, uncertainty, and acquisition premiums. *Administrative Science Quarterly* 39: 391–411.

Haveman, H. 1993. Ghosts of managers past: Managerial succession and organizational mortality. *Academy of Management Journal* 36: 864–81.

Hayes, R. H., and Abernathy, W. J. 1980. Managing our way to economic decline. *Harvard Business Review* 58 (July-August): 67–77.

Hayes, R. H., and Hoag, G. H. 1974. Post-acquisition retention of top management. *Mergers and Acquisitions* 9(2): 8–18.

Healey, P. M. 1985. The effect of bonus schemes on accounting decisions. *Journal of Accounting and Economics* 7: 85–107.

Helmich, D. L. 1980. Board size variations and rates of success in the corporate presidency. *Journal of Business Research* 8: 51–63.

Helmich, D. L., and Brown, W. B. 1972. Successor type and organizational change in the corporate enterprise. *Administrative Science Quarterly* 17: 371–78.

Hempel, C. G. 1966. *Philosophy of natural science*. Englewood Cliffs, N.J.: Prentice-Hall.

Henderson, A. D., and Fredrickson, J. W. 1993. Managerial complexity of a determinant of CEO compensation. Working paper, University of Texas, Austin.

Hermalin, B. E. and Weisbach, M. S. 1988. The determinants of board composition. *Rand Journal of Economics* 19: 589–606.

Hermalin B. E. and Weisbach, M. S. 1991. The effects of board composition and direct incentives on firm performance. *Financial Management* 20(4): 101–12.

Herman, E. S. 1981. *Corporate control, corporate power*. Cambridge: Cambridge University Press.

Hicks, J. 1963. *The theory of wages*. New York: St. Martin's Press.

Hickson, D. J., Pugh, D. S., and Pheysey, D. 1969. Operations technology and organization structure: An empirical reappraisal. *Administrative Science Quarterly* 14: 378–97.

Hill, C. W. L., Hitt, M. A., and Hoskisson, R. E. 1988. Declining U. S. competitiveness: Reflections on a crisis. *Academy of Management Executive* 2: 51–60.

Hill, C. W. L., and Phan, P. 1991. CEO tenure as a determinant of CEO pay. *Academy of Management Journal* 34: 707–17.

Hill, C. W. L., and Snell, S. A. 1988. External control, corporate strategy, and firm performance in research-intensive industries. *Strategic Management Journal* 9: 577–90.

Hinings, C. R., Hickson, D. J., Pennings, J. M., and Schneck, R. E. 1974 Structural conditions of intraorganizational power. *Administrative Science Quarterly* 189: 22–44.

Hirsch, B. T. 1982. The interindustry structure of unionism, earnings, and earnings dispersion. *Industrial and Labor Relations Review* 36 (1): 22–39.

Hirsch, P. M. 1986. From ambushes to golden parachutes: Corporate takeovers as an instance of cultural framing and institutional integration. *American Journal of Sociology* 91: 800–37.

Hite, G. L., and Long, M. S. 1982. Taxes and executive stock options. *Journal of Accounting and Economics* 4: 3–14.

Hitt, M. A., and Tyler, B. B. 1991. Strategic decision models: Integrating different perspectives. *Strategic Management Journal* 12: 327–51.

Hodgkinson, G. F. 1992. Development and validation of the strategic locus of control scale. *Strategic Management Journal* 13(4): 311–17.

Hodgkinson, G. F. 1993. Doubts about the conceptual and empirical status of context-free and firm-specific control expectancies: A reply to Boone and De Brabander. *Strategic Management Journal* 14(8): 627–31.

Hofer, C. W. 1975. Toward a contingency theory of business strategy. *Academy of Management Journal* 18: 784–810.

Hofer, C. W. 1980. Turnaround strategies: An examination. *Journal of Business Strategy* 1: 19–31.

Hofer, C. W. and Schendel, D. 1978. *Strategy formulation: Analytical concepts*. St. Paul: West Publishing.

Hoffman, L. R. 1959. Homogeneity of member personality and its effect on group problem solving. *Journal of Abnormal and Social Psychology* 58: 227–32

Hoffman, L. R. and Maier, N. 1961. Quality and acceptance of problem solutions by members of homogeneous and heterogeneous groups. *Journal of Abnormal and Social Psychology* 2: 401–07.

Hofstede, G. 1980. *Culture's consequences: International differences in work-related values.* Beverly Hills and London: Sage Publications.

Hogan, T., and McPheters, L. 1980. Executive compensation: Performance versus personal characteristics. *Southern Economic Journal* 46: 1060–68.

Holderness, C. G., and Sheehan, D. P. 1988. The role of majority shareholders in publicly held corporations. *Journal of Financial Economics* 20: 317–46.

Holmstrom, B. 1979. Moral hazard and observability. *Bell Journal of Economics* 10: 74–91.

Holmstrom, B. 1982. Managerial incentive problems—a dynamic perspective. In *Essays in Economics and Management in Honor of Lars Wahlbeck.* 209–30. Helsinki: Swedish School of Economics.

Holmstrom, B. 1987. Incentive compensation: Practical design from a theory point of view. In *Incentives, cooperation, and risk sharing: Economic and psychological perspectives on employment contracts*, ed. Haig R. Nalbantian. 176–85. Totoya, N.J.: Rowman and Littlefield.

Holmstrom, B., and Milgrom, P. 1990. Regulating trade among agents. *Journal of Institutional and Theoretical Economics* 146 (1): 85–105.

Homans, G. C. 1961. *Social behavior: Its elementary forms.* New York: Harcourt Brace Jovanovich.

Hoskisson, R. E., and Hitt, M A. 1988. Strategic control systems and relative R&D intensity in large multiproduct firms. *Strategic Management Journal* 9: 605–22.

Hoskisson, R. E., and Hitt, M. A. 1994. *Downscoping: How to tame the diversified firm.* New York: Oxford University Press.

Hoskisson, R. E., Hitt, M. A., and Hill, C. W. L. 1993. Managerial incentives and investment in R&D in large multiproduct firms. *Organization Science* 4: 325–41.

Hoskisson, R. E., Johnson, R. A., and Moesel, D. D. 1994. Corporate divestiture intensity in restructuring firms: Effects of governance, strategy, and performance. *Academy of Management Journal* 37: 1207–51.

Hoskisson, R. E., Hitt, M. A., Turk, T. A., and Tyler, B. B. 1989. Balancing corporate strategy and executive compensation: Agency theory and corporate governance. In *Research in personnel and human resources management*, ed. G. R. Ferris, and K. M. Roland. vol. 7: 25–58, Greenwich, Conn.: JAI Press.

House, R. J. 1977. A 1976 theory of charismatic leadership. In *Leadership: The cutting edge*, ed. J. G. Hunt and L. L. Larson. 189–207. Carbondale, Ill.: Southern Illinois University Press.

House, R. J., Spangler, W. D., and Woycke, J. 1991. Personality and charisma in the U. S. presidency: A psychological theory of leader effectiveness. *Administrative Science Quarterly* 36: 364–96.

Howard, A., Shudo, K., and Umeshima, M. 1983. Motivation and values among Japanese and American managers. *Personnel Psychology* 36: 883–98.

Huff, A. S. 1982. Industry influences on strategy reformulation. *Strategic Management Journal* 3: 119–31.

Huff, A. S., ed. 1990. *Mapping strategic thought.* Chichester, England: John Wiley.

Hurst, D. K., Rush, J. C., and White, R. E. 1989. Top management teams and organizational renewal. *Strategic Management Journal* 10 (Special Issue): 87–105.

Iacocca, L. 1984. *Iacocca: An autobiography*. New York: Bantam.

Isabella, L. A. and Waddock, S. A. 1994. Top management team certainty: Environmental assessments, teamwork, and performance implications. *Journal of Management* 20: 835–58.

Isenberg, D. J. 1981. Some effects of time-pressure on vertical structure and decision-making accuracy in small groups. *Organizational Behavior and Human Performance* 27(1): 119–34.

Isenberg, D. J. 1984. Managers' knowledge structures. Working paper, Harvard Business School.

Jackson, S. E. 1992. Consequence of group composition for the interpersonal dynamics of strategic issue processing. In *Advances in strategic management*, ed. P. Shrivastava, A. Huff, and J. Dutton. vol. 8, 345–82. Greenwich, Conn.: JAI Press.

Jackson, S. E., Brett, J. F., Sessa, F. I., Cooper, D. M., Julin, J. A., and Peyronnin, K. 1991. Some differences make a difference: Individual dissimilarity and group heterogeneity as correlates of recruitment, promotions, and turnover. *Journal of Applied Psychology* 76: 675–89.

Jacob, P. E., Flink, J. J., and Shuchman, H. L. 1962. Values and their function in decision-making. *American Behavioral Scientist* 9 (Supplement 9): 6–38.

Jacobs, M. T. 1991. *Short-term America: The causes and cures of our business myopia*. Boston: Harvard Business School Press.

James, D. R., and Soref, M. 1981. Profit constraints in managerial autonomy: Managerial theory and the unmaking of the corporation president. *American Sociological Review* 46: 1–18.

Janis, I. L. 1972. *Victims of groupthink: A psychological study of foreign policy decisions and fiascoes*. Boston: Houghton Mifflin.

Jensen, M. C. 1984. Takeovers: Folklore and science. *Harvard Business Review* 62(6): 109–21.

Jensen, M. C. 1986. Agency costs of free cash flow, corporate finance and takeovers. *American Economic Review* 76: 323–29.

Jensen, M. C. 1989. Eclipse of the public corporation. *Harvard Business Review* 67: 61–74.

Jensen, M. C., and Meckling, W. 1976. Theory of the firm: Managerial behavior, agency costs, and ownership structure. *Journal of Financial Economics* 3: 305–60.

Jensen, M. C., and Murphy, K. J. 1990. Performance pay and top management incentives. *Journal of Political Economy* 98: 225–64.

Jensen, M. C., and Ruback, R. 1983. The market for corporate control: The scientific evidence. *Journal of Financial Economics* 11: 5–50.

Jensen, M. C., and Zimmerman, J. L. 1985. Management compensation and the managerial labor market. *Journal of Financial Economics* 7: 3–9.

Johnson, R. A., Hoskisson, R. E., and Hitt, M. A. 1993. Board of director involvement in restructuring: The effects of board versus managerial controls and characteristics. *Strategic Management Journal* 14 (Special Summer Issue): 33–50.

Johnson, W., Magee, R., Nagarajan, N., and Newman, H. 1985. An analysis of the stock price reaction to sudden executive deaths. *Journal of Accounting and Economics* 7: 151–78.

Joskow, P., Rose, N., and Shepard, A. 1993. *Regulatory constraints on CEO compensation.* Washington, DC: National Bureau of Economic Research.

Judge, W. Q. and Zeithaml, C. P. 1992. Institutional and strategic choice perspectives on board involvement in the strategic decision process. *Academy of Management Journal* 35 (4): 766-794.

Kanter, R. M. 1977. *Men and women of the corporation.* New York: Basic Books.

Kao, J. 1985. Lou Gerstner. Boston: Harvard Business School Case Services.

Kaplan, S. N., and Rishus, D. 1990. Outside directorships and corporate performance. *Journal of Financial Economics* 27: 389–410.

Katz, R. 1982. The effects of group longevity on project communication and performance. *Administrative Science Quarterly* 27: 81–104.

Keats, B. W. and Hitt, M. A. 1988. A causal model of linkages among environmental dimensions, macro organizational characteristics, and performance. *Academy of Management Journal* 31: 570–98.

Keck, S. L., and Tushman, M. L. 1993. Environmental and organizational context and executive team structure. *Academy of Management Journal* 36: 1314–44.

Keck, S. L. 1990. Determinants and consequences of top executive team structure. Unpublished Ph.D. dissertation, Columbia University, New York.

Kefalas, A., and Schoderbeck, P. 1973. Scanning the business environment: Some empirical results. *Decision Sciences* 4: 63–74.

Keirsey, D. W. and Bates, M. 1978. *Please understand me.* Del Mar, Calif.: Prometheus.

Kerr, J. 1985. Diversification strategies and managerial rewards: An empirical study. *Academy of Management Journal* 28: 155–79.

Kerr, J., and Bettis, R. A. 1987. Boards of directors, top management compensation, and shareholder returns. *Academy of Management Journal* 30: 645–64.

Kerr, J., and Kren, L. 1992. Effect of relative decision monitoring on chief executive compensation. *Academy of Management Journal* 35: 370–97.

Kerr, J., and Slocum, J. W. 1987. Managing corporate cultures through reward systems. *Academy of Management Executive* 1: 99–107.

Kesner, I. F. 1987. Directors' stock ownership and organizational performance: An investigation of Fortune 500 companies. *Journal of Management* 13: 499–508.

Kesner, I. F., and Dalton, D. R. 1994. Top management turnover and CEO succession: An investigation of the effects of turnover on performance. *Journal of Management Studies* 31: 701–13.

Kesner, I. F., and Sebora, T. C. 1994. Executive succession: Past, present and future. *Journal of Management* (Special Issue): 327–72.

Kets de Vries, M. F. R. 1994. The leadership mystique. *Academy of Management Executive* 8(3): 73–92.

Kets de Vries, M. F. R., and Miller, D., 1984. Neurotic style and organizational pathology. *Strategic Management Journal* 5: 35–55.

Khandwalla, P. N. 1977. *The design of organizations.* New York: Harcourt Brace Jovanovich.

Kiesler, S. B., and Sproull, L. 1982. Managerial response to changing environments: Perspectives on problem sensing from social cognition. *Administrative Science Quarterly* 27: 548–70.

Kim, W. S., Lee, L. W., and Francis, J. C. 1988. Investment performance of common stocks in relation to insider ownership. *Financial Review,* 23(1): 53–64.

Kimberly, J. R., and Evanisko, M. J. 1981. Organizational innovation: The influence of individual, organizational, and contextual factors on hospital adoption of technological and administrative innovations. *Academy of Management Journal* 24(4): 689–713.

Kluckhohn, C., 1951. Values and value-orientations in theory of action: An exploration of definition and classification. In *Toward a general theory of action,* ed. T. Parsons and E. A. Shils. 388–433. Cambridge: Harvard University Press.

Koenig, T., Gogel, R. and Sonquist, J. 1979. Models of the significance of interlocking corporate directorates. *American Journal of Economics and Sociology* 38: 173–86.

Korn/Ferry International and Columbia University, 1989. *Reinventing the CEO: 21st century report.* New York.

Korsgaard, M. A., Schweiger, D. M., and Sapienza, H. J. 1995. Building commitment, attachment, and trust in strategic decision-making teams: The role of procedural justice. *Academy of Management Journal* 38: 60–84.

Kosnik, R. D. 1987. Greenmail: a study of board performance in corporate governance. *Administrative Science Quarterly* 32: 163–85.

Kosnik, R. D. 1990. Effects of board demography and directors' incentive on corporate greenmail decisions. *Academy of Management Journal* 33: 129–50.

Kotter, J. P. 1982. *The general managers.* New York: Free Press.

Kotter, J. P. 1988. *The leadership factor.* New York: Free Press.

Kraus, D. 1976. The "devaluation" of the American executive. *Harvard Business Review* 54 (3): 84–94.

Krueger, H. W. 1985. Opportunities and pitfalls in designing executive compensation: The effects of the golden parachute tax penalties. *Taxes* 63: 846–61.

Lambert, R. A., and Larcker, D. F. 1984. Stock options and managerial incentives. Working paper, Northwestern University, J. L. Kellog Graduate School of Management.

Lambert, R. A., and Larcker, D. F. 1985. Executive compensation, corporate decision-making, and shareholder wealth: A review of the evidence. *Midland Corporate Finance Journal* 2: 6–22

Lambert, R. 1986. Executive effort and selection of risky projects. *Rand Journal of Economics* 17: 77–88.

Lambert, R. A., and Larcker, D. F. 1987. An analysis of the use of accounting and market measures of performance in executive compensation contracts. *Journal of Accounting Research* 25: 85–125.

Lambert, R. A., Larcker, D. F., and Verrecchia, R. E. 1991. Portfolio considerations in the valuation of executive compensation. *Journal of Accounting Research* 29: 129–49.

Lambert, R. A., Larcker, D. F., and Weigelt, K. 1991. How sensitive is executive compensation to organizational size? *Strategic Management Journal* 12: 395–402.

Lambert, R. A., Larcker, D. F., and Weigelt, K. 1993. The structure of organizational incentives. *Administrative Science Quarterly* 38: 438–61.

Larcker, D. F. 1983. The association between performance plan adoption and corporate capital investment. *Journal of Accounting and Economics* 5: 9–30.

Larcker, D. F. 1984. Short-term compensation contracts, executive expenditure decisions, and corporate performance: The case of commercial banks. Working paper, Northwestern University, J. L. Kellogg Graduate School of Management, Evanston, Ill.

Lawler, E. E., III. 1966. The mythology of management compensation. *California Management Review* 9 (1): 11–22.

Lawler, E. E., III. 1971. *Pay and organizational effectiveness: A psychological view.* New York: McGraw-Hill.

Lawler, E. E., III., and Jenkins, G. D. 1992. Strategic reward systems. In *The handbook of industrial and organizational psychology*, ed. M. Dunnette. 2d ed. 1009–55. Palo Alto, Calif.: Consulting Psychologists Press.

Lawrence, B. S. 1991. The black box of organizational demography. Unpublished working paper, University of California, Los Angeles.

Lawrence, P. R. and Lorsch, J. W. 1967. *Organization and environment.* Boston: Graduate School of Business Administration, Harvard University.

Lazear, E. P. 1989. Pay equality and industrial politics. *Journal of Political Economy* 97: 561–80.

Lazear, E. P. 1991. Labor economics and the psychology of organizations. *Journal of Economic Perspectives* 5(Spring): 89–110.

Lazear, E. P., and Rosen, S. 1981. Rank-order tournaments as optimum labor contracts. *Journal of Political Economy* 89: 841–64.

Learned, E. P., Christensen, C. R., and Andrews, K. R. 1961. *Problems of general management-business policy.* Homewood, Ill.: Irwin.

Lee, R. 1975. The relationship between managerial values and managerial behavior: A cross-cultural, cross-validation study. Unpublished Ph.D. dissertation, University of Minnesota.

Lenski, G. E. 1966. *Power and privilege.* New York: McGraw Hill.

Leonard, J. S. 1990. Executive pay and firm performance. *Industrial and Labor Relations Review* 43: 13S–29S.

Leontiades, M. 1982. Choosing the right manager to fit the strategy. *Journal of Business Strategy* 3(2): 58–69.

Leontiades, M., and Tezel, A. 1981. Some connections between corporate-level planning and diversity. *Strategic Management Journal* 2: 413–18.

Leventhal, G. S. 1976. The distribution of rewards and resources in groups and organizations. In *Advances in experimental social psychology*, ed. L. Berkowitz. vol. 9, 91–131. New York: Academic Press.

Leventhal, G. S., Michaels, J. W., and Sanford, C. 1972. Inequity and interpersonal conflict: Reward allocation and secrecy about reward as methods of preventing conflict. *Journal of Personality and Social Psychology* 23: 88–102.

Levinson, B. 1974. Don't choose your own successor. *Harvard Business Review* 52: 53–62.

Lewellen, W. G., and Huntsman, B. 1970. Managerial pay and corporate performance. *American Economic Review* 60: 710–20.

Lewin, K. 1936. *A dynamic theory of personality*. New York: McGraw-Hill.

Lieberson, S., and O'Connor, J. F. 1972. Leadership and organizational performance: A study of large corporations. *American Sociological Review* 37: 117–30.

Lloyd, W. P., Jahera, Jr., J. S., and Goldstein, S. J. 1986. The relationship between returns, ownership structure, and market value. *Journal of Financial Research,* 9(2): 1986, 171–77.

Lohr, S. 1994. On the road with chairman Lou. *New York Times* 2 June, Section 3:1.

Lorsch, J. 1989. *Pawns or potentates: The reality of America's boards*. Boston: Harvard Business School Press.

Lorsch, J. W., and Allen, S. A. 1973. *Managing diversity and interdependence*. Boston: Division of Research, Harvard Business School.

Lott, B. E., and Lott, A. J. 1965. Group cohesiveness and interpersonal attraction: A review of relationships with antecedent and consequent variables. *Psychological Bulletin* 4: 259–309.

Louis, M. R., Posner, B. Z., and Powell, G. N. 1983. The availability and helpfulness of socialization practices. *Personnel Psychology* 36: 857–66.

Lubatkin, M., Chung, K., Rogers, R., and Owers, J. 1989. Stockholder reactions to CEO changes in large organizations. *Academy of Management Journal* 32: 47–68.

MacAvoy, P. W., Cantor, S., Dana, J., and Peck, S. 1983. ALI proposals for increased control of the corporation by the board of directors: An economic analysis. In *Statement of the Business Roundtable on the American Law Institute's proposed principles of corporate governance and structure: Restatement and recommendations*. New York: Business Roundtable.

Mace, M. L. 1971. *Directors: Myth and reality*. Boston: Harvard University Press.

MacMillan, I. C. 1991. The emerging forum for business policy scholars. *Strategic Management Journal* 12, 161–65.

Magnet, M. 1993. What activist investors want. *Fortune* May: 59–63.

Mahoney, Thomas A. 1964. Compensation preferences of managers. *Industrial Relations* 3: 135–144.

Maier, N. R. F. 1970. *Problem solving and creativity in individuals and groups*. Belmont, Calif.: Brooks/Cole.

Main, B., O'Reilly, C., and Wade, J. 1993. Top executive pay: tournament or teamwork? *Journal of Labor Economics* 11: 606–28.

Main, B. O'Reilly, C., and Wade, J. 1994. The CEO, the board of directors and executive compensation: Economic and psychological perspectives. Unpublished manuscript, Stanford University, Stanford, Calif.

Mallette, P., and Fowler, K. L. 1992. Effects of board composition and stock owner-ship on the adoption of poison pills. *Academy of Management Journal* 35: 1010–35.

March, J. G. 1966. The power of power. In *Varieties of political theory*, ed. D. Easton. 39–70. Englewood Cliffs, N.J.: Prentice-Hall.

March, J. G. 1984. Notes on ambiguity and executive compensation. *Scandinavian Journal of Management Studies* August: 53–64.

March, J. C., and March, J. G. 1977. Almost random careers—the Wisconsin school superintendency, 1940–1972. *Administrative Science Quarterly* 22(3): 377–409.

March, J. G., and Simon, H. A. 1958. *Organizations*. New York: Wiley.

Marcus, A. A., and Goodman, R. S. 1986. Airline deregulation: Factors affecting the choice of firm political strategy. *Policy Studies Journal* 15(2): 231–46.

Mariolis, P., and Jones, M. H., 1982. Centrality in corporate interlock networks: Reliability and stability. *Administrative Science Quarterly* 27: 571–84.

Marris, R. 1964. *Managerial capitalism*. New York: Free Press.

Martin, J. 1981. Relative deprivation: A theory of distributive injustice for an era of shrinking resources. In *Research in organizational behavior*, ed. L. L. Cummings, and B. M. Staw. vol. 3, 53–107. Greenwich, Conn.: JAI Press.

Maruyama, M. 1982. Mindscapes, management, business policy, and public policy. *Academy of Management Review* 7: 612–17.

Mason, R., and Mitroff, I. 1981. *Challenging strategic planning assumptions*. New York: Wiley.

Mathews, J. 1993. Kodak ousts chairman, a company veteran. *Washington Post*, 7 August, B1.

McCain, B., O'Reilly, C. A., and Pfeffer, J. 1983. The effects of departmental demography on turnover. *Administrative Science Quarterly* 26: 626–41.

McCall, M. W., and Segrist, C. A. 1980. In pursuit of the manager's job: Building on Mintzberg. Technical Report 14. Greensboro, N.C.: Center for Creative Leadership.

McClelland, D. C. 1972. The role of money in managing motivation. In *Managerial motivation and compensation*, ed. H. K. Tosi, R. J. House, and M. D. Dunnette. 523–39. East Lansing: Michigan State University.

McClelland, D. C. 1975. Power: The inner experience. New York: Irving Press.

McClelland, D. C., and Boyatzis, R. E. 1982. Leadership motive pattern and long-term success in management. *Journal of Applied Psychology* 67: 737–43.

McEachern, W. 1975. *Managerial control and performance*. Lexington, Mass.: Lexington Books.

McGrath, J. E. 1984. *Groups: Interaction and performance*. Englewood Cliffs, N.J.: Prentice-Hall.

McGuire, J. W., Chiu, J. S. Y., and Elbing, A. D. 1975. Executive incomes, sales and profits. *American Economic Review* 52: 753–61.

Meeks, G., and Whittington, G. 1975. Directors' pay, growth, and profitability. *Journal of Industrial Economics* (September): 1–14.

Meindl, J. R., Ehrlich, S. B., and Dukerich, J. M. 1985. The romance of leadership. *Administrative Science Quarterly* 30: 521–51.

Merchant, K. A. 1989. *Rewarding results: Motivating profit center managers*. Boston: Harvard University Business School Press.

Merton, R. K. 1968. *Social theory and social structure*. New York: Free Press.

Meyer, A. D., and Starbuck, W. H. 1992. Interactions between ideologies and politics in strategy formation. In *New challenges to understanding organizations: high reliability organizations*, ed. K. Roberts. New York: MacMillan, 203–223.

Micelli, M. P., and Near, J. P. 1994. Whistleblowing: Reaping the benefits. *Academy of Management Executive* 8(3): 65–72.

Michel, J. G., and Hambrick, D. C. 1992. Diversification posture and top management team characteristics. *Academy of Management Journal* 35: 9–37.

Miles, R. E., and Snow, C. C. 1978. *Organizational strategy, structure, and process*. New York: McGraw-Hill.

Miles, R. H. 1982. *Coffin nails and corporate strategies*. Englewood Cliffs, N.J.: Prentice-Hall.

Miller, D. 1987. The genesis of configuration. *Academy of Management Review* 12: 686–702.

Miller, D. 1991. Stale in the saddle: CEO tenure and the match between organization and environment. *Management Science* 37: 34–52.

Miller, D. 1993. Some organizational consequences of CEO succession. *Academy of Management Journal* 36: 644–59.

Miller, D., and Droge, C. 1986. Psychological and traditional determinants of structure. *Administrative Science Quarterly* 31: 539–60.

Miller, D., Droge, C., and Toulouse, J. M. 1988. Strategic process and content as mediators between organizational context and structure. *Academy of Management Journal* 31: 544–69.

Miller, D., Kets de Vries, M. F. R., and Toulouse, J. 1982. Top executive locus of control and its relationship to strategy-making, structure, and environment. *Academy of Management Journal* 4: 221–35.

Miller, D., and Toulouse, J. M. 1986a. Chief executive personality and corporate strategy in small firms. *Management Science* 32: 1389–1409.

Miller, D., and Toulouse, J. M. 1986b. Strategy, structure, CEO personality, and performance in small firms. *American Journal of Small Business* 10(3): 47–62.

Miller, L., and Hamblin, R. 1963. Interdependence, differential rewarding, and productivity. *American Sociological Review* 28: 768–78.

Milliken, F. 1990. Perceiving and interpreting environmental change: An examination of college administrators' interpretation of changing demographics. *Academy of Management Journal* 33: 42–63.

Mintz, B., and Schwartz, M. 1981. The structure of intercorporate unity in American business. *Social Problems* 29: 87–103.

Mintzberg, H. 1973. *The nature of managerial work*. New York: Harper and Row.

Mintzberg, H. 1976. Planning on the left side and managing on the right. *Harvard Business Review* 54(4): 49–58.

Mintzberg, H. 1978. Patterns in strategy formation. *Management Science* 24: 934–48.

Mintzberg, H. 1979. *The structuring of organizations.* Englewood Cliffs, N.J.: Prentice-Hall.

Mintzberg, H. 1983. *Power in and around Organizations.* Englewood Cliffs, N.J.: Prentice-Hall.

Mintzberg, H. 1985. Strategy formation in an adhocracy. *Administrative Science Quarterly* 30: 160–97.

Mintzberg, H., Raisinghani, D., and Theoret, A. 1976. The structure of unstructured decision processes. *Administrative Science Quarterly* 21: 246–75.

Mischel, W. 1968. *Personality and assessment.* New York: Wiley.

Mischel, W. 1977. The interaction of person and situation. In *Personality at the crossroads: Current issues in interactional psychology,* ed. D. Magnusson and N. S. Endler. Hillsdale, N.J.: Erlbaum.

Mitchell, T. R., and Silver, W. S. 1990. Individual and group goals when workers are interdependent: Effects on task strategies and performance. *Journal of Applied Psychology* 75: 185–193.

Mizruchi, M. S. 1982. *The American corporate network: 1904–1974.* Beverly Hills: Sage Publications.

Mizruchi, M. S. 1983. Who controls whom? An examination of the relation between management and board of directors in large American corporations. *Academy of Management Review* 8: 426–35.

Mizruchi, M. S., and Stearns, L. B. 1988. A longitudinal study of the formation of interlocking directorates. *Administrative Science Quarterly* 33: 194–210.

Mizruchi, M. S., and Stearns, L. B. 1994. A longitudinal study of borrowing by large American corporations. *Administrative Science Quarterly* 39: 118–40.

Molz, R. 1988. Managerial domination of boards of directors and financial performance. *Journal of Business Research* 16: 235–50.

Morck, R., Schleifer, A., and Vishny, R., 1988. Management ownership and market valuation: An empirical analysis. *Journal of Financial Economics* 20: 293–315.

Morck, R., Shleifer, A., and Vishny, R. 1989. Alternative mechanisms for corporate control. *American Economic Review* 79: 842–52.

Mortimer, J. T., and Lorence, J. 1979. Work longitudinal study. *American Journal of Sociology* 84: 1361–85.

Mueller, R. K. 1979. *Board compass.* Lexington, Mass.: D. C. Heath.

Mueller, R. K. 1981. *The incomplete board: The unfolding of corporate governance,* Lexington, Mass.: Lexington Books.

Murphy, K. J. 1986. Incentives, learning, and compensation: A theoretical and empirical investigation of managerial labor contracts. *Rand Journal of Economics* 17: 59–76.

Murphy, K. J. 1994. Reporting choice and the 1992 proxy disclosure rules. Unpublished manuscript, Harvard Business School, Boston.

Murray, A. I. 1989. Top management group heterogeneity and firm performance. *Strategic Management Journal* 10: 125–41.

Murthy, K. R., and Salter, M. 1975. Should CEO pay be linked to results?. *Harvard Business Review* 53 (3): 66–73.

Myers, I. B. 1982. *Introduction to type*. Palo Alto, Calif.: Consulting Psychologists Press.

Myers, C. A. 1983. Top management featherbedding? *Sloan Management Review,* 24(4): 55–8.

Myerson, A. R. 1993. American Express chairman quits after days of corporate turmoil. *New York Times* 31 January: Section 1: 32.

Napier, N. K., and Smith, M. 1987. Product diversification, performance criteria and compensation at the corporate level. *Strategic Management Journal* 8: 195–201.

Narayanan, V. K., and Fahey, L. 1990. Evolution of revealed cause maps during organizational decline: A case study of Admiral. In *Mapping strategic thought*, ed. A. S. Huff, 109–33. Chichester, England: Wiley.

Nemeth, C. J. 1986. Differential contributions of majority and minority influence. *Psychological Review* 91: 23–32.

Nemeth, C. J. and Staw, B. M. 1989. The trade-offs of social control and innovation in groups and organizations. *Advances in Experimental Social Psychology* 22: 175–210.

Newell, S. E. 1989. An interpretive study of the public statements and strategic actions of the CEOs of U.S. Steel and the Presidents of the USWA: 1945–1985. Unpublished Ph.D. dissertation, University of Massachusetts-Amherst.

New York Times. 1995a. Agee leaving Morrison Knudsen. 2 February: D1.

New York Times. 1995B. A celebrity boss faces exile from second corporate kingdom. 10 February: A1.

Nohria, N., and Berkley, J. D. 1994. Whatever happened to the take-charge manager? *Harvard Business Review* 72(1): 128–39.

Norburn, D. 1986. GOGOs, YOYOs, and DODOs: Company directors and industry performance. *Strategic Management Journal,* 7: 101–18.

Norburn, D., and Birley, S. 1988. The top management team and corporate performance. *Strategic Management Journal* 9: 225–37.

Nutt, P. C. 1984. Types of organizational decision-processes. *Administrative Science Quarterly* 29: 414–50.

Nutt, P. C. 1986a. Decision style and strategic decisions of top executives. *Technological Forecasting and Social Change* 30: 39–62.

Nutt, P. C. 1986b. Tactics of implementation. *Academy of Management Journal* 29: 230–61.

Nutt, P. C. 1987. Identifying and appraising how managers install strategy. *Strategic Management Journal* 8: 1–14.

Nutt, P. C. 1989. Selecting tactics to implement strategic plans. *Strategic Management Journal* 10: 145–61.

Nutt, P. C. 1993. Flexible decision styles and the choices of top executives. *Journal of Management Studies* 30(5): 695–721.

Ocasio, W. 1994. Political dynamics and the circulation of power: CEO succession in U. S. industrial corporations, 1960–1990. *Administrative Science Quarterly* 39: 285–312.

Olson, M. 1982. *The rise and decline of nations: Economic growth, stagflation, and social rigidities*. New Haven: Yale University Press.

O'Reilly, C. A., Caldwell, D. F., and Barnett, W. P. 1989. Work group demography, social integration, and turnover. *Administrative Science Quarterly* 34: 21–37.

O'Reilly, C. A. and Flatt, S. 1989. Executive team demography, organizational innovation and firm performance. Working paper, University of California, Berkeley.

O'Reilly, C. A., Main, B. G., and Crystal, G. S. 1988. CEO compensation as tournament and social comparison: A tale of two theories. *Administrative Science Quarterly* 33: 257–74.

O'Reilly, C. A., Snyder, R. C., and Boothe, J. N. 1993. Executive team demography and organizational change. In *Organizational change and redesign: Ideas and insights for improving performance*, ed. G. P. Hunter and W. H. Glick. New York: Oxford.

Oster, S. 1990. *Modern strategic analysis* New York: Oxford University Press.

Oswald, S. L., and Jahera, J. S. Jr., 1991. The influence of ownership on performance: An empirical study. *Strategic Management Journal* 12: 31–326 .

Ouichi, W. G., and Jaeger, A. M. 1978. Type Z organization: Stability in the midst of mobility. *Academy of Management Review* 3(2): 305–14.

Palepu, K. 1985. Diversification strategy, profit performance, and the entropy measure. *Strategic Management Journal* 6: 239–55.

Palmer, D. 1983. Broken ties: interlocking directorates and intercorporate coordination. *Administrative Science Quarterly* 28: 40–55.

Palmer, D. A., Jennings, P. D., and Zhou, X. 1993. Late adoption of the multidivisional form by large U.S. corporations: Institutional, political, and economic accounts. *Administrative Science Quarterly* 38: 100–31.

Patton, A. 1961. *Men, money, and motivation*. New York: McGraw-Hill.

Patton, A. 1971. Motivating tomorrow's executives. In *The arts of top management*, ed. R. Mann. 192–204. New York: McGraw-Hill.

Patton, A. and Baker, J. C. 1987. Why do directors not rock the boat? *Harvard Business Review* 65: 6–18.

Pavett, C. M., and Lau, A. W. 1982. Managerial roles, skills and effective performance. *Academy of Management Proceedings* 95–99.

Pearce, J. A., II, and Zahra, S. A. 1991. The relative power of CEOs and boards of directors. *Strategic Management Journal* 12: 135–53.

Pearce, J. A., and Zahra, S. A., 1992. Board composition from a strategic contingency perspective. *Journal of Management Studies* 29(4): 411–38.

Peers, A., and Kansas, D. 1994. Inside track: Some brokerage-firm chairmen receive hefty options grants. *Wall Street Journal* 9 February: C1.

Pennings, J. 1980. *Interlocking directorates*. Washington, D.C.: Jossey-Bass.

Perrow, C. 1986. *Complex organizations: A critical essay*. New York: Random House.

Peters, T. J., and Waterman, R. H., II. 1982. *In search of excellence*. New York: Harper & Row.

Pettigrew, A. 1973. *The politics of organizational decision making*. London: Tavistock.

Pettigrew, A. 1992. On studying managerial elites. *Strategic Management Journal* 13(Winter, Special Issue): 163–82.

Pfeffer, J. 1972. Size and composition of corporate boards of directors: The organization and its environment. *Administrative Science Quarterly* 17: 218–29.

Pfeffer, J. 1973. Size, composition, and function of hospital boards of directors: A study of organization-environment linkage. *Administrative Science Quarterly* 18: 349–64.

Pfeffer, J. 1981a. *Power in organizations*. Boston: Pitman.

Pfeffer, J. 1981b. Management as symbolic action: The creation and maintenance of organizational paradigms. In *Research in organizational behavior*, ed. L. L. Cummings and B. M. Staw. vol. 3: 1–52. Greenwich, Conn.: JAI Press.

Pfeffer, J. 1982. *Organizations and organization theory*. Boston: Pitman.

Pfeffer, J. 1983. Organizational demography. In *Research in organizational behavior*, ed. L. L. Cummings and B. M. Staw. vol. 5: 299–357. Greenwich, Conn.: JAI Press.

Pfeffer, J. 1993. Barriers to the advance of organizational science: Paradigm development as a dependent variable. *Academy of Management Review* 18: 599–620.

Pfeffer, J., and Davis-Blake, A. 1986. Administrative succession and organizational performance: How administrator experience mediates the succession effect. *Academy of Management Journal* 29: 72–83.

Pfeffer, J., and Davis-Blake, A. 1990. Determinants of salary dispersion in organizations. *Industrial Relations* 29: 38–57.

Pfeffer, J., and Davis-Blake, A. 1992. Salary dispersion, location in the salary distribution, and turnover among college administrators. *Industrial and Labor Relations Review* 45: 753–63.

Pfeffer, J., and Langton, N. 1988. Wage inequality and the organization of work: The case of academic departments. *Administrative Science Quarterly* 33: 588–606.

Pfeffer, J., and Langton, N. 1993. The effect of wage dispersion on satisfaction, productivity, and working collaboratively: Evidence from college and university faculty. *Administrative Science Quarterly* 38: 382–407.

Pfeffer, J., and Moore, W. 1980. Average tenure of academic department heads: The effects of paradigm, size, and departmental demography. *Administrative Science Quarterly* 25: 387–405.

Pfeffer, J., and Salancik, G. R. 1978. *The external control of organizations: A resource dependence perspective*. New York: Harper and Row.

Pinder, C., and Moore, L. F., eds. *Middle range theory and the study of organizations*. Leiden, Netherlands: Martinus Nijhoff.

Pinfield, L. T. 1986. A field evaluation of perspectives on organizational decision making. *Administrative Science Quarterly* 31: 365–88.

Pitts, R. A. 1974. Incentive compensation and organization design. *Personnel Journal* (March): 49–57.

Pitts, R. A. 1976. Toward a contingency theory of multibusiness organization design. *Academy of Management Review* 3: 203–10.

Platt, J. R. 1964. Strong inference. *Science* 146: 347–53.

Porter, J. 1957. The economic elite and the social structure in Canada. *Canadian Journal of Economics and Political Science* 23: 376–94.

Porter, M. E. 1980. *Competitive strategy: Techniques for analyzing industry and competitors.* New York: Harper and Row.

Postman, J., Bruner, J. S., and McGinnies, E. 1948. Personal values as selective factors in perception. *Journal of Abnormal and Social Psychology* 43 (2): 142–54.

Power, C. 1987. Shareholders aren't rolling over anymore. *Business Week* 27 April: 32–33.

Prahalad, C. K., and Bettis, R. A. 1986. The dominant logic: A new linkage between diversity and performance. *Strategic Management Journal* 7: 485–501.

Prahalad, C. K., and Hamel, G. 1990. The core competence of the corporation. *Harvard Business Review* 6: 79–93.

Priem, R. 1990. Top management team group factors, consensus, and firm performance. *Strategic Management Journal* 11: 469–78.

Priem, R. L. 1994. Executive judgment, organizational congruence, and firm performance. *Organization Science* 5(3): 421–37.

Price, J. L. 1963. The impact of governing boards on organizational effectiveness and morale. *Administrative Science Quarterly* 8: 361–78.

Provan, J. G. 1980. Board power and organizational effectiveness among human service agencies. *Academy of Management Journal* 23: 221–36.

Prowse, S. D. 1990. Institutional investment patterns and corporate financial behavior in the United States and Japan. *Journal of Financial Economics* 27: 43–66.

Puffer, S., and Weintrop, J. 1991. Corporate performance and CEO turnover: A comparison of performance indicators. *Administrative Science Quarterly* 36: 1–19.

Quinn, J. B. 1980. *Strategies for change: Logical incrementalism.* Homewood, Ill.: Irwin.

Rajagopalan, N., and Finkelstein, S. 1992. Effects of strategic orientation and environmental change on senior management reward systems. *Strategic Management Journal* 13 (Special Issue): 127–42.

Rajagopalan, N., and Prescott, J. E. 1990. Determinants of top management compensation: Explaining the impact of economic, behavioral, and strategic constructs and the moderating effects of industry. *Journal of Management* 16: 515–38.

Rajagopalan, N., Rasheed, A. M. A., and Datta, D. K. 1993. Strategic decision processes: Critical review and future directions. *Journal of Management* 19: 349–84.

Ramanan, R., Simon, D. T., and Harris, D. 1993. Chief executive compensation surrounding strategic divestitures. *International Journal of Management* 10: 256–63.

Rappaport, A. 1978. Executive incentives versus corporate growth. *Harvard Business Review* 56 (4): 81–88.

Raskas, D. F., and Hambrick, D. C. 1992. Multifunctional managerial development: A framework for evaluating the options. *Organizational Dynamics* 21(2): 5–17.

Ratcliff, R. E. 1980. Banks and corporate lending: An analysis of the impact of internal structure of the capitalist class on the lending behavior of banks. *American Sociological Review* 45: 553–70.

Raviv, A. 1985. Management compensation and the managerial labor markets: An overview. *Journal of Accounting and Economics* 7: 239–45.

Rawls, J. R. and Nelson, O. T., Jr. 1975. Characteristics associated with preferences for certain managerial positions. *Psychology Reports* 36: 911–18.

Rechner, P. L., and Dalton, D. R. 1991. CEO duality and organizational performance: A longitudinal analysis. *Strategic Management Journal* 12: 155–60.

Rediker, K. J., and Seth, A. 1995. Boards of directors and substitution effects of alterantive governance mechanisms. *Strategic Management Journal*, 16: 85–100.

Reed, R L. 1978. Organizational change in the American foreign service, 1925–1965: The utility of cohort analysis. *American Sociological Review* 43: 404–21.

Reger, R. P., and Huff, A. S. 1993. Strategic groups: A cognitive perspective. *Strategic Management Journal* 14: 103–24.

Reinganum, M. 1985. The effects of executive succession on stockholder wealth: A reply. *Administrative Science Quarterly* 30: 375–76.

Rhodes, S. R., and Steers, R. M. 1981. Conventional versus worker-owned organizations. *Human Relations* 34: 1013–35.

Roberts, D. R. 1959. *Executive compensation*. Glencoe, Ill.: Free Press.

Roberts, E. B., and Berry, C. A. 1985. Entering new businesses: Selecting strategies for success. *Sloan Management Review* 27(3): 57–71.

Roberts, J. L., and Smith, R. 1993. The plot thickens: Who gets the blame for Paramount gaffes? *Wall Street Journal,* 13 December, A1.

Roberts, K. H. and O'Reilly, C. A. 1979. Some correlates of communication roles in organizations. *Academy of Management Journal* 22: 42–57.

Roche, G. R. 1975. Compensation and the mobile executive. *Harvard Business Review* 53 (6): 53–62.

Rogers, E. M., and Shoemaker, F. 1971. *Communication of innovations*. New York: Free Press.

Rokeach, M. 1969a. Value systems in religion. *Review of Religious Research* 11: 3–23.

Rokeach, M. 1969b. Religious values and social compassion. *Review of Religious Research* 11: 24–38.

Rokeach, M. 1973. *The nature of human values*. New York: Free Press.

Rokeach, M., and Parker, S. 1970. Values as social indicators of poverty and race relations in America. *Annals of the American Academy of Political and Social Science* 388: 97–111.

Romanelli, E., and Tushman, M. L. 1988. Executive leadership and organizational outcomes: An evolutionary perspective. In *The executive effect: Concepts and methods for studying top managers*, ed. D. Hambrick. Greenwich, Conn.: JAI Press.

Rosen, S. 1986. Prizes and incentives in elimination tournaments. *American Economic Review* 76: 701–15.

Rosenstein, S., and Wyatt, J. G. 1990. Outside directors, board independence, and shareholder wealth. *Journal of Financial Economics* 26: 175–91.

Ross, S. 1973. The economic theory of agency: The principal's problem. *American Economic Review* 63: 134–39.

Rotter, J. B. 1966. Generalized expectancies for internal versus external control of reinforcement. *Psychological Monographs: General and Applied* 80:(609): (whole).

Rubin, J. Z. and Brockner, J. 1975. Factors affecting entrapment in waiting situations: The Rosencrantz and Guildenstern effect. *Journal of Personality and Social Psychology* 31: 1054–63.

Rumelt, R. P. 1974. *Strategy, structure and economic performance*. Boston: Harvard University Press.

Salancik, G. R., and Pfeffer, J. 1977. Constraints on administrative discretion: The limited influence of mayors on city budgets. *Urban Affairs Quarterly* 12: 475–98.

Salancik, G. R., and Pfeffer, J. 1980. Effects of ownership and performance on executive tenure in U. S. corporations. *Academy of Management Journal* 23: 653–64.

Salter, M. A. 1973. Tailor incentive compensation to strategy. *Harvard Business Review* 51: 94–102.

Sampson, E. E. 1975. On justice as equality. *Journal of Social Issues* 31: 45–64.

Saunders, C. B. and Thompson, J. C. 1980. A survey of the current state of business policy research. *Strategic Management Journal* 1: 119–30.

Schein, E. H. 1968. Attitude change during management education. *Administrative Science Quarterly* 13: 601–21.

Schellenger, M. H., Wood, D. D. and Tashakori, A. 1989. Board of director composition, shareholder wealth, and dividend policy. *Journal of Management* 15: 457–87.

Schendel, D. E., and Hofer, C. W., eds. 1979. *Strategic management: A new view of business policy and planning*. Boston: Little, Brown.

Schifrin, M. 1994. Last legs. *Forbes*, 12 September, 159–60.

Schmidt, R. 1977. The board of directors and financial interests. *Academy of Management Journal* 20(10): 677–82.

Schmidt, S. M., and Kochan, T. 1972. The concept of conflict: Toward conceptual clarity. *Administrative Science Quarterly* 17: 359–70.

Schmidt, W. H. 1974. Conflict: A powerful process for (good or bad) change. *Management Review* 63: 4–10.

Schmidt, W. H., and Posner, B. Z. 1983. *Managerial values in perspective*. New York: American Management Associations.

Schneier, C. E. 1979. Measuring cognitive complexity: Developing reliability, validity, and norm tables for a personality instrument. *Educational and Psychological Measurement* 39: 599–612.

Scholes, M. 1992. Stern Stewart roundtable on management incentive compensation and shareholder value. *Journal of Applied Corporate Finance* 5: 110–30.

Schotter, A., and Weigelt, K. 1992. Behavioral consequences of corporate incentives and long-term bonuses: An experimental study. *Management Science* 38: 1280–98.

Schweiger, D. M., Sandberg, W. R., and Rechner, P. L. 1989. Experiential effects of dialectical inquiry, devil's advocacy, and consensus approaches to strategic decision making. *Academy of Management Journal* 32: 745–72.

Schwenk, C. R. 1989. Devil's advocacy and the board: A modest proposal. *Business Horizons* 32(4): 22–27.

Schwenk, C. R. and Dalton, D. R. 1991. The changing shape of strategic management research. In *Advances in strategic management*, ed. P. Shrivastava, A. Huff, and J. Dutton. vol. 7, 277–300. Greenwich, Conn.: JAI Press.

Selznick, P. 1949. *TVA and the grass roots.* Berkeley: University of California Press.

Selznick, P. 1957. *Leadership in administration.* New York: Harper & Row.

Shavell, S. 1979. Risk sharing and incentives in the principal and agent relationship. *Bell Journal of Economics* 10: 55–73.

Shaw, M. E. 1981. *Group dynamics.* New York: McGraw-Hill.

Shaw, M. E., and Harkey, B. 1976. Some effects of congruency of member characteristics and group structure upon group behavior. *Journal of Personality and Social Psychology* 34: 412–18.

Shirley, R. C. 1975. Values in decision-making—their origin and effects. *Managerial Planning* 23(4): 1–5.

Shleifer, A., and Vishny, R. W. 1986. Large shareholders and corporate control. *Journal of Political Economy* 94: 461–84.

Shrivastava, P., and Lim, G. E. 1989. A profile of doctoral dissertations in strategic management: A note. *Journal of Management Studies* 26: 531–40.

Shrivastava, P., and Nachman, S. A. 1989. Strategic leadership patterns. *Strategic Management Journal* 10: 51–66.

Shull, F. A., Delbecq, A. L., and Cummings, L. L. 1970. *Organizational decision making.* New York: McGraw-Hill.

Simon, H. A. 1945. *Administrative behavior.* New York: Free Press.

Simon, H. A. 1957. The compensation of executives. *Sociometry* 20: 32–35.

Sims, H. P., and Gioia, D. A. 1986. *The thinking organization.* San Francisco: Jossey-Bass.

Singh, H., and Harianto, F. 1989a. Management board relationships, takeover risk, and the adoption of golden parachutes. *Academy of Management Journal* 32: 7–24.

Singh, H., and Harianto, F. 1989b. Top management tenure, corporate ownership structure and the magnitude of golden parachutes. *Strategic Management Journal* 10 (Summer): 143–56.

Sloan, R. 1991. Accounting earnings and top executive compensation. Working paper, University of Pennsylvania, Philadelphia.

Smart, J. C., and Pascarella, E. T. 1986. Self-concept development and educational degree attainment. *Higher Education* 15: 3–15.

Smith, C. W., and Watts, R. L. 1982. Incentive and tax effects of U. S. executive compensation plans. *Australian Journal of Management* 7: 139–57.

Smith, J. E., Carson, K. P., and Alexander, R. A. 1984. Leadership: It can make a difference. *Academy of Management Journal* 27: 765–76.

Smith, K. G., Smith, K. A., Olian, J. D., Sims, Jr., H. P., O'Bannon, D. P., and Scully, J. A. 1994. Top management team demography and process: The role of social integration and communication. *Administrative Science Quarterly* 39: 412–38.

Smith, M., and White, M. 1987. Strategy, CEO specialization, and succession. *Administrative Science Quarterly* 32: 263–80.

Snider, H. K. and Bird, A. 1994. CEO pay and firm performance in Japan. Working paper, New York University.

Snyder, M., and Ickes, William. 1985. Personality and social behavior. In *Handbook of Social Psychology,* ed. G. Lindzey and E. Aronson. 2d ed.

Solomon, J., Washington, F., and Stokes, M. 1992. One more pink slip. *Newsweek, 2* November 70.

Song, J. H. 1982. Diversification strategies and the experience of top executives of large firms. *Strategic Management Journal* 3: 377–80.

Sonnenfeld, J. 1988. *The hero's farewell: What happens when CEOs retire.* New York: Oxford University Press.

Sorenson, T. 1968. *Decision making in the White House.* New York: Columbia University Press.

Spender, J. C. 1989. *Industry recipes: The nature and sources of managerial judgement.* Oxford: Basil Blackwell.

Srivastava, S., and Associates. 1983. *The executive mind.* San Francisco: Jossey-Bass.

Starbuck, W. 1976. Organizations and their environments. In *Handbook of industrial and social psychology*, ed. M. Dunnette. 1069–1123. Chicago: Rand McNally.

Starbuck, W. H., Greve, A., and Hedberg, B. L. T. 1978. Responding to crisis. *Journal of Business Administration* 9: 111–37.

Starbuck, W., and Hedberg, B. 1977. Saving an organization from a stagnating environment. In *Strategy + Structure = Performance*, ed. H. Thorelli. Bloomington: Indiana University Press.

Starbuck, W., and Milliken, F. 1988. Executives' perceptual filters: What they notice and how they make sense. In *The executive effect: Concepts and methods for studying top managers*, ed. D. Hambrick. 35–65. Greenwich, Conn.: JAI Press.

Stasser, G. 1993. Pooling of unshared information during group discussions. In *Group process and productivity*, ed. S. Worchel, W. Wood, and J. Simpson. 48–76. Newbury Park, Calif.: Sage Publications.

Staw, B. M. 1976. Knee-deep in the big muddy: A study of escalating commitment to a chosen course of action. *Organizational behavior and human performance* 16: 27–44.

Staw, B. M., McKechnie, P. I., and Puffer, S. M. 1983. The justification of organizational performance. *Administrative Science Quarterly* 28: 582–600.

Staw, B. M., Sandelands, L. E., and Dutton, J. E. 1981. Threat-rigidity effects in organizational behavior: A multi-level analysis. *Administration Science Quarterly* 26: 501–24.

Stearns, L. B., and Mizruchi, M. S. 1993. Board composition and corporate financing: The impact of financial institution representation on borrowing. *Academy of Management Journal* 36: 603–18.

Steiner, I. D. 1972. *Group process and productivity.* New York: Academic Press.

Stewart, R. 1967. *Managers and their jobs: A study of the similarities and differences in the ways managers spend their time.* London: MacMillan.

Stigler, G. J. 1971. The theory of economic regulation. *Bell Journal of Economics and Management Science* 2 (Spring): 3–21.

Sundaramurthy, C., and Wang, W. 1993. *The impact of board attributes and stock ownership on the adoption of classified boards.* Paper presented at the Academy of Management meetings, Atlanta.

Sutcliffe, K. M. 1994. What executives notice: Accurate perceptions in top management teams. *Academy of Management Journal* 37: 1360–78.

Sutton, F. X., Harris, S. E., Kaysen, C., and Tobin, J. 1956. Value orientations and the relationship of managers and scientists. *Administration Science Quarterly* 10: 39–51.

Sutton, R. I. 1987. The process of organizational death: Disbanding and reconnecting. *Administrative Science Quarterly* 32: 542–69.

Szilagyi, A., and Schweiger, D. 1984. Matching managers to strategies: A review and suggested framework. *Academy of Management Review* 9: 626–37.

Taggart, W., and Robey, D. 1981. Minds and managers: On the dual nature of human information processing and management. *Academy of Management Review* 6(2): 187–95.

Tashakori, A., and Boulton, W. R. 1983: A look at the board's role in planning. *Journal of Business Strategy* 3(2): 64–70

Teece, E. J. 1980. Economics of scope and the scope of the enterprise. *Journal of Economic Behavior and Organization* 1 (3): 223–47.

Tehranian, H., and Waegelein, J. F. 1985. Market reaction to short-term executive compensation plan adoption. *Journal of Accounting and Economics* 7: 131–44.

Thomas, A. S., Litschert, R. J., and Ramaswamy, K. 1991. The performance impact of strategy-manager coalignment: An empirical examination. *Strategic Management Journal* 12: 509–22.

Thomas, J. B., Clark, S. M., and Gioia, D. A. 1993. Strategic sense-making and organizational performance: Linkages among scanning, interpretation, action, and outcomes. *Academy of Management Journal* 36: 239–70.

Thompson, J. D. 1967. *Organizations in action.* New York: McGraw-Hill.

Thompson, J. D., and McEwen, W. J. 1958. Organizational goals and environment: Goal-setting as an interaction process. *American Sociological Review* 23: 23–31

Tichy, N. M., and Devanna, M. A. 1986a. *The transformational leader.* New York: Wiley.

Tichy, N. M., and Devanna, M. 1986b. The transformational leader. *Training and Development Journal* 40: 27–32.

Tichy, N. M., and Sherman, S. 1993. *Control your destiny or someone else will.* New York: Currency Doubleday.

Tosi, H. L., and Gomez-Mejia, L. R. 1989. The decoupling of CEO pay and performance: An agency theory perspective. *Administrative Science Quarterly* 34: 169–89.

Tosi, H. L., and Gomez-Mejia, L. R. 1994. CEO compensation monitoring and firm performance. *Academy of Management Journal* 37: 1002–16.

Triandis, H., Hall, E., and Ewen, R. 1965. Member heterogeneity and dyadic creativity. *Human Relations* 18: 33–55.

Tsui, A. S. 1984. A role set analysis of managerial reputation. *Organizational Behavior and Human Performance* 34: 64–96.

Tsui, A. S., Egan, T. D., and O'Reilly, C. A. 1992. Being different: Relational demography and organizational attachment. *Administrative Science Quarterly* 37: 549–79.

Tushman, M., and Anderson P. 1986. Technological discontinuities and organizational environments. *Administrative Science Quarterly* 31: 439–65.

Tushman, M. L., and Keck, S. 1990. Environmental and organization context and executive team characteristics: An organizational learning approach. Working paper, Graduate School of Business, Columbia University, New York.

Tushman, M. L., and Romanelli, E. 1985. Organizational evolution: A metamorphosis model of convergence and reorientation. In *Research in organizationl behavior*, ed. L. L. Cummings and B. M. Staw. vol. 7, 171–222. Greenwich, Conn.: JAI Press.

Tushman, M. L., Virany, B., and Romanelli, E. 1985. Executive succession, strategic reorientation, and organization evolution. *Technology in Society* 7: 297–314.

Ungson, G., and Steers, R. M. 1984. Motivation and politics in executive compensation. *Academy of Management Review* 9: 313–23.

Useem, M. 1979. The social organization of the American business elite and participation of corporation directors in the governance of American institutes. *American Sociological Review* 44: 553–72.

Useem, Michael 1984. *The inner circle*. New York: Oxford University Press.

Useem, M., and Karabel, J. 1986. Pathways to top corporate management. *American Sociological Review* 51: 184–200.

Vance, S. C. 1955. *Functional control and corporate performance in large scale industrial enterprise*. Amherst: University of Massachusetts Press.

Vance, S. C. 1964. *Board of directors: Structure and performance*. Eugene: University of Oregon Press.

Vance, S. C. 1983. *Corporate leadership: Boards, directors, and strategy*. New York: McGraw-Hill.

Vancil, R. F. 1979. *Decentralization: Managerial ambiguity by design*. New York: Financial Executives Research Foundation.

Vancil, R. F. 1987. *Passing the baton*. Boston: Harvard Business School Press.

Van de Ven, A. H., Hudson, R., and Schroeder, D. M. 1984. Designing new business start-ups: Entrepreneurial, organizational, and ecological considerations. *Journal of Management* 10: 87–107.

Van Nuys, K. 1993. Corporate governance through the proxy process: Evidence from the 1989 Honeywell proxy solicitation. *Journal of Financial Economics* 34: 101–32.

Virany, B., and Tushman, M. L. 1986. Top management teams and corporate success in an emerging industry. *Journal of Business Venturing* 1: 261–74.

Virany, B., Tushman, M., and Romanelli, E. 1992. Executive succession and organization outcomes in turbulent environments: An organizational learning approach. *Organizational Science* 3: 72–91.

Vroom, V. H., and Pahl, B. 1971. Relationship between age and risk-taking among managers. *Journal of Applied Psychology* 55(5): 399–405.

Wade, J., O'Reilly, C. A., III, and Chandratat, I. 1990. Golden parachutes: CEOs and the exercise of social influence. *Administrative Science Quarterly* 35: 587–603.

Waegelein, J. F. 1983. The impact of executive compensation on managerial decisions: An empirical investigation. Working paper, School of Management, Boston College, Chestnut Hill, Mass.

Wagner, W. G., Pfeffer, J., and O'Reilly, C A. 1984. Organizational demography and turnover in top management groups. *Administrative Science Quarterly* 29: 74–92.

Wagner, J. A., III. 1995. Studies of individualism-collectivism: Effects on cooperation in groups. *Academy of Management Journal* 3: 152–72.

Wagner, W. G., Pfeffer, J., and O'Reilly, C. A. 1984. Organizational demography and turnover in top-management groups. *Administrative Science Quarterly* 29: 74–92.

Wall Street Journal. 1995a. William Agee will leave Morrison Knudsen. 2 February, B1.

Wall Street Journal. 1995b. Call to duty: Why Morrison board fired Agee. 13 February, B1.

Wall Street Journal. 1995c. In a cost-cutting era, many CEOs enjoy imperial perks. 7 March, B1.

Waller, M J., Huber, G. P., and Glick, W. H. In press. Functional background as a determinant of executives' selective perception. *Academy of Management Journal*.

Wally, S., and Baum, J. R. 1994. Personal and structural determinants of the pace of strategic decision making. *Academy of Management Journal* 37: 932–56.

Walsh, J. P. 1986. Cognitive simplification processes in managerial decision making. Unpublished manuscript, Dartmouth College.

Walsh, J. P. 1989. Doing a deal: Merger and acquisition negotiations and their impact upon target company top management turnover. *Strategic Management Journal* 10: 307–22.

Walsh, J. P. 1995. Managerial and organizational cognition: Notes from a trip down memory lane. *Organization Science*, 6: 280–321.

Walsh, J. P., and Ellwood, J. W. 1991. Mergers, acquisitions, and the pruning of managerial deadwood: An examination of the market for corporate control. *Strategic Management Journal* 12: 201–18.

Walsh, J. P. and Kosnik, R. D. 1993. Corporate raiders and their disciplinary role in the market for corporate control. *Academy of Management Journal* 36(4): 671–700.

Walsh, J. P. and Seward, J. K. 1990. On the efficiency of internal and external corporate control mechanisms. *Academy of Management Review* 15: 421–58.

Wanous, J. P. and Youtz, M. A. 1986. Solution diversity and the quality of group decisions. *Academy of Management Journal* 29: 149–58.

Warner, J. B., Watts, R. L., and Wruck, K. H. 1988. Stock prices and top management changes. *Journal of Financial Economics* 20: 461–92.

Warner, W. L., and Abegglen, J. 1955. *Big business leaders in America*. New York: Harper.

Weber, M. 1946. *From Max Weber: Essays in sociology*. ed. H. H. Gerth and C. W. Mills. New York: Oxford University Press.

Weick, K. E. 1969. *The social pyschology of organizing*. Reading: Addison-Wesley.

Weick, K. E. 1979. Cognitive processes in organizations. In *Research in organizational behavior*, ed. B. M. Staw. 41–74. Greenwich, Conn.: JAI Press.

Weick, K. E. 1983. Managerial thought in the context of action. *The executive mind*, ed. S. Srivastava, San Francisco: Jossey-Bass.

Weick, K. E., and Bougon, M. G. 1986. Organizations as cognitive maps: Charting ways to success and failure. In *the thinking organization*, ed. H. P. Sims and D. A. Gioia. 102–135. San Francisco: Jossey-Bass.

Weidenbaum, M. 1985. The best defense against the raiders. *Business Week* 23 September: 21.

Weiner, N., and Mahoney, T. A. 1981. A model of corporate performance as a function environmental, organizational, and leadership influences. *Academy of Management Journal* 24: 453–70.

Weisbach, M. 1988. Outside directors and CEO turnover. *Journal of Financial Economics* 20: 431–60.

Weiss, H. M., and Adler, S. 1984. Personality and organizational behavior. In *Research in organizational behavior*, ed. B. M. Staw and L. L. Cummings. vol. 6, 1–50. JAI Press.

Welsh, M. A., and Slusher, E. E. 1986. Organizational design as a context for political activity. *Administrative Science Quarterly* 31: 389–402.

Westphal, J. D., and Zajac, E. J. 1994. Substance and symbolism in CEOs' long-term incentive plans. *Administrative Science Quarterly* 39: 367–90.

Westphal, J. D., and Zajac, E. J. 1995. Who shall govern? CEO/board power, demographic similarity, and new director selection. working paper, Northwestern University, Evanston, Ill.

Whistler, T. L. 1984. *Rules of the game: Inside the corporate boardroom*. Homewood, IL: Dow Jones-Irwin.

Whistler, T. L., Meyer, H., Baum, B. H., and Sorensen, P. F., Jr. 1967. Centralization of organizational control: An empirical study of its meaning and measurement. *Journal of Business* 40: 10–26.

Whitehill, A. M. 1991. *Japanese management: Tradition and transition*. London: Routledge.

Whitley, W., and England, G. W. 1980. Variability in common dimensions of managerial values due to value orientation and country differences. *Personal Psychology* 33: 77–89.

Whyte, W. F. 1955. *Money and motivation: An analysis of incentives in industry*. New York: Harper.

Wiener, Y. 1982. Commitment in organizations: A normative view. *Academy of Management Review* 7: 418–25.

Wiersema, M. F., and Bantel, K. A. 1992. Top management team demography and corporate strategic change. *Academy of Management Journal* 35: 91–121.

Wiersema, M. F., and Bantel, K. A. 1993. Top management team turnover as an adaptation mechanism: The role of the environment. *Strategic Management Journal* 14: 485–504.

Wiersema, M. F., and Bird, A. 1993. Organizational demography in Japanese firms: Group heterogenity, individual dissimilarity, and top management team turnover. *Academy of Management Journal* 36(5): 996–1025.

Williamson, O. E. 1963. Managerial discretion and business behavior. *American Economic Review* 53: 1032–1057.

Williamson, O. E. 1964. The economics of discretionary behavior: Managerial objectives in a theory of the firm. Englewood Cliffs, N.J.: Prentice-Hall.

Williamson, O. E. 1975. *Markets and hierarchies: Analysis and antitrust implications.* New York: MacMillan-Free Press.

Williamson, O. E. 1983. Organization form, residual claimants, and corporate control. *Journal of Law and Economics* 26: 351.

Williamson, O. E. 1985. *The economic institutions of capitalism.* New York: Free Press.

Wissema, J. G., Van der Pol, H. W., and Messer, H. M. 1980. Strategic management archetypes. *Strategic Management Journal* 1: 37–47.

Wolfson, N. 1984. *The modern corporation: Free market versus regulation.* New York: McGraw-Hill.

Woolridge, B., and Floyd, S. W. 1990. Strategy process, middle management involvement, and organizational performance. *Strategic Management Journal* 11: 231–42.

Worrell, D. L., Davidson, W. N., and Glascock, J. L. 1993. Stockholder reactions to departures and appointments of key executives attributable to firings. *Academy of management Journal* 36: 387–401.

Zahra, S. A., and Chaples, S. S. 1993. Blind spots in competitive analysis. *Academy of Management Executive* 7: 7–28.

Zahra, S. A., and Pearce, J. A., II. 1989. Boards of directors and corporate financial performance: A review and integrative model. *Journal of Management* 15: 291–344.

Zahra, S. A., and Stanton, W. W. 1988. The implications of board of directors' composition for corporate strategy and performance. *International Journal of Management* 5 (2): 229–36.

Zajac, E. J. 1990. CEO selection, succession, compensation, and firm performance: A theoretical integration and empirical analysis. *Strategic Management Journal* 11: 313–30.

Zajac, E. 1992. *CEO preferences for incentive compensation: An empirical analysis.* Paper presented at the Academy of Management meetings, Las Vegas.

Zajac, E. J., and Westphal, J. C. In press. Who shall rule after a CEO succession? The likelihood and direction of changes in CEO characteristics. *Administrative Science Quarterly.*

Zald, M. N. 1965. Who shall rule? A political analysis of succession in a large welfare organization. *Pacific Sociological Review* 8: 52–60.

Zald, M. N. 1967. Urban differentiation, characteristics of boards of directors, and organizational effectiveness. *American Journal of Sociology* 73: 261–72.

Zald, M. N. 1969. The power and functions of boards of directors. *American Journal of Sociology* 5: 97–111.

Zaleznik, A., and Kets de Vries, M. F. R. 1975. *Power and the corporate mind.* Boston, Houghton-Mifflin.

Zander, A. 1977. *Groups at work.* San Francisco: Jossey-Bass.

Zenger, T. R. and Lawrence, B. S. 1989. Organizational demography: The differential effects of age and tenure distributions on technical communication. *Academy of Management Journal* 32: 353–76.

INDEX